Conflict of Laws

WEST ACADEMIC PUBLISHING'S LAW SCHOOL ADVISORY BOARD

BLACK LETTER OUTLINES

Conflict of Laws

TENTH EDITION

Peter Hay
Emory School of Law Distinguished Professor Emeritus
L.Q.C. Lamar Professor of Law Emeritus
Emory University

Alumni Distinguished Professor of Law Emeritus
and former Dean
University of Illinois

BLACK LETTER SERIES®

WEST ACADEMIC

860 Blue Gentian Road, Suite 350
Eagan, MN 55121
1-877-888-1330

Published in the United States of America

ISBN: 979-8-89545-712-2

Preface

This Tenth Edition of the **Conflict of Laws Black Letter** retains the structure of the earlier editions. However, all of the material has been updated through the fall of 2025 and, in parts, has been substantially rewritten. With respect to Jurisdiction, both the sections on the exercise of general jurisdiction (*Goodyear*, *Daimler,* now with *Mallory* (2023)) and on specific jurisdiction (*Ford v. Montana* (2021)) have been rewritten. In Family Law, material on same-sex relationships, on the Respect for Marriage Act (enacted in late 2022), and on polygamous relationships has been added or expanded. Continued attention has been given to federal court problems and to international matters, for instance the new Hague Convention on recognition of judgments. Where relevant, references to and discussion of new rules or approaches proposed or already approved by the membership of the American Law Institute for the forthcoming Restatement (Third) of Conflict of Laws have also been included.

Appendix C with review and practice exam questions (and suggested answers to them) has been substantially revised. Both the "Capsule Summary" and the "Glossary" have been expanded to permit a quick first orientation and overview with respect to particular problems and terms.

Comments and suggestions from students and colleagues have been of great help over the years and again with the respect to this edition. I again do thank them very much.

PETER HAY

Emory University
Atlanta, Georgia
January 2026

Summary of Contents

PREFACE III

Capsule Summary **1**

Perspective **19**

PART ONE. INTRODUCTION

Chapter I. Overview and General Background **25**
I. The Conflicts Case 26
II. Sources 27
III. Introduction to Choice of Law 27
IV. Review Questions 30

Chapter II. Domicile and Habitual Residence **31**
I. The Significance of the Domicile Concept in the Conflict of Laws 33
II. Domicile and Habitual Residence Defined 34
III. Analogies in the Case of Corporate Entities 40
IV. Review Questions 41

PART TWO. LITIGATIONAL MATTERS

Chapter III. Jurisdiction to Adjudicate **45**
I. Overview 48
II. General *In Personam* Jurisdiction: The Exercise of Jurisdiction Without Regard to Claim-Related Contacts or Relationships 51
III. Specific Jurisdiction: Contacts Related to the Litigation 57
IV. Limitations on the Exercise of Personal Jurisdiction 77
V. Continuing Jurisdiction 82
VI. Note: Contacts for Personal Jurisdiction and for Choice of Law 83
VII. Jurisdiction over Things 83
VIII. Review Questions 87

Chapter IV. Recognition and Enforcement of Foreign Judgments and Decrees **91**
I. Basic Concepts and Overview 93
II. Interstate Recognition of Foreign Judgments 96
III. Recognition of Foreign-Country Judgments 113
IV. Arbitral Awards 117
V. Review Questions 117

PART THREE. DOMESTIC RELATIONS

Chapter V. The Creation of Status and Its Consequences 123
I. Introduction 124
II. Traditional Marriage 124
III. Contemporary Issues 131
IV. Legitimation 133
V. Adoption 134
VI. Review Questions 135

Chapter VI. Dissolution of Domestic Relationships and Its Consequences (Support, Custody) 137
I. Introduction and Summary: Issues and Problems Addressed in This Part; Definitions 139
II. Interstate Divorces: *Ex Parte* 140
III. Interstate Divorces: Bilateral 144
IV. Incidents of Divorce: Support and Custody 145
V. Annulment 148
VI. International Situations 149
VII. Review Questions 153

PART FOUR. CHOICE OF LAW: BASIC CONSIDERATIONS

Chapter VII. Pervasive Problems 157
I. Introduction 158
II. Characterization: Subject Matter 159
III. Characterization: Substance or Procedure 160
IV. Renvoi 163
V. Public Policy 166
VI. Proof of Foreign Law 167
VII. Review Questions 168

Chapter VIII. Approaches to Choice of Law: Theory 171
I. Introduction 173
II. The Traditional Approach 173
III. Interest Analysis 175
IV. Restatement (Second): Most Significant Relationship 181
V. Restatement (Third): Some Rules and the Search for the "Most Appropriate Law" 186
VI. Leflar's Choice-Influencing Considerations, Particularly Also the "Better Rule of Law" 187
VII. Other Approaches 190
VIII. Conclusion: The Choice-of-Law Continuum 193
IX. The Future: The Coming Restatement (Third) 194
X. Overview 195
XI. Review Questions 195

PART FIVE. PARTICULAR CHOICE-OF-LAW PROBLEMS

Chapter IX. Choice of Law by Subject Matter 199
I. Introduction 201
II. Torts 201

III. Contract 206
IV. Property 217
V. Succession 219
VI. Trusts 223
VII. Probate and Administration of Estates 224
VIII. Corporations 225
IX. Review Questions 227

Chapter X. Constitutional Limitations on State Choice of Law 229
I. Introduction 230
II. Due Process and Full Faith and Credit: The Early Cases 231
III. *Hague, Shutts,* and *Wortman* 234
IV. Court Closing 238
V. Other Constitutional Provisions 239
VI. Conclusions 241
VII. Review Questions 242

PART SIX. ISSUES OF FEDERALISM

Chapter XI. State Law in Federal Court 245
I. The *Erie* Doctrine 246
II. *Erie* and the Federal Rules of Civil Procedure 249
III. *Erie* and Choice of Law 253
IV. Determining State Decisional Law 256
V. Review Questions 256

Chapter XII. Federal Common Law as the Rule of Decision 259
I. Introduction: Sources of Federal Law 260
II. Federal Common Law 260
III. Review Questions 268

Appendix A. Answers to Review Questions 269

Appendix B. Glossary 283

Appendix C. Sample Examination Questions 301

TABLE OF CASES 327

Table of Contents

PREFACE III

Capsule Summary 1

Perspective 19

PART ONE. INTRODUCTION

Chapter I. Overview and General Background 25
I. The Conflicts Case 26
  A. Introduction 26
  B. The Elements; Definitions 26
  C. Interstate Versus International Conflicts Cases 27
II. Sources 27
III. Introduction to Choice of Law 27
  A. Introduction 27
  B. A Look at History 28
  C. Modern Approaches 29
IV. Review Questions 30

Chapter II. Domicile and Habitual Residence 31
I. The Significance of the Domicile Concept in the Conflict of Laws 33
  A. The Need for "Connecting Factors" 33
  B. Domicile as a Pervasive Concept 33
II. Domicile and Habitual Residence Defined 34
  A. In General 34
    1. What Domicile Is Not (but May Become) 34
      a. Residence 34
      b. "Habitual Residence" 34
      c. Residence and Nationality 34
      d. Statutory References 35
    2. The Central Concept 35
  B. Types of Domicile 35
    1. Domicile of Origin 35
    2. Domicile of Choice 35
    3. Domicile by Operation of Law 36
  C. Acquisition of Domicile of Choice 36
    1. In General; Capacity 36
    2. Physical Presence 36
      a. Presence at a Specific Rather than at a General Location 36
      b. In Transit 37
    3. Intent to Remain Indefinitely 37
      a. In General 37
      b. Intent and Motive 37
      c. Factors for the Determination of Intent 37

4. The Forum Determines the Existence of a Domicile of Choice 38
D. Domicile by Operation of Law 39
1. Derivative Domicile: Children 39
2. Derivative Domicile: Married Individuals 39
E. Special Situations 39
1. Incompetent, Institutionalized, and Incarcerated Persons 39
2. Military Service Personnel 40
F. Habitual Residence 40
III. Analogies in the Case of Corporate Entities 40
IV. Review Questions 41

PART TWO. LITIGATIONAL MATTERS

Chapter III. Jurisdiction to Adjudicate 45
I. Overview 48
A. Introduction: Importance of the Jurisdictional Inquiry 48
1. Basic Definition 48
2. Judicial Jurisdiction as Distinguished from Subject Matter Jurisdiction 48
3. Judicial Jurisdiction as Distinguished from Legislative Jurisdiction 48
4. Jurisdiction and the Notice Requirement 49
5. Jurisdiction and Recognition of Judgments 49
B. Categories of Jurisdiction 50
1. *In Personam* (Personal) Jurisdiction 50
a. Specific Jurisdiction 50
b. General Jurisdiction 50
2. Jurisdiction over Things 50
a. *In Rem* Jurisdiction 50
b. *Quasi In Rem* Jurisdiction 51
II. General *In Personam* Jurisdiction: The Exercise of Jurisdiction Without Regard to Claim-Related Contacts or Relationships 51
A. Enterprises: Required Forum Connection 51
1. A Single Transaction Does Not Support General Jurisdiction 51
2. Quality of Defendant-Forum Contacts 52
B. Natural Person 52
1. Domicile 52
2. Citizenship 53
a. National Citizenship 53
b. State Citizenship 54
3. Service Within the Jurisdiction 54
a. *Pennoyer v. Neff* 54
b. Transient Jurisdiction 54
C. Corporations: "At Home" in the Forum or "Consent" by Registering for Doing Business 55
D. Notice Requirement 57
III. Specific Jurisdiction: Contacts Related to the Litigation 57
A. Introduction 57
1. The Territorial Approach 57
2. Shifting the Focus to the "Individual Liberty Interest" 57

B. Voluntary Submission 58
1. Waiver Through Appearance 58
a. Special and General Appearance 58
b. Federal Rules 58
c. Plaintiff's Implied Consent 58
d. Defendant's Implied Consent 59
2. Express Consent 59
a. Forum Selection Clauses 59
b. Appointment of an Agent for Service 59
c. Cognovit Clauses 60
C. By Service Within the Forum State 61
D. By Service Outside the Forum: The Requirements of "Minimum Contacts," "Foreseeability" or "Relatedness" of Business Activity, and Fairness 61
1. "Minimum Contacts" and Long-Arm Statutes 61
a. The Need for a Long-Arm Statute 61
b. Case Categories Under the Long-Arm Statutes 62
c. Reaching the Parent Corporation Through Service on Its Subsidiary 63
2. The Tests of *International Shoe, World-Wide Volkswagen*, and *J. McIntyre* 64
3. Considerations to Be Taken into Account: In General 66
a. Requirement That the Action Arise from Claim-Specific Contacts or Relationships 66
b. The Contact Must Have Been Established by the Defendant 66
c. Benefits Derived from the Forum 67
d. Reasonableness 67
e. Forum State Interest; Jurisdiction by Necessity 68
f. "National Contacts": Jurisdiction and *Erie* 68
4. Specific Jurisdiction in the Case Law 69
a. Products Liability: Injury in the Forum 69
b. Products Liability and "Relatedness:" *Ford v. Montana* 71
c. Defamation 72
d. Contracts 73
e. Domestic Relations 73
5. Jurisdiction and the Internet 74
6. Jurisdiction and Complex Litigation 75
a. Interpleader 75
b. Impleader 75
c. Class Actions 76
d. Multiparty, Multiforum Actions 77
IV. Limitations on the Exercise of Personal Jurisdiction 77
A. Forum-Selection Clauses 77
B. The Inappropriate Forum 79
1. Dismissal or Stay for *Forum Non Conveniens* 79
2. Federal Transfer 81
C. Defenses 82
1. Fraudulent Inducement at Common Law 82
2. Immunity of Parties 82
3. Witness Immunity 82
4. Notice and Opportunity to Appear 82
V. Continuing Jurisdiction 82

VI. Note: Contacts for Personal Jurisdiction and for Choice of Law 83
A. Common Features 83
B. Differences 83
VII. Jurisdiction over Things 83
A. *In Rem* Jurisdiction 83
1. Introduction 83
2. *In Rem* Jurisdiction over Land 83
3. *In Rem* Jurisdiction over Chattels 84
4. Intangibles 84
B. *Quasi In Rem* Jurisdiction 85
1. Introduction 85
2. Post-*Shaffer Quasi In Rem* Jurisdiction 86
a. *Seider*-Type Actions 86
b. Creditor with Prior Judgment 86
c. Intangible as Collateral 86
d. Federal Interpleader 87
e. Maritime Attachment 87
f. Anticybersquatting Consumer Protection Act 87
VIII. Review Questions 87

Chapter IV. Recognition and Enforcement of Foreign Judgments and Decrees 91
I. Basic Concepts and Overview 93
A. The Policy of Preclusion 93
1. Introduction 93
2. Res Judicata: Merger and Bar (*Claim Preclusion*) 93
3. Res Judicata: Collateral Estoppel (*Issue Preclusion*) and Mutuality 93
B. Preclusion and the Enforcement of Interstate Judgments 94
1. "Foreign Judgment" Defined 94
2. Preclusion 95
C. Preclusion and the Enforcement of International Judgments 95
D. Methods of Enforcement 96
II. Interstate Recognition of Foreign Judgments 96
A. Foreign Proceedings Entitled to Recognition 96
1. Finality 96
2. Equity Decrees 97
3. Foreign Decrees Relating to Land 97
4. Persons Affected 98
5. Nature of the Proceedings; Cross Reference 98
B. Enforcing Interstate Judgments 99
1. Full Faith and Credit 99
a. The Constitutional and Statutory Texts 99
b. Judgments Covered 99
c. Method of Enforcement 100
2. Registration and Summary Proceedings 100
a. Federal Judgments in Federal Courts 100
b. State Court Judgments 100
C. Defenses to the Enforcement of Sister-State Judgments 100
1. Lack of Jurisdiction of the Rendering Court (F-1) 100
a. Basic Principle 100

b. Particular Problems 101
i. Default Judgments 101
ii. Subject Matter Jurisdiction 102
2. Erroneous Judgments 102
3. Summary and Review of Previous Sections 102
4. Foreign Judgment Not on the Merits 103
a. "On the Merits" and Preclusion 103
b. "Opportunity to Litigate" and Preclusion 104
c. Greater Preclusion in F-2 than in F-1 104
d. Defining the Reach of Preclusion: Worker Compensation Awards 105
e. Preclusion in Federal Court 107
5. Public Policy, Penal Judgments, Tax Judgments, and Lack of a Competent Court 107
a. Public Policy 107
b. No Competent Court in F-2 108
c. Tax and Penal Judgments 109
6. Other Defenses 110
a. Judgment Obtained by Fraud and Equitable Defenses 110
b. Non-Final Judgments 111
c. Inconsistent Judgments 111
d. Injunctions Against Enforcement or Prohibiting Action 112
e. Reversal of Prior Judgment 112
f. Payment 112
g. Statutes of Limitation 112
III. Recognition of Foreign-Country Judgments 113
A. Recognition and Enforcement 113
1. The *Hilton* Doctrine 113
2. Modern Recognition Practice 114
B. Defenses to Foreign-Country Judgments 115
1. Jurisdiction 115
2. Foreign Judgment for Taxes or Penalties 115
3. Public Policy 116
IV. Arbitral Awards 117
V. Review Questions 117

PART THREE. DOMESTIC RELATIONS

Chapter V. The Creation of Status and Its Consequences 123
I. Introduction 124
II. Traditional Marriage 124
A. Recognition 124
1. The General Rule 124
2. Special Problems 125
a. Non-Age 125
b. "Incestuous" Marriages 126
c. Polygamous Marriages 126
d. Remarriage After Divorce 126
B. Interspousal Property Rights 127
1. By Operation of Law 127
a. Common Law and Community Property Systems Described 127

b. What Law Applies? 127
c. Effect of Change of Domicile 129
i. Traditional Approaches 129
ii. Legislative Responses 129
iii. Foreign Country Situations 130
d. Debts 130
2. By Contract 130
III. Contemporary Issues 131
A. Same-Sex Marriage 131
B. Non-Marital Partnerships 132
IV. Legitimation 133
V. Adoption 134
A. Jurisdiction 134
B. Incidents 135
VI. Review Questions 135

Chapter VI. Dissolution of Domestic Relationships and Its Consequences (Support, Custody) 137
I. Introduction and Summary: Issues and Problems Addressed in This Part; Definitions 139
A. Dissolution of Domestic Relationships 139
B. Support and Custody 139
II. Interstate Divorces: *Ex Parte* 140
A. The *Williams* Cases 140
B. The Definition of Domicile for Divorce Jurisdiction 141
1. State or Federal Law? 141
2. The *In Rem* Approach and "Minimum Contacts" 141
C. Parties to Collateral Attack 141
D. Is Domicile Really Needed? 142
E. Divisible Divorce 143
III. Interstate Divorces: Bilateral 144
A. The *Sherrer* Doctrine 144
1. The Parties 144
2. Third Parties 144
B. Effect of Collateral Determinations of Invalidity 144
IV. Incidents of Divorce: Support and Custody 145
A. Support 145
B. Custody 146
V. Annulment 148
VI. International Situations 149
A. Dissolution of Marriage 149
1. By Judicial Proceeding 149
2. Non-Judicial Divorces 151
B. Support 152
C. Child Custody 152
D. Legitimation and Adoption 153
VII. Review Questions 153

PART FOUR. CHOICE OF LAW: BASIC CONSIDERATIONS

Chapter VII. Pervasive Problems **157**
I. Introduction 158
A. Jurisdiction and Choice of Law 158
B. Sources for the Choice-of-Law Decision 158
C. Pervasive Problems 159
II. Characterization: Subject Matter 159
III. Characterization: Substance or Procedure 160
A. In General 160
B. What Law Determines How an Issue Should Be Characterized? 160
C. Statute of Frauds 161
D. Statute of Limitations 161
1. The Traditional Approach 161
2. Modern Approaches 162
a. Case Law 162
b. The Uniform Conflict of Laws Limitations Act 163
c. Restatement (Second) and (Third) 163
d. Dépeçage 163
IV. Renvoi 163
A. In General: Statutory and Restatement Directives 163
B. Conflicting Choice-of-Law Rules: The *Renvoi* Problem 164
V. Public Policy 166
VI. Proof of Foreign Law 167
VII. Review Questions 168

Chapter VIII. Approaches to Choice of Law: Theory **171**
I. Introduction 173
II. The Traditional Approach 173
A. The Territorial Focus: Vested Rights 173
B. Application 174
C. Illustration 175
III. Interest Analysis 175
A. Introduction 175
B. "False" Versus "True" Conflicts 176
1. Currie's Methodology 176
2. Criticism 177
3. Application 178
4. Interest Analysis and "Pervasive Problems" 179
C. "Comparative Impairment" 180
IV. Restatement (Second): Most Significant Relationship 181
A. Overview 181
B. Determining the State of the Most Significant Relationship: Applying the Restatement (Second) 181
C. Application 182
D. Restatement (Second) and Pervasive Problems 183
E. Narrow Rules: New York's Tort Approach 184
1. From *Babcock* to *Neumeier* 184
2. From *Neumeier* to *Schultz* to *Edwards* 185

V. Restatement (Third): Some Rules and the Search for the "Most Appropriate Law" 186
A. Overview 186
B. Rules and General Approach 187
VI. Leflar's Choice-Influencing Considerations, Particularly Also the "Better Rule of Law" 187
A. In General 188
B. The "Better Rule of Law" 189
VII. Other Approaches 190
A. Functional Analysis 190
B. "Lex Fori" 191
C. "Principles of Preference" 191
VIII. Conclusion: The Choice-of-Law Continuum 193
IX. The Future: The Coming Restatement (Third) 194
X. Overview 195
XI. Review Questions 195

PART FIVE. PARTICULAR CHOICE-OF-LAW PROBLEMS

Chapter IX. Choice of Law by Subject Matter 199
I. Introduction 201
II. Torts 201
A. Introduction: Overview, Answering Exam Questions 201
B. The Traditional Approach 202
C. Modern Approaches 203
D. Particular Problems and Issues 204
1. Multistate Torts 204
2. Fraud and Misrepresentation 205
3. Common Law Tort of Unfair Competition 205
4. Worker Compensation 205
5. No-Fault Insurance 205
6. Admiralty 206
III. Contract 206
A. Introduction 206
B. The Traditional Approach 207
1. Validity 207
a. Express Choice by the Parties 207
b. Applicable Law Absent Party Stipulation 207
c. Exceptions: Special Problems 208
2. Performance 209
3. Current Practice 209
C. Modern Approaches 209
1. Express Choice by the Parties 209
2. The Applicable Law in the Absence of an Express Choice 211
a. False Conflicts 211
b. True Conflicts: Pure Interest Analysis 212
c. True Conflicts: Comparative Impairment 212
d. Restatement (Second): Most Significant Relationship 213
e. The Restatement (Third): Most Appropriate Law 214
D. Particular Contracts and Contract Issues 214
1. Interest in Land 215

2. Sale of Goods 215
3. Insurance 215
4. Surety 215
5. Loans, Negotiable Instruments 215
6. Services, Including Employment Contracts 216
7. Other Contracts and Issues 216

IV. Property 217
A. Introduction 217
B. Interests in Land (Immovables) 217
C. Tangible Movable Property 218
D. Intangibles 219

V. Succession 219
A. Introduction 219
B. Intestate Succession 219
1. Immovables 219
2. Movables 220
C. Testate Succession 220
1. Immovables 220
a. Formal Validity 220
b. Equitable Conversion 221
2. Movables 221
a. Formal Validity 221
b. Substantive Validity 222
c. Testator's Choice 222
3. Forced Shares 222
4. Family Allowance 223

VI. Trusts 223
A. Validity 223
B. Other Issues 223

VII. Probate and Administration of Estates 224
A. Probate 224
B. Administration 224
C. Creditors' Rights 225
D. Distribution 225

VIII. Corporations 225
A. Existence and Internal Affairs 225
B. Other Issues 226
C. Regulation by the Forum 226

IX. Review Questions 227

Chapter X. Constitutional Limitations on State Choice of Law 229

I. Introduction 230
A. Overview 230
B. Function of Due Process and Full Faith and Credit in Choice of Law 230

II. Due Process and Full Faith and Credit: The Early Cases 231
A. Due Process 231
B. Full Faith and Credit 232
C. Conclusion 234

III. *Hague*, *Shutts*, and *Wortman* 234
A. The Test 234
B. *Hague* 235

C. *Shutts* 236
D. *Wortman* 236
1. Constitutional Limitations on Choice of Law and Characterization: Statutes of Limitations 237
2. *Wortman*'s Choice of the Applicable Substantive Law 237
IV. Court Closing 238
V. Other Constitutional Provisions 239
A. Privileges and Immunities; Equal Protection 239
B. Commerce Clause: *Bendix* 240
VI. Conclusions 241
VII. Review Questions 242

PART SIX. ISSUES OF FEDERALISM

Chapter XI. State Law in Federal Court 245
I. The *Erie* Doctrine 246
A. The Rationale for *Erie R.R. v. Tompkins* 246
B. When Does *Erie* Apply? Substance Versus Procedure 247
C. "Countervailing Considerations": *Byrd* 248
II. *Erie* and the Federal Rules of Civil Procedure 249
A. *Hanna* 249
B. *Walker* 250
C. *Semtek* 251
D. Summary 251
E. *Forum Non Conveniens* 252
F. The Federal Rules in International Cases 252
III. *Erie* and Choice of Law 253
A. *Klaxon* and *Challoner* 253
B. Special *Erie* Problems 253
1. Interstate Forum Shopping 253
a. Interpleader 253
b. The 100-Mile Bulge Rule 254
c. Supplemental Jurisdiction 254
d. Federal Transfer 255
e. Complex Litigation 255
2. When Federal Law Is Applicable 255
IV. Determining State Decisional Law 256
V. Review Questions 256

Chapter XII. Federal Common Law as the Rule of Decision 259
I. Introduction: Sources of Federal Law 260
II. Federal Common Law 260
A. Introduction: Definition; Source of Federal Common Law 260
B. Federal Common Law: The Prerequisite of a Federal Interest 261
1. Government Obligations 261
2. Contractual Relations with the Government 262
3. Tort-Related Issues 262
4. Private Disputes over Government-Created Rights 263
5. Foreign Relations 264
C. Intermediate Summary: When Is Federal Common Law Appropriate? 267
D. When Does Federal Legislation Displace Federal Common Law? 267

III. Review Questions 268

Appendix A. Answers to Review Questions 269

Appendix B. Glossary 283

Appendix C. Sample Examination Questions 301

TABLE OF CASES 327

Capsule Summary

Note: The Glossary in Appendix B not only defines terms—as a dictionary would—but also provides short explanations. For fast review purposes, you might want to combine reading this Summary and reading the Glossary. The main part of the book then provides further detail if needed.

■ PART ONE. INTRODUCTION

CHAPTER I. OVERVIEW AND GENERAL BACKGROUND

I. The Conflicts Case

Conflicts law deals with cases in which the parties or the event (or transaction) or both are connected with a "foreign" jurisdiction (sister-states or foreign countries are "foreign" to the "forum," which is the state in which the case is being considered). The principal areas of inquiry concern *jurisdiction* over the out-of-state party, the *choice of the law applicable to the case*, and the *recognition and enforcement of a judgment* rendered outside of the local (forum) state.

II. Sources

Conflicts law is mainly state law, subject only to federal constitutional limitations. Isolated federal statutes and federal treaties provide special conflicts rules for a few subject matters as well as for some international situations and of course take precedence over state conflicts law.

III. Introduction to Choice of Law

Comity, the international "golden rule," is used to explain why one state would give effect to the law of another. At one time, the U.S. Constitution's Full Faith and Credit Clause was thought to mandate (some) deference to sister state law in interstate cases. Underlying this assumption was probably the "vested rights theory" of the First Restatement, which held that rights and obligations acquired or liability incurred in one state will "vest" and must therefore be recognized by all other states unless against their public policy. Today, there are only minimal federal constitutional limits on a state's choice of the applicable law. These limits flow principally from the Constitution's Due Process Clause: it does not mandate application of a particular law but rather sets limits to a state's application of its *own* law when there is an insufficient connection to the case. What law to apply? Modern approaches take a more differentiated view than did the First Restatement. They analyze underlying party interests and state policies in order to make a functionally appropriate choice of law. The Restatement (Second) casts this inquiry into the search for the "law of the place of the most significant relationship to the parties and the particular issue." Another approach, "interest analysis," stresses the consideration of "governmental" (societal) interests of the involved states to have their law applied. The forthcoming Restatement (Third) is more specific than the Second Restatement: it provides/suggests some rules, supplemented by approaches to determine the law that should be applied in the absence of a rule or which, for an overriding interest or reason, should displace an otherwise applicable rule.

CHAPTER II. DOMICILE AND HABITUAL RESIDENCE

I. The Significance of the Domicile Concept in the Conflict of Laws

In order to decide many questions of jurisdiction and of choice of law, all legal systems select one principal factor ("connecting factor") that connects a person to a particular jurisdiction more than other possible, but more casual factors. In many countries around the world, this principal connecting factor is a person's nationality. In the countries of the Common Law, including the United States, it has been a person's domicile. To bridge the differences between nationality and domicile, many international agreements and increasing numbers of national laws now look to a person's "habitual residence" as the relevant connecting factor.

II. Domicile and Habitual Residence Defined

Domicile—in the Common Law—does not equal residence nor even the increasingly popular concept of "habitual residence." Domicile is the closest connection a person has to a state; therefore, a person can only have one domicile at a time. A person starts with a *domicile of origin* at birth (derived from his or her custodial parent(s)) and thereafter, assuming capacity, may acquire a *domicile of choice* by 1) abandoning the previous domicile, 2) arriving at the new domicile, and 3) having no present intent to leave the new domicile (or, stated differently, having the intent to remain indefinitely). Since a person can have only one domicile at a time, all three prerequisites must be met before one's domicile changes. Domicile of choice is thus derived from *facts* and a person's *intent*. Minor children derive their domicile from the custodial parent; special rules apply to incompetent, institutionalized, and incarcerated persons. Federal diversity jurisdiction requires diversity of citizenship: a person is a citizen of the state where he or she "resides," U.S. Const. amend. 14 § 1, but the latter term has been interpreted to mean "domicile." Determining a person's intent is not easy. In the case of intestate succession, doing so for purposes of determining the decedent's law of domicile at death is obviously impossible. The forthcoming Restatement (Third) now drops the intent criterion and instead bases the determination only on objective facts: where is or was a person's "center of life?" Objective facts may include religious or social affiliations, principal place of work, a family's main residence, and the like.

"Habitual residence" is used increasingly in international treaty practice and in more modern foreign codifications of conflicts law. This connecting factor emphasizes the *facts* surrounding residence of a substantial duration and does not focus on intent, as does the older concept of domicile.

III. Analogies in the Case of Corporate Entities

The state of incorporation furnishes the law applicable to issues concerning internal corporate affairs. By analogy to the concept of domicile, it may also be the place where general jurisdiction may be exercised over the corporation. For diversity jurisdiction, a corporation is also a "citizen" of the place where it has its principal business activity. The new Restatement (Third) also refers to the state law of a company's principal place of business to determine the law applicable to a particular issue.

■ PART TWO. LITIGATIONAL MATTERS

CHAPTER III. JURISDICTION TO ADJUDICATE

I. Overview

"Jurisdiction" (judicial jurisdiction, "jurisdiction to adjudicate," as distinguished from "legislative jurisdiction") is the power of the court to bind the defendant personally or to affect the defendant's interest in local property. The assertion of jurisdiction to adjudicate is subject to the federal constitutional Due Process limitation that the defendant or the transaction from which the claim arises have sufficient contact with the forum state and that the court have control over, or sufficient contact with the property it wishes to affect. In addition, due process requires that the plaintiff perfect the court's jurisdiction by giving sufficient notice to the defendant, so as to enable the latter to defend. The existence of proper jurisdiction (in the constitutional sense) in the court rendering a judgment is also a precondition for its judgment to be entitled to recognition in other states under the mandate of the Full Faith and Credit Clause of the Constitution (Art. IV, Sec. I). Jurisdiction is either personal (*in personam*) or over things (*in rem*). When exercising *quasi in rem* jurisdiction, a court uses the defendant's assets to vindicate or satisfy the plaintiff's personal claim.

II. General *In Personam* Jurisdiction: The Exercise of Jurisdiction Without Regard to Transaction-Related Contacts

When a plaintiff's claim is unrelated to a specific defendant-contact with the forum, the court must have *general jurisdiction* over the defendant. For natural persons this means that the defendant generally must be domiciled within the forum state. Service of process within the forum state on the defendant, even while only casually present—"transient jurisdiction"—is also a sufficient basis for the exercise of general jurisdiction. General jurisdiction over a corporation may be exercised in its state of incorporation, at its principal place of business, and, additionally, whenever it is so closely related to a state through its activities that it is practically "at home" in the state or when it has consented to be subject to general jurisdiction (even when such consented was mandated by statute, as in *Mallory*). How much and what activity makes it "at home" and whether statutory mandates are permissible are still open questions.

III. Specific Jurisdiction: Contacts Related to the Litigation

In the absence of general jurisdiction, the defendant has an "individual liberty interest" to be protected against being subjected to jurisdiction at a place with which he or she has insufficient or no contact. The defendant may waive the objection through appearance or may consent to jurisdiction, including by consent in advance (choice-of-court clauses). (Exceptions: legislation may limit the use of choice-of-court clauses in certain consumer transactions; contracts may also provide for mandatory individual arbitration in lieu of litigation.)

Where there is no general jurisdiction, waiver, or consent, the defendant and the cause of action must have "minimum contacts" with or be so related to the forum state, that it is "foreseeable" to the defendant that he or she could be subjected to litigation at the forum. These contacts must have been established by the defendant himself or herself. They can result from the fact that the defendant has derived benefits from, or has acted with respect to, the forum. Specific jurisdiction on the basis of minimum contacts or the defendant's relation to the cause of action must be asserted by the forum state's long-arm statute; even if this is done, its assertion in a given case may nevertheless be considered unreasonable and therefore constitute a violation of due process. Special problems exist with respect to the assertion of specific jurisdiction in products liability cases ("stream-of-commerce jurisdiction," still an open question), in interpleader, and in class actions.

IV. Limitations on the Exercise of Personal Jurisdiction

Even when the exercise of jurisdiction does not violate the constraints of the Due Process Clause, it may still be inappropriate. This may be the case when the parties have, by express agreement, chosen another court to have exclusive jurisdiction (choice-of-court clause or "forum selection" clause), when the forum in which the plaintiff sues is seriously inconvenient or otherwise inappropriate (*forum non conveniens*), when litigation is already pending elsewhere (*lis pendens*), or when federal law permits transfer to another federal court in diversity cases (federal transfer). Additionally, a defendant may move to dismiss for fraudulent inducement, on the basis of immunity, or for insufficient notice and opportunity to appear.

V. Continuing Jurisdiction

Once a court has validly assumed jurisdiction in a cause (for instance, in the administration of an estate), its jurisdiction continues until final resolution of the cause, even though the defendant moves away from the state and would no longer be subject to jurisdiction in an initial proceeding.

VI. Note: Contacts for Personal Jurisdiction and for Choice of Law

Jurisdiction determines the place of suit; choice of law determines the applicable substantive law. Of these, the latter may result in liability, while the former may involve an inconvenient place of trial. The exercise of jurisdiction requires at least"*minimum* contacts" or a relevant relationship of the cause of action to the forum; the application of forum law "*significant* contacts." These concepts are elastic; often there are no definite rules or standards. The factual circumstances to be analyzed and evaluated will often be the same, and the resulting analysis may lead to the same conclusion. However, "contacts" for purposes of jurisdiction and choice of law must be analyzed separately.

VII. Jurisdiction over Things

A court has jurisdiction over things within its territory, whether land, chattels, or intangibles represented by a certificate or other kind of documentation. In theory, this jurisdiction is exclusive, especially as developed historically with respect to a state's jurisdiction over local land. However, while the state cannot affect interests in foreign land, it can, through the exercise of personal jurisdiction, adjudicate the respective rights and obligations of the parties before it. Moreover, the same is true for personal property where a state that has jurisdiction as a consequence of the location of the chattel may nonetheless choose to apply another state's law to the merits of the dispute. *Quasi-in-rem* jurisdiction today survives mainly in favor of a creditor with a prior valid *in personam* judgment. Special rules apply to federal interpleader and to maritime attachment.

CHAPTER IV. RECOGNITION AND ENFORCEMENT OF FOREIGN JUDGMENTS AND DECREES

I. Basic Concepts and Overview

There is a *pervasive* policy in all legal systems that there not be repetitive litigation of claims and issues. When there has been fair litigation, or jurisdiction and a fair opportunity to litigate, the parties are precluded from further litigation. The concept of res judicata encompasses both "claim preclusion"—the ideas of *merger* (the claim merges with the judgment) and *bar* (the judgment bars renewal of the claim) in the older decisions—and "issue preclusion" (also expressed as "collateral estoppel" in older decisions).

The policy of preclusion also underlies the law of recognition and enforcement of foreign judgments. Judgments of sister states benefit from the Full Faith and Credit Clause of the Federal Constitution. International judgments must depend on the applicability of uniform laws or on state-law principles of preclusion and comity for their recognition.

II. Interstate Recognition of Foreign Judgments

The Full Faith and Credit Clause of the Federal Constitution requires states to recognize judgments of sister states. The judgment creditor sues on the judgment in the state in which recognition is sought and that state enters its own judgment, which is then enforceable within the state. State court judgments are also entitled to recognition in federal court, and federal judgments in state court. Many states also provide a summary proceeding for the recognition of sister-state judgments.

Defenses to the recognition and enforcement of sister-state judgments include that the issuing court lacked jurisdiction, that the judgment was not "on the merits," that it has limited preclusive effect, that it was obtained by fraud, that it is not final or has been reversed in the issuing state, that there exists a subsequent inconsistent valid judgment rendered in another jurisdiction, and that the recognition and enforcement of the judgment would violate local public policy. Additionally, the judgment debtor may of course show that the judgment has been satisfied or that the statute of limitations has run on its enforcement. The public policy defense and the objection that the claim is for taxes or penalties are not available when the claim has been reduced to a money judgment in the other jurisdiction. This results from the merger doctrine (above No. I). Note, however, that assertion of some defenses—for instance, lack of jurisdiction of the rendering court—may itself be precluded (e.g., if litigated in the first court). The Full Faith and Credit Clause does not extend to foreign country judgments. See No. IV below.

III. Recognition of Foreign—Country Judgments

An older Supreme Court decision declared that foreign country judgments relating to land and status (e.g., divorce) would be recognized as a matter of course but that money judgments in favor of a foreign plaintiff and against an American defendant would be recognized only as a matter of comity on the condition that the foreign country would accord reciprocity to American judgments (*Hilton*). Recognition of foreign country judgments is now a matter of state law, and most states (but not all) recognize these judgments on the same basis as sister-state judgments (subjecting them also to the same defenses) and do not impose a reciprocity requirement. However, a foreign country judgment does not merge the underlying cause of action (see No. I above). As a result, a judgment may be denied recognition when the foreign cause of action or the law applied offends the recognizing state's public policy (*Matusevitch*).

IV. Arbitral Awards

The Federal Arbitration Act and the United Nations Arbitration Convention, to which the United States is a party, deal with arbitration and arbitral awards in interstate and international commerce. Agreements to arbitrate, if validly concluded, must be specifically enforced by the courts, and arbitration awards must be recognized and enforced.

■ PART THREE. DOMESTIC RELATIONS

CHAPTER V. THE CREATION OF STATUS AND ITS CONSEQUENCES

I. Introduction

The determination of a person's status (for instance, as a "surviving spouse" or as an "adopted child") is often necessary for the resolution of other questions, such as whether a particular person is the heir of an intestate decedent. In other words, questions of status usually do not arise by themselves (in the abstract), but are "preliminary questions" for the resolution of the main problem.

II. Traditional Marriage

A marriage which is valid where contracted is usually regarded as valid everywhere. Even when a marriage would not be recognized for the purpose of allowing people to live together (for instance, because the marriage is incestuous or polygamous), it may still be recognized for some other purposes, for instance to allow one "spouse" to inherit from the other. The distinction thus is between the status itself and its consequences ("incidents").

Property rights between spouses follow either the common law or the community property system. The property rights are determined as of the time of the acquisition of the asset, according to the law of the domicile of the spouses (in the case of movable property) or the law of the situs (in the case of immovable property). Difficult problems may arise if the spouses change their domicile, and one of them then dies intestate. If the change of domicile is from a common law to a community property state, the surviving spouse could be left without protection: if no community property is created after the move, then there might be nothing in which he or she could claim an interest.

Three states permit parties to enter into a "covenant marriage." Its main feature is to make dissolution more difficult to obtain (counseling and waiting period requirements). It will be recognized interstate like any other marriage, but a divorce proceeding will be governed by the law of the party's or parties' new state of domicile, which might not apply/enforce the restrictions of the covenant regarding divorce. Finally, some states still permit informal marriages ("common law marriage"). If valid where contracted, such a marriage will usually be recognized in other states as well.

III. Same-Sex Marriages

In two decisions (*Windsor* in 2013 and *Obergefell* in 2015), the United States Supreme Court held provisions of the federal Defense of Marriage Act (DOMA) unconstitutional. That act had not recognized same-sex marriage for purposes of federal benefits and had permitted states not to allow and not to recognize same-sex marriage. These decisions solved many conflicts problems that had arisen from divergent treatment of same-sex relationships by the states of the Union. The Respect for Marriage Act of 2022 now makes same-sex marriage validity and interstate recognition a matter of federal statutory law. Differences (and therefore recognition problems) still exist internationally in relation to countries that do not recognize (or even prohibit) same-sex marriage or other formalized same-sex relationships.

IV. Legitimation

Legitimation is the conferral of legitimacy after a child's birth, either by the parents' subsequent marriage or upon recognition by the father. The consequences of legitimation (for instance, inheritance rights) are determined by the forum state, which will ordinarily treat all legitimated children alike, regardless of where the acts of legitimation occurred.

V. Adoption

Jurisdiction for adoption exists at the domicile of the child. It might also exist at the domicile of the adoptive parents, and at other places. An adoption decreed by a court with competent jurisdiction will be recognized everywhere. The consequences of an out-of-state adoption will be the same as of a local adoption.

CHAPTER VI. DISSOLUTION OF DOMESTIC RELATIONSHIPS AND ITS CONSEQUENCES (SUPPORT, CUSTODY)

I. Introduction and Summary: Issues and Problems Addressed in This Part; Definitions

Divorces are granted according to the law of the forum; they therefore only raise questions concerning the court's jurisdiction. It is an open question whether the forum will honor the stricter standards of an out-of-state "covenant marriage" (below p. 125), but unlikely. The status decision (the divorce) is different from the determination of the consequences ("incidents"), such as support and custody. While a court may grant a divorce on less than personal jurisdiction over the defendant, personal jurisdiction is necessary for the determination of some incidents, for instance support.

II. Interstate Divorces: *Ex Parte*

An "*ex parte*" divorce is one in which only the petitioner is before the court. The Supreme Court held in the *Williams* cases that the domicile of the plaintiff suffices for divorce jurisdiction: the marriage, like a thing, was at the domicile of the plaintiff and thus became subject to the jurisdiction of the court. It has not been definitely stated by the Supreme Court whether another close connection to the forum, short of domicile, also makes for *ex parte* divorce jurisdiction.

In an *ex parte* divorce, the respondent is not subject to the court's jurisdiction, so the court cannot affect personal rights and obligations of the parties (incidents), such as support. This is the "divisible divorce" concept in *ex parte* divorces: there is jurisdiction to grant the divorce but not to deal with incidents (*Estin*).

III. Interstate Divorces: Bilateral

When both parties are before the court (bilateral divorce), the jurisdictional issue becomes res judicata, whether raised in that proceeding or not, and cannot be raised collaterally. The Supreme Court has extended this res judicata effect to third parties, such as children. For international cases, see No. VI below.

IV. Incidents of Divorce: Support and Custody

A court has jurisdiction to make support decisions when the defendant is before it. If the defendant is absent, the Uniform Interstate Family Support Act (UIFSA) now provides for interstate judicial cooperation, allowing the plaintiff to sue in his or her state with the defendant being summoned to respond in his or her state.

Custody, at common law, presented a number of problems, chief among them the fact that custody decrees are never final but remain modifiable. This led disappointed ex-spouses to snatch the child from (or not return him or her to) the custodial parent and to seek modification in his or her own home state instead. The Uniform Child Custody Jurisdiction Act (UCCJA) and the Federal Parental Kidnapping Prevention Act provide uniform rules for initial jurisdiction and for subsequent modification of a custody decree. The Uniform Child Custody Jurisdiction and Enforcement Act (UCCJEA) has replaced the UCCJA in all states except Massachusetts (where a bill to do so was again introduced in 2025); it gives priority to the original home state to make the initial custody determination as well as to modify it subsequently. An international treaty makes similar provisions for international cases.

V. Annulment and Separate Maintenance

Annulment (the determination that the marriage never existed) may be decreed at the common domicile of the parties, the domicile of the petitioner (in analogy to *ex parte* divorce jurisdiction), and even where there is mere personal jurisdiction over the parties (in analogy to the bilateral divorce). Separate maintenance follows the rules for personal jurisdiction.

VI. International Situations

Foreign country divorces are recognized on the same basis as sister-state divorces. A number of foreign countries grant divorces upon the plaintiff's petition and the mere appearance of the defendant in person or by counsel. In a few countries, no period of residence may be required ("quickie divorce"). While a number of states will not recognize such a divorce, some others do. Once the foreign divorce is recognized in an American proceeding, for instance as part of a support determination, it becomes an American decision that is thereinafter entitled to Full Faith and Credit.

Foreign country judgments which reduce a support obligation to a money judgment are recognized in the United States. In addition, a number of states cooperate with foreign nations under arrangements entered into under the Uniform Reciprocal Enforcement of Support Act. Similarly, the Uniform Child Custody Jurisdiction and Enforcement Act extends recognition to foreign-country custody decrees rendered pursuant to the principles of the acts.

The Hague Convention on Civil Aspects of International Child Abduction, in force in the United States, provides for the return of a child to its "home state," as defined by the Convention. The federal International Parental Kidnapping Act makes it a crime to remove a child from the United States with intent to obstruct parental rights.

■ PART FOUR. CHOICE OF LAW: BASIC CONSIDERATIONS

CHAPTER VII. PERVASIVE PROBLEMS

I. Introduction

In choosing what law to apply to the case pending before it, the court will follow the statutory direction of its own state or the choice-of-law approach adopted by its case law. Some statutory directions, for instance, may be found in the Uniform Commercial Code. The choice-of-law decision is analytically different from the question of whether the court has jurisdiction, although the contacts required for either may overlap and both may be present in the particular case. Certain problems are pervasive to the entire choice-of-law process; they are the subject of this chapter.

II. Characterization: Subject Matter

The choice of the applicable law will be affected by the type of case that is presented. The court must therefore identify ("characterize") the subject matter of the case or issue as sounding in contract, tort, or whatever.

III. Characterization: Substance or Procedure

Even when the forum's choice-of-law rule refers to the law of another state, the court will only apply the substantive law of that state; it will use its own procedural law. This will require the court to determine ("characterize") whether an issue is substantive or procedural. The Statute of Frauds is usually characterized as substantive. This means that the court will apply the same law that it applies to the merits, for instance the law of the state having the most significant relationship to the issue. Until recently, statutes of limitations were considered procedural unless they were "built in" the statutory claim or unless a borrowing statute imported another state's limitation. As a result, the forum would apply its own statute, regardless of whether it was shorter or longer than the other state's. More recently, some states have adopted a substantive characterization by case law or statute. The Restatements (Second) and (Third) generally follow the procedural position, except when another state's statute is the applicable law and contains a time limitation or, however rarely, when an exception is necessary.

IV. Renvoi

Occasionally, a court will be directed by statute to apply the "whole law" of another jurisdiction, meaning that state's substantive law and its conflicts rules. In the absence of such a statutory directive, the question arises whether a court should consider the other state's conflicts law, either in circumstances where the other state's law would refer back to the forum (remission) or when it would refer to yet another state (transmission). As a general rule, American courts do not engage in *renvoi* (do not follow the other state's conflicts rule). The Restatement (Second) advocates limited use of *renvoi*. The new Restatement (Third) is even more limited in allowing its use. A reference to a third state's law will only be followed if both the forum and the second state want to achieve that result. If the other (the second) state's law refers back to the forum this could indicate that the issue presents a "false conflict" and that the forum should therefore apply its own law (see below Chapter

VIII(III-B)). See also Appendix B (the "Glossary"). However, the Restatement (Third) does not examine the other state's conflicts law for that purpose.

V. Public Policy

A state will not apply another state's law that offends its local public policy. However, the public policy defense has been construed narrowly: mere differences in law are not to be regarded as offending the forum's public policy.

VI. Proof of Foreign Law

At common law, the content of foreign law (including the law of sister states) was regarded as a question of fact and had to be pleaded and proved as such; the determination of the foreign law was therefore not subject to review on appeal. The U.S. Supreme Court continues to regard foreign country law as "fact," but advises federal courts how to proceed. Statutory changes now provide for judicial notice of sister-state law. A uniform act and a federal rule provide that the court, with the assistance of the parties, is to determine foreign law, that its decision is to be treated as one on a question of law, and that it is therefore subject to review. When proof fails or the foreign law cannot be determined, a court may engage in presumptions, for instance that the foreign rule is the same as that of the forum.

CHAPTER VIII. APPROACHES TO CHOICE OF LAW: THEORY

I. Introduction

When the forum has a case with foreign elements (parties, events, transactions), it must decide whether to apply its own law (if constitutionally permissible) or the law of another involved state. One reason for not applying forum law in all cases is that doing so would allow plaintiffs to engage in forum shopping, contrary to the goal of fostering interstate and international certainty and predictability. Traditionally, courts applied fixed, predetermined choice-of-law rules for the selection of the law applicable to the case. Modern American approaches emphasize a policy-oriented analysis for the selection of the applicable law. They also seek to determine an applicable law for individual issues of a case rather than for the case in its entirety. The issue-by-issue approach is known as "dépeçage." Both the current Restatement (Second) and the new Restatement (Third) follow this method for determining the applicable law.

II. The Traditional Approach

The First Restatement, which represents the traditional approach, adopted a territorially-focused "vested rights" approach. For instance, it applied the law of the state where the injury occurred in a tort case, or where a contract was made, or where the alleged breach of contract occurred. A court utilizing the traditional approach would first characterize the subject matter as, for instance, involving tort, and would then select the choice-of-law rule applicable to that area of the law (for instance, the place-of-injury rule in tort). It would then ask which issues were substantive or procedural to determine whether the other state's or its own law applied. In rare cases, it might reject the other law on the ground that it offended local public policy. The traditional approach has been criticized as mechanical and as ignoring many important policy considerations. The overwhelming majority of states have abandoned it.

III. Interest Analysis

Interest analysis and all other policy-focused approaches first ask whether the case really presents a (true) conflict or whether it is a "false conflict." A conflict is "false" when the potentially applicable laws do not differ or when one law—by its own terms or policies—is not intended to apply to the situation. When a false conflict has been identified, the inapplicable law drops out, thus resolving the choice-of-law problem. In the event of a "true conflict," pure interest analysis (based on the writings of *Brainerd Currie*) calls for the application of forum law on the ground that courts may not weigh conflicting state policies, but must effectuate the policies of their own state. A modification of the pure interest analysis approach is the "comparative impairment" approach. It *does* weigh and will apply the law of that jurisdiction whose policies would be more impaired if its law were not applied. See also Appendix B (the "Glossary").

IV. Restatement (Second): Most Significant Relationship

The Restatement (Second) retains many of the fixed references of the First Restatement but in a number of important areas calls for the application of the "law of the place of the most significant relationship" with respect to the parties and the particular issue. This is the case for the important areas of contract and tort. The Restatement (Second) establishes a number of "general principles" and, in the context of particular areas of the law, lists a number of "contacts" that should be considered to determine the place of the "most significant relationship" with respect to the parties and the particular issue. In tort, for instance, the place of the injury is now only one among several contacts to be considered in the selection of the applicable law. New York, on the basis of long experience in reshaping choice of law, developed new rules (the "*Neumeier*-Rules," subsequently modified in *Schultz*). So have Nevada and some other states. While policy-centered, these rules are more narrowly drawn than the flexible approach of the Restatement (Second).

V. Restatement (Third)

The new Restatement (Third) provides rules for tort cases based on the distinction between conduct-regulating and loss-allocating rules. As a default rule, it calls for the application of the "most appropriate law," providing a list of contacts and policies to consider—that resembles the list of the current Restatement (Second). For contract cases, the Draft also provides some rules and, when none exists or applies, calls for the application of the law of the state that has the dominant interest, again providing a non-exclusive checklist. See also Section IX, below.

VI. Choice-Influencing Considerations, Particularly Also the "Better Rule of Law"

The "choice-influencing considerations" of Professor *Leflar* overlap in most respects with the "general principles" contained in § 6 of the Restatement (Second). However, one "consideration" is different and has had decisive influence on the choice-of-law approach of at least two to three states. This approach advocates that courts should select the "better rule of law" for the solution of the problem at hand. In the to or three states using this approach, the "better rule of law" has usually been found to be forum law.

VII. Other Approaches

Other proposals advance a number of additional approaches: the identification of the "predominantly concerned" state and the articulation of special rules for multi-state problems (*von Mehren* and *Trautman*), the identification of particular policies relevant to a functional analysis ("consequences-based" approach, *Weintraub*), the application of the "lex fori" in most cases in which there is no express legislative directive to do something else *(Ehrenzweig),* the assignment of priorities to different policies for the purpose of identifying "principles of preference" *(Cavers),* and a greater return to territorialism than advocated by the Restatement (Second) *(Twerski).* With the exception of Weintraub's functional analysis, these approaches today find scant mention in the case law, although they may well be reflected in the way that a court applies the criteria of the Restatement (Second).

VIII. Conclusion: The Choice-of-Law Continuum

The approaches examined in this chapter may be thought of as located somewhere on a continuum, one extreme of which is represented by the fixed and mechanical rules of the First Restatement, and the other by the result-selective approach of the "better rule of law" proposal. Interest analysis, the Restatement (Second), and the coming Restatement (Third) occupy the middle ground, and will usually be used by many or most courts that have abandoned the rules of the First Restatement. The emphasis on contacts and policies of the Restatements makes it possible for courts to be result-selective in the choosing the applicable law.

IX. The Future: The Coming Restatement (Third)

The drafting of a Restatement (Third) is still on its way. Many specific rules as well as general policy provisions have already been approved by the membership of the American Law Institute but a number of drafts and proposals of the Reporter and Associate Reporters are still pending consideration. Completion will take some more time.—The sections so far approved or proposed provide some important and welcome new or changed rules. Absent specific rules, the new Restatement provides guidance for how the applicable law should be determined. These guidelines or approaches are more concrete than those of the Restatement (Second) but some—it is suggested in this book—do not provide a great more certainty than do those of the Restatement (Second). For the new rules or approaches to replace those of current approaches and particularly those of the Restatement (Second) requires their adoption by the states' appellate and ultimately by their highest courts. All that is still in the future.

■ PART FIVE. PARTICULAR CHOICE-OF-LAW PROBLEMS

CHAPTER IX. CHOICE OF LAW BY SUBJECT MATTER

I. Introduction

This chapter summarizes specific choice-of-law rules or approaches. Since Chapter VIII presents a great many tort illustrations, it should also be consulted for choice of law in tort. For domestic relations, you should also review Part Three (regarding Chapters V and VI) above.

II. Torts

The traditional approach, exemplified by the First Restatement, applies the law of the "place of the wrong" to torts. The place of the wrong usually is defined as the place where the injury was suffered. When a state has regulatory concerns, the place of the wrong may also be defined as the state where the tortious conduct occurred. States that depart from the fixed rules of the First Restatement follow various approaches (see Chapter VIII) to make choice-of-law decisions on the basis of policy analysis, while protecting the defendant against "unfair surprise." Particularly difficult problems are raised by multi-state torts such as in products liability, multistate libel, and multistate or multi-person disasters. The Restatement (Second) suggests application of the "most significant relationship" test to these, although—in products liability—some cases follow a plaintiff-favoring approach. In fraud and misrepresentation, the courts apply the law of the place where the plaintiff relied. Worker compensation and no-fault insurance are statutory, as are claims arising from maritime injuries. For the Draft Restatement (Third), see *supra* Chapter VIII (IV) and (IX) as well Appendix B (the "Glossary").

III. Contract

The traditional approach (First Restatement) gives weight to the express choice of the parties, otherwise it calls for application of the law of contract formation to questions of validity and to the law of the intended performance to questions of breach. Modern approaches put principal emphasis on the protection of party expectations, especially on upholding (validating) the contract. Both the Restatement Second and the Uniform Commercial Code permit the parties to select the applicable law (choice-of-law clauses). Consumer protective legislation may limit this freedom (for instance, U.C.C. § 2A–106).

In the absence of a choice by the parties, states make a choice on the basis of their general approach to choice of law (Chapter VIII). Substantial agreement does exist with respect to a number of specific contracts and contract issues. Thus, contracts for an interest in land are usually governed by the law of the situs. Much of the case law has interpreted the Uniform Commercial Code as calling for the application of the law of the most significant relationship to the sale of goods. For the Draft Restatement (Third), see *supra,* Chapter VIII (V) and (IX) as well Appendix B (the "Glossary").

Contracts for the international sale of goods may be governed by the UN (Vienna) Convention on the International Sale of Goods (CISG), to which the United States is a party. Life insurance contracts are governed by the law of the insured's domicile, casualty insurance contracts by the location of the insured risk, and liability insurance by the law applicable to the tort. Service contracts are governed by the law of the place where the services are to be rendered, where the contract was formed, or where it has its center of gravity. Modern approaches consider the Statute of Frauds to be substantive.

IV. Property

Interests in land (immovable property) are governed by the law of the situs. The Restatement (Second) adopts the most-significant-relationship test for the validity and effect of the transfer of movable property; the Uniform Commercial Code (§ 9–301) provides choice-of-law rules for the perfection of security interests and their effects. The assignability of a claim (intangible property) is governed, according to the Restatement (Second), by the law of the place of the most significant relationship which, however, will ordinarily be the law applicable to the original transaction.

V. Succession

Intestate succession to immovable property is governed by the law of its situs, while the law of the decedent's domicile at death applies to intestate succession to movable property. The validity of a will (testate succession) traditionally is also governed by situs and domiciliary law, respectively. However, in order to effectuate the intent of the testator, most states provide for alternative references, for instance to the law of the place where the will was executed or where the testator was domiciled. The same applies to testamentary trusts. The right of the surviving spouse to take a statutory share is also determined by situs and domiciliary law, respectively; however, the situs may choose to recognize the greater interest of the domicile in this issue and to defer to its law. The Draft Restatement (Third) provides for a unitary approach for the determination of the applicable law in succession, particularly intestate succession. Following the civil law approach, it would regard the estate as a unit, governed by one law, while technical problems (such as the registration of title changes) need still be done at the situs.

VI. Trusts

Testamentary trusts depend for their formal validity on the validity of the will that established them. Inter vivos trusts of land are governed by situs law, while those relating to movables are valid if valid where made.

VII. Probate and Administration of Estates

Principal administration takes place at the decedent's domicile (domiciliary administration); ancillary administration takes place in those other states in which the decedent also left assets. The authority of an administrator is limited to the state of his or her appointment. Debtors of the estate who make payment to the administrator who has not qualified locally may nevertheless be protected under certain circumstances. Creditors may file wherever there is administration. When the overall estate is insolvent, but local assets would be sufficient to pay those who filed locally, modern cases may view the estate as a unit and treat all creditors equally. Thus, a "surplus" state would allow only proportionate satisfaction of claims pending there and then remit the balance to the domiciliary administration for the benefit of claims pending in deficit states. With the promulgation of the Restatement (Third), the foregoing will change if and when courts change to the unitary administration of a decedent's estate.

VIII. Corporations

The existence and dissolution of a corporation, as well as its "internal affairs" (validity of stock issues, bylaws, voting rights, management, dividends), are governed by the law of incorporation. A corporation may need to comply with a state's "qualification statute" in order to do intrastate business in that state. Whether compliance with the registration requirement may constitutes consent to general jurisdiction in the particular state was very much disputed. The U.S. Supreme Court approved such mandated consent in 2023 (*Mallory*), Chapter III, Sections II, III(2)(b)). In some states, "pseudo-foreign corporation" statutes provide for the application of forum law to out-of-state corporations not listed on national securities exchanges that do a specified significant amount of business within the state. These statutes may conflict with the "internal affairs" rule upheld by the Supreme Court in *CTS* (Chapter IX, Section VIII).

CHAPTER X. CONSTITUTIONAL LIMITATIONS ON STATE CHOICE OF LAW

I. Introduction

This chapter focuses on the question of whether a state is entirely free in its choice of the applicable law (most usually: its own) or whether there are constitutional limitations or mandates that it must observe. The two principal constitutional provisions relevant in this context are the Due Process and Full Faith and Credit Clauses. The first protects the defendant against the unfair and arbitrary application of an unrelated law, while the latter addresses the interests of other states in the application of their laws.

II. Due Process and Full Faith and Credit: The Early Cases

In early cases, the Supreme Court undertook to endorse the vested rights approach and to prescribe what law a state had to apply; non-application of that law was said to deprive the defendant of due process rights. Similarly, under the Full Faith and Credit Clause, the Court required the use of another state's law (for instance, where the employment relationship had been formed) unless doing so would be "obnoxious" to the forum. Subsequent decisions abandoned this approach. The Court no longer prescribes the applicable law; rather, it places limits upon a state's freedom to choose the applicable law. What remains from the early cases is that a state may not apply its own law when it has no contact with the defendant or the transaction other than being the place of suit. Furthermore, the case law now treats the due process and full faith and credit inquiries to be co-extensive for practical purposes.

III. *Hague, Shutts,* and *Wortman*

Hague and *Shutts* established the modern test that "for a state's substantive law to be selected in a constitutionally permissible manner, that state must have a significant contact or significant aggregation of contacts, creating state interests, such that choice of its law is neither arbitrary nor fundamentally unfair." In *Wortman,* the Court permitted the forum to interpret the other state's law in such a manner as to have it come out the same as forum law (which it could not have applied directly). The dissent considered *Wortman* to diminish the authority of the two previous cases.

IV. Court Closing

A state may not discriminate against claims arising under the law of another state by closing its courts to those claims. However, it may apply its own procedural rules to those claims and, moreover, need not entertain claims unknown to its own legal system.

V. Other Constitutional Provisions

Both the Privileges and Immunities and the Equal Protection Clauses prohibit the application of discriminatory forum law to out-of-state parties unless the distinctions drawn exist for a legitimate purpose. In addition, the imposition on a non-resident of a disadvantageous rule of local law which does not apply to residents may constitute an impermissible burden on interstate commerce.

VI. Conclusion

With few possible exceptions, there are no constitutionally mandated choice-of-law rules, only constitutional limits. Again with only few possible exceptions, these limits will ordinarily arise from the application of the Due Process Clause.

■ PART SIX. ISSUES OF FEDERALISM

CHAPTER XI. STATE LAW IN FEDERAL COURT

I. The *Erie* Doctrine

The decision in *Erie R.R. Co. v. Tompkins* overturned *Swift v. Tyson*, which had permitted federal courts, sitting in diversity, to make federal common law in the absence of an applicable state statute. First, *Swift* was held to be unconstitutional to the extent that it permitted federal courts to exercise lawmaking powers not granted by the Constitution to the legislative branch of the federal government. Secondly, *Swift* had also produced undesirable differences in result between state and federal courts sitting in the same state. Therefore, for constitutional and policy (intrastate uniformity) reasons, *Erie* requires a federal court sitting in diversity to apply the law of the state in which it sits when there is no applicable federal law or federal lawmaking authority. With respect to the policy aspects of *Erie*, decisions often refer to the "twin aims" of *Erie*: " . . . discouragement of forum-shopping and avoidance of inequitable administration of the laws" (*Hanna*).

The *Erie* doctrine applies to issues that are substantive "for *Erie* purposes." An issue is substantive in this sense when it is outcome determinative (*Guaranty Trust v. York*). However, "countervailing considerations" of policy may justify adoption of a federal rule, provided there is constitutional authority to do so *(Byrd)*. The substantive-procedural analysis and the weighing of policy interests may produce mixed procedures—those governed in part by state and in part by federal law (*Gasperini*; see also below, No. II).

II. *Erie* and the Federal Rules of Civil Procedure

As part of its power to establish federal courts, Congress has lawmaking power to regulate the procedure in these courts. The Rules Enabling Act exercises this power and is the basis upon which the Federal Rules of Civil Procedure have been promulgated. Whenever a validly promulgated Federal Rule "clashes" with an inconsistent rule of state law, the Federal Rule takes precedence *(Hanna)*. Whether it "clashes" is to be determined on the basis of an analysis of the respective functions of the federal and state rules and of the Congressional intent *(Walker)*.

A 1996 U.S. Supreme Court decision (*Gasperini*) takes a Solomonic approach: the jury mandate of the Seventh Amendment applies in federal court (*Byrd*), but state law is to be followed and state-law standards are to be used for the review of the jury's award for excessiveness by the trial court, but not upon appeal. See also *Semtek*.

III. *Erie* and Choice of Law

The state "law" which a federal court must apply in consequence of the *Erie* decision encompasses the *choice-of-law* rules of the state in which it sits *(Klaxon, Challoner)*.

The application of the *Erie* doctrine raises potential problems of forum shopping in some cases in which federal courts have jurisdiction when state courts could not have entertained the case (for lack of jurisdiction). This may be a problem in federal interpleader, the 100-mile bulge rule, in supplemental jurisdiction, and in some federal transfers.

IV. Determining State Decisional Law

Where in force, the Uniform Certification of Questions of Law Act permits a federal court to obtain a ruling on state decisional law from the state supreme court. In the absence of such help, the federal court must decide the state-law issue as it thinks that the state supreme court would, taking into account existing precedents.

CHAPTER XII. FEDERAL LAW AS THE RULE OF DECISION

I. Introduction: Sources of Federal Law

Federal law consists of the Constitution, federal statutes, treaties with foreign nations, and federal decisional law. The latter either interprets and applies the written federal law or declares new federal law ("federal common law"). The last of these can be divided further into "federal courts law" (i.e., applicable only in federal court) or general federal common law—see next section. Federal law is the "supreme law of the land." It may claim exclusive application, preempt previously applicable state law, or grant state law concurrent application.

II. Federal Common Law

The federal courts may make federal common law whenever the Constitution gives lawmaking power to the federal government. However, the policy considerations underlying *Erie* do not make it appropriate to create federal common law whenever there is authority to do so. Instead, the creation of federal common law must advance a federal interest. Thus, the Supreme Court has created federal common law to define the government's liability with respect to commercial paper and in tort, to regulate the government's relation with its contractors, and to ensure uniform application of government-created rights. Some rules of foreign relations law are also derived from federal common law.

The Supreme Court has shown great restraint in creating federal common law. In addition, it has held that federal common law is displaced when Congress addresses the particular area legislatively. In 2022, it restricted the Environmental Protection Agency from developing rules in the absence of specific direction by Congress to do so.

Where does federal common law come from? In some cases (see *Clearfield*), the Court will make its own rule. In others, it may adopt a (or the particular) state law definition as the federal rule (at least for that case); see *Williams II*, *Semtek*.

Perspective

■ I. WHAT IS CONFLICT OF LAWS?

Conflict of Laws (also "**conflicts**") comprises three main subject areas that may be important in dealing with a case that has an *out-of-state party,* concerns *out-of-state events*, deals with out-of-state *transactions*, or has other out-of-state aspects. "Out-of-state" in this context means any state or foreign country, other than the state that we are in. What are the principal question? (1) Does the local court (the "**forum**") have jurisdiction over the parties, (2) if so, what law—its own or another state's or country's—does it apply, and (3) in circumstances in which a case was litigated and decided in *another* state or country, is the other court's judgment entitled to recognition in the forum? Of these, the second area—choice of law—is particularly difficult because different considerations often apply depending on whether the case involves—for example—a tort, a support claim, the construction of a will, or some other area of the law.

■ II. THE CONFLICTS COURSE AND OTHER COURSES

All conflicts courses will touch on jurisdiction, choice of law, and the enforcement of judgments, although the sequence (and relative emphasis) will vary from casebook to casebook and from one instructor to another. Additionally, the course will usually address how conflicts cases are handled in federal court (the *Erie* doctrine).

One will have studied jurisdiction in the Civil Procedure course. Its review for the conflicts course is essential because, in appropriate cases, courts may choose and apply their own law. In those cases, for practical purposes, the choice of the court amounts to a choice of the law that will be applied. For this reason, conflicts courses often review jurisdiction. The *Erie* doctrine and issues raised by the Federal Rules of Civil Procedures are also treated in Civil Procedure and in Federal Courts but are important to be reviewed in Conflicts.

Because of the review of jurisdiction and procedural law, and because the choice-of-law segment of the course cuts across so many fields of substantive law, one may find that Conflict of Laws is a very good capstone course.

■ III. ABOUT THIS BOOK

The organization of this book groups the material in discrete parts. The first part further introduces you to the subject and deals with the concept of **domicile**, which is pervasive in all of conflicts law. Matters of litigation—**jurisdiction** and **recognition of judgments**—are presented together in Part Two because they raise no choice-of-law issues. Part Three deals with domestic relations because many issues also do not involve choice of the applicable law, but only jurisdiction and recognition of judgments, and are therefore related to the material in Part Two.

The very difficult topic of choice of law is presented in Part Four. An understanding of Chapter VIII is essential.

Federal-State problems conclude the book in Part Five. See also the last paragraph of Section IV, immediately following.

IV. HOW TO STUDY

The material summarized in Parts One through Three is difficult but does not call for different ways of studying from those you have developed so far: studying and understanding procedural rules, identifying the constitutional limits within which state law may operate, and making judgment calls in close cases on the basis of the understanding of the law and the underlying policy which you have gained. The review questions that follow each chapter will help you in your search for confident "judgment calls."

Choice of Law (Part Four) is a new—and for many students, lawyers, and courts, a confusing—experience. This is so because there are often different (competing, also inconsistent) approaches as to how to choose the applicable law. There are *some* rules, but often the choice of what law to apply involves an analysis of competing party interests and legal policies. To master choice-of-law analysis, you must practice it extensively. This is best done by taking the cases studied in the course and analyzing their facts on the basis of *each* of the choice-of-law approaches. This will show you how and why different approaches reach similar or inconsistent results. Chapter VIII gives you the theoretical background for your own practice.

Each chapter ends with a section containing review questions. Answers to these questions may be found in Appendix A. A glossary (Appendix B) presents short definitions and explanations of terms and concepts used in conflicts law. Sample comprehensive, final exam-type questions are presented in Appendix C, followed by suggested answers. A Table of Cases lets you find the page(s) in the text on which a particular case is discussed.

V. REFERENCES; FURTHER READING

The **Restatement** of Conflict of Laws has been very influential. As you will see, there are important differences between the First Restatement (1934) and the Restatement (Second) (1971). The text refers to both, indicating whether the reference is to the "**First Restatement**" or to the "**Restatement (Second)**." For a few years now, work has been under way in the American Law Institute to promulgate a **Restatement (Third)**. Many proposals have already been adopted my the membership, others already exist in "tentative draft" form. Where relevant, the new provisions—already adopted or proposed—are discussed.

A text of this size cannot deal with all aspects of the conflict of laws, nor even treat comprehensively, and with attention to all nuances, all the subjects it does address. The cases cited may help you further. You will find more detailed and comprehensive textual treatment in **Hay, Borchers, Symeonides & Whytock, Conflict of Laws** (7th ed. 2026, West Hornbook Series). References to this book are contained in the text—abbreviated as ***"Hornbook § ___."*** An important older treatise is **Weintraub, Commentary on the Conflict of Laws** (6th ed. 2010, Foundation Press). See also **Hay,**

Advanced Introduction to Private International Law and Procedure (Edward Elgar, 2018, 2nd ed. 2023).

Part One

Introduction

■ ANALYSIS

I. Overview and General Background

II. Domicile and Habitual Residence

Chapter I

Overview and General Background

■ ANALYSIS

I. **The Conflicts Case**
   - A. Introduction
   - B. The Elements; Definitions
   - C. Interstate Versus International Conflicts Cases

II. **Sources**

III. **Introduction to Choice of Law**
   - A. Introduction
   - B. A Look at History
   - C. Modern Approaches

IV. **Review Questions**

I. The Conflicts Case

A. Introduction

Many legal disputes are purely local. For instance: The question of whether a contractor has or has not substantially performed when the location of an interior wall was off by six inches will usually be decided by local courts and according to local contract law.

Increasingly, however, disputes may have a **foreign element**.

Note: In conflicts law, "foreign" does not necessarily mean "foreign country." Instead, "foreign" means *everything that is not local.* Thus, for instance, "foreign" parties are parties from another state of the United States *or* from a foreign country. Similarly, a "foreign" transaction is one which took place outside the local state. A case with "foreign elements" might involve a product manufactured in another state or country that causes injury locally.

The victim in such a product liability case would like to sue locally, rather than have to travel to where the defendant tortfeasor is located. Does the local court have jurisdiction? Also, the victim would like, if possible, to have the court apply local law (for instance, because it provides for strict liability). Assume that the victim does recover in his or her home state, but that the foreign (out-of-state) defendant owns no property there. The judgment creditor will now have to seek recognition and enforcement of the judgment in the defendant's home state (or in another state where there are assets belonging to the defendant).

Conflicts law thus has an ordering function: When the case is connected with more than one legal system—when it is an interstate or international case—conflicts law decides who has the power to decide the case, according to whose law the case should be decided, and what effect the resulting judgment has elsewhere.

B. The Elements; Definitions

In legal language, the foregoing statement asks (1) what state has **jurisdiction** over the parties and the subject matter, (2) what is the appropriate **choice of law**, and (3) under what circumstances is an out-of-state judgment entitled to **recognition and enforcement**? The recognition of a judgment often contains further questions with respect to the extent of its effect: *who* is bound and with respect to *what issues?*

Conflict of Laws ("Conflicts"—but **not** "Conflicts of Law") deals with all of the above elements of an interstate or international case.

Note: The term "conflicts" is sometimes also used when only choice of law is meant.

When we look at a conflicts case, we usually look at it from the *perspective of the local state and court* (where the case is pending). They are called the "**forum**" (also: "forum state" or "forum court").

Refer to the products liability example in Section A above. The questions are: does the victim's home state have jurisdiction over the out-of-state manufacturer? If so, what substantive law should the forum apply? What will be the effect of its judgment?

Note: The law of the forum state is also called the "**lex fori**," especially in older decisions.

C. Interstate Versus International Conflicts Cases

As a general rule, American conflicts law does not differentiate between interstate and international cases. With few exceptions, the same rules with respect to jurisdiction, choice of law, and the recognition of judgments apply to both.

Exceptions: 1) Regarding jurisdiction, the international nature of a case may make litigation in an American court inappropriate. For *forum non conveniens*, see below Chapter III(IV-B).

2) Although the Full Faith and Credit Clause does not apply to foreign-country judgments, *most* states accord those judgments the same recognition as sister-state judgments, but provide for additional defenses. See below at p. 113.

3) The United States has entered into a number of treaties that apply to *international cases only*. Examples: Intercountry Adoptions, International Sales Convention, Civil Aspects of International Child Abduction, Service of Documents, Taking of Evidence Abroad, Liability in Civil Aviation (Warsaw Convention).

II. Sources

As a general rule, **conflicts law is state law**.

Federal law—statutory or federal common law—may displace state law. In such a case, state conflicts law becomes irrelevant because of the existence of a uniform federal *substantive* rule. Note that federal statutory law may preserve state conflicts law. For example, the Federal Tort Claims Act provides for liability "in accordance with the law of the place where the act or omission occurred." 28 U.S.C.A. § 1346(b)(1) (West 2024). This has been interpreted to include the conflicts rules of that place. *Richards v. United States*, 369 U.S. 1, 82 S. Ct. 585, 7 L. Ed. 2d 492 (1962). See also *Schalliol v. Fare*, 206 F. Supp. 2d 689 (E.D. Pa. 2002) (applying *Richards*).

Federal law, especially **federal constitutional law**, establishes the **outer limits** within which a state is free to adopt or apply its own substantive law and rules of procedure (jurisdiction).

Example: The Due Process Clause establishes limits for the assertion of state court jurisdiction over nonresident defendants. See below at p. 71. Similarly, the Due Process Clause and, possibly, the Full Faith and Credit Clause, limit a state court's freedom to apply the law of the forum to a case with which it has little or no connection, see p. 234.

Exception: The United States has entered into a number of treaties that establish *conflicts rules for international cases* to which they apply. For examples, see above at p. 8. When a treaty exists (which is federal law and preempts state law under the Supremacy Clause), the state conflicts rule applies to interstate cases, while the treaty (federal) rule usually applies only to international cases.

III. Introduction to Choice of Law

A. Introduction

You are used to analyzing facts to identify issues. When you have the issue, you then apply a rule of law to resolve it. Things are more complex in conflicts cases. When we have found the issue in a conflicts case—e.g., "did the defendant's conduct create liability?"—we must choose between or among two or more legal systems (the laws of sister states or of foreign nations) to furnish the substantive rule of law for the resolution of our issue. In other words, there is an additional step between issue identification and application of a rule of law: it is deciding *which* rule of law to apply.

It would be relatively easy if there were rules about which rule of law to select. As you will see, there are *some* choice-of-law *rules.* But for several important subjects (torts, contracts), most states have found the traditional rules to be too narrow and too mechanical to yield just results. They therefore seek to choose the applicable law through a process of analysis: by making *value and policy judgments.* When courts weigh policies, comparing their state's policy to that of another, outcomes may differ from state to state; policy analysis and interest weighing make for less certainty than a fixed rule. Learning to analyze competing interests and policies makes the choice-of-law part of Conflicts Law difficult.

B. A Look at History

A look at the history of conflicts law will help you understand the origin of some of today's rules and approaches, not to mention the language and reasoning of some of the older cases.

Cross reference: For greater detail, see *Hornbook* Chapter II.

Early conflicts law (in the Italian city-states of the 12th and 13th centuries) distinguished between *real* and *personal* statutes. The former were territorial in nature, for instance rules of law dealing with land. Personal rules of law followed the person wherever he or she went, and in that way claimed universal application. An example of such a rule is a person's capacity to contract.

The seventeenth century Dutch scholar *Huber* emphasized the *territorial nature of all law.* He solved the need for international cooperation with the concept of "comity." *Joseph Story,* the "father" of American conflicts law, made comity the cornerstone of his 1834 *Commentaries* on conflicts. *Acting with comity means recognizing—giving local effect—to acts valid where done and rights acquired under another state's law.*

Foreign-country judgments are not covered by the Constitution's Full Faith and Credit Clause. According to an older U.S. Supreme Court decision, they were nevertheless recognized as a matter of comity. Today, most states recognize foreign-country judgments like sister-state judgments. Some decisions still refer to the comity concept. Sometimes they invoke it erroneously, as a reason *not* to recognize a foreign act or law. In addition, since a foreign-country judgment also does not merge the underlying cause of action, such a judgment may also be subject to more extensive public policy review.

Territoriality and comity are somewhat inconsistent concepts. They hold, in combination, that a law is at the same time limited (territorially), yet entitled to some recognition or deference beyond the territory. The **vested rights** theory sought to overcome this inconsistency: a right validly created by the law of one state is valid (to be recognized) everywhere. In the United States, its chief proponent was *Joseph Beale,* who later became the reporter for the First Restatement. This explains the **vested rights orientation of the First Restatement** (1934).

C. Modern Approaches

The vested rights approach dominated choice of law thinking in the United States for over a generation. Beginning in the 1950s, there was much criticism of the First Restatement. It was acknowledged that the First Restatement provided predictable and certain choice of law rules, but it was also felt that they were mechanistic and could therefore produce unjust results.

Example: Driver and guest from State A take a Sunday drive, which is to take them through a small area of State B. They have an accident in B involving no other car, and the guest is injured. Back in A, the guest wishes to sue the driver for negligence (the driver carries insurance that would cover his liability). If B has a guest statute (barring guests from suing their host-drivers), the choice-of-law rule of the First Restatement would select the law of the place of the accident and bar the guest. Critics would say, what does B have to do with these parties? No B people were injured, and no B personnel will go uncompensated if the guest recovers. In contrast, if the guest may not sue, and if the guest should be indigent, it will be A's taxpayers who will provide the support.

As a result of this kind of potentially unfair outcome, a number of new approaches to choice of law were developed. All retain some of the rules of the First Restatement for some areas of the law where certainty and predictability are the most important considerations. Examples include land transactions, succession, and trusts. Beyond these areas, however, the new approaches focus on a variety of factors: the expectations of the parties, the policies underlying particular legal rules (e.g., compensation, deterrence, shielding a charity or a manufacturer from liability), and the relative weight of the concerns of the states involved. The most influential of the new approaches has been represented by the Restatement (Second) of Conflict of Laws (1971) ("**Restatement (Second)**"). It calls for continued application of traditional rules for many types of cases. But for some types of cases, particularly in contract and tort, and for some particular issues, it calls for application of the law of "the most significant relationship" to the parties and/or to the transaction. It provides guidelines as to how to determine that place. Other approaches seek to determine the state with the predominant "governmental interest," or—a bit subjectively—as providing the "better [substantive] law." The great majority of states now apply one of these modern approaches. Yet recently, still more than nine states had retained the traditional approach in tort and contract conflict cases.[1]

The Restatement (Second) is also not ideal. There have been many critical comments, particularly with respect to differences in how courts make the value judgments for which it calls. As a result, the American Law Institute (ALI) is currently working on a "**Restatement (Third)**," of which many sections have been approved, while others are still in the form of tentative drafts. The ALI's General Assembly will finally approve and promulgate the whole new Restatement (Third). It will then be up to the courts of the states whether they adopt the new Restatement or some of its sections to replace approaches or Restatement (Second) sections that have been applied heretofore. We will therefore deal with both the Restatement (Second) and with

[1] **See** John F. Coyle, William S. Dodge & Aaron D. Simowitz, *Choice of Law in the American Courts in 2024: Thirty-Eighth Annual Survey*,73 Am.J.Comp.L. 485 (2025). See also *Hornbook* § 2.21A.

changes that may result as some or many states begin to adopt differences contained in the new Restatement (Third).

IV. Review Questions

1. Define "forum" and "lex fori."
2. A "foreign party" or other "foreign element" (event or transaction) is:
   a. A non-United States citizen or an event that took place abroad,
   b. A party from another State of the Union or an event that occurred in such a state,
   c. Both of the above.
3. "Conflicts" means:
   a. Choice of law,
   b. The problem areas of jurisdiction, choice of law, and recognition and enforcement of judgments, which are involved in a conflicts case,
   c. Both of the above.
4. a. T or F: With few exceptions, American conflicts law does not differentiate between interstate and international cases.
   b. T or F: The Full Faith and Credit Clause mandates the recognition and enforcement of all "foreign" judgments.
   c. T or F: Many choice of law rules are derived from federal law.
   d. T or F: The concept of comity was used to explain why one state would recognize the territorially limited law or judgment of another.
   e. T or F: The First Restatement is associated with the vested rights approach to choice of law.
   f. T or F: The Restatement (Second) calls for an evaluation of the potentially "conflicting" laws and for the ultimate application of the law that is substantively better (best) than the other(s).
   g. T or F: When adopted by the American Law Institute, the Restatement (Third) will replace the Restatement (Second) in the states that had followed it.
   h. T or F: The coming Restatement (Third) provides rules as well as policy guidance for the determination of the law that is appropriate for the particular issue.
5. Does federal law provide conflicts rules or enforcement standards?
   a. Yes or no?
   b. Explain.
   c. Assume that the UCC requires a writing (statute of frauds) and that the Convention on Contracts for the International Sales of Goods (CISG) does not. Which standard prevails when a contract falls within the subject matter coverage of both?

Chapter II

Domicile and Habitual Residence

■ ANALYSIS

I. **The Significance of the Domicile Concept in the Conflict of Laws**
   A. The Need for "Connecting Factors"
   B. Domicile as a Pervasive Concept
II. **Domicile and Habitual Residence Defined**
   A. In General
      1. What Domicile Is Not (but May Become)
         a. Residence
         b. "Habitual Residence"
         c. Residence and Nationality
         d. Statutory References
      2. The Central Concept
   B. Types of Domicile
      1. Domicile of Origin
      2. Domicile of Choice
      3. Domicile by Operation of Law
   C. Acquisition of Domicile of Choice
      1. In General; Capacity
      2. Physical Presence
         a. Presence at a Specific Rather than at a General Location
         b. In Transit
      3. Intent to Remain Indefinitely
         a. In General
         b. Intent and Motive
         c. Factors for the Determination of Intent
      4. The Forum Determines the Existence of a Domicile of Choice
   D. Domicile by Operation of Law
      1. Derivative Domicile: Children
      2. Derivative Domicile: Married Individuals
   E. Special Situations
      1. Incompetent, Institutionalized, and Incarcerated Persons
      2. Military Service Personnel
   F. Habitual Residence

III. **Analogies in the Case of Corporate Entities**
IV. **Review Questions**

I. The Significance of the Domicile Concept in the Conflict of Laws

A. The Need for "Connecting Factors"

Every legal system must use some kind of link or trigger to determine when it may exercise its sovereign powers with respect to a person, event, or transaction (or when another state's law should be applied). "Sovereign power," in this context, may be the exercise of judicial power (jurisdiction). Alternatively (or additionally), it may be the application of a local or a foreign law to local or foreign parties or transactions.

The particular link needed will often depend on the purpose for which a state wishes to exercise its powers over a person. Thus, very little by way of a link may be needed for a state to exercise the power to tax; the fact that revenue was derived from an in-state transaction may be enough. A different, more substantial link to the forum state may be needed when a state requires a person to defend himself or herself in its courts, that is, to exercise jurisdiction over that person. Still other, perhaps even more substantial links may be needed (or seem appropriate) when a state seeks to impose substantive liability upon a person under its laws, or when it is asked to dissolve a marriage or other domestic relationship.

For these and many other purposes, legal systems establish "connecting factors." In the United States, as we will see, the U.S. Supreme Court speaks, in various contexts, of "minimum contacts," "significant contacts," "affiliating circumstances," and the like.

From among the many connecting factors that may be used to establish the necessary link between a person and the forum (or other) state, all legal systems will identify one as the most important. That one link will serve as the connecting factor in virtually all circumstances and for many purposes. Other connecting factors will play a more subsidiary role, being usually restricted to specific situations. In the United States and in the other countries that follow the common law tradition, a person's *domicile* is the single most important connecting factor. In contemporary practice, and especially in international practice, "habitual residence" is becoming the main connecting factor. One notable exception is in family law, for which many civil-law countries still often look to the law of the parties' nationality. For title to real property, the situs state has jurisdiction and its law applies.

B. Domicile as a Pervasive Concept

The concept of domicile is pervasive in American conflicts law. It is one of the bases upon which a state may exercise *jurisdiction* over a person. Domicile may also furnish the connecting factor for the selection of the law that should be applied to a particular issue or case (*choice of law*). Thus, a state will ordinarily apply the law of the state in which the decedent was domiciled at death to determine succession to his or her movable property in the absence of a valid testamentary disposition. Although the exercise of a state's authority could be based on other grounds as well, domicile is often invoked when a state taxes a person on his or her property, determines eligibility for certain benefits, or undertakes to regulate conduct.

II. Domicile and Habitual Residence Defined

A. In General

Domicile is a pervasive concept in the conflict of laws. Many critics have questioned its usefulness, claiming that it is not a unitary concept. This is true, as it would be for any term or concept that is called upon to do multiple service. The problem is recognized by the Restatement (Second): "the core of domicil[e] is everywhere the same. But in close cases, decision of a question of domicil[e] may sometimes depend upon the purpose for which the domicil[e] concept is used in the particular case." § 11 cmt. *o*. The coming Restatement (Third) also refers to the determination of a person's domicile "for the purpose of deciding a particular conflict-of-laws issue." § 2.03(3).

1. What Domicile Is Not (but May Become)

a. Residence

Domicile does *not* equal *residence*. A person may have two or more residences but, as subsequent discussion will make plain, a person can have *only one domicile at a time*. Under current law, one of the ingredients of domicile is a person's intent (*infra* at pp. 11, 13). Intent must often be derived from facts. A person's residence is a fact, and the use of one residence from among two or several as a principal residence may well suggest that he or she intended to make it his or her domicile. Thus, there may be a *relationship* between a person's (principal) residence and domicile but the two are *not the same*. See Section B(2) below.

b. "Habitual Residence"

Apart from the United States, "habitual residence" is used in the national conflicts law of many countries, as well as in international conventions. This concept is discussed below at Section F.

c. Residence and Nationality

As is the case with residence, a person's nationality by itself says nothing about the location of his or her domicile. Thus, a person may be a citizen of state A by birth, and by choice have acquired quite a different domicile for the rest of his or her life. Again, a person may possess dual or multiple citizenship (for instance, because of his or her birth in one country and the automatic—derivative—acquisition of the different citizenship of his or her parents). Again, and as in the case of residence, a person's citizenship may be a factor to consider in the domicile determination. Thus, the fact that a person retained his citizenship while changing his home to another country may raise the question whether he really intended to abandon his former domicile and acquire a new one. This is a matter of proof and persuasion.

In American law, the only direct relationship between citizenship and domicile is that *state citizenship* (for instance, for purposes of federal diversity jurisdiction) is derived from domicile. However, domicile *is not* derived from citizenship. Thus, the Fourteenth Amendment to the U.S. Constitution provides that persons are citizens of the United States and "of the state wherein they reside." Residence, in that context, has been held to mean domicile.

d. Statutory References

Statutes sometimes use the terms "resident" or "residence." In many instances, particularly in statutes relating to divorce or probate, these references may mean domicile. In other cases, for instance in statutes dealing with the use and occupancy of real property, the context will make it clear that the statute means to address and to regulate actual residence or occupancy rather than domicile. In still other cases (for instance, with respect to divorce), "residence" may impose a waiting requirement, regardless of the person's domicile.

2. The Central Concept

Domicile is the closest connection a person has to a state. It is the place where he or she maintains his or her home; it is the center of his or her life. "Center of a person's life" will be the definition of "domicile" in the future Restatement (Third) of Conflict of Laws (also see below at Section B-2). Therefore, every person has a domicile. It is possible to be stateless, i.e., not to possess a citizenship, but it is impossible not to have a domicile. From this, it also follows that a person can only have *one* domicile at a time. But see above Section A at the end.

B. Types of Domicile

1. Domicile of Origin

An infant derives his or her domicile from his or her parents (or custodial parent) at birth. Restatement (Third) § 2.04(1). This derivative domicile is therefore one illustration of a domicile by operation of law (for others, see below at Section III). In the United States, the domicile of origin is lost when, in the exercise of one's capacity to make a choice (Section C-1, below), the person abandons the domicile of origin and acquires a domicile of choice. Such a domicile of choice continues until the acquisition of yet another domicile of choice.

In England, in contrast, the domicile of origin revives upon the abandonment of a domicile of choice and until such time as a new domicile of choice has been perfected. *Udny v. Udny,* [1869] H.L. 441 (Scot.). See also Section F, below.

2. Domicile of Choice

Every person with capacity to do so (see below, Sections C-1 and E) may change his or her present domicile—whether this is the domicile of origin, another domicile by operation of law, or the previously acquired domicile of choice—by acquiring a *domicile of choice.* The traditional criteria for the perfection of a domicile of choice are (1) *abandonment* of the previous domicile; (2) *arriving* (some physical presence) at the *intended* new domicile; and (3) the *intent to remain* at the new domicile for an *indefinite* time, or the *lack of a present intent to leave* at a specified time. In American conflicts law, cases involving a person's domicile of choice are by far the most numerous. The Restatement (Third) of Conflict of Laws no longer includes a person's subjective intent in its definition of domicile. Instead, a person's domicile is "the place where the person's life is centered," as determined by "objective evidence of the person's domestic, familial, social, religious, economic, professional, and civil activities." Tentative Draft No. 2, § 2.03(1)–(2) (approved 2021).

3. Domicile by Operation of Law

As stated initially, "domicile" is a pervasive concept in American conflicts law and furnishes the connecting factors for resolving several issues. Every person is therefore said to have a domicile. If one is incapable of acquiring one by the exercise of his or her own volition, a domicile will be assigned: this is the domicile *by operation of law*. Today, this applies principally to minor children and to the various living circumstances in which they may find themselves (children of separated or divorced parents, children born out of wedlock, adopted children, married minor children). The old common law concept of a derivative domicile of a married woman has been abolished. Special considerations apply to people not capable of forming the requisite intent to establish a domicile of choice, such as military service personnel and incarcerated or institutionalized persons. See also Section C-1, immediately following.

C. Acquisition of Domicile of Choice

1. In General; Capacity

As noted above, a domicile of choice is a combination of fact (physical presence) and intent (for a more objective test, see Section B-2, *supra*). Legal capacity results from reaching the age of majority, unless a minor child has been emancipated earlier by marriage or by becoming economically independent from his or her parents (see below). Mental capacity simply means the understanding required to choose a "home." If even such minimal understanding is lacking, the person will either retain his or her previous domicile of choice, or if indicated, derive his or her domicile from the person charged with his or her custody. See Restatement (Second) § 23.

2. Physical Presence

a. Presence at a Specific Rather than at a General Location

To perfect a (new) domicile of choice, a person must arrive (be physically present) at the new location. The physical presence need not be of any particular duration; the factual requirement for domicile (presence) may be satisfied by physical presence of only one instance. Arriving at the specific location which was the intended destination will of course best meet the requirement. However, arrival in the general area of the intended new home, for instance, in the state but not yet in the city, has been held to satisfy the requirement of physical presence as well. See *Winans v. Winans,* 91 N.E. 394, 396 (Mass. 1910); *In re Harrison's Estate,* 89 A.2d 293, 296 (N.J. Hudson Cnty. Ct. 1952). Occasionally, a court will dispense with the presence requirement because of special circumstances, but this is not the general rule. See, e.g., *Mitchell v. Mackey*, 915 F. Supp. 388 (M.D. Ga. 1996) (parents moved from Georgia to Florida while student was living at Georgia school; student had Florida domicile for diversity suit, despite never having set foot in Florida); *Glasford v. Schreier*, No. 03 Civ. 9494, 2004 WL 1469469, at *3 (S.D.N.Y. June 30, 2004) (financial dependence of college student on parent domiciled in another state). See also Restatement (Third) § 2.03(1).

b. In Transit

It has been suggested occasionally that the new domicile of choice comes into being when the old one has been abandoned and the person is en route (*in itinere*) to the new one. That view does not comport with the view of the overwhelming majority of American cases, which is that a domicile of choice is displaced only upon the actual perfection of the new domicile of choice. It also does not comport with the new Restatement (Third) definition of domicile as a person's center of life (Section B-2, *supra*). Query whether a "center of life" can be anticipated, even though the facts might show that the old one no longer continues.

3. Intent to Remain Indefinitely

a. In General

The intent traditionally required for the acquisition of a domicile of choice is the *intent to stay indefinitely* (animus manendi). To state it the other way around, there must not be a present intent to leave at a specific future time or even an indeterminate future time (animus revertendi). However, a "floating intent"—a feeling or nostalgic wish that a person might perhaps, some day in the future, return to his or her homeland—is not enough to overcome facts showing active and lasting ties with the present community. Such facts suggest an intent to remain indefinitely, or at least, the lack of a real intent to leave. See *Penn Mutual Life Insurance Co. v. Fields,* 81 F. Supp. 54 (S.D. Cal. 1948). Again, note that the "intent" factor—to the extent that it seeks to determine a person's subjective intent—should be replaced by the objective determination of a person's "center of life" in the domicile definition of the new Restatement (Third) (see Section B-2, *supra*).

b. Intent and Motive

Motive, the reason why a person wishes to acquire a particular domicile, is not the same as "intent." It is only the latter that is traditionally required for the establishment of domicile, for whatever motive. A person's motive, if it can be proved, may at best be a factor for the determination of whether he or she really had the requisite intent (or where is the person's "center of life" as the new Restatement (Third) provides in § 2.03(2).).

c. Factors for the Determination of Intent

The question of intent (or his or her "center of life," see above) arises often in circumstances where the person can no longer be asked (for instance, the determination of the domicile at death of the testator or intestate decedent). At other times, domicile might be claimed to gain particular advantages, e.g., entitlement to pay in-state tuition, and the validity of the claim is therefore in issue. The courts will deduce intent (or the person's "center of life") from the circumstances of a person's life. The circumstances may include, among others, where the person lives (or lives predominantly); where he or she is a citizen, or votes, or maintains property; or whether he or she has moved his or her property to a new location; or whether property in the old location has been liquidated; or the length of stay in the new location (even though, theoretically, a mere instance will be enough for the creation of domicile); or where his or her business, social, and civic ties are. See *Penn Mutual Life Insurance Co. v. Fields,* 81 F. Supp. 54 (S.D. Cal. 1948); *Estate of Dorrance,* 163 A. 303 (Pa. 1932).

4. The Forum Determines the Existence of a Domicile of Choice

To determine domicile is to evaluate and to decide facts (physical presence and the person's intent, usually as deduced from facts). As a determination of fact, the determination of domicile is for the trier of facts—the court (or jury) of the forum state.

It follows from the foregoing that courts in different states, looking at the same set of facts, may come to different conclusions. Thus, in the famous litigation concerning the *Estate of Dorrance,* 163 A. 303 (Pa. 1932) and 170 A. 601 (N.J. Prerog. Ct. 1934), the courts of Pennsylvania and New Jersey both concluded that Dr. Dorrance had died domiciled in their respective state for the purpose of permitting the (domiciliary) state to levy estate taxes. This was so, not because they rejected the concept that a person can have but a single domicile, but because they differed as to where, as a matter of fact, Dr. Dorrance's single domicile had been. Because the Eleventh Amendment of the Constitution prohibits suits against states, there was no way to join the authorities of one state in the litigation pending in the other, so as to preclude subsequent litigation on the same issue. A due process problem was not involved because no one's property was being taken (heirs are entitled to property only after the settlement of the estate).

In cases in which the total estate proved insufficient to pay multiple state taxes, the U.S. Supreme Court has assumed original jurisdiction to determine the issue as between the states (since one of them stood to lose collecting on its claim). *Texas v. Florida,* 306 U.S. 398, 59 S. Ct. 563, 83 L. Ed. 817 (1939); *California v. Texas,* 457 U.S. 164, 102 S. Ct. 2335, 72 L. Ed. 2d 755 (1982). The *Dorrance* litigation also illustrates how the concept of "domicile" serves multiple purposes (see above). Surely there was enough contact, in the *Dorrance* case, with both New Jersey and Pennsylvania to permit the states to exercise their jurisdiction to tax without resorting to the difficult concept of domicile. In the area of estate taxation, the *Dorrance* problem has been resolved by several states through participation in interstate compacts that allocate death taxes. An example is the settlement of the obligations of the estate of Charles Lindbergh.

When exercising diversity jurisdiction, a federal court's jurisdiction is based on satisfaction of the required jurisdictional amount in controversy (greater than $75,000) and the diversity of *citizenship* of the parties, whereby "citizenship" is synonymous with their domicile. In this context, the existence of domicile ("citizenship") is a requirement of *federal* law. The federal court therefore does not apply state law standards under *Erie* principles but rather applies *federal* standards. *Kantor v. Wellesley Galleries, Ltd.,* 704 F.2d 1088, 1090 (9th Cir. 1983). See also *Rodriguez-Diaz v. Sierra-Martinez,* 853 F.2d 1027 (1st Cir. 1988); *Hearts with Haiti, Inc. v. Kendrick,* 856 F.3d 1 (1st Cir. 2017).

Diversity jurisdiction requires that the parties be citizens of different states. As discussed above, a U.S. citizen is also a citizen of the state in which he or she resides. What if a stateless person resides—has his or her "center of life"—in a state and wishes to sue someone who is a citizen of a neighboring state for

$80,000: have the requirements for diversity of citizenship been met? The courts in *Kantor* and *Yousef v. James River Ins. Co.*, No. 21–160, 2021 WL 2010768 (E.D. La. May 20, 2021), said "no": state citizenship requires United States citizenship, hence plaintiff was not a citizen of the state of his residence.

As noted earlier, the finding of domicile is a factual determination. Therefore, when it arises in a second state (F-2), the issue of domicile may be *precluded by prior litigation* in a prior state (F-l). Thus, in the *Dorrance* litigation mentioned above, if the New Jersey tax authorities had voluntarily participated in the Pennsylvania proceeding, the Pennsylvania determination would have been conclusive and would have precluded a subsequent inconsistent determination in New Jersey. See also Restatement (Third) § 2.09. For discussion of "preclusion by prior litigation" see *infra* Chapter IV(II-C-4).

D. Domicile by Operation of Law

1. Derivative Domicile: Children

Today, the principal example of a person deriving his or her domicile from another relates to the domicile of a minor. As a general rule, the domicile of a legitimate minor child is that of the father. If the parents are separated or divorced, the minor's domicile will be that of the custodial parent. If both parents have died, the minor child will derive his or her domicile from the custodian. An illegitimate child will derive his or her domicile from the mother, if she is alive, or, otherwise, from the person having custody. Even though a child is a minor, it is possible that he or she will gain capacity to establish his or her own domicile of choice. This will be so when the child is emancipated, i.e., no longer under the control and authority of the parents. Emancipation may be the result of marriage. It may also result from economic independence from the parents and a concomitant acknowledgment by the parents that the child is on his or her own. For the Hague Child Abduction Convention, see below at Section F.

2. Derivative Domicile: Married Individuals

In the United States, married individuals acquire their own domicile of choice. Older cases assumed (or engaged in the presumption) that a married woman's domicile was the same as her husband's during marriage and while they lived together. This "assumption," however, did not make her domicile one "by operation of law." Today, it is entirely clear that spouses can, and at times do, have different domiciles (for instance, when university students from different states marry, while not intending to make the college town their home).

E. Special Situations

1. Incompetent, Institutionalized, and Incarcerated Persons

Institutionalized, incompetent and incarcerated persons may or may not have the necessary intent to establish a domicile. However, they lack the capacity to move about freely and therefore cannot physically make the choice (at least, they lack the capacity to make an alternative choice). They therefore retain whatever domicile they had prior to their institutionalization or incarceration.

As noted earlier, an incompetent may have sufficient capacity to understand the meaning of choosing a place to call home. If so, the physical facts of making a place a home combined with the intent to do so will give him or her a domicile there. If the incompetent person lacks this minimal capacity to form a domiciliary intent, whatever previous domicile existed (domicile of choice or even the domicile of origin) will continue.

2. Military Service Personnel

Military personnel similarly may lack capacity to acquire a (new) domicile of choice since they may control neither the location nor the time of their being stationed at a given place. As a rule, military personnel therefore also retain the prior domicile. However, divorce jurisdiction is traditionally grounded upon domicile (see below at p. 141 *seq.*), a rule which would therefore deny to military personnel the ability to obtain a divorce at the place where stationed during the duration of the military service. By statute, a number of states have therefore introduced a durational residence requirement, as an alternative to domicile, as a basis for divorce jurisdiction. For further discussion see *infra* at p. 142.

F. Habitual Residence

The Hague Conference on Private International Law sponsors conventions (treaties) to harmonize or unify conflict of laws rules with respect to a variety of subject matters. The United States is a member of the Hague Conference and has adopted several of its conventions. To bridge the gap between the use of nationality as a connecting factor by civil law countries (compare above at p. 33 and below at p. 52) and the use of domicile as a connecting factor by common law countries, Hague conventions now increasingly utilize the concept of *"habitual residence."* This concept comes very close to the traditional definition of domicile, but is not exactly the same. It expresses factual circumstances alone (where *is* a person habitually resident—usually, principally, most of the time?), while the domicile determination additionally requires a finding as to the person's *intent.* For international practice, the habitual residence concept will no doubt become the functional equivalent of domicile and the forthcoming Restatement (Third) of Conflict of Laws will adopt a similar definition.

In construing "habitual residence" for purposes of the Hague Child Abduction Convention, the Second Circuit looked to the parents' last "shared intent" and then inquired whether the child had acclimatized to the (present) new location, so as to have acquired a new habitual residence, notwithstanding the parents' last shared intent. *Gitter v. Gitter*, 396 F.3d 124 (2d Cir. 2005); *Guzzo v. Cristofano*, 719 F.3d 100 (2d Cir. 2013). See also *Monasky v. Taglieri*, 589 U.S. 68, 140 S. Ct. 719, 206 L. Ed. 2d 9 (2020) (rejecting "categorical requirements for establishing a child's habitual residence," in this case, an "actual-agreement" of intent and establishing clear error as the appropriate standard of appellate review, at 730).

III. Analogies in the Case of Corporate Entities

The case law makes frequent references to the "domicile" of corporations. The thought (no doubt) is that just as natural persons have a domicile, so should legal persons. As Justice Ginsburg put it in the *Goodyear* and *Daimler* decisions, see Chapter III(II-C) *infra*, the test is whether a corporation is so closely affiliated with a state to be considered "at home" there. The new Restatement (Third) now also uses "domicile" in the case of legal persons (corporations, limited liability companies, and the like). The states of incorporation and principal place of business meet that test. In the context of corporations and other business entities, "domicile" also connotes a relationship to the forum state that justifies or enables the forum state to exercise some particular kind of regulatory control. As in the case of natural persons (above II(A)(2)), the new Restatement (Third) emphasizes that the "domicile" of a juridical person "depends on its activities relevant to the particular conflict-of-laws matter to be resolved." § 2.08(1). It is thus not one and the same for all purposes: its purpose is to provide context for a particular issue.

Thus, the state of incorporation furnishes the law applicable to issues concerning internal corporate affairs (see *infra* Chapter IX(VIII)), and—by analogy to the concept of domicile—might be a place where the corporation is subject to general jurisdiction (see *infra* Chapter III(II-C)).

"Domicile," for purposes of "citizenship" in the context of diversity of citizenship for federal jurisdiction, also has been tied to the corporation's place of incorporation. However, since that place may have nothing to do with the corporation's present center of business, diversity jurisdiction depends upon (or may be destroyed) by a finding of principal business activity in the forum state or, in contrast, in another state. Thus, 28 U.S.C.A. § 1332(c) (West 2024) provides that for diversity jurisdiction purposes, a corporation is a citizen of the state in which it is incorporated *and* of the state in which it has its principal place of business.

An "artificial" domicile of corporations is used by statutes defining "pseudo-foreign" corporations (e.g., in California and New York). These are state statutes subjecting foreign corporations—i.e., corporations incorporated under the law of another state and thus technically "domiciled" there—to many aspects of the law of the forum state if ownership by forum state residents exceeds a percentage of total ownership, or if in-state revenues exceed a stated percentage of total revenues.

IV. Review Questions

1. a. T or F: Domicile is a basis both for the assertion of personal jurisdiction *and* for the choice of the applicable law for several conflicts cases.

b. T or F: Under the older definition, where a person has his or her domicile is a matter of intent.

c. T or F: Where a person has his or her domicile is a matter both of facts and intent.

d. T or F: A person who regularly spends three winter months in Florida therefore has his or her domicile there.

e. T or F: The domicile of a United States citizen in the United States also determines his or her state citizenship.

f. T or F: A person *cannot* have more than one domicile at a time, but courts may differ, as a matter of fact, as to *where* that domicile is.

2. List the elements of domicile.

3. Define "domicile of origin," "derivative domicile," and "domicile of choice."

4. A corporation is a "citizen" of what state for purposes of determining whether diversity jurisdiction exists?

5. After growing up in state A, P attended college and law school in state B and is about to graduate. She has already accepted a permanent job in state C and bought a condominium there.

a. T or F: It is clear that state B never became her domicile since she only attended school there.

b. T or F: Even if she considers state C her new home, state C has become her domicile only if she has already gone there to establish a new domicile.

c. T or F: Even if state C has now become her new domicile, she could still maintain her old domicile in state A.

d. T or F: Even if she lost her old domicile in state A, she could have retained her status as a resident of that state.

Part Two

Litigational Matters

■ ANALYSIS

III. Jurisdiction to Adjudicate
IV. Recognition and Enforcement of Foreign Judgments and Decrees

Chapter III

Jurisdiction to Adjudicate

■ ANALYSIS

I. **Overview**
  A. Introduction: Importance of the Jurisdictional Inquiry
    1. Basic Definition
    2. Judicial Jurisdiction as Distinguished from Subject Matter Jurisdiction
    3. Judicial Jurisdiction as Distinguished from Legislative Jurisdiction
    4. Jurisdiction and the Notice Requirement
    5. Jurisdiction and Recognition of Judgments
  B. Categories of Jurisdiction
    1. *In Personam* (Personal) Jurisdiction
      a. Specific Jurisdiction
      b. General Jurisdiction
    2. Jurisdiction over Things
      a. *In Rem* Jurisdiction
      b. *Quasi In Rem* Jurisdiction
II. **General *In Personam* Jurisdiction: The Exercise of Jurisdiction Without Regard to Claim-Related Contacts**
  A. Enterprises: Required Forum Connection
    1. A Single Transaction Does Not Support General Jurisdiction
    2. Quality of Defendant-Forum Contacts
  B. Natural Persons
    1. Domicile
    2. Citizenship
      a. National Citizenship
      b. State Citizenship
    3. Service Within the Jurisdiction
      a. *Pennoyer v. Neff*
      b. Transient Jurisdiction
  C. Corporations: "At Home" in the Forum or "Consent" by Registering for Doing Business
  D. Notice Requirement
III. **Specific Jurisdiction: Contacts Related to the Litigation**
  A. Introduction
    1. The Territorial Approach

2. Shifting the Focus to the "Individual Liberty Interest"

B. Voluntary Submission

1. Waiver Through Appearance

a. Special and General Appearance

b. Federal Rules

c. Plaintiff's Implied Consent

d. Defendant's Implied Consent

2. Express Consent

a. Forum Selection Clauses

b. Appointment of an Agent for Service

c. Cognovit Clauses

C. By Service Within the Forum State

D. By Service Outside the Forum: The Requirements of "Minimum Contacts," "Foreseeability" of Litigation or "Relatedness" of Business Activity, and of Fairness

1. "Minimum Contacts" and Long-Arm Statutes

a. The Need for a Long-Arm Statute

b. Case Categories Under the Long-Arm Statutes

c. Reaching the Parent Corporation Through Service on Its Subsidiary

2. The Tests of *International Shoe, World-Wide Volkswagen*, and *J. McIntyre*

3. Considerations to Be Taken into Account: In General

a. Requirement That the Claim Arise from the Contact

b. The Contact Must Have Been Established by the Defendant

c. Benefits Derived from the Forum

d. Reasonableness

e. Forum State Interest; Jurisdiction by Necessity

f. "National Contacts": Jurisdiction and *Erie*

4. Specific Jurisdiction in the Case Law

a. Products Liability: Injury in the Forum

b. Products Liability and "Relatedness:" *Ford v. Montana*

c. Defamation

d. Contracts

e. Domestic Relations

5. Jurisdiction and the Internet

6. Jurisdiction and Complex Litigation

a. Interpleader

b. Impleader

c. Class Actions

d. Multiparty, Multiforum Actions

IV. Limitations on the Exercise of Personal Jurisdiction

A. Forum-Selection Clauses

B. The Inappropriate Forum

1. Dismissal or Stay for *Forum Non Conveniens*

2. Federal Transfer

C. Defenses

1. Fraudulent Inducement at Common Law

2. Immunity of Parties

3. Witness Immunity

4. Notice and Opportunity to Appear

V. Continuing Jurisdiction

VI. Note: Contacts for Personal Jurisdiction and for Choice of Law

A. Common Features

B. Differences

VII. Jurisdiction over Things

A. *In Rem* Jurisdiction

1. Introduction
2. *In Rem* Jurisdiction over Land
3. *In Rem* Jurisdiction over Chattels
4. Intangibles

B. *Quasi In Rem* Jurisdiction

1. Introduction
2. Post-*Shaffer Quasi In Rem* Jurisdiction

a. *Seider*-Type Actions

b. Creditor with Prior Judgment

c. Intangible as Collateral

d. Federal Interpleader

e. Maritime Attachment

f. Anticybersquatting Consumer Protection Act

VIII. Review Questions

I. Overview

A. Introduction: Importance of the Jurisdictional Inquiry

In the conflict of laws, the question of whether a court has "jurisdiction" is important because the court is being asked to decide a case involving foreign parties or facts or both. (*Reminder*: all out-of-state parties are "foreign parties.") The jurisdictional inquiry seeks to determine whether the court has been *granted jurisdiction*, whether it *may constitutionally exercise* it under the Federal Constitution and, if it may, *whether it should do so according to the laws and policies of its state.*

Determining whether a court has jurisdiction is also important for the question (below at p. 100) of whether its resulting judgment is entitled to recognition in other states of the Union under the Constitution's Full Faith and Credit Clause.

1. Basic Definition

Judicial jurisdiction (also called "jurisdiction to adjudicate") is the power of a court to enter a judgment which binds the defendant personally or which affects a defendant's interest in property The limits of that power are set by the Due Process Clause of the 14th Amendment to the Federal Constitution. The exercise of jurisdiction does not violate due process if there are sufficient contacts between the forum state (the state in which the court sits) and the defendant, the transaction from which the claim arises, or the property in which an interest is sought to be affected. The view of what type and quality of contacts are "sufficient" has changed over time and requires further analysis, below.

2. Judicial Jurisdiction as Distinguished from Subject Matter Jurisdiction

Subject matter jurisdiction is the power of a court to hear and determine particular *types of cases.*

For example, some states provide by statute that only certain courts have matrimonial subject matter jurisdiction (to hear and determine actions seeking separation, annulment, or divorce). Likewise, federal courts are limited in their subject matter jurisdiction by Article III of the United States Constitution to cases involving federal questions or in which there is diversity of citizenship between the parties. Diversity jurisdiction is further limited by statute to cases in which the amount in controversy exceeds $75,000.

The definition of *jurisdiction to adjudicate,* given in Section 1, above, assumes the existence of subject matter jurisdiction. Further inquiry into subject matter jurisdiction is generally beyond the scope of this book.

3. Judicial Jurisdiction as Distinguished from Legislative Jurisdiction

Jurisdiction to adjudicate, as defined in Section 1 above, may be contrasted with *legislative* jurisdiction. The chapters of this book that deal with *choice of law* involve the question of whether a state allows or requires its courts to apply its own *law* (legislative jurisdiction). This issue concerns the *reach* of one's own law: whether the use of the forum's law is constitutionally permissible, and if so, whether doing so would be an appropriate or desirable choice.

The question whether a state may apply its own law is often interrelated with the question whether it may exercise jurisdiction to adjudicate. Both inquiries, as we shall see, focus on the forum state's contacts with or relationship to the defendant, the transaction or the claim. However, while these questions are interrelated, they are not the same. Thus, a court may have sufficient contact with the defendant to exercise *judicial jurisdiction* in circumstances where the transaction or claim is so unrelated to the forum that it may not constitutionally apply its own law. See *infra* Chapter X, Section III.

4. Jurisdiction and the Notice Requirement

Before a court may exercise the *jurisdiction to adjudicate* ("jurisdiction") that it has, due process requires that *notice* of litigation be given to the defendant to afford him or her an opportunity to defend.

Notice is normally given by service of process on the defendant (for instance, by physical delivery of a summons to the defendant, by delivery of a summons to an agent who receives process on behalf of the defendant, or by publication of the summons). The due process requirement of the Federal Constitution does not require *actual* notice in all cases, but the method of giving notice must be "such as one desirous of actually informing the absentee might reasonably adopt to accomplish it." *Mullane v. Central Hanover Bank & Trust Co.,* 339 U.S. 306, 315, 70 S. Ct. 652, 657, 94 L. Ed. 865 (1950). State law may require a higher standard of notice (for actions in state court) than that demanded by federal due process.

It is important to remember that the giving of notice *does not give a court jurisdiction* when it is otherwise lacking. Instead, the giving of notice is a requirement to *perfect* the jurisdiction that a court has and is otherwise empowered to exercise. Thus, both the existence of jurisdiction and compliance with the notice requirement are necessary for the valid exercise of jurisdiction.

5. Jurisdiction and Recognition of Judgments

A judgment rendered by a court that lacked jurisdiction within the meaning of the Due Process Clause *is void where rendered.* It is therefore *not entitled to recognition* in other states under the Constitution's Full Faith and Credit Clause. Indeed, the recognition of a void judgment would, in turn, violate due process. However, since the existence of jurisdiction and its proper exercise depend on facts, the litigation of these facts in F-1 (or the opportunity to have litigated such facts, upon proper service) will become res judicata and preclude review by F-2 of F-1's jurisdiction. See further *infra* Chapter IV(II-C).

To the extent that the exercise of jurisdiction in the state of rendition complied with due process requirements, the resulting judgment is entitled to recognition under the Full Faith and Credit Clause. This is so even if the state in which recognition is sought, had it been the state in which the claim was first litigated, would have taken a much narrower view of jurisdiction and would not have entertained the claim. For purposes of *recognition* of a sister-state judgment, *federal due process* is virtually the *only* constitutional standard for the validity of the exercise of jurisdiction. Older decisions occasionally also referred to other constitutional provisions, but do not furnish independent grounds for a refusal of recognition today. The recognition of judgments is treated in detail in Chapter IV.

B. Categories of Jurisdiction

1. *In Personam* (Personal) Jurisdiction

Personal jurisdiction (also: *in personam* jurisdiction) is the power of a court to determine the rights and duties of the parties to a lawsuit and to bind them personally. The power of a court to exercise personal jurisdiction is seen either in territorial terms (the power of a court over people within the territory of the forum state) or as a function of the contacts (many or few) which an absent defendant and the claim had with the forum state. The territorial element of jurisdiction will be discussed further below at p. 54 *et seq.* In its decision in *Helicopteros Nacionales de Colombia, S.A. v. Hall,* 466 U.S. 408, 104 S. Ct. 1868, 80 L. Ed. 2d 404 (1984), the United States Supreme Court expressly used the distinction between *specific* and *general* jurisdiction.

a. Specific Jurisdiction

Specific jurisdiction is ***contact or relationship-specific***. Unless a court has general jurisdiction (see below), its jurisdiction is *limited to claims arising from the specific relationship between the defendant and the claim to the forum state* (for instance, the defendant's conduct, or a transaction undertaken by the defendant). One example of such contacts is claims arising from a tort committed in the forum state. This type of personal jurisdiction is discussed further in Part Three below.

b. General Jurisdiction

When the defendant has very substantial contacts with the forum state, the courts of that state may exercise *general* jurisdiction. This means that they may adjudicate *all* claims against the defendant, including those that are *unrelated* to a specific contact with the forum state.

For ***general*** jurisdiction, the focus is on the relationship of the *defendant to the forum,* while in ***specific*** jurisdiction the focus is on the relationship of the forum to the *defendant* <u>and</u> *the transaction* or *occurrence* from which the claim arises. Thus, for instance, an individual may be sued in the state of his or her domicile (and a corporation at its place of incorporation and its chief place of business) in addition to the (different) state where a tort was committed or caused injury, or where a contract was to be performed. See further *infra* Section II-C.

Even when a court lacks general or specific jurisdiction, a defendant may always *consent* or voluntarily *submit* to jurisdiction. See Section II(C) below.

2. Jurisdiction over Things

a. *In Rem* Jurisdiction

When a court exercises jurisdiction based on the presence of the defendant's property within the forum state *for claims relating to that property,* it is exercising *in rem* jurisdiction. The court focuses on the property, the *res,* and exercises its power over it; the court determines rights *in the thing,* but does not use it as a medium to address *other* personal claims.

In adjudicating rights in the *res,* the court has power "to bind the world." Examples are quiet title actions, libels against ships, seizures of drugs, and—by peculiar reasoning and understood only in the historical context—the exercise of divorce jurisdiction. The last of these, divorce, will be discussed separately in Chapter VI below.

b. *Quasi In Rem* Jurisdiction

A court exercises *quasi in rem* jurisdiction when it bases its jurisdiction on the presence, within the forum state, of property belonging to a defendant who is not subject to the court's personal jurisdiction, even though the property is unrelated to the claim.

When the plaintiff's claim has not been reduced to judgment in a previous (local or foreign) action, in which a court had personal jurisdiction over the defendant, the assertion of *quasi in rem* jurisdiction is unconstitutional. *Shaffer v. Heitner,* 433 U.S. 186, 97 S. Ct. 2569, 53 L. Ed. 2d 683 (1977); *Rush v. Savchuk,* 444 U.S. 320, 100 S. Ct. 571, 62 L. Ed. 2d 516 (1980). But see *infra* at Section VII(B-2-f) and Chapter VI(II-B-2).

When the plaintiff's claim has previously been reduced to judgment by a court with valid personal jurisdiction, such a judgment can be enforced, under the Full Faith and Credit Clause (or as a matter of comity in the case of a foreign country judgment), against the defendant's property, wherever it is located. The plaintiff need not obtain personal jurisdiction over the defendant anew.

II. General *In Personam* Jurisdiction: The Exercise of Jurisdiction Without Regard to Claim-Related Contacts or Relationships

A. Enterprises: Required Forum Connection

1. A Single Transaction Does Not Support General Jurisdiction

When a plaintiff's claim is unrelated to a specific contact of the defendant with the forum, the court must have *general* jurisdiction over the defendant. In *Helicopteros Nacionales de Colombia, S.A. v. Hall,* 466 U.S. 408, 104 S. Ct. 1868, 80 L. Ed. 2d 404 (1984), the United States Supreme Court said that general jurisdiction requires more than a single transaction (even when that transaction, as in this case, has several elements, e.g., purchase of helicopters, pilot training). Specific jurisdiction—that the claim arose out of the particular contact—had not been argued by the parties, and therefore was not before the Court, which the Court noted. The extensive discussion in the case about whether a claim must "arise out of" or need only be "related to" the contact would have been relevant if the issue had been specific jurisdiction. Under the circumstances, it was obiter dictum. It became the central issue in *Ford v. Montana, infra* in Section III(D-4) for specific jurisdiction. After *Goodyear* and *Daimler, infra* in Section II(C), general jurisdiction is seems limited, such that the single-transaction question may no longer arise.

2. Quality of Defendant-Forum Contacts

General jurisdiction requires that the defendant have substantial contacts with the forum. For natural persons, their being *domiciled* within the forum state satisfies this requirement (see below at Section B-1).

For business enterprises, the determination of "substantial" contacts is more difficult. A business enterprise's principal place of business may be equated with a natural person's domicile. In the absence of a principal place of business, an early decision of the United States Supreme Court required that a corporation carry on a "continuous and systematic, but limited, part of its general business" in the forum state. *Perkins v. Benguet Consolidated Mining Co.,* 342 U.S. 437, 72 S. Ct. 413, 96 L. Ed. 485 (1952). In two recent decisions, the Supreme Court narrowed this test considerably, requiring such close contacts with the state that the corporation can be considered to be "at home" there. *Goodyear Dunlop Tire Operations, S.A. v. Brown,* 564 U.S. 915, 131 S. Ct. 2846, 180 L. Ed. 2d 796 (2011); *Daimler AG v. Bauman*, 571 U.S. 117, 134 S. Ct. 746, 187 L. Ed. 2d 624 (2014). For imposed consent to general jurisdiction (*Mallory*) and further, more detailed discussion, see Section C below.

B. Natural Person

In many civil law countries, the primary connecting factor, for both jurisdiction and many choice-of-law questions, traditionally has been a person's *nationality.* Increasingly, many civil law countries now refer to "habitual residence" as the primary connecting factor. In Anglo-American law, the primary connecting factor is *domicile,* while "habitual residence" is often used in international conventions to which the United States is (or may become) a party.

1. Domicile

The domicile of a natural person, at the time that suit is commenced, is a sufficient basis for general jurisdiction, even if the domiciliary is not physically present in the state at that time. *Milliken v. Meyer,* 311 U.S. 457, 61 S. Ct. 339, 85 L. Ed. 278 (1940). The original rationale was that the domicile of a person represents his or her closest connection to a state, in view of the Anglo-American doctrine that a person can only have one domicile at a time. Since it is convenient that there be at least one place where a person can be sued on any cause of action, subjecting him or her to jurisdiction at the domicile is a fair way to achieve that goal: the defendant will not be unfairly surprised.

Criticism, however, points out that this traditional definition of domicile is essentially based on a single contact combined with intent, and that some people may have only an attenuated relationship to their technical domicile while having the focal point of their life in a different community. Especially in England, it has therefore been argued that domicile should be replaced by another test—such as a person's *habitual residence*—for the determination of whether the contact with the forum state is substantial enough to permit the exercise of general jurisdiction.

"Habitual residence" is the standard reference in modern conflicts treaties, especially those elaborated by the Hague Conference on Private International Law (the United States is a member). For decisions applying the concept in the context of the Convention on the Civil Aspects of International Child Abduction, see *Gitter v. Gitter*, 396 F.3d 124 (2d Cir. 2005), and *Marks ex rel. SM v. Hochhauser,* 876 F.3d 416 (2d Cir. 2017).

In the United States, however, the case law so far continues to regard domicile, as traditionally defined, as a sufficient basis for general jurisdiction. In the work on the Restatement (Third) of Conflict of Laws, the membership of the ALI approved a new definition of domicile in 2021. Domicile would be defined as a person's center of life, as determined by objective facts. When the Restatement (Third) is ultimately promulgated, courts may well embrace this welcome change, which would eliminate the difficult determination of a person's "intent" (especially if deceased).

The coming Restatement (Third) also uses a domicile concept for "juridical persons," i.e., corporations, which is the state with which they are centrally linked—usually, the states of their incorporation and principal place of business. However, since the Restatement (Third) emphasizes the issue-by-issue approach, as did its predecessor (*dépeçage*, see below Chapter VII(III-D-2-d)), the location of the principal place of business may vary, depending on the issue. This then raises the question whether a company can be "at home" (in the *Goodyear* sense, Section C below) in different places for purposes of general jurisdiction as a result of a particular, unrelated issue. If the U.S. Supreme Court meant to limit general jurisdiction, the foregoing obviously cannot work. See also *Mallory* in Section C.

2. Citizenship

a. National Citizenship

United States citizenship may be sufficient for the exercise of personal jurisdiction by federal courts over an absent defendant in matters involving federal law. Restatement (Second) § 31; *Blackmer v. United States,* 284 U.S. 421, 52 S. Ct. 252, 76 L. Ed. 375 (1932) (upholding the constitutionality of a federal statute requiring U.S. citizens to return to the U.S. when subpoenaed as witnesses in federal criminal proceedings); *United States v. Belfast,* 611 F.3d 783, 809 (11th Cir. 2010) (allowing prosecution of U.S. citizen for engaging in acts abroad that were prohibited by U.S. law); *U.S. v. Lawrence,* 727 F.3d 386 (5th Cir. 2013) (same).

28 U.S.C.A. § 1783(a) (West 2024) permits a court to compel an American citizen, currently located abroad, to appear in a United States proceeding and to testify. See *SEC v. Sabhlok,* No. C 08-4238, 2009 WL 3561523 (N.D. Cal. Oct. 30, 2009); *Cadence Design Sys., Inc. v. Pounce Consulting, Inc.,* No. CV-19-05404, 2019 WL 11504668 (C.D. Cal. Sept. 26, 2019).

The Supreme Court has not passed on the question of whether national citizenship is a sufficient basis for general personal jurisdiction in the absence of a federal statute. However, it has been suggested that, in analogy to domicile, national citizenship should be considered as furnishing a sufficient link for the exercise of national jurisdiction. Restatement (Second) § 31 cmt. *d.* In light of more recent case law (see Section I-B, above), it is highly unlikely that this suggestion would be adopted today.

The existence of a statute, as in *Blackmer,* was also said to provide adequate notice to the absent citizen.

b. State Citizenship

The Fourteenth Amendment provides that "[a]ll persons, born or naturalized in the United States, and subject to the jurisdiction thereof, are citizens of the United States and the State wherein they reside." The phrase, "the State wherein they reside" has been interpreted to mean the state of domicile. *In re Slaughter-House Cases,* 83 U.S. (16 Wall.) 36, 21 L. Ed. 394 (1872). State citizenship, being identical with domicile, therefore does not furnish an independent basis for personal jurisdiction apart from that already provided by the domicile concept.

3. Service Within the Jurisdiction

a. *Pennoyer v. Neff*

The early United States Supreme Court decision in *Pennoyer v. Neff,* 95 U.S. (5 Otto) 714, 24 L. Ed. 565 (1877) adopted a *territorial* approach to jurisdiction, which it derived from principles of public international law of that time, for granting or withholding recognition of another state's or country's judgment. Every state, the Court wrote, "possesses exclusive jurisdiction and sovereignty over persons and property within its territory." Thus, a judgment rendered against a non-resident was not entitled to recognition elsewhere, and under the Due Process Clause of the then recently adopted Fourteenth Amendment, was also invalid in the state in which it was rendered.

Thus, (a) recognition would be denied to such a judgment elsewhere because the judgment "would be deemed an encroachment upon the independence of the State in which the [non-resident defendants] are domiciled . . . ," *Pennoyer* at 723; and (b) the invalidity of the judgment in the state of rendition follows from the violation of the defendant's due process rights.

Conversely, the notion of a state's territorial sovereignty meant that the state would acquire *general* in personam *jurisdiction* over defendants served with process within its territory. Much of this—from judgment recognition to general jurisdiction—has of course changed over the last century and a half, but not all of it: see (b) immediately following, for instance.

b. Transient Jurisdiction

Jurisdiction obtained by service within the state, and not based on any other defendant or transaction contacts with the state, is also known as *transient* (or *tag*) *jurisdiction.* The harshness of transient jurisdiction—forcing a defendant to trial wherever he or she may have been casually present when served with process—is still a viable and strong rule of law with regard to natural persons. See *Burnham v. Superior Court,* 495 U.S. 604, 110 S. Ct. 2105, 109 L. Ed. 2d 631 (1990). Decisions subsequent to *Pennoyer* have pushed the notion of territorial sovereignty to absurd extremes. See, e.g., *Grace v. MacArthur,* 170 F. Supp. 442 (E.D. Ark. 1959) (service in an airplane while flying over the state).

Transient jurisdiction has been much criticized in the domestic literature, and especially internationally. The 2019 Hague Convention on jurisdiction and judgment recognition does not provide for the recognition of judgments based on transient jurisdiction. The Convention has been adopted by the required number of contracting states and entered into force on August 1, 2023. The United States has signed it but has not ratified it so far.

C. Corporations: "At Home" in the Forum or "Consent" by Registering for Doing Business

Corporations are often incorporated in states in which they transact no business, for instance in Delaware. Nevertheless, the state of incorporation, having created the corporate entity, may subject it to *general in personam* jurisdiction.

Additionally, a corporation may be subjected to general jurisdiction in a state with which it maintains substantial contacts or which requires consent as a condition for doing business in it. The state of the *principal place of business* satisfies the substantial contact standard (for instance, General Motors will be subject to general jurisdiction in Michigan).

If the corporation is less closely connected with the forum state, the question will become how much business activity is necessary to support general jurisdiction.

In *Perkins v. Benguet Consolidated Mining Co.,* 342 U.S. 437, 72 S. Ct. 413, 96 L. Ed. 485 (1952), the United States Supreme Court said that the defendant Philippine corporation carried on a "continuous and systematic, but limited, part of its general business" in Ohio, and was therefore subject to (general) jurisdiction for an unrelated claim. In *Bryant v. Finnish National Airline,* 208 N.E.2d 439 (N.Y. 1965), New York upheld general *in personam* jurisdiction on the basis of the maintenance of a small reservations office by a Finnish airline, at which no tickets were sold and no money was accepted. The office did a certain amount of publicity work and the airline maintained a small bank account out of which to pay local employees.

Bryant and decisions like it used such a broad interpretation of the *Perkins* language that a company conducting nationwide business, with even minimal connections to a state (for instance, maintaining only a warehouse there), might have been subject to jurisdiction virtually anywhere on claims that had nothing to do with the forum. *Helicopteros Nacionales de Colombia, S.A. v. Hall,* 466 U.S. 408, 104 S. Ct. 1868, 80 L. Ed. 2d 404 (1984), provided an initial limitation on such an expansive application of *Perkins.* The Court held that the purchase of helicopters worth approximately $4 million in the forum, the sending of employees to the forum for training and familiarization with supply organizations, and the maintenance of a $5 million bank account in the forum—all part of a single transaction—did not constitute "continuous and systematic business" with the Texas forum to support general jurisdiction over a claim unrelated to the forum. The Court did not consider whether the single transaction would have supported the exercise of specific jurisdiction (see below at p. 66 et seq.) because this issue had not been raised below.

Goodyear Dunlop Tires Operations, S.A. v. Brown, 564 U.S. 915, 131 S. Ct. 2846, 180 L. Ed. 2d 796 (2011), and *Daimler AG v. Bauman,* 571 U.S. 117, 134 S. Ct. 746, 187 L. Ed. 2d 624 (2014), are more recent pronouncements of the Court on the subject. In *Goodyear,* the domestic plaintiff sought to establish jurisdiction over foreign subsidiaries of a domestic corporation for foreign-based claims. In *Daimler,* foreign plaintiffs sought to establish jurisdiction over a foreign corporation, by way of its local subsidiary, to assert foreign-based claims.

In *Goodyear*, two U.S. residents were killed in a bus accident in France, allegedly due to failure of the defendant's tires. The defendant had sold tires into the United States, including the forum state, but that was not enough to establish jurisdiction. The out-of-state defendant's contacts with the forum must be so substantial that it could be considered to be virtually "at home" in the forum. 564 U.S. at 919.

In *Daimler*, Argentinian residents sued the German defendant in California, a place where its subsidiary sold vehicles, alleging various tort claims based on the defendant's alleged actions in Argentina. The "at home" language was used again, and the exercise of general jurisdiction denied. Its author in both decisions, Justice Ginsburg, stated that "at home" was not necessarily restricted to the states of incorporation or place of principal business of the company, but did not elaborate further. What else would qualify? How substantial contacts must be to satisfy the test is an open question and remains to be defined by future case law.

The California subsidiary also was not an "agent" of the German defendant for service of process when the claim had nothing to do with its California functions for the principal. At the end of its opinion in *Goodyear*, the Court noted the suggestion that a parent and its subsidiaries be regarded as a single economic unit (the "enterprise theory"). Viewed as an entity (i.e., disregarding the parties' corporate separateness), all parts of the entity would be subject to the jurisdiction established in the forum (e.g., the principal place of business of any part of the entity). However, this approach had not been raised below, and therefore was not part of the Court's review. What is the bottom line? The broad application of the *Perkins* line of cases seemed out: A company's conduct of local business must be systematic and continuous (*Helicopteros*) and *very substantial* (to satisfy the "at home" test).

General jurisdiction thus seemed substantially limited, therefore directing one's attention to the reach of specific jurisdiction (Section III below). Yet *Mallory v. Norfolk So. Ry. Co.*, 600 U.S. 122, 143 S.Ct. 2028, 216 L.Ed.2d 815 (2023), now provides an opportunity for states to broaden their general jurisdiction over out-of-state business enterprises. In that decision, the defendant railway company, incorporated in Virginia and with principal place of business in that state, was sued in Pennsylvania by a former employee who, while living in Virginia and employed by the defendant there, was diagnosed with cancer which he attributed to exposure to carcinogens while working for the defendant. The plaintiff retired to Pennsylvania and sued there. The railroad company operated in several states, including in Pennsylvania, and as an out-of-state enterprise had to register in each state. The Pennsylvania registration statute provided that a registered company is subject to general jurisdiction. The U.S. Supreme Court upheld Pennsylvania's exercise of jurisdiction: a minority of four Justices based this on the defendant's "consent" through registration. They and another Justice—thus a majority—also adhered to *Penn Fire Ins. Co. v. Gold Mining & Milling Co.*, 243 U.S. 93 (1917) as precedent, In *Penn Fire,* Georgia had construed two provisions of its registration statute, when considered together, as providing for general jurisdiction and thus informing registering enterprises of it. In addition to authoring the "consent" argument, Justice Gorsuch also briefly elaborated about "tag jurisdiction" (*supra* Section III (B)(3)(b)), but did not seem to make this part of his decision. The fifth Justice who joined only on the precedent grounds raised the question whether imposing consent on general jurisdiction on out-of-state enterprises might not raise a "dormant Commerce Clause" question, i.e. the prohibition for states to regulate interstate commerce which the Constitution has delegated to the Federation. This issue had not been raised below and therefore was not before the Court, but of course may be in the future. The dissent disagreed that submitting to a registration requirement constituted "consent" to general jurisdiction (as distinguished from providing a means for service of process when there was assertion of specific jurisdiction for claims arising from in-state activities). Today's dividing line between general and specific jurisdiction seems to become less clear. For further discussion, see below at Section III (D). For further discussion of *Mallory*, see 38 Emory Int'l L. Rev. 95 (2024).

D. Notice Requirement

The exercise of general (as well as specific) jurisdiction still requires that the individual defendant or the company be given adequate notice, and with it, an opportunity to be heard. In the case of an absent defendant (for instance, a temporarily absent domiciliary), such notice is usually given by substituted service outside of the forum state or by publication ("constructive service"). *Mullane v. Central Hanover Bank & Trust Co.*, 339 U.S. 306 (1950).

III. Specific Jurisdiction: Contacts Related to the Litigation

A. Introduction

1. The Territorial Approach

As outlined above (at p. 54), the territorial approach of *Pennoyer v. Neff,* 95 U.S. (5 Otto) 714, 24 L. Ed. 565 (1877), defined a court's jurisdiction in terms of its *power* over persons and property in its territory: the forum had this power, other states did not, and—in turn—the forum had no power over persons and property beyond its borders. Indeed, an attempt to exercise such *extraterritorial* jurisdiction would be an encroachment on the sovereignty of the other states. This approach expressed both a court's power over the person of the defendant and a principle of federalism, viz. that the states of the Union are coequal.

2. Shifting the Focus to the "Individual Liberty Interest"

In *World-Wide Volkswagen Corp. v. Woodson,* 444 U.S. 286, 100 S. Ct. 559, 62 L. Ed. 2d 490 (1980), the Supreme Court still wrote that "the Due Process Clause, acting as an instrument of interstate federalism, may sometimes act to divest the State of its power to render a valid judgment." 444 U.S. at 294. However, in *Insurance Corp. of Ireland, Ltd. v. Compagnie des Bauxites de Guinee,* 456 U.S. 694, 102 S. Ct. 2099, 72 L. Ed. 2d 492 (1982), the Court stated that interstate federalism is *not* an independent restriction on the exercise of jurisdiction; if it were otherwise, an individual defendant could not waive jurisdictional objections. Instead, "[t]he restriction on state sovereign power . . . must be seen as ultimately a function of the individual liberty interest preserved by the Due Process Clause. That Clause is the only source of the personal jurisdiction requirement . . . ." 456 U.S. at 702 n.10. After *Insurance Corp. of Ireland,* the only focus of the jurisdictional inquiry seemed to be on due process to be afforded the defendant for the protection of his or her individual liberty interest. However, in a number of subsequent cases, including in the more recent decision in *Ford v. Montana* (*infra* at p. 71), the Court continues to refer to "interstate federalism."

Considerations of territoriality and state sovereignty of course continue to have currency in those international cases that have a public law/public interest element. The extraterritorial effect of (and its limits on) American antitrust law is the best example. See *Hartford Fire Ins. Co. v. California*, 509 U.S. 764, 113 S. Ct. 2891, 125 L. Ed. 2d 612 (1993); *F. Hoffmann-La Roche Ltd. v. Empagran S.A.,* 542 U.S. 155, 124 S. Ct. 2359, 159 L. Ed. 2d 226 (2004). See also *Kiobel v. Royal Dutch Petroleum Co.*, 569 U.S. 108, 133 S. Ct. 1659, 185 L. Ed. 2d 671 (2013) (Alien Tort Statute does not apply to conduct outside the U.S.); *.Austria GmbH v. Hectronic International, Inc*, 600 U.S. 412, 143 S.Ct. 2522, 2528 (2023); *RJR Nabisco, Inc. v. European Community*, 579 U.S. 325, 136 S. Ct. 2090, 195 L. Ed. 2d 476 (2016) (Racketeer Influenced and Corrupt Organizations Act (RICO) may apply extraterritorially, but plaintiff must prove an injury within the U.S.); *Abernathy v. Carlyle Group, Inc.*, 2024 WL 5331993 (D.C. 2024); *Medical Marijuana, Inc. v. Horn*, 604 U.S. 593, 145 S.Ct. 931, 933 (2025).

B. Voluntary Submission

1. Waiver Through Appearance

a. Special and General Appearance

In the procedural law of some states, jurisdictional defenses can be maintained only if the defendant makes a "special appearance," in which only jurisdictional issues may be raised. If the defendant loses on the jurisdictional issue, other (substantive) defenses may then be raised. For the need to raise such defenses at this time, see *infra* at pp. 58, 101. Pleading to the merits automatically waives the jurisdictional defense, even if this had not been the defendant's intent. A defense that raises the merits thus constitutes a "general appearance." See *Cargill, Inc. v. Sabine Trading & Shipping Co.,* 756 F.2d 224 (2d Cir. 1985).

b. Federal Rules

The Federal Rules of Civil Procedure ("Fed. R. Civ. P.") do not provide for special appearances. Jurisdictional defenses and defenses going to the merits may be raised together. Nonetheless, they do provide that if preliminary motions are made, they must contain jurisdictional defenses. If they are not raised at that time, jurisdictional defenses—other than those relating to the court's subject matter jurisdiction—are lost. If more than one preliminary motion is made, the jurisdictional defense must be contained in the first motion. Fed. R. Civ. P. 12.

When the defendant alleges lack of personal jurisdiction, the plaintiff thereupon may request and obtain a discovery order directed at establishing jurisdictional facts. If the defendant fails to comply with the order, the trial court—under Fed. R. Civ. P. 37(b)(2)(A)—may regard the jurisdictional fact as established. *Insurance Corp. of Ireland, Ltd. v. Compagnie des Bauxites de Guinee,* 456 U.S. 694, 102 S. Ct. 2099, 72 L. Ed. 2d 492 (1982), explained further in *Kohler v. Bank of Bermuda, Ltd.*, 2003 WL 289640 (S.D.N.Y. 2003).

c. Plaintiff's Implied Consent

A plaintiff impliedly consents to the court's jurisdiction by commencing the action. The plaintiff's implied consent includes consent to all permissible counterclaims and cross-actions that the defendant might assert and which are permissible under the law of the state where the plaintiff commenced the main action. *Adam v. Saenger,* 303 U.S. 59, 58 S. Ct. 454, 82 L. Ed. 649 (1938).

d. Defendant's Implied Consent

Early statutes provided that by using the state's highways, a nonresident motorist would be deemed to have appointed the state's secretary of state as his agent for the receipt of service of process for an action growing out of an accident caused by the nonresident in the state. *Hess v. Pawloski,* 274 U.S. 352, 47 S. Ct. 632, 71 L. Ed. 1091 (1927). Later cases correctly pointed out that this assertion of jurisdiction did not depend on the defendant's "implied consent" at all. Rather, it derived, as it was explained then, from the state's police power: the state can regulate the use of its highways and hence attach conditions and consequences to a person's doing so. *Olberding v. Illinois Central R. Co.,* 346 U.S. 338, 340, 74 S. Ct. 83, 85, 98 L. Ed. 39 (1953).

Today, the provisions of long-arm statutes allowing the assertion of jurisdiction on the basis of the commission of a tortious act within the state replace the early fiction of "implied consent." For the "commission of a tortious act" provision of long-arm statutes and for the reach of specific jurisdiction generally, see below at Section III.

2. Express Consent

a. Forum Selection Clauses

A party may always consent to be subject to the jurisdiction of a court, and may give such consent in advance of litigation by means of a contractual choice-of-court clause. Restatement (Second) of Conflict of Laws §§ 32, 43 (1971). For limits of such clauses, and for the effect of such clauses on the exercise of jurisdiction by courts *other* than the one chosen by the parties, see below at Section IV.

b. Appointment of an Agent for Service

Many states have legislation requiring foreign corporations to "qualify" before doing business within the state. Such legislation often requires that a foreign corporation file a copy of its articles of incorporation, as well as designate a local agent for the receipt of service of process.

Originally designed to facilitate the exercise of local jurisdiction, these statutes may achieve no more than long-arm statutes can also accomplish. In particular, qualification statutes probably cannot enlarge the jurisdiction of a state. Unless the foreign corporation has substantial contacts with the state (that satisfy the "at home" test for general jurisdiction), service on the agent appointed pursuant to such a statute will ordinarily be for the purpose of perfecting *specific jurisdiction.* Service on an appointed agent, without more, will not perfect *general jurisdiction.* See *Daimler, supra* at p. 56. *But see* immediately following.

Does registration to do business in a state, together with the appointment of an agent to receive service (as required by state law), constitute consent to general jurisdiction? The Georgia Supreme Court held in 2021 that it does. *Cooper Tire & Rubber Co. v. McCall*, 863 S.E.2d 81 (Ga. 2021). In interpreting its statute, the New York Court of Appeals held that it did not provide for general jurisdiction. *Aybar v. Aybar*, 177 N.E.3d 1257 (N.Y. 2021). The Pennsylvania Supreme Court went further, holding its statute unconstitutional: no general jurisdiction unless the company is virtually at "home" in the sense of *Goodyear*. *Mallory v. Norfolk So. Ry. Co.*, 266 A.3d 542 (Pa. 2021). Going beyond *Aybar*, a New York federal court also considered basing general jurisdiction on a company's registration in the state to be precluded by the U.S. Supreme Court's decisions. *SUEZ Water N.Y. Inc. v. E.I. du Pont de Nemours & Co.*, No. 20-cv-10731, 578 F. Supp. 3d 511, (S.D.N.Y. 2022).

The Pennsylvania decision in *Mallory* was reversed by the U.S. Supreme Court, thereby also contradicting the New York decisions just mentioned. *Mallory* is discussed in detail above in Section II(C). The consent to general jurisdiction was imposed by the requirement to register for doing business in-state. The divided U.S. Supreme Court treated registration as consent and thus permitted the exercise of general jurisdiction.

The dividing line between general and specific jurisdiction (the latter for in-state claims) seems to become somewhat blurred. For instance, *National Equipment Rental, Ltd. v. Szukhent,* 375 U.S. 311, 84 S. Ct. 411, 11 L. Ed. 2d 354 (1964) held that the appointment of an in-state agent satisfied the requirements of Fed. R. Civ. P. 4(d)(1). Service on the agent is the equivalent of service on the principal within the forum state. However, the Supreme Court's decisions in *Goodyear* and *Daimler*, *supra* at p. 55, cast doubt upon whether the appointment of a general agent satisfies the substantial connection with the forum state required by those decisions. Again: *but see* the Supreme Court's decision in *Mallory* (discussed in II(C) above). So far, States have not made their registration statutes as explicit as Pennsylvania's in *Mallory*. But the constructive interpretation of state statutes, as in *Penn Fire* (Sec. II(C)), may present an option.

A mere choice-of-law clause, without additional contacts (such as the appointment of an agent or a provision for service), does not confer jurisdiction. This follows from *Burger King v. Rudzewicz,* 471 U.S. 462, 105 S. Ct. 2174, 85 L. Ed. 2d 528 (1985). See also *Dynamic Software Services v. Cyberbest Technology, Inc.*, No. C-13-04217 DMR, 2014 WL 3373924 (N.D. Cal. July 9, 2014).

c. Cognovit Clauses

In signing a cognovit clause (also called a confession-of-judgment clause) as part of a specific transaction, the defendant authorizes an attorney of record (engaged by the other party) to confess judgment on his or her behalf in a specific court or even in "any court of record." The confession-of-judgment clause also typically waives the right to receive notice that a judgment is being confessed against the defendant. The Supreme Court has held that in general, a defendant can waive its due process rights to notice and a hearing if the waiver is made "voluntarily, intelligently and knowingly [and] with full awareness of the legal consequences." *D.H. Overmyer Co. v. Frick Co.,* 405 U.S. 174, 187, 92 S. Ct. 775, 783, 31 L. Ed. 2d 124 (1972).

The *Overmyer* rule is limited to a voluntary waiver; it does not address contracts of adhesion, overreaching, great disparity of bargaining power, or situations in which the defendant receives nothing in return for agreeing to the cognovit provision. Thus, in *Swarb v. Lennox,* 405 U.S. 191, 92 S. Ct. 767, 31 L. Ed. 2d 138 (1972), the Supreme Court approved the adoption, by the trial court, of a rebuttable presumption that confession contracts entered into by persons with less than $10,000 annual income were the result of coercion, and hence lacked genuine consent. *Overmyer* has been consistently upheld. For a more recent case to rule that a defendant may waive due process rights to notice and a hearing if the waiver is made voluntarily, intelligently, and knowingly, see *1st Summit Bank v. Samuelson,* 580 N.W.2d 132 (N.D. 1998). In *Mallory, supra,* the Pennsylvania court also emphasized the need for express consent but was overruled by the U.S. Supreme Court (see the discussion at Section II(C) above.

By statute, many states invalidate or severely restrict the availability of cognovit clauses. See, e.g., § 1.201(8)(b)–(e) of the Uniform Consumer Credit Code (resident consumer's agreement to out-of-state jurisdiction and service invalid in credit transaction). However, even though a state's law would invalidate a cognovit clause entered into locally, the Full Faith and Credit Clause still requires the recognition and enforcement of a money judgment obtained in another state, on the basis of a cognovit clause, which was valid there and comports with the constitutional standard established by *Overmyer.*

C. By Service Within the Forum State

Unless the claim arises from or directly relates to the defendant's presence within the forum state, or unless the defendant is subject to the forum's general jurisdiction, service on such a defendant represents the exercise of transient jurisdiction. "Transient jurisdiction" (above at Section B-3-b) still is a form of general jurisdiction.

D. By Service Outside the Forum: The Requirements of "Minimum Contacts," "Foreseeability" or "Relatedness" of Business Activity, and Fairness

1. "Minimum Contacts" and Long-Arm Statutes

a. The Need for a Long-Arm Statute

The assertion of judicial jurisdiction on a basis other than the historic bases of presence and domicile (i.e., of general jurisdiction) or consent requires specific authority by statute. The United States Supreme Court's decisions on jurisdiction define the outer limits for the assertion of state court jurisdiction. State statutes, in turn, define how much jurisdiction a state intends to exercise within federal constitutional limits. Some statutes are quite specific; others merely incorporate the federal standard by providing for jurisdiction "to the limits of due process," and are therefore not very helpful. To be valid, the exercise of jurisdiction by a state court must satisfy both the state statute and federal constitutional limits. The state statutes are commonly known as *long-arm statutes.*

b. Case Categories Under the Long-Arm Statutes

Although state long-arm statutes differ with respect to the detail and number of subcategories of cases for which jurisdiction over non-resident defendants is claimed, three principal categories are involved: *causing tortious injury* within the state, *transacting business* in the state, and *having an interest in local real property*.

Causing tortious injury encompasses both torts committed by the defendant or his agent when physically in the state and injury resulting within the state caused by acts committed outside the state. *Gray v. American Radiator & Standard Sanitary Corp.,* 176 N.E.2d 761 (Ill. 1961) was the leading older case for in-state injury caused by out-of-state activity. The decision in *Gray* was adopted by § 37 of the Restatement (Second) and was cited with apparent approval in the United States Supreme Court's decision in *World-Wide Volkswagen* (*infra*). But see the discussion of *Asahi*, *J. McIntyre*, and *Ford*, *infra* Section III(D-2).

In *Gray,* the Ohio defendant, a valve manufacturer, sold a safety valve to American Standard outside Illinois. American Standard incorporated the valve into a water heater, which was sold into Illinois, where it exploded and injured the plaintiff. The Illinois Supreme Court upheld jurisdiction under the Illinois long-arm statute, and with it the constitutionality of the "tortious injury" provision. Since the defendant had acted outside Illinois and had not itself shipped the defective product into Illinois, the decision adopted a stream-of-commerce approach. It is in this way that it was cited by the United States Supreme Court in *World-Wide Volkswagen*: a state may assert jurisdiction over a corporation "that delivers its products into the stream of commerce with the expectation that they will be purchased by consumers in the forum State." 444 U.S. at 298. The Supreme Court's decision in *J. McIntyre, infra,* continues to leave open whether (and under what circumstances) placing a product into the "stream of commerce" can be a sufficient basis for specific jurisdiction. At a minimum, that decision very much casts doubt on the broad statement in the *Volkswagen* case.

Transacting business in the state has also received varying interpretations in the courts. Consistent with the adoption of the specific-jurisdiction concept, single business transactions give rise to jurisdiction for claims arising from them.

Examples include placing a purchase order, later confirmed by telephone, *State ex rel. White Lumber Sales, Inc. v. Sulmonetti,* 448 P.2d 571 (Or. 1968); placing a bid in a New York auction over a telephone line set up at the non-resident defendants request, *Parke-Bernet Galleries, Inc. v. Franklyn,* 256 N.E.2d 506 (N.Y. 1970); mailing a reinsurance certificate to an insured in California upon succeeding to the previous insurance carrier's obligations, *McGee v. International Life Insurance Co.,* 355 U.S. 220, 78 S. Ct. 199, 2 L. Ed. 2d 223 (1957). See also *Burger King v. Rudzewicz,* 471 U.S. 462, 105 S. Ct. 2174, 85 L. Ed. 2d 528 (1985), though the Court there also stressed that the parties had contemplated a long-term relationship. In *J. McIntyre, infra* p. 70, one opinion stated that a single transaction would not suffice for jurisdiction, citing to *Helicopteros, supra* Section II(A). However, in *Helicopteros*, the issue was *general* jurisdiction, and a footnote in it expressly noted that specific jurisdiction (the claim arising from the contact) had not been raised and therefore was not considered. So while forum connection in the above cases may be tenuous, the claim did arise from the contact, and when it does, it supports the assertion of specific jurisdiction.

An interest in property within the state was the basis for jurisdiction under the U.S. Supreme Court's decision in *Harris v. Balk,* 198 U.S. 215, 25 S. Ct. 625, 49 L. Ed. 1023 (1905). To the extent that the presence of property within the state forms the basis for the assertion of jurisdiction for a claim *unrelated* to that property, this kind of jurisdiction (*quasi in rem* jurisdiction) was held to be unconstitutional. *Shaffer v. Heitner,* 433 U.S. 186, 97 S. Ct. 2569, 53 L. Ed. 2d 683 (1977). The presence of property will now support jurisdiction only with respect to claims *related to the specific property*, for instance in a quiet title action (for further discussion see below) and with respect to claims *arising from* the ownership of property. An example of the latter is a damage claim for injury sustained from the improper maintenance of an apartment house. See *Dubin v. City of Philadelphia,* 34 Pa. D. & C. 61 (Ct. Com. Pl. 1938). Additionally, a defendant's in-state property may be used to satisfy a judgment previously entered against the defendant by a court of the forum or of a sister state with valid personal jurisdiction over the defendant.

c. Reaching the Parent Corporation Through Service on Its Subsidiary

A foreign corporation may be subject to personal jurisdiction in the forum state through service of process effected upon its subsidiary, over which the forum does have jurisdiction. This is clearly the case when the subsidiary acted as the *agent* of the parent. *Frummer v. Hilton Hotels Int'l, Inc.,* 227 N.E.2d 851 (N.Y. 1967). See also Goldsmith v. Sotheby's, Inc., 14 Misc. 3d 1223(A) (N.Y. Sup. Ct. 2007). But, as the Supreme Court emphasized in *Daimler, supra* at p. 56, being an agent for one purpose does not mean that the subsidiary is an agent for general jurisdiction.

Apart from assuming an agency relationship, the forum court may also disregard the separate corporate existence of the two corporations (i.e., "pierce the corporate veil"), so that jurisdiction over the subsidiary equals jurisdiction over the parent. The court may do this when the parent so dominates, controls, and directs the subsidiary that the two are really one and the same. *Taca Int'l Airlines v. Rolls-Royce of England, Ltd.,* 204 N.E.2d 329 (N.Y. 1965); *Ex parte Volkswagenwerk Aktiengesellschaft,* 443 So. 2d 880 (Ala. 1983). See also *Ex parte Boyles,* 70 So. 3d 1233, 1235 (Ala. 2011) (Murdock, J., concurring) (citing *Volkswagenwerk* and explaining the standard under Alabama law).

The fact that the subsidiary is wholly owned by the parent, by itself, is not enough to justify piercing. Restatement (Second) § 52 cmt. *b.* Note that in *Goodyear, supra* at p. 55, the plaintiff argued that the "enterprise theory" (regarding several interrelated companies as one—which also would disregard their corporate separateness) would support the exercise of jurisdiction over the American company's foreign subsidiaries. The U.S. Supreme Court did not address this argument because it had not been raised below. Piercing was denied in *Armstrong v. Atrium Med. Corp. et al.,*

No. 1:22-cv-03007-MKD, 2022 WL 16648824 (E.D.Wash. Oct. 26, 2022, slip opinion) because the interrelationship of the companies had not been proved. See also *Lewis v. Vail Results, Inc.,* 2025 WL 306369, **5–6 (W.D. Wash. 2025, slip. op.).

The United States Supreme Court held in *Volkswagenwerk Aktiengesellschaft v. Schlunk,* 486 U.S. 694, 108 S. Ct. 2104, 100 L. Ed. 2d 722 (1988), that the Hague Convention on the Service of Documents (to which the United States is a party, and which specifies the manner of service on parties of member countries) does not apply when the domestic subsidiary of a foreign parent is the latter's "involuntary agent" under state law.

The Illinois state court's decision, that the subsidiary was the foreign corporate defendant's "involuntary agent" for service, amounted to piercing of the corporate veil. The defendant did not challenge piercing and service on Due Process grounds, and the Supreme Court therefore did not address this issue.

Schlunk, like the other decisions mentioned above, should be re-evaluated in light of *Goodyear* and *Daimler.* While neither case addressed agency directly, or even considered the enterprise theory, it is clear that a substantial connection—in terms of its *own activities*—must exist between the foreign corporation and the forum, and that this connection is not supplied merely through a parent-subsidiary relationship with a forum company, as some of the lower court decisions have already emphasized.

2. The Tests of *International Shoe, World-Wide Volkswagen,* and *J. McIntyre*

The territorial focus of the older jurisdictional cases, such as *Pennoyer v. Neff* (*supra* at p. 54), proved inadequate for a society that became increasingly mobile and economically interdependent.

It would disallow jurisdiction, for instance, in a situation where a person entered the forum state, committed some wrong there, but left the state before process could be served. Conversely, jurisdiction would be lacking when the defendant sends a harm-causing defective product into the state, but never itself enters that state and therefore cannot be served there.

In *International Shoe Co. v. Washington,* 326 U.S. 310, 316, 66 S. Ct. 154, 158, 90 L. Ed. 95 (1945), the Supreme Court announced a new standard for specific *in personam* jurisdiction. It said that a state may assert jurisdiction when there exist "minimum contacts" between the defendant and the forum state, such that the assertion of jurisdiction would not "offend traditional notions of fair play and substantial justice" (quoting *Milliken v. Meyer,* 311 U.S. 457, 463, 61 S.Ct. 339, 342 (1941)).

The defendant International Shoe Company had sent sales representatives to the state of Washington to solicit orders for shoes. The sales personnel took samples with them and travelled throughout the state, but had no authority to conclude contracts. Orders were sent to the company for approval at its headquarters in St. Louis. The State of Washington attempted to impose a tax on the sales representatives' activities for its unemployment compensation fund. It sued International Shoe for the taxes in local state court. International Shoe, inter alia, contested the assertion of jurisdiction by the Washington courts. The Supreme Court held that the contacts of the company with the state were sufficient to support jurisdiction for a claim that arose out of those contacts. In subsequent cases, the Supreme Court has struggled with the application of the "minimum contacts" test. These cases will be discussed in specific contexts below.—Note that Congress can establish federal subject matter jurisdiction for federal courts which the latter may exercise without requiring "minimum contacts." *CC/Devas (Mauritius) Ltd. v. Antrix Corp. Ltd.*, 605 U.S. 223, 145 S.Ct. 1572 (2025). The "minimum contacts" requirement of *International Shoe* derived from the 14th Amendment and addressed the judicial authority of the individual States. The Federal Sovereign Immunity Act (28 U.S.C.A. § 1602 et seq.), involved in *CC/Devas* addressed the judicial authority of the federal government. The Court left open whether the 5th Amendment due process requirement imposes limitations in this type of case because the issue had not been raised below.

In the Supreme Court's recent *Mallory* decision (above Section II(C) Justice Gorsuch wrote that *International Shoe* introduced consent to jurisdiction through action. However, Washington—unlike Pennsylvania in *Mallory*—did not condition doing business in the state on consenting to general jurisdiction. It exercised its power to tax International Shoe's business activity and then sought to collect the taxes that were due. Jurisdiction was based on, and its exercise justified by the defendant's instate activity.

While adhering to the "minimum contacts" test, requiring—to put it differently—that there be "affiliating circumstances" between the defendant and the forum, the Court held in *World-Wide Volkswagen Corp. v. Woodson,* 444 U.S. 286, 100 S. Ct. 559, 62 L. Ed. 2d 490 (1980), that just *any* connection to the forum state will not be enough. It held that *litigation in the forum* must have been *"foreseeable"* for the defendant. Note that foreseeability is (or may also be) a factor in products liability cases invoking the "stream of commerce" idea. The *Volkswagen* court mentioned stream of commerce. But see Section III(D-4) *infra*.

In *World-Wide Volkswagen,* plaintiffs had bought an Audi automobile in New York and were travelling toward their new home in Arizona when they were involved in an accident in Oklahoma. A resulting fire severely injured three of the plaintiffs. They sued four parties in Oklahoma state court on a design-defect theory: the manufacturer, the importer, the regional distributor, and the dealer. The first two parties did not contest jurisdiction; the Supreme Court held that there was no jurisdiction over the two latter parties.

The motor vehicle had been sold in New York. That it might cause *injury* wherever it was taken was foreseeable. However, the Court emphasized that *foreseeability of injury* is not the test. Rather, it is *foreseeability of being "haled into court,"* in this case, in Oklahoma. The regional East Coast distributor, and even more so the local dealer, could not "foresee" (in the sense of *anticipate*) that a local sale would result in their being subjected to jurisdiction in Oklahoma.

The Court has also consistently stated that the defendant must have "purposefully" established minimum contacts with the forum. This reference permits us to translate the reference to the "foreseeability" of litigation into the idea that the defendant must have *anticipated*—because of its own acts (including the market it contemplated or targeted)—that litigation could be brought in the forum. Foreseeability of litigation in the forum introduces a fairness test, which became very important in the decision in *Ford v. Montana, infra* at p. 71.

In *Volkswagen,* market orientation and the permissible exercise of jurisdiction run parallel. Market orientation + acting with respect to that market = jurisdiction there. On the other hand, the *J. McIntyre* plurality, *infra* p. 70, does not accept a general market orientation. There, it seems that the defendant must have had contact with the particular market. Assertion of jurisdiction there will then have been foreseeable. Recent decisions of lower courts raise the question whether *targeting* a specific market (without actually making contact with it), is enough. See further *infra.*

3. Considerations to Be Taken into Account: In General

a. Requirement That the Action Arise from Claim-Specific Contacts or Relationships

Specific jurisdiction, as outlined earlier, looks to the specific contact(s) or relationship that the defendant has with the forum to determine whether the forum may properly subject him or her to jurisdiction for claims *arising from that contact or relationship.*

Because the issue was not raised by the parties, the Court in *Helicopteros, supra,* declined to comment on whether specific jurisdiction might lie when the claim does not directly *arise out of* the particular contacts but *relates* to them, for instance, when the tort claim arose out of the overall transactional relationship of the parties. The question was answered affirmatively many years later—in *Ford v. Montana* (*infra* in subsection 4(b)). Today, "relatedness" of contact(s) for specific jurisdiction (as distinguished from required that they *caused* what is at issue) blurs the distinction to general jurisdiction somewhat. An example is *Moki Mac River Expeditions v. Drugg,* 221 S.W.3d 569 (Tex. 2007). In *Moki Mac,* the defendant's contacts with Texas did not cause the plaintiffs' son's death on a river-rafting cruise; an employed guide's negligence did, so plaintiffs lost. But the defendant's instate activities—advertising the cruise, communicating with plaintiffs and receiving and accepting the application for participation—were related to the boy's death so that today (after *Ford*) jurisdiction for a wrongful death claim against the defendant company might have been upheld.

b. The Contact Must Have Been Established by the Defendant

In *Kulko v. Superior Court,* 436 U.S. 84, 98 S. Ct. 1690, 56 L. Ed. 2d 132 (1978), the defendant had allowed his children to move to California and to live there with his former wife. When sued in California for increased child support, he contested the California court's jurisdiction. The United States Supreme Court held that by allowing his children to move to California, he had not himself "purposefully availed himself" of the "benefits and protection" of California's laws. The financial benefit he received because of the absence of the children from his household did not result from their being in California, but rather from their not being with him in New York. California law or considerations might be relevant for determining whether the support obligation should be increased but to do that local courts had to have personal jurisdiction first, and they did not. See also Chapter Six, Section IV.

c. Benefits Derived from the Forum

Language in *International Shoe* referred to *benefits* derived by the defendant from the forum state as establishing the requisite nexus to the forum. "[A]ppellant received the benefits and protection of the laws of the state, including the right to resort to the courts for the enforcement of its rights." 326 U.S. at 320, 66 S. Ct. at 160.

The derivation of financial or related benefits is a persistent theme in jurisdiction cases after *International Shoe*. The lack of purposeful availment and lack of derivation of benefits were major factors in the determination that Florida lacked jurisdiction in *Hanson v. Denckla,* 357 U.S. 235, 78 S. Ct. 1228, 2 L. Ed. 2d 1283 (1958). Reference to the benefits criterion is also contained in *Burger King Corp. v. Rudzewicz,* 471 U.S. 462, 105 S. Ct. 2174, 85 L. Ed. 2d 528 (1985). In contrast, the court said in *World-Wide Volkswagen* that "whatever marginal revenues petitioners may receive by virtue of the fact that their products are capable of use in Oklahoma is far too attenuated a contact to justify that State's exercise of *in personam* jurisdiction over them." 444 U.S. at 299, 100 S. Ct. at 568.

The benefits criterion thus is an important part of the "foreseeability" test. Again, however, derivation of benefits may not be a substitute for the defendant's forum connection and the requirement that the claim arise from or be related to that connection. These issues have become somewhat blurred with the decision in *Ford v. Montana, infra* at p. 71.

d. Reasonableness

Fairness and reasonableness traditionally had not been considerations separate from minimum contacts. The latter concept, just as the notion of the foreseeability of litigation introduced by *World-Wide Volkswagen,* served as a means of testing fairness.

Yet in *Asahi Metal Industry Co. v. Superior Court,* 480 U.S. 102, 107 S. Ct. 1026, 94 L. Ed. 2d 92 (1987), the Supreme Court struck down—as *unreasonable*—the assertion of jurisdiction by California over a Japanese manufacturer of a component part. The principal Taiwanese defendant, the manufacturer of the defective product, which incorporated the component part, sought indemnification from the Japanese manufacturer by way of a cross-complaint. Since the injured American plaintiff had settled with the defendant, the lower courts concluded, and the Supreme Court agreed, that it would be "unreasonable" to have the Japanese company defend against the Taiwanese company in an American court, with respect to a claim that arose abroad and to which foreign law would apply. "Reasonableness" was used as yet another aspect of the jurisdictional inquiry, to be separately determined. The Court mentioned reasonableness again in *Daimler, supra* p. 55, and in *J. McIntyre, infra,* but the emphasis on actual and substantial defendant contact with the forum suggests that the cases did not turn on this point.

In Asahi, application of the *forum non conveniens* doctrine (*infra,* Section IV(B)(1)) would have led to the same result: despite the presence of contacts, a state interest on the part of the forum was lacking, and the foreign elements were so numerous, even exclusive, as to make the American forum inappropriate. See also *infra* with respect to *forum non conveniens.* The result might have been different if the question had been whether the California court had jurisdiction in a suit by the injured American plaintiff against the Japanese manufacturer of the component part (i.e., in a direct suit against the third party in *Asahi*).

e. Forum State Interest; Jurisdiction by Necessity

The Supreme Court has stated that on some occasions, the interest of a forum state may justify application of *forum law,* but not the exercise of jurisdiction. See *Kulko,* above. This seems appropriate: if the focus of the jurisdictional inquiry is the *defendant's* "individual liberty interest" (above), forum state interest by itself cannot overcome this due process concern. Conversely, however, the *lack* of forum state interest may well suggest that the forum is inappropriate for the particular litigation. See *Asahi,* above, and below. The latter conclusion should then support a dismissal for *forum non conveniens* (*infra* Section IV(B)).

The foregoing also suggests an answer to the question whether a court may exercise *jurisdiction by necessity* when there is no other American forum available to the plaintiff. In *Helicopteros, supra* at pp. 51, 55, 62, the Court "decline[d] to consider adoption of a doctrine of jurisdiction by necessity—a potentially far-reaching modification of existing law . . . ." 466 U.S. at 419 n.13, 104 S. Ct. at 1874 n.13. However, it did so "in the absence of a more complete record" since the "respondents failed to carry their burden of showing that all three defendants could not be sued together in a single forum." Id.

Thus, while the "individual liberty interests" of defendants should not be balanced against the interest of the forum in providing a local plaintiff with an American court, it may be that the Court, in an appropriate case, will adopt a limited rule of jurisdiction by necessity when (1) there is no alternative forum *anywhere* (i.e., not just no other forum in the United States: *Helicopteros*); and (2) the defendant has some contact with the United States, as in *Helicopteros.* This has been the position of other legal systems, especially for cases of the first type. In the European Union, in an action for maintenance, for instance, a court has jurisdiction "by necessity" if (1) no other court in the EU would have jurisdiction, and (2) an action could "not reasonably be brought" in a third state. Art. 7, Regulation (EC) No. 4/2009, [2009] Official Journal L 7/1. Similarly, EU law provides for jurisdiction over child custody on the basis of the mere presence of the child when no other court appears to have jurisdiction.

f. "National Contacts": Jurisdiction and *Erie*

A "national contacts" approach differs from "jurisdiction by necessity." The former inquires whether there are sufficient contacts with the United States, in the *aggregate,* to permit the exercise of jurisdiction in conformity with the constitutional standard of *International Shoe.* The latter, on the other hand, seeks to provide a forum when there are some, but not enough, contacts with the forum, but the special circumstances of the case require a resolution.

"National contacts" jurisdiction would have to be exercised by federal courts, representing the national sovereign. However, in the absence of a statute authorizing nation-wide or world-wide service, Fed. R. Civ. P. 4 governs service, and that rule incorporates state law. The permissibility of service out of the forum therefore depends on the constitutionality of such service if it were made by a state court. As the previous discussion showed, state court jurisdiction so far requires *forum-specific,* not national, contacts.

The question then remained whether national contacts would satisfy the due process requirement of the Fifth Amendment in cases involving *federal* causes of action, for which Congress authorized nationwide or world-wide service. Since 1993, an amendment to the Federal Rules of Civil Procedure permits the exercise of jurisdiction to the maximum permitted by the Constitution "for a claim that arises under federal law." Fed. R. Civ. P. 4(k)(2). See *ISI Int'l, Inc. v. Borden Ladner Gervais LLP*, 256 F.3d 548, 552 (7th Cir. 2001); *Mwani v. Osama Bin Laden*, 417 F.3d 1 (D.C. Cir. 2005) (Bin Laden's aggregate contacts with U.S. sufficient for jurisdiction in suit by Kenyan victims of bombing of U.S. Embassy). Courts have answered the constitutional question (does exercise of jurisdiction comply with Fifth Amendment due process?) by applying the same tests used to evaluate state court jurisdiction. See *Safra v. Palestinian Authority*, 82 F. Supp. 3d 37 (D.D.C. 2015) (no jurisdiction; defendant's conduct with the United States too attenuated); *Triple Up Ltd. v. Youku Tudou Inc.*, 235 F. Supp. 3d 15 (D.D.C. 2017) (no purposeful availment). For detailed discussion, see also the dissent in *Fuld v. Palestine Liberation Organization*, 101 F.4th 190, 219 et seq. (2nd Cir. 2024).

4. Specific Jurisdiction in the Case Law

a. Products Liability: Injury in the Forum

In *World-Wide Volkswagen Corp. v. Woodson,* 444 U.S. 286, 100 S. Ct. 559, 62 L. Ed. 2d 490 (1980), the Court held that it was not foreseeable for the regional distributor and the local dealer that they would be subjected to jurisdiction in Oklahoma. The appeal did not involve the question of whether the manufacturer and the importer were subject to jurisdiction. At the time of the decision, they probably would have been considered to be subject to jurisdiction: they manufactured and introduced the motor vehicle into the American market, intended that the cars manufactured and imported would be used nationwide, derived benefit from marketing these cars in the United States, and as a result, could anticipate litigation in states such as Oklahoma. In numerous cases, the courts held that a manufacturer who targets a market will be subject to jurisdiction there. After the decision in *J. McIntyre*, below, this became less clear. The more recent decision in *Ford* (also below) again makes it more likely. Oklahoma could not have asserted general jurisdiction at the time, given the limitations declared by *Goodyear* and *Daimler*, above at pp. 55, 56 (the "at home" test). *Mallory* now lets states revise their registration statutes to provide for general jurisdiction over out-of-state enterprises required to register to do business instate. See above Section II(C) and Section III(B)(2)(b).

Whether there is jurisdiction over a manufacturer who has not (directly or by means of an agent) marketed the product in the United States, but whose product reaches the United States in the ordinary "stream of commerce" *and* causes injury here, may still be an open question. In *Asahi,* 480 U.S. 102, 107 S. Ct. 1026, 94 L. Ed. 2d 92 (1987), four Justices, including Justices O'Connor and Powell, considered "stream-of-commerce" jurisdiction to exceed *World-Wide Volkswagen* limits and therefore to be invalid. Four Justices would consider the exercise of such jurisdiction to be valid. Justice Stevens declined to reach the question, but seemed to favor stream-of-commerce jurisdiction, at least in circumstances where the defendant has derived economic benefit from the American market over a period of time.

J. McIntyre Machinery, Ltd. v. Nicastro, 564 U.S. 873, 131 S. Ct. 2780, 180 L. Ed. 2d 765 (2011), did not settle the question. Machines manufactured by the British defendant were advertised and marketed nationwide in the United States; the defendant also attended an American trade fair. The defendant did not sell directly in the United States, but did so through an independent distributor. A machine sold by the latter into New Jersey caused grievous injury there and gave rise to this action. A plurality of the Supreme Court, echoing Justice O'Connor in *Asahi*, rejected jurisdiction based on "stream of commerce" notions, but required that the defendant have established contact to the forum itself before being subject to jurisdiction there. Two Justices agreed that there was no jurisdiction, in part because established case law had not so extended the jurisdictional reach, and in part because perhaps more needed to be known about modern marketing arrangements. Justice Ginsburg, joined by two other Justices, wrote a vigorous dissent, also citing this author. She criticized the ability of foreign manufacturers to shield themselves through the use of intermediaries, as the plurality opinion would facilitate, and also showing in detail the contrary result reached by other legal systems, notably the European Union.

Subsequent lower court decisions have undertaken to distinguish *J. McIntyre* and to uphold the forum's exercise of jurisdiction. For example, in *Soria v. Chrysler Canada, Inc.,* 958 N.E.2d 285 (Ill. App. Ct. 2011), leave denied, 963 N.E.2d 250 (Ill. 2012), 82% of the market of the Canadian defendant, a vehicle assembler, was in the U.S., and it knew the final destination of each vehicle that it assembled. "Targeting," as was already seen in *World-Wide Volkswagen*, here becomes the same as direct contact in *J. McIntyre*. The main difficulty is what is meant by "targeting."

When a manufacturer markets the product itself, it is of course targeting the market. When it employs an exclusive distributor, whom it controls, it may do so as well. *Oswalt v. Scripto, Inc.,* 616 F.2d 191 (5th Cir. 1980). Here, a court may cross the line to what *J. McIntyre* forbids. But what does that decision forbid? A rejection of jurisdiction on the basis of "stream of commerce" drew only four votes; it is not the holding. A lower court therefore felt free to examine and to decide for itself whether "stream of commerce" could be a sufficient basis for the exercise of jurisdiction, and concluded that it could. See *Johnson v. Chrysler Canada, Inc.,* 24 F.Supp.3d

1118 (N.D.Ala. 2014); *Estate of Moore v. Carroll,* 159 F. Supp. 3d 1002 (D.S.D. 2016); *Sims v. BMW of North America, LLC,* 2023 WL 5279340 (M.D. Fla. 2023).

b. Products Liability and "Relatedness:" *Ford v. Montana*

The decisions reviewed above required specific forum contacts for the exercise of specific jurisdiction in product liability cases. At the same time, the U.S. Supreme Court limited the exercise of general jurisdiction severely in its *Goodyear* and *Daimler* decisions, *supra* at pp. 52, 55, 56. *Ford Motor Co. v. Montana,* 592 U.S. 351, 141 S. Ct. 1017, 209 L. Ed. 2d 225 (2021), however, loosened the test for specific jurisdiction. Both the restriction of general jurisdiction and the broadening of specific jurisdiction are welcome developments, even though the dividing line between the two has become somewhat blurred. An interesting question is whether some of the earlier cases would have come out differently under the new approach (see *infra* this page).

In *Ford,* the decedent had purchased a car in another state, before moving to Montana, where the vehicle crashed due to an alleged defect. The owner-driver died from the crash. The U.S. Supreme Court upheld the exercise of specific jurisdiction over Ford: it sold and serviced the same model car in Montana, as well as advertised and did substantial business nationally—including in Montana. Ford *benefited* from Montana, it *targeted* that marketed, and it could *foresee* being sued in Montana in a products liability case. Ford is a large company, so it was *not unfair* to be have to defend in Montana. What's more, Montana had an *interest* in providing a forum for the estate of a local resident to sue for damages resulting from an injury suffered in the state.

The italicized words are elements or aspects that the Court mentioned in many of the cases reviewed above. However, none of them had anything to do directly with the case at hand. The car was not brought into Montana by the defendant automaker; it was bought out-of-state. Thus, Ford did not benefit from doing business in Montana insofar as the alleged defect is concerned. Foreseeability of being sued in Montana had nothing to do with this decedent, who bought the car elsewhere and did not indicate where she would be moving. The Court applied a "relatedness" test (urged by Justice Brennan in *Helicopteros*) against a backdrop of fairness: the claim arose from the type of business Ford was doing in Montana, as it did everywhere; the claim involved a model of car that Ford sold in-state; Ford could have expected to be sued wherever the car caused injury; and the state of injury had an interest in providing a forum. The claim was *related* to Ford's business, was not unfair, and Montana's interest in providing a forum did not infringe on interstate federalism (i.e., the interest of another state).

The foregoing may answer the question asked earlier: Would the older cases have come out differently if *Ford* had been on the books? Probably not. In none (*Worldwide Volkswagen, Asahi, J. McIntyre)* did the defendant itself introduce the product into the forum state, or do substantial business in the forum state with like products: in other words, it did not derive direct benefits. Fairness was an important consideration in the first two cases, *Volkswagen* also raised interstate federalism as a reason for denying jurisdiction to Oklahoma, and the plurality in *J. McIntyre* again rejected the "stream of commerce" rationale for jurisdiction. Later cases, as discussed, got around this rejection by showing that the forum was targeted or foreseen as a place where the product might end up. This might have been true in *Asahi*, but the exercise of jurisdiction was considered unfair.

Ford certainly broadened specific jurisdiction, which Justice Gorsuch welcomed in his concurrence. He disliked the way in which enterprises doing nationwide business benefitted from being somewhat insulated by the restrictions on general jurisdiction. Nonetheless, *Ford*'s relatedness test contains elements that are often present in cases that involve big enterprises nationally engaged in selling the same products, but which may be lacking in many other cases. The relatedness test, as Justice Gorsuch also mentioned, is a continuum—a sliding scale—that future case law must still flesh out.

Justice Gorsuch expanded jurisdiction over out-of-state enterprises further in his reasoning (accepted by three other justices) in *Mallory* (*supra* Section II(C) that registering to do intrastate business may, by statute, constitute consent of an out-of-state enterprise to general jurisdiction.

c. Defamation

The United States Supreme Court (*Keeton*, immediately following, and *Calder*, below) addressed a state's jurisdiction in defamation cases in two 1984 decisions. In *Keeton v. Hustler Magazine, Inc.,* 465 U.S. 770, 104 S. Ct. 1473, 79 L. Ed. 2d 790 (1984), the magazine carrying the defamatory material had been distributed nationwide, including 10,000–15,000 copies in New Hampshire. Plaintiff Keeton had originally brought suit for libel and invasion of privacy in Ohio, where the magazine is published. Her claim had been dismissed there on statute-of-limitations grounds. However, the dismissal was not on the merits (see *infra* Chapter IV(II-C-4)), thus leaving her free to sue elsewhere. New Hampshire, at that time, was the only state in the Union in which the statute of limitations had not yet run.

At common law, a person was libeled every time the defamation was "published" (communicated to another). Thus, the publishers of Hustler magazine would commit a tort in every state in which the magazine is distributed. Specific jurisdiction would therefore also lie in New Hampshire *for the tort committed in New Hampshire.* The more modern approach is reflected in the "single publication rule": all damage suffered by a plaintiff in all states in which a publication occurred is aggregated and recoverable under the substantive law of one state. Even though relatively few issues of Hustler magazine had been distributed in New Hampshire, compared with the number of copies sold nationwide, the tort did have a connection with New Hampshire. The United States Supreme Court therefore upheld New Hampshire's jurisdiction over Hustler magazine.

In *Calder v. Jones,* 465 U.S. 783, 104 S. Ct. 1482, 79 L. Ed. 2d 804 (1984), the United States Supreme Court upheld California's jurisdiction over the defendant reporters who had written a libelous article in Florida for the National Enquirer, a Florida publication with nationwide distribution. The Court focused on the plaintiff's California residence and the fact that the libel would therefore cause the greatest harm there. The defendants' "intentional conduct in Florida [was] calculated to cause injury to [plaintiff] in California." Id. at 791, 1488. Thus, through their actions, the defendants brought themselves into relation with California, making the exercise of jurisdiction there fair. See *Hornbook* §§ 7.11, 7.12.

The contacts with the forum are to be evaluated individually for each defendant, said the Court, finding that the defendants themselves were "primary participants in an alleged wrongdoing intentionally directed at a California resident . . . ." Id. at 790, 1487. Finally, the Court rejected a defense based on the First Amendment. It does not enter into the jurisdictional analysis because First Amendment protection is already taken into account in the limitations placed upon the substantive law governing libel actions.

d. Contracts

The defendants in *Burger King Corp. v. Rudzewicz,* 471 U.S. 462, 105 S. Ct. 2174, 85 L. Ed. 2d 528 (1985) operated a Burger King franchise in Michigan. When they stopped making payments to Burger King in Miami, Burger King sued in Florida, relying on the Florida long-arm statute, which provides for jurisdiction in contract cases when the contract was made in Florida. The United States Supreme Court upheld jurisdiction.

In applying the test of *World-Wide Volkswagen* (*supra* at p. 65), the Court pointed to contract negotiations that had taken place at Burger King's Miami headquarters, the 20-year relationship contemplated by the franchise agreement, the supervision that Burger King exercises over its franchisees, and the presence in the contract of a clause choosing Florida law for disputes arising from the contract. While a *choice-of-law* clause ordinarily does not make for *jurisdiction,* it is nevertheless relevant. It shows that the parties, including the defendants, "purposefully availed themselves of the benefits" of Florida law. In combination, these contacts made it "foreseeable" that litigation might occur in Florida; the defendants could "reasonably anticipate" it. For discussion of the case, see *Clark v. Podesta,* No. 1:15-cv-00008-ELJ-CWD, 2015 WL 5721796 (D. Idaho Sept. 14, 2015), and *Sanchez v. State Farm Fire & Cas. Co.*, No. 14-CV-0433 MCA/RHS, 2015 WL 12864232 (D.N.M. Mar. 31, 2015), both stressing that even a single contact could constitute a substantial connection. See also *Martinez v. N. Ariz. Univ.*, 553 F. Supp. 3d 908 (D.N.M. 2021) (direct contact by defendant is necessary).

e. Domestic Relations

The jurisdiction of courts and the recognition of judgments and decrees in domestic relations matters is the subject of separate treatment in this book. See *infra* Part Three. The present subsection provides a brief summary only.

A court has *divorce* jurisdiction when the forum is the domicile of the petitioner. *Williams v. North Carolina (II),* 325 U.S. 226, 65 S. Ct. 1092, 89 L. Ed. 1577 (1945). This is so because a court's divorce jurisdiction is viewed similar to a court's jurisdiction over a thing, a *res,* located in its territory: the *status* of marriage is before the court (in this case, for purposes of dissolution), and that status is "located" wherever a spouse is domiciled.

Additionally, a court has divorce jurisdiction when *both* parties participate. *Sherrer v. Sherrer,* 334 U.S. 343, 68 S. Ct. 1087, 92 L. Ed. 1429 (1948). This is so because the respondent could have raised the question of lack of jurisdiction (for instance, that neither party was domiciled in the forum). When the jurisdictional defense is not raised, it is lost for purposes of collateral attack. See also *infra* at p. 75. For the recognition of *international divorces,* some courts have accepted jurisdiction based on the presence of both parties before the foreign court, even if lack of domicile could not have been raised as a defense in the foreign country. *Rosenstiel v. Rosenstiel,* 209 N.E.2d 709 (N.Y. 1965). See *Hornbook* § 15.20. Foreign religious divorces will generally be recognized if valid where rendered. See further below at p. 151.

When divorce jurisdiction is based only on the domicile of the petitioner, and the court has no other personal jurisdiction over the respondent, its jurisdiction extends solely to the dissolution of the marriage (*ex parte* divorce). It has no power to affect other aspects of the parties' relations, such as the award of alimony. The non-status aspects, also called the "incidents" of the marriage status, thus are split off from the status determination. This is the "divisible divorce" concept. *Estin v. Estin,* 334 U.S. 541, 68 S. Ct. 1213, 92 L. Ed. 1561 (1948).

Jurisdiction for the *annulment* of a marriage exists wherever divorce jurisdiction exists as well as in the court with personal jurisdiction over both parties. *Whealton v. Whealton,* 432 P.2d 979 (Cal. 1967).

Jurisdiction to award or to modify *support* exists in courts having personal jurisdiction over both parties. When such jurisdiction is lacking, the plaintiff may be able to utilize the interstate cooperative procedures provided by the *Uniform Interstate Family Support Act (UIFSA).* For further discussion see *infra* Chapter VI, at IV(A).

Jurisdiction to award *custody* exists in courts having jurisdiction over both parents, *May v. Anderson,* 345 U.S. 528, 73 S. Ct. 840, 97 L. Ed. 1221 (1953), but may also be exercised by courts at the residence of one parent when the child is physically present there. To curb the abuses of interstate child snatching, custody today is governed by the *Uniform Child Custody Jurisdiction and Enforcement Act* and by the *Federal Parental Kidnapping Prevention Act.* For further discussion see *infra* Chapter VI, at IV(B).

5. Jurisdiction and the Internet

The maintenance of websites and communication via the Internet raise new jurisdictional questions. Typically, the plaintiff will assert *specific* jurisdiction because some on-line deal went awry. The question is whether the maintenance of a website (with or without return communication capability) subjects the Internet participant to jurisdiction in any place where the site can be accessed.

Weber v. Jolly Hotels, 977 F. Supp. 327 (D.N.J. 1997) addressed three different fact situations: (1) defendants actively do (solicit) business via the Internet; (2) a website gives information but also allows interactivity with the host; and (3) the website is passively informative only. The court found the third fact pattern to characterize the case (i.e., no jurisdiction). Under these tests, jurisdiction would clearly exist in fact pattern no. 1, while no. 2 would require a case-specific analysis and evaluation. See also *CompuServe Inc. v. Patterson*, 89 F.3d 1257 (6th Cir. 1996), and *Zippo Mfg. Co. v. Zippo Dot Com, Inc.*, 952 F. Supp. 1119 (W.D. Pa. 1997) (establishing a sliding continuum approach to Internet jurisdiction, the "Zippo test"). The "Zippo test," however, has been rejected by a number of other courts. A leading decision requires that the defendant purposefully directed its activity to the forum (a notion not dissimilar from the rationale in products liability cases, above). See *Shrader v. Biddinger*, 633 F.3d 1235 (10th Cir. 2010). See also *Claimsolution, Inc. v. Claim Solutions, LLC*, No. 17-2005-JWL, 2017 WL 2831330 (D. Kan. June 30, 2017); Allergy Research Group LLC v. Rez Candles, Inc., 2021 WL 3862326, *4, (D. Utah Aug 30, 2021).

As an alternative to personal jurisdiction, the Anticybersquatting Consumer Protection Act provides that the owner of a trademark may bring an *in rem* action against an infringing domain name where the domain registrar, domain registry, or "other domain name authority" is located. 15 U.S.C.A. § 1125(d)(2) (West 2022). See also *Mattel, Inc. v. Barbie-Club.com,* 310 F.3d 293, 306 (2d Cir. 2002); *Jacobs Private Equity, LLC v. <JPE.com>*, No. 1:16–cv–01331, 2017 WL 830397 (E.D. Va. Feb. 2, 2017), *enforced,* 2017 WL 831150 (E.D. Va. Mar. 2, 2017).

6. Jurisdiction and Complex Litigation

a. Interpleader

When two or more parties claim the same asset, the obligor naturally desires protection against potential double liability. However, in view of the constitutional limitations upon the reach of state court jurisdiction, the obligor may be unable to get all of the parties into the same court. See *New York Life Insurance Co. v. Dunlevy,* 241 U.S. 518, 36 S. Ct. 613, 60 L. Ed. 1140 (1916). The Federal Interpleader Act, first adopted in 1917 and since then expanded, gives federal courts nationwide service of process. "Statutory interpleader" enables an obligor/stakeholder to bind all interested parties in a single proceeding. For "rule interpleader" (under Fed. R. Civ. P. 22), in contrast, traditional rules of jurisdiction must be observed.

b. Impleader

State practice permits a defendant to bring in, as a further defendant, a party against whom the principal defendant believes to have a claim over if found liable to the plaintiff. The situation in *Gray* (*supra*) illustrates the point: if found liable to the Illinois plaintiff, American Standard will want to invoke the liability of the manufacturer of the defective component, the safety valve. If American Standard cannot have the liability of the component part manufacturer established in the same lawsuit, it runs the risk of inconsistent judgments: liable to the Illinois plaintiff but no recovery, for whatever reason, against the component part manufacturer.

Unlike the case of the stakeholder with potential multiple liability, which the interpleader legislation addressed (*supra*), there exists no interstate procedure for impleader. Thus, in the absence of federal legislation addressing this problem, it remains true that "[t]he requirements of *International Shoe* . . . must be met as to each defendant over whom a state court exercises jurisdiction." *Rush v. Savchuk,* 444 U.S. 320, 332, 100 S. Ct. 571, 579, 62 L. Ed. 2d 516 (1980).

c. Class Actions

(i) In general, class actions are the procedure by which one or more parties, as representatives of a larger class of claimants or defendants, are permitted to bring suit (or be sued) in circumstances where the number of those interested in the litigation is so great as not to permit joinder in the traditional sense, or where individual claims are so small as to make it uneconomical for parties to litigate their claims individually.

All members of the class will be affected by the judgment entered in the suit brought by the class representatives. They will not be able to litigate the matter anew. The question therefore arises whether absent members of the class must affirmatively "opt in" (in the sense of submitting to the court's jurisdiction), or whether the class can also be certified, and the absent members of the class be bound by a judgment, if they merely fail to exercise their right to "opt out." In *federal* practice, Fed. R. Civ. P. 23 provides for two types of class actions: one where a member of the class must be given notice and an opportunity to opt out, and one where there is no opt-out opportunity.

In *Phillips Petroleum Co. v. Shutts,* 472 U.S. 797, 105 S. Ct. 2965, 86 L. Ed. 2d 628 (1985), which arose under a *state* class action statute, the United States Supreme Court expressly sanctioned the exercise of state jurisdiction when absent members of the plaintiff class had not opted in, but had been given notice and an adequate opportunity to "opt out." The Court distinguished the position of members of a plaintiff class from *absent* defendants, and expressly declined to address jurisdictional issues in class actions not for money but for equitable relief, as well as actions asserted against a *defendant class.*

(ii) Class actions in state courts—limitations. Legislation adopted in 2005 severely limits the extent to which class actions may be brought in state court (typically, any state in which the injury occurred) and moves most multiparty, multistate class actions to federal court. The expectation is that federal courts are more likely to deny class action certification (because the potential applicability of different state laws means that the required "common questions of law or fact" requirement is not met), and that if an action is entertained in federal court, recoveries will tend to be lower than in plaintiff-friendly state courts. Class Action Fairness Act of 2005, Pub. L. No. 109–2, 119 Stat. 4 (codified at 28 U.S.C.A. §§ 1332(d), 1453, 1711–15 (West 2022)).

(iii) When Rule 23 conflicts with state law, the Rule prevails. In *Shady Grove Orthopedic Associates, P.A. v. Allstate Ins. Co.,* 559 U.S. 393, 130 S. Ct. 1431, 178 L. Ed. 2d 311 (2010), New York law imposed penalties for nonpayment of statutory interest on overdue payments of medical benefits, but barred class actions seeking to recover penalties. The Supreme Court held that Fed. R. Civ. P. 23 provided a remedy for the enforcement of substantive rights, that it was *procedural* (i.e., that it did not impinge on New York substantive law), and that it thus prevailed for actions in federal court. Confirmed in *Berk v. Choy*, 607 U.S. ___, 2026 WL 135974 (2026).

Similarly, for Fed. R. Civ. P. 56 (summary judgment), see *Scola v. Publix Supermarkets, Inc.,* 557 Fed. App'x 458 (6th Cir. 2014); *Sec'y of U.S. Dep't of Labor v. American Made Bags, LLC,* No. 5:19CV863, 2022 WL 479790 (N.D. Ohio Feb. 15, 2022) (slip op.).

(iv) In international cases, class certification may be denied because choice-of-law problems may make it unlikely that there are common questions of law. Also, the likelihood that a resulting U.S. judgment would not be recognized abroad may be a factor against certification in the first place. See *In re Vivendi Universal S.A. Securities Litigation*, 242 F.R.D. 76 (S.D.N.Y. 2007); *Anwar v. Fairfield Greenwich Ltd.*, 289 F.R.D. 105 (S.D.N.Y. 2013), *rev'd on other grounds, St. Stephen's School v. PriceWaterhouseCoopers Accountants N.V.*, 570 Fed. App'x 37 (2d Cir. 2014).

d. Multiparty, Multiforum Actions

Ordinarily, federal diversity jurisdiction requires "full diversity": no opposing parties may share the same citizenship. This creates a problem when, for instance, as the result of an airplane crash, a number of parties wish to join to bring an action. The Multiparty, Multiforum Trial Jurisdiction Act of 2002, 28 U.S.C. § 1369, provides that federal courts have jurisdiction if there is "minimal diversity" in an action arising from a single accident in which at least 75 persons have died. In such a case, there must be diversity as to at least one party on each side. The provision does not apply when a substantial number of plaintiffs and the primary defendants are from one state and that state's law also applies to the claims. For removal under the Act, see *Wallace v. Louisiana Citizens Property Ins. Corp.*, 444 F.3d 697 (5th Cir. 2006).

IV. Limitations on the Exercise of Personal Jurisdiction

A. Forum-Selection Clauses

Forum-selection clauses are a form of jurisdiction by consent. They confer personal jurisdiction on the designated court and eliminate the need to inquire whether the court would otherwise have jurisdiction. See also *supra.*

Parties will adopt forum-selection clauses to gain certainty about the location of future litigation, and also to centralize or localize litigation in a single place, for instance in the case of an interstate or international business. As a consequence, parties to a forum selection clause often intend that *only the designated court* have jurisdiction, and that other courts *not* exercise the jurisdiction they otherwise might have.

Traditionally, American courts have accepted the grant of jurisdiction contained in a forum selection clause, but many were hostile to the exclusion of their jurisdiction when they were not the designated court. It was said that the parties, by private agreement, cannot "oust the jurisdiction of a court" which it otherwise has, as some older decisions put it. Today, only three states (Iowa, Idaho, and Montana) continue to regard forum-selection clauses as unenforceable.

In *M/S Bremen v. Zapata Off-Shore Co.,* 407 U.S. 1, 92 S. Ct. 1907, 32 L. Ed. 2d 513 (1972), the United States Supreme Court upheld a forum-selection clause in favor of

England and reversed the trial court's refusal to honor the clause on "ouster" grounds. The Supreme Court's decision was rendered in an admiralty case.

Subsequent decisions extended *Zapata* to other federal-question cases: *Scherk v. Alberto-Culver Co.,* 417 U.S. 506, 94 S. Ct. 2449, 41 L. Ed. 2d 270 (1974) (arbitration in securities case); *Mitsubishi Motors Corp. v. Soler Chrysler-Plymouth, Inc.,* 473 U.S. 614, 105 S. Ct. 3346, 87 L. Ed. 2d 444 (1985) (arbitration of antitrust claim); *Vimar Seguros y Reaseguros, S.A. v. M/V Sky Reefer,* 515 U.S. 528, 115 S. Ct. 2322, 132 L. Ed. 2d 462 (1995) (Carriage of Goods by Sea Act).

In *Carnival Cruise Lines, Inc. v. Shute,* 499 U.S. 585, 111 S. Ct. 1522, 113 L. Ed. 2d 622 (1991), another admiralty case (that is, a federal question case), the Supreme Court upheld a forum selection clause in a contract of passage that clearly was not bargained for. It did so on the grounds, inter alia, that it was reasonable for the defendant to wish to have a central place for litigation, and that it is not unreasonable to expect an American plaintiff to travel to another state of the United States. In *Carnival Cruise Lines, Inc. v. Superior Court,* 286 Cal. Rptr. 323 (Cal. Ct. App. 1991), a California appellate court declined to enforce a forum selection clause in a mass tort case as to all plaintiffs who had not had sufficient notice of the clause prior to entering into the contract of passage, a point expressly left unaddressed in *Shute.* For a similar decision, see *Casavant v. Norwegian Cruise Line, Ltd.*, 829 N.E.2d 1171 (Mass. App. Ct. 2005), *cert. denied,* 546 U.S. 1173, 126 S. Ct. 1337, 164 L. Ed. 2d 52 (2006). The *Shute* decision was followed in *Monsanto Co. v. McFarling,* 302 F.3d 1291 (Fed. Cir. 2002), *cert. denied,* 537 U.S. 1232, 123 S. Ct. 1357, 155 L. Ed. 2d 196 (2003).

Forum-selection clauses are often contained in a provider's "terms of use" on the Internet. In *Berkson v. Gogo LLC,* 97 F. Supp. 3d 359 (E.D.N.Y. 2015), *appeal withdrawn,* No. 15-1407, 2016 WL 11785988 (2d Cir. May 16, 2016), the court reviewed the various ways in which "terms of use" might appear: by requiring the user to scroll down the page ("scrollwrap"), by deeming a user's act of signing into a website to be agreement to terms made available elsewhere, such as on another webpage ("sign-in-wrap"), or by simple announcement that continued use of the website constitutes acceptance of the "terms of use," the content of which the user would also have to call up by him/herself. Since the user in this case did not have actual knowledge of the terms of use, and it was not likely that the user realized the need to seek information, the court concluded that the "contract scenario in *Carnival Cruise* should not be analogized to electronic websites' contracts of adhesion." Id. at 404. See likewise *Applebaum v. Lyft, Inc.,* 263 F. Supp. 3d 454, 464 (S.D.N.Y. 2017); *TopstepTrader, LLC v. OneUp Trader, LLC,* No. 17 C 4412, 2018 WL 1859040 (N.D. Ill. Apr. 18, 2018).

Federal courts apply *Zapata* principles to forum-selection clauses arising in **diversity** cases. See *Lambert v. Kysar,* 983 F.2d 1110, 1117 n.10 (1st Cir. 1993). In a case arising on a motion to transfer, the United States Supreme Court agreed that federal law governed. However, the applicable standard was the federal transfer statute, not the federal common law rule of *Zapata* and the other federal question cases. *Stewart Organization, Inc. v. Ricoh Corp.,* 487 U.S. 22, 108 S. Ct. 2239, 101 L. Ed. 2d 22 (1988); *Atlantic Marine Const. Co. v. U.S. District Court,* 571 U.S. 49, 59, 134 S. Ct. 568, 579, 187 L. Ed. 2d 487 (2013) (restating *Stewart*).

"The forum-selection clause, which represents the parties' agreement as to the most proper forum, should receive neither dispositive consideration (as respondent might have it) nor no consideration (as Alabama law might have it), but rather the consideration for which Congress provided in [the federal transfer statute]." 487 U.S. at 31, 108 S. Ct. at 2245. For federal transfer see below.

What if no federal rule is involved, and the federal court, sitting in diversity, needs to decide whether to follow *Zapata* or the more restrictive law of the forum state? The U.S. Supreme Court has not decided the issue, but the majority of the federal circuit courts of appeals now apply the federal rule. See *GITA Sports Ltd. v. SG Sensortechnik GmbH & Co. KG*, 560 F. Supp. 2d 432 (W.D.N.C. 2008). In *international* cases arising in diversity, and not under federal law, and to which the federal transfer statute of course does not apply, federal courts also continue to apply the federal common law rule of *Zapata*. See, e.g., *Interamerican Trade Corp. v. Companhia Fabricadora de Pecas,* 973 F.2d 487 (6th Cir. 1992); *GITA Sports, supra.* Federal law has also been applied—in diversity—when its standards were more permissive than the state law of the forum. See *Esfeld v. Costa Crociere, Sp.A.*, 289 F.3d 1300 (11th Cir. 2002) (involving *forum non conveniens*); *Seguros Universales, S.A. v. Microsoft Corp.*, 32 F. Supp. 3d 1242 (S.D. Fla. 2014) (same).

In determining whether to give effect to the forum selection clause, the *Zapata* Court inquired whether the clause was contained in a contract between economic equals, whether it seemed to have been bargained for (as distinguished from being boilerplate), and whether it was a reasonable stipulation. See also § 80 of the Restatement (Second). In reviewing the reasonableness of the stipulation, it may be important whether the chosen court is at the place of business of either party or whether there was some other good reason for choosing it. In *Zapata,* for instance, the parties had chosen English courts because of their special expertise in maritime matters. For consumer protection, see the discussion of cognovit clauses, *supra* p. 60. Forum-selection clauses raise similar issues. See also U.C.C. § 2A–106.

When a forum-selection clause is valid, but suit has been brought in another court in breach of the stipulation (and the federal transfer statute is inapplicable), the appropriate remedy in the latter court is a motion for dismissal or the granting of a stay. The latter remedy may be given to assure a local forum if the designated court, for whatever reason, does not provide an appropriate remedy. In federal practice, the U.S. Supreme Court held that the proper remedy is not dismissal for improper venue but transfer to the court designated in the forum selection clause. Transfer is not automatic; it is at the discretion of the court. However, the federal district court should only consider public factors (such as evasion of mandatory norms of forum law); it should not weigh private factors and interests, which the parties themselves are presumed to have done in making their agreement. *Atl. Marine Constr. Co., Inc. v. U.S. Dist Ct.*, 571 U.S. 49, 57, 134 S. Ct. 568, 578, 187 L. Ed. 2d 487 (2013); *MKM Healthcare Solutions, LLC v. Biotronic Inc.*, No. CV-20-00255-TUC-CKJ, 2020 WL 5111137 (D. Ariz. Aug. 31, 2020) (slip op.). For denial of a motion to transfer because the forum selection clause violated a statutory provision of the forum, see *Lakeside Surfaces, Inc. v. Cambria Co., LLC,* 16 F.4th 209 (6th Cir. 2021). For an overview, see Hay, Forum Selection Clauses, 35 Emory Int'l L. Rev. 1, 9 *et seq.* (2021).

B. The Inappropriate Forum

1. Dismissal or Stay for *Forum Non Conveniens*

Even though a court has jurisdiction over the parties, considerations of justice and convenience may lead the court, in its discretion, to refuse to exercise its jurisdiction, thereby forcing the plaintiff to sue in a more appropriate forum. This is the doctrine of *forum non conveniens.* The leading decision, also followed widely in state practice, is *Gulf Oil Corp. v. Gilbert,* 330 U.S. 501, 67 S. Ct. 839, 91 L. Ed. 1055 (1947).

The *forum non conveniens* inquiry begins with a preference for the plaintiff's choice of the forum. The defendant has the burden of showing that another forum is readily available (see also *infra*), that the present forum is seriously and burdensomely inconvenient, and that the other forum is more convenient. In interstate practice, it is impermissible, however, to refuse to exercise jurisdiction only because the cause of action arises under the laws of a sister state, in the absence of a showing that the claim violates the public policy of the forum. A dismissal for this reason, under the guise of *forum non conveniens,* would violate the Full Faith and Credit Clause, and possibly deny the claimant equal protection. See *Hughes v. Fetter,* 341 U.S. 609, 71 S. Ct. 980, 95 L. Ed. 1212 (1951).

In *Piper Aircraft Co. v. Reyno,* 454 U.S. 235, 102 S. Ct. 252, 70 L. Ed. 2d 419 (1981), the United States Supreme Court approved a "distinction between resident or citizen plaintiffs and foreign plaintiffs. . . . When the home forum has been chosen, it is reasonable to assume that this choice is convenient. When the plaintiff is foreign, however, this assumption is much less reasonable. . . . a foreign plaintiff's choice deserves less deference." Id. at 255 56. This distinction is necessary to counteract the attractiveness of American procedure and substantive tort law for foreign plaintiffs. See also *In re Union Carbide Corp. Gas Plant Disaster,* 809 F.2d 195 (2d Cir. 1987), *cert. denied,* 484 U.S. 871, 108 S. Ct. 199, 98 L. Ed. 2d 150 (1987) (the Bhopal disaster). For more recent applications, see *Guidi v. Inter-Continental Hotels Corp.,* 224 F.3d 142 (2d Cir. 2000); *Iragorri v. United Technologies Corp.,* 274 F.3d 65 (2d Cir. 2001); *Chirag v. MT Marida Marguerite Schiffahrts,* 983 F. Supp. 2d 188 (D. Conn. 2013); *Wave Studio, LLC v. General Hotel Management Ltd.,* 712 Fed. App'x 88 (2d Cir. 2018); *Zanghi v. Ritella,* No. 19 Civ. 5830, 2021 WL 4392756 (S.D.N.Y. Sept. 24, 2021) (slip op.); *.Cohen v. Key Safety Systems, Inc,* 2023 WL 2561372 (M.D.Fla. 2023); *AdvanFort Co. v. Zamil Offshore Services Co.,* 134 F.4th 760 (4th Cir. 2025). For foreign retaliatory legislation, see *infra* at p. 81.

Courts carefully distinguish between, and then balance, the private and public interest involved. Private interests include access to proof, including witnesses, costs, and the like, while public interests also consider judicial dockets, connection of the case to the forum, and difficulties in the determination of applicable foreign law. Increasingly, courts tend to accord greater weight to the private interests involved. See *Iragorri, supra; In re Bridgestone/Firestone Inc.,* 190 F. Supp. 2d 1125 (S.D. Ind. 2002); *Windt v. Qwest Communications Int'l, Inc.,* 529 F.3d 183 (3d Cir. 2008) (interest in having litigation seeking redress for corporate wrongdoing—RICO claims—proceed in the United States outweighed by slight connection to New Jersey and pendency of significant related litigation and presence of evidence in the Netherlands); *Incubadora Mexicana, SA de CV v. Zoetis, Inc.,* 116 F. Supp. 3d 519 (E.D. Pa. 2015) (upholding choice of Pennsylvania forum on private interest grounds). But see *Fresh Results, LLC v. ASF Holland, B.V.,* 921 F.3d 1043 (11th Cir. 2019) (district court abused discretion by not adequately considering public factors).

The fact that the alternative forum would apply a different law, possibly a law less favorable to the plaintiff, is not a consideration for the *forum non conveniens* determination. *Piper Aircraft, supra* (no strict liability under Scottish law, the applicable law in the alternate forum). But see *Holmes v. Syntex Laboratories, Inc.*, 202 Cal. Rptr. 773 (Cal. Ct. App. 1984): whether the alternative forum is "suitable" is to be determined with reference to the possibility that the applicable law in the alternative forum will be less favorable to the plaintiff. This is a minority view, and was subsequently disapproved by the California Supreme Court in *Stangvik v. Shiley Inc.*, 819 P.2d 14, 27 (Cal. 1991) (en banc). See also *Wimbledon Financing Master Fund, Ltd. v. Molner*, No. B276434, 2018 WL 1325618, at *10 (Cal. Ct. App. Mar. 15, 2018). The matter may be different when the foreign legal system lacks effective remedies, so that a *forum non conveniens* dismissal might amount to a denial of access to justice. Cf. *Lubbe v. Cape PLC*, [2002] 1 W.L.R. 1545 (English House of Lords): factors considered in the denial of a *forum non conveniens* dismissal were the unavailability of legal aid in support of litigation expenses in the foreign legal system in combination with a publication of retainers on a contingent fee basis.

In a diversity action, what law applies? See *Esfeld v. Costa Crociere S.P.A.*, 289 F.3d 1300 (11th Cir. 2002).

New York law provides that a case may not be dismissed if there is a choice-of-court clause in favor of New York, the case involves obligations of $1 million in the aggregate, and New York law has also been chosen. Similarly, Texas law forbids a *forum non conveniens* dismissal if the plaintiff is a Texas resident. Tex. Civ. Prac. & Rem. Code Ann. § 71.051(e) (West 2021). See also *In re Mahindra, USA Inc.*, 549 S.W.3d 541 (Tex. 2018) (extensive discussion of § 71.051).

When the court grants relief for *forum non conveniens,* it will dismiss, sometimes on the condition or stipulation that the defendant submit to jurisdiction in the other forum, and if necessary, also waive any defense with respect to the statute of limitations. The conditional dismissal is the functional equivalent, in state practice, of the transfer available to federal courts. Note, however, that the second court in a *forum non conveniens* dismissal then makes its own determination as to the applicable law, while a transferee court does not. See below at p. 248 *et seq.*

Retaliatory legislation in some countries attempts to divest local courts of jurisdiction when the action was dismissed abroad on *forum non conveniens* grounds. In these circumstances, an American court might conclude that the foreign forum is not available (see above at p. 80) and therefore decline to dismiss, lest its actions have the effect of denying the plaintiff access to justice. See, e.g., *Paulowina Plantations v. Rajamannan*, 757 N.W.2d 903 (Minn. Ct. App. 2008), *rev'd*, 793 N.W.2d 128 (Minn. 2009) (Panama). However, other American courts seem less willing to dissipate judicial resources on lawsuits rebuffed by countries to which they are more closely connected. See, e.g., *Aranda v. Philip Morris*, 183 A.3d 1245, 1251–54 (Del. 2018) (rejecting the requirement of an alternative forum before dismissing a case on *forum non conveniens* grounds); *Scotts Co. v. Hacienda Loma Linda*, 2 So. 3d 1013 (Fla. Dist. Ct. App. 2008) ("a plaintiff in a lawsuit dismissed [in Florida] for forum non conveniens may not render an alternative forum 'unavailable' [by] relying on foreign laws . . . plainly calculated to preclude dismissal in Florida . . . ."). Id. at 1017–18.

2. Federal Transfer

By statute (28 U.S.C.A. § 1404(a)), a federal court—"for the convenience of parties and witnesses"—may transfer a civil case to any other federal court in which the case could have been brought in the first place. A state court finding of *forum non conveniens* is not res judicata on the question of federal transfer because different questions with respect to docket status and place of trial may be involved in the state court finding and in the federal decision. *Parsons v. Chesapeake & Ohio Ry. Co.,* 375 U.S. 71, 84 S. Ct. 185, 11 L. Ed. 2d 137 (1963).

The Federal Transfer Statute (§ 1404(a)) has displaced the common law dismissal for *forum non conveniens* in federal practice whenever it applies. *Forum non conveniens* continues to remain important for international cases to which § 1404(a) of course does not apply. See *American Dredging Co. v. Miller,* 510 U.S. 443, 449 n.2, 114 S. Ct. 981, 986 n.2, 127 L. Ed. 2d 285 (1994).

Cross reference: For federal transfer and forum-selection clauses, see above at p. 77; for federal transfer and choice of law, see below at p. 222 *et seq.*

C. Defenses

1. Fraudulent Inducement at Common Law

There was no jurisdiction at common law over a defendant who had been lured into the state by fraud or brought into the state by force. See Restatement (Second) §§ 82, 115.

2. Immunity of Parties

Foreign government officials and accredited diplomats are immune from service of process under principles of public international law. Restatement (Second) § 83. Immunity is also generally accorded a person who voluntarily enters the forum for the purpose of defending another case. These exceptions apply only to persons who would otherwise be subject to jurisdiction on the basis of their presence (transient jurisdiction)—not to persons over whom jurisdiction may be asserted on some other basis.

3. Witness Immunity

Immunity from process also extends to witnesses entering a state, subject to the same limitation as under (2) above.

4. Notice and Opportunity to Appear

As noted above, due process requires that before a court may assert jurisdiction, notice of litigation must be given to the defendant. That notice must be reasonably calculated to inform him or her of the pending action and to afford an opportunity to appear therein. The notice requirement must be satisfied even though the relational circumstances which give a court jurisdiction are present.

V. Continuing Jurisdiction

Once a court has acquired valid jurisdiction, the jurisdiction continues until the cause of action is adjudicated, even though the facts originally creating jurisdiction may have changed ("continuing jurisdiction").

For example, jurisdiction continues even though the defendant leaves the forum after commencement of the action. Similarly, once the plaintiff has commenced his or her action, the court has continuing jurisdiction over him or her with respect to any permissible counterclaim which the defendant may assert. See *Michigan Trust Co. v. Ferry,* 228 U.S. 346, 33 S. Ct. 550, 57 L. Ed. 867 (1913): The court-appointed administrator of a decedent's estate is subject to the jurisdiction of the court until he is discharged. Accord Restatement (Second) § 26. The concept is also very important for such areas as support and custody, i.e., areas in which formal decrees are not issued, but in which courts will entertain petitions for modification.

VI. Note: Contacts for Personal Jurisdiction and for Choice of Law

A. Common Features

Choice of law, just as the exercise of jurisdiction, is subject to constitutional limitations. These are also expressed in terms of *contacts.* Many of the contacts relevant for jurisdiction are also relevant for choice of law.

B. Differences

As we have seen, the contacts necessary for the permissible exercise of state court *jurisdiction* focus on the contacts that the state has to the defendant or to the transaction. In *choice of law* (*infra* at p. 158 *et seq.*), the emphasis is on the connection between the transaction or occurrence and the forum state, so as to allow the forum to apply its own law.

While the same contacts will often permit a state to exercise jurisdiction and to apply its own law, there may be cases when this is not so.

For instance, a state may have general jurisdiction over a corporation at its place of incorporation but have insufficient contact with a claim which arose elsewhere and for that reason may grant a motion for dismissal for *forum non conveniens.* Similarly, a state may have jurisdiction in a class action, for instance in circumstances like *Phillips Petroleum v. Shutts* (*infra* at p. 76), yet not be able to apply its own law to claims that arose elsewhere. Conversely, a state may have a legitimate interest in applying its law, for instance for the award of compensation in favor of a locally resident car accident victim, yet be unable to assert jurisdiction over the non-resident defendant. Constitutional limitations on choice of law are discussed *infra* in Chapter X.

VII. Jurisdiction over Things

A. *In Rem* Jurisdiction

1. Introduction

Historically, a state had jurisdiction over all things within its borders since it had *power* over these things, for instance to enforce a judgment against them. Since *Shaffer v. Heitner,* 433 U.S. 186, 97 S. Ct. 2569, 53 L. Ed. 2d 683 (1977), discussed below, a state's jurisdiction over local things has been sharply curtailed when the plaintiff's claim is not related to the thing.

2. *In Rem* Jurisdiction over Land

A state has jurisdiction over local land. Thus, in a quiet title action, the state has power to award full (indefeasible) title to local land to a claimant as against the owner as well as all others. The jurisdiction exists on the basis of the presence of the land, and personal jurisdiction over the owner is not necessary. He or she may be brought into the suit through service by publication. Similarly, a state may exercise its powers of eminent domain and take over land for public purposes.

However, the state's power is limited. It extends only to *title-related claims* to local land. It has no power to adjudicate the personal rights and obligations between parties, even if related to the land (such as the question whether a mortgage has been paid off), unless it has personal jurisdiction over the parties.

For instance, the court at the situs of the land may find that the owner has defaulted on a mortgage obligation, proceed with a foreclosure and award the land to the mortgagee or a buyer at public auction. The (absent) owner will have lost title to the land but will still be able to litigate, in a proceeding with personal jurisdiction over both parties, whether there was a default on the mortgage or whether, possibly, it had been paid off. If he prevails in the personal action, he then has a claim in restitution against the mortgagee. See *Fitch v. Huntington,* 102 N.W. 1066 (Wis. 1905).

Similarly, a state cannot directly affect title to land in another state. It cannot give title to, directly impose a lien upon, or partition foreign land. However, it can, in a proceeding with personal jurisdiction over the parties, bind the *personal rights* of these parties. To the extent that its decree adjudicates personal obligations of the parties, it is entitled to full faith and credit in the state in which the land is situated. In the absence of intervening rights of third parties not bound by the first judgment, the situs state should then give its own remedy, for instance by recognizing the prevailing party's claim to the land and then quieting title to that land in that party. See *In re Marriage of Kowalewski,* 182 P.3d 959 (Wash. 2008); *OneWest Bank, FSB v. Erickson,* 367 P.3d 1063, 1071–72 (Wash. 2016) (en banc).

3. *In Rem* Jurisdiction over Chattels

A state similarly has jurisdiction over chattels within its boundaries, especially if such chattels are not only casually within the state or in transit. Thus, there exists jurisdiction to litigate ownership of equipment, furniture, cattle, and the like. Again, however, such jurisdiction extends only to *title* claims and not to the personal rights and obligations of the competing parties unless the state also has personal jurisdiction over them.

When a chattel is only temporarily within the state or in transit, the Supreme Court's decision in *Shaffer v. Heitner,* 433 U.S. 186, 97 S. Ct. 2569, 53 L. Ed. 2d 683 (1977), suggests that considerations of fairness to the (absent) owner may restrict the historically absolute power of a state over local property, including chattels.

4. Intangibles

An intangible asset may be represented by a document. In that case, rights to the document, for instance a promissory note or a bond, may be adjudicated where the document is located. Restatement (Second) § 363. If the intangible is not represented by a document, it is in the nature of a personal debt relationship. Litigation concerning the intangible then takes the form of attachment or garnishment: the court will exercise *quasi in rem* jurisdiction, rather than *in rem* jurisdiction. For discussion see the section immediately following.

Jurisdiction to *escheat unclaimed property* was originally governed by the rule of *Texas v. New Jersey,* 379 U.S. 674, 85 S. Ct. 626, 13 L. Ed. 2d 596 (1965) (state of creditor's last known address). Federal legislation now provides for jurisdiction to escheat in the state where the instrument (money order, traveler's check, or similar instrument) was purchased or, if unknown, in the state of the principal place of business of the holder. 12 U.S.C.A. § 2503 (West 2022). See also the Uniform Unclaimed Property Act, 1981, 8 U.L.A. Supp.

For the Anticybersquatting Consumer Protection Act, see *supra* at Section III-D-5 and *infra* at Section B-2-f.

B. *Quasi In Rem* Jurisdiction

1. Introduction

Quasi in rem jurisdiction is the exercise of judicial power over a person's local property in circumstances where the claimant has *no specific claim against the property* but seeks it for the satisfaction of an *unrelated claim.* The claimant will assert his claim by seizing the defendant's local tangible property (*attachment*) or by *garnishing* an obligation owing to the defendant.

For instance, a creditor may have a claim against a non-resident debtor. The debtor, in turn may have intangible assets within the state, for instance a bank account. In order to reach the debtor's property for the satisfaction of the claim he has against him, the creditor may garnish the debt (bank account) owed by the *garnishee* (the bank) to the absent debtor. The plaintiff is the *garnishor.*

The procedure in the foregoing illustration was originally expressly approved by the United States Supreme Court in *Harris v. Balk,* 198 U.S. 215, 25 S. Ct. 625, 49 L. Ed. 1023 (1905). The Court held there that the garnishee would be protected against double liability (namely against being sued again by the absent party) if the absent debtor had been given notice sufficient to enable him to come and to defend in a case in which the underlying debt or its extent was in dispute. This procedure put the absent debtor to the difficult choice of staying out and losing his property or, by appearing, to subject himself to personal jurisdiction.

Shaffer v. Heitner, 433 U.S. 186, 97 S. Ct. 2569, 53 L. Ed. 2d 683 (1977), effectively overruled *Harris v. Balk.* The Court held that the garnishment of intangibles with a local situs is an insufficient basis for the exercise of personal jurisdiction in the absence of the affiliating contacts required to satisfy *International Shoe,* 326 U.S. 310, 66 S. Ct. 154, 90 L. Ed. 95 (1945), *supra* at p. 64. It stated that "all assertions of state-court jurisdiction must be evaluated according to the [minimum contacts] standards set forth in International Shoe." 433 U.S. at 212, 97 S. Ct. at 2584. See also *Tennessee ex rel. Sizemore v. Surety Bank,* 200 F.3d 373 (5th Cir. 2000).

2. Post-*Shaffer Quasi In Rem* Jurisdiction

a. *Seider*-Type Actions

In *Seider v. Roth,* 216 N.E.2d 312 (N.Y. 1966), New York exercised jurisdiction over a Quebec defendant, in favor of a New York plaintiff, for a claim arising from a Vermont auto accident, on the basis of attachment of a "debt" owed the defendant in New York. The "debt" was the insurance obligation owed the defendant, in the event of his potential liability, by an insurance company doing business in New York. A New York decision subsequent to *Shaffer* continued to approve of *Seider*, on the bases that the *Seider* procedure was a permissible "direct action" against the insurance carrier, and that the defendant's exposure was limited to the amount of the insurance coverage.

In *Rush v. Savchuk,* 444 U.S. 320, 100 S. Ct. 571, 62 L. Ed. 2d 516 (1980), the United States Supreme Court reversed a Minnesota decision employing the *Seider* procedure.

The plaintiff-passenger was injured in a single car accident in Indiana. The defendant-driver was an Indiana resident, and the car was insured under a policy issued in Indiana by State Farm. Indiana's guest statute would have barred this plaintiff's claim. About one and one-half years after the accident, the plaintiff moved to Minnesota, and after another year brought suit. Since there were no contacts to support personal jurisdiction, the plaintiff sought to invoke *quasi in rem* jurisdiction by garnishing State Farm's obligation to defend and indemnify the defendant.

The Supreme Court rejected the characterization of *Seider*-type actions as direct action equivalents because the garnishee, who had forum contacts, becomes indebted to the defendant only when the defendant, who has no forum contacts, is found liable. Furthermore, the insurance carrier, which might do business in any state of the Union, does not link the defendant with the forum state. Defendant contacts must be brought about by the *defendant himself.*

b. Creditor with Prior Judgment

Shaffer does not apply to the enforcement of a judgment (rendered by a court of another state with valid personal jurisdiction over the defendant) against the defendant's property in the forum, even if that property is unrelated to the original claim. The Due Process Clause protects the defendant, in the sense that the first court must have had valid personal jurisdiction to reduce a claim to judgment. The Full Faith and Credit Clause subsequently protects the plaintiff, in letting him or her seek out the defendant's property and enforce against it the judgment he or she has gained on the basis of proper jurisdiction.

c. Intangible as Collateral

When accounts receivable or general intangibles (as defined by UCC § 9–102) are used as collateral in a secured transaction, they are assigned a situs for the purpose of determining the law which governs the perfection (or the effect of non-perfection) of the security interest. See UCC § 9–301(1) (debtor's location).

d. Federal Interpleader

When a stakeholder faces competing claims over the same property, (statutory) federal interpleader provides protection. See *supra* Chapter III, at VII(B-2-d).

e. Maritime Attachment

Rule B of the Supplemental Rules for Certain Admiralty and Maritime Claims of the Federal Rules of Civil Procedure provides a procedure for the attachment of a defendant's goods and chattels or the garnishment of his credits in the hands of local garnishees for admiralty or maritime claims *in personam*. On its face, Rule B is inconsistent with the decision in *Shaffer v. Heitner, supra*. However, a number of lower federal courts have assumed its continued validity, viewing personal jurisdiction in admiralty on the basis of attachment of local property to be an exception sanctioned by history and the special needs of admiralty litigation.

f. Anticybersquatting Consumer Protection Act

"Cybersquatting" is the registering of an Internet domain name that potentially infringes on someone else's trademark. Since domain name registration can be effected electronically, the whereabouts of the registrant may be unknown and personal jurisdiction may be difficult to obtain. For the latter case, and restricted to it, the Anticybersquatting Consumer Protection Act (ACPA) provides for *in rem* jurisdiction in the "judicial district in which the domain name registrar, domain name registry, or other domain name authority . . . is located." 15 U.S.C.A. § 1125(d)(2) (West 2022). To assure that the action is indeed *in rem* and not *in personam*, and therefore incompatible with *Shaffer*, the remedies under the ACPA are limited to the cancellation of the offending domain name or to its transfer to the owner of the mark.

VIII. Review Questions

1. a. T or F: Notice to an out-of-state defendant of pending litigation in the forum by registered mail will establish jurisdiction over the defendant.

   b. T or F: A court has jurisdiction to adjudicate title to property within the forum state.

   c. T or F: "Transient jurisdiction" describes the assertion of general jurisdiction on the basis of service of process on the defendant while casually present within the forum state.

   d. T or F: A court may assert jurisdiction over an out-of-state defendant in a personal injury action by attaching the defendant's in-state property.

   e. T or F: A defendant can waive a court's lack of jurisdiction (for instance, by appearance).

   f. T or F: The continued validity of transient jurisdiction is controversial.

g. T or F: A court may exercise jurisdiction over a nonresident defendant on the basis of "minimum contacts" regardless of whether there is an applicable long-arm statute.

h. T or F: A court may subject a nonresident's local property to execution for the satisfaction of a valid personal judgment.

i. T or F: A federal court may transfer a case to any other federal court where trial may be more convenient.

j. T or F: A conditional dismissal for *forum non conveniens* is functionally the state-law counterpart to federal transfer.

k. T or F: Once a court has acquired valid personal jurisdiction, it continues until the case is concluded.

l. T or F: Due process requires notice in addition to jurisdiction.

m. T or F: Notice can be waived, for instance in a cognovit (confession-of-judgment) clause, so long as the waiver is the result of genuine consent.

n. T or F: There is nationwide service of process under the Federal Interpleader Act ("statutory interpleader") and under Fed. R. Civ. P. 22 ("rule interpleader").

o. T or F: Absent members of a plaintiff class will be bound by the result of a class action seeking money, even if they did not specifically "opt in," so long as they had notice and an opportunity to opt out.

2. Assume that a product manufactured outside the forum reaches the forum and there injures the plaintiff, who now wishes to bring suit. Which of the following is true or perhaps false? If in doubt, state why.

a. T or F: There is general jurisdiction on stream-of-commerce grounds.

b. T or F: There is specific jurisdiction on stream-of-commerce grounds.

c. T or F: There is specific jurisdiction if injury in the forum was foreseeable.

d. T or F: There is general jurisdiction if the defendant does continuous and systematic business in the forum, for instance by maintaining several warehouses.

e. T or F: There is general jurisdiction in the state of a company's incorporation.

f. T or F: There is general jurisdiction if the defendant company's president was served in the forum state while attending a meeting there.

g. T or F: Litigation at the forum is foreseeable if the defendant targets that market.

h. T or F: If the foreign-country defendant's contacts with the forum are insufficient, its contacts with the nation as a whole can be aggregated to support jurisdiction in a diversity action.

i. T or F: The "enterprise theory" permits consideration of a parent company and its subsidiaries as a single unit so that jurisdiction over one draws in the others as well.

j. T or F: Specific jurisdiction, in the hypothetical given, may be based on the defendant's forum contact of maintaining a local bank account.

k. T or F: A plaintiff may successfully resist a foreign country defendant's motion for dismissal on grounds of *forum non conveniens* by:

a. showing that under the law of the foreign country, there is no cause of action for his or her particular claim (for instance, for wrongful death);

b. that the foreign legal system does not provide for damages for pain and suffering nor for punitive damages.

l. T or F: An American court that takes jurisdiction of a case after it was dismissed on *forum non conveniens* grounds in a previous action in a sister-state court will apply the law that the latter would have applied had it kept the case.

3. Define "general" and "specific" jurisdiction.

4. T or F: A court deciding a federal question case will uphold a forum selection clause in a form contract, at least when the plaintiff had notice of the clause.

5. Does the Anticybersquatting Consumer Protection Act run afoul of *Shaffer* by permitting action against a (possibly) non-resident on an infringement claim?

Chapter IV

Recognition and Enforcement of Foreign Judgments and Decrees

■ ANALYSIS

I. **Basic Concepts and Overview**
- A. The Policy of Preclusion
  - 1. Introduction
  - 2. Res Judicata: Merger and Bar (*Claim Preclusion*)
  - 3. Res Judicata: Collateral Estoppel (*Issue Preclusion*) and Mutuality
- B. Preclusion and the Enforcement of Interstate Judgments
  - 1. "Foreign Judgment" Defined
  - 2. Preclusion
- C. Preclusion and the Enforcement of International Judgments
- D. Methods of Enforcement

II. **Interstate Recognition of Foreign Judgments**
- A. Foreign Proceedings Entitled to Recognition
  - 1. Finality
  - 2. Equity Decrees
  - 3. Foreign Decrees Relating to Land
  - 4. Persons Affected
  - 5. Nature of the Proceedings; Cross Reference
- B. Enforcing Interstate Judgments
  - 1. Full Faith and Credit
    - a. The Constitutional and Statutory Texts
    - b. Judgments Covered
    - c. Method of Enforcement
  - 2. Registration and Summary Proceedings
    - a. Federal Judgments in Federal Courts
    - b. State Court Judgments

C. Defenses to the Enforcement of Sister-State Judgments
1. Lack of Jurisdiction of the Rendering Court (F-1)
a. Basic Principle
b. Particular Problems
i. Default Judgments
ii. Subject Matter Jurisdiction
2. Erroneous Judgments
3. Summary and Review of Previous Sections
4. Foreign Judgment Not on the Merits
a. "On the Merits" and Preclusion
b. "Opportunity to Litigate" and Preclusion
c. Greater Preclusion in F-2 than in F-1
d. Defining the Reach of Preclusion: Worker Compensation Awards
e. Preclusion in Federal Court
5. Public Policy, Penal Judgments, Tax Judgments, and Lack of a Competent Court
a. Public Policy
b. No Competent Court in F-2
c. Tax and Penal Judgments
6. Other Defenses
a. Judgment Obtained by Fraud and Equitable Defenses
b. Non-Final Judgments
c. Inconsistent Judgments
d. Injunctions Against Enforcement or Prohibiting Action
e. Reversal of Prior Judgment
f. Payment
g. Statutes of Limitation

III. Recognition of Foreign-Country Judgments
A. Recognition and Enforcement
1. The *Hilton* Doctrine
2. Modern Recognition Practice
B. Defenses to Foreign-Country Judgments
1. Jurisdiction
2. Foreign Judgment for Taxes or Penalties
3. Public Policy

IV. Arbitral Awards

V. Review Questions

I. Basic Concepts and Overview

A. The Policy of Preclusion

1. Introduction

All legal systems share the policy that there be an end to litigation of claims and issues. The basic goal is to resolve disputes through final adjudication, binding arbitration, or alternative dispute resolution. In other words, there must be a point when party expectations from prior proceedings are protected, when defendants are no longer exposed to liability, and when judicial resources are freed for other tasks. These considerations underlie the *policy of preclusion*: "One trial of an issue is enough." *Treinies v. Sunshine Mining Co.*, 308 U.S. 66, 78, 60 S. Ct. 44, 51, 84 L. Ed. 85 (1939).

2. Res Judicata: Merger and Bar (*Claim Preclusion*)

When a court renders judgment, the issues that were litigated, *or which could have been litigated* (by parties subject to the court's jurisdiction), become binding on the parties when the time for appeal *(direct attack)* has expired or when an appeal has been unsuccessful. This is the *res judicata* effect of the judgment: it describes the effect of the prior litigation on a subsequent case involving the same claim(s) or issue(s) that a party may bring.

Many foreign legal systems restrict *res judicata* to issues and claims actually litigated, therefore permitting a subsequent action on issues that could have been but were not litigated in the first action. This difference between the American and the civil law *definition of res judicata* could be a problem in the context of recognizing foreign country judgments.

The American definition of *res judicata* encompasses *merger* and *bar*. Once a judgment has been issued, the plaintiff's cause of action is *merged in the judgment*; it is gone. The plaintiff may not relitigate the same claim (for instance, to win a higher award), but may enforce the earlier judgment. The defendant may interpose the prior judgment as a *bar* against a second action by the plaintiff on the same claim. See, e.g., *Brown v. Kansas City Live, LLC*, 931 F.3d 712 (8th Cir. 2019) (federal case barred when plaintiff asserted the same claims against the same defendants as had been dismissed in state court). Traditionally, a foreign-country judgment does *not* merge the cause of action. See further below.

Merger and bar thus define the effect of earlier litigation on subsequent litigation between the same parties (or their privies) concerning the same cause of action. This *res judicata* effect is known today as "*claim preclusion*." For the preclusive effect of a state court judgment in federal court, see *infra* in Section II-C-4.

3. Res Judicata: Collateral Estoppel (*Issue Preclusion*) and Mutuality

When an issue determined in prior litigation arises subsequently in a *different* action, the party who participated in the earlier litigation and had an opportunity to be heard there may be precluded from relitigating that issue. This is the doctrine of *collateral estoppel*: it results in *issue preclusion*. The nature of the prior action—whether *in rem* or *in personam*—does not matter, so long as the party to be estopped had litigated the particular issue in the prior action. *Harnischfeger Sales Corp. v. Sternberg Dredging Co.*, 191 So. 94 (Miss. 1939).

Historically, collateral estoppel would operate only as between the same parties to the prior litigation, or their privies, because the courts required *mutuality*: if one party is to be estopped, the other party would also have to be estopped under similar circumstances. Today, however, collateral estoppel may apply even as between different parties if the party to be estopped by the prior litigation had a fair and adequate opportunity to be heard there. This extension of the doctrine permits the *offensive* use of collateral estoppel. See, for instance, *United States v. United Air Lines, Inc.,* 216 F. Supp. 709 (E.D. Wash. 1962), *aff'd in part and modified in part sub nom, United Air Lines, Inc. v. Wiener*, 335 F.2d 379 (9th Cir. 1964), *cert. dismissed,* 379 U.S. 951, 85 S. Ct. 452, 13 L. Ed. 2d 549 (1964) (defendant airline, after adverse judgment in California, held collaterally estopped from denying liability in an action by other plaintiffs in another forum arising out of the same airplane accident). See also *Hart v. American Airlines,* 304 N.Y.S.2d 810 (N.Y. Sup. Ct. 1969) (same).

Non-mutual offensive use of collateral estoppel, as in *United Airlines* and *Hart, supra,* is not permitted against the United States. Otherwise, the first decision rendered against the government would freeze its liability, and at that point require review by the U.S. Supreme Court. This, in turn, would deprive the Court of the benefit of different views of courts of appeals, and would eliminate the possibility of not granting review until there appears to be a conflict among the circuits. *United States v. Mendoza,* 464 U.S. 154, 104 S. Ct. 568, 78 L. Ed. 2d 379 (1984). *Mendoza* has been extended to apply to state agencies. *Coleman v. California Bd. of Prison Terms,* 228 Fed. App'x 673, 675 (9th Cir. 2007); *Demaree v. Fulton Cnty. School Dist.*, 515 Fed. App'x 859 (11th Cir. 2013); *In re Exercise Tax Litigation*, 2024 WL 3552580 (D. Virgin Isl. 2024). But see *Jones v. Cannizzaro*, No. 18-503, 2019 WL 2289470, at *6 (E.D. La. May 28, 2019) (*Mendoza* distinguished; allowed non-mutual offensive collateral estoppel against state governmental entity when opinions at issue "did not consider widely-applicable questions of law or policy"), followed in *Reeder v. Williams*, 2014 WL 5195314 (E.D.La. 2024), slip op.

B. Preclusion and the Enforcement of Interstate Judgments

1. "Foreign Judgment" Defined

For purposes of the recognition and enforcement of judgments, a "foreign judgment" is *any judgment rendered outside the forum.* The term therefore includes judgments from other American jurisdictions (sister states, the District of Columbia, United States territories and possessions, Native American tribal courts), as well as judgments rendered by courts of foreign countries. Because a judgment is "foreign" to the forum, it has no direct effect in the forum. Instead, the judgment creditor must utilize the procedures provided by the forum for the recognition and enforcement of the judgment. It is in the manner of enforcement that there is a technical difference between sister state judgments and foreign-country judgments because the Full Faith and Credit Clause of the United States Constitution does not apply to the latter. However, as we shall see, modern recognition practice of most states treats foreign-country judgments quite similarly to sister-state judgments.

2. Preclusion

When the forum is asked to recognize and enforce a foreign judgment, it must determine the preclusive effect of the prior judgment. This may be particularly difficult when there are differences between the jurisdictions as to what is precluded by prior litigation.

For instance, if the first jurisdiction provides for compulsory counterclaims but the present forum does not, may the judgment debtor now raise the counterclaim which he or she failed to raise in the prior litigation? The problem raised by this example concerns the determination of what part of the prior judgment was "on the merits." This is considered *infra* in Section II-C-4.

When an issue goes to the merits, the broad reach of the Full Faith and Credit requirement of the United States Constitution mandates recognition of the preclusive effect in all other states of the Union. Thus, in the interstate setting, the U.S. Supreme Court has held that all aspects of the prior determination, including questions of personal jurisdiction, subject matter jurisdiction, and of the correct application of the law, are entitled to recognition in the second forum (assuming that both parties participated). *The proper procedure to obtain review of a judgment rendered by a court with proper jurisdiction is to appeal it, not to draw it into question collaterally.*

The usual standard of American *state law* considers all issues precluded that *were* or *could* have been litigated in the previous case between the same parties on a claim arising from the same facts. See *Storey v. Cello Holdings, L.L.C.*, 182 F. Supp. 2d 355 (S.D.N.Y. 2002), *vacated and remanded*, 347 F.3d 370 (2d Cir. 2003) (prior judicial resolution as a defense to recognition of a subsequent inconsistent arbitral award). For a recent application, see *Mohamad v. Rajoub*, No. 17 Civ. 2385 (LAP), 2018 WL 1737219, at *7–8 (S.D.N.Y. Mar. 12, 2018), *aff'd*, 767 Fed. App'x 91 (2d Cir. 2019).

C. Preclusion and the Enforcement of International Judgments

The Full Faith and Credit Clause (*infra* at 99) does not apply to foreign-country judgments. An early U.S. Supreme Court decision therefore concluded that such judgments were not entitled to recognition as of right, but only on the basis of *comity*. *Hilton v. Guyot*, 159 U.S. 113 (1895), discussed *infra*. The comity requirement then translated into a *reciprocity* requirement: we would enforce the foreign-country judgment if the country of origin similarly accorded recognition to American judgments. Almost all states of the Union subsequently departed from the reciprocity requirement, although a few have reintroduced it by statute.

Normally, American courts will give a foreign-country judgment, based on proper jurisdiction, the same preclusive effect that they accord to judgments of sister states. However, foreign-country judgments have been treated differently in some important respects. One difference—much criticized—has been retained by § 95 of the Restatement (Second). In contrast to the rule in interstate practice, the cause of action underlying a foreign-country judgment is thought *not* to have merged in the judgment. Thus, the successful plaintiff in the prior foreign-country litigation would remain free to sue upon the original cause of action *or* upon the judgment. For an application of the non-merger doctrine, see *infra*. Also, if the cause of action underlying the foreign-country judgment offends public policy, the American court will not enforce it. The nature of the underlying cause of action normally is not relevant in U.S. interstate recognition practice with respect to a sister-state *money* judgment.

Res judicata may be defined differently in a foreign legal system (see *supra*). In the case of recognition and enforcement of a foreign-country judgment in an American court, which preclusion law applies? That of the American court or that of the foreign country? This question is important if a party seeks to raise an issue that would be precluded here but is not under the law of the rendering court. American case law does not provide a uniform answer because international judgment recognition is a matter of state, not federal law. Note, however, that the merger rule does not apply to claims reduced to an international judgment.

D. Methods of Enforcement

As noted above, a foreign judgment has no force of its own in the forum. The common law method of enforcement is for the judgment creditor to bring an action upon the judgment, invoking the Full Faith and Credit Clause (in the case of interstate judgments), to obtain the recognition and enforcement that the Clause mandates. The forum will then enter its own judgment which, of course, has direct operative effect within the forum state. By federal statute, a judgment for "money or property" rendered by one federal district court may be registered in another, giving it the same effect as a judgment rendered by the second court. For discussion see *infra* Section II(B)(2). A similar procedure exists in those states which have adopted the Uniform Enforcement of Foreign Judgments Act, discussed *infra*.

By 2025, 30 states and the District of Columbia had adopted the Uniform Foreign-Country Money Judgments Recognition Act. Eight states still had the prior version. It essentially puts foreign-country money judgments on the same footing, for purposes of recognition and enforcement, as judgments of sister states, spelling out in statutory form the preconditions that apply as a matter of constitutional law in the interstate setting. See *infra* Section II-B.

II. Interstate Recognition of Foreign Judgments

A. Foreign Proceedings Entitled to Recognition

1. Finality

The Full Faith and Credit Clause (*infra* at p. 99) refers to "judicial proceedings," not to final judgments. Thus, the court in the second forum (F-2) might be thought obliged to enforce all judgments, including a judgment that is still modifiable in the first state (F-1), and grant the same recognition to any modifications which F-1 may subsequently make. In addition, it might entertain the same requests for modification in its courts that could have been advanced in F-1. This is generally the procedure followed with respect to the recognition and subsequent modification of *support decrees,* discussed in greater detail *infra* Chapter VI, at IV(A).

Generally, however, it is assumed that the recognition of interstate judgments is constitutionally required only for *final judgments*. The underlying reason is that F-2 is not required to give a judgment greater effect than it has where rendered. Thus, it is the law of F-1, the state of rendition, that determines when a judgment is conclusive and final and thereby entitled to recognition and enforcement in other states.

There is a presumption that a judgment is final unless the contrary is clearly demonstrated. *Barber v. Barber,* 323 U.S. 77, 65 S. Ct. 137, 89 L. Ed. 82 (1944). Declaratory judgments are also considered conclusive with respect to the matters addressed.

2. Equity Decrees

Historically, equity decrees for the *payment of money* and *divorce decrees* were entitled to recognition on the same basis as judgments at law. However, the enforceability of other equity decrees was uncertain because of historic notions that an equity court only bound the "defendant's conscience," and that an equity decree did not "merge" the claim.

It appears, however, that there are different reasons why some equity decrees were unenforceable in the past and may still be now. First, many equity decrees may not be final (see No. 1, above). Second, the F-1 court might lack subject matter jurisdiction. This might be the case, for instance, if the F-1 court attempted to affect title to F-2 land. Third, the F-1 equity decree might violate F-2's public policy. This might occur when F-1 attempts (impermissibly) to interfere with the F-2 judicial process, for instance, by seeking to enjoin litigation there.

When special circumstances are not present, an F-1 decree that is final and was rendered by a court with competent jurisdiction should be accorded recognition in F-2; labeling the F-1 decree as one "at law" or "in equity" is not helpful. The relevant question is only whether a claim or an issue was finally *adjudicated as between the parties.*

In *Baker v. General Motors Corp.*, 522 U.S. 222, 118 S. Ct. 657, 139 L. Ed. 2d 580 (1998), the U.S. Supreme Court agreed that Missouri did not have to honor a Michigan decree, enjoining a person from testifying elsewhere, when the plaintiffs seeking the person's testimony in a Missouri action had not been parties to the Michigan action. The majority confirmed, in *dictum*, that equity decrees may enjoy full-faith-and-credit effects but denied such effect to the injunction in issue. It adduced various considerations, including the public policy of the forum. However, the real basis supporting the ultimate decision seems to be that the present plaintiffs had not been parties to the earlier Michigan proceedings, and therefore could not be bound by the Michigan witness-protective order.

3. Foreign Decrees Relating to Land

The F-1 court cannot *directly* affect land situated in F-2, for instance by quieting title in the plaintiff before it. See *Fall v. Eastin,* 215 U.S. 1, 30 S. Ct. 3, 54 L. Ed. 65 (1909). However, it does not follow that the non-situs court (F-l) has no power (indirectly, through its power over the parties) to affect interests in F-2 land.

Thus, F-1 can exercise its personal jurisdiction to compel a party before it to convey title to F-2 land, and such a conveyance, if actually made, will be effective and not subject to a defense of duress. See *Massie v. Watts,* 10 U.S. (6 Cranch) 148, 3 L. Ed. 181 (1810). Even if the defendant does not convey, or if the F-1 court merely established one party's entitlement to the F-2 land, this adjudication of the rights and obligations of the parties is entitled to recognition in F-2. See *Weesner v. Weesner,* 95 N.W.2d 682 (Neb. 1959); *Baker v. General*

Motors Corp., 522 U.S. 222, 118 S. Ct. 657, 139 L. Ed. 2d 580 (1998) (dictum); *Boghosian v. Boghosian*, No. FM-09-1515-08, 2009 WL 2486583, at *6 (N.J. Super. Ct. App. Div. Aug. 17, 2009); *In re Marriage of Kowalewski*, 182 P.3d 959 (Wash. 2008).

Similarly, in *Durfee v. Duke*, 375 U.S. 106, 84 S. Ct. 242, 11 L. Ed. 2d 186 (1963), the issue concerned the Nebraska court's subject matter jurisdiction over land, the location of which was in dispute. The Supreme Court emphasized that the Nebraska court did no more than determine title to the land *"as between the parties."*

The decision in *Fall v. Eastin, supra,* is not inconsistent with the foregoing. In *Fall,* the Washington court had attempted to enforce its decree by giving its own deed to Nebraska land. This it could not do. Moreover, the Washington decree, which, as the foregoing showed, would be binding *as between the parties,* could not have an effect on a *third party,* to whom the defendant had conveyed the Nebraska property in disregard of the Washington decree, but who had not been before the Washington court. Whether—absent personal jurisdiction over the third party in the Washington court—the Washington decree raised any equities in favor of the Washington plaintiff and against the third party is a question of property law, to be determined by the situs, Nebraska.

A number of modern decisions give direct effect, at the situs, to sister state decrees purporting to adjudicate title, as between the parties, to situs land. See *Matter of Estate of Mack,* 373 N.W.2d 97 (Iowa 1985).

4. Persons Affected

A person is ordinarily not affected by a judgment *in personam* unless he or she has been made a party to it by service of process or is in privity with a party. In *Phillips Petroleum Co. v. Shutts,* 472 U.S. 797, 105 S. Ct. 2965, 86 L. Ed. 2d 628 (1985), the U.S. Supreme Court approved an exception, with respect to absent members of a plaintiff class in a class action under *state law.* In a class action, fewer burdens are placed on plaintiffs than on defendants, and court supervision ensures adequate representation of the interests of the class. To be bound by the resulting determination, due process therefore only requires that absent members of a plaintiff class (a) receive notice of the action, and (b) be given an opportunity to "opt out" (i.e., to file a declaration that they do not wish to be part of the class). *An absent member of the plaintiff class need not "opt in"; he or she will be bound upon failure to "opt out."* For class actions in state court, see *supra* Chapter III(D)(6)(c).

Federal practice provides for class actions without any opt-out opportunity (as well as class actions that do afford that opportunity). Fed. R. Civ. P. 23, *supra* Chapter III(D)(6)(c).

Persons not parties to a prior proceeding may be able to benefit from it by holding an adversary estopped from relitigating an issue previously determined. On non-mutual offensive estoppel, see *supra.*

5. Nature of the Proceedings; Cross Reference

The F-1 judgment or decree must have been rendered by an impartial tribunal, which had proper jurisdiction, and gave the defendant reasonable notice and an opportunity to be heard. These are recurrent themes and will be addressed in further detail in Section C below, which deals with defenses to the enforcement of sister-state judgments.

B. Enforcing Interstate Judgments

1. Full Faith and Credit

a. The Constitutional and Statutory Texts

Article IV, Section 1 of the United States Constitution provides:

> Full faith and credit shall be given in each State to the public Acts, Records, and Judicial Proceedings of every other State. And the Congress may by general laws prescribe the Manner in which such Acts, Records, and Proceedings shall be proved, and the Effect thereof.

Title 28 of the U.S. Code provides the implementing legislation envisioned by the Constitution at § 1738. The first two paragraphs deal with the manner in which records and judgments are to be authenticated. The third provides:

> Such Acts, records and judicial proceedings or copies thereof, so authenticated, shall have the same full faith and credit in every court within the United States and its Territories and Possessions as they have by law or usage in the courts of such State, Territory or Possession from which they are taken.

Additional Implementing Legislation:

— § 1738A: Federal Parental Kidnapping Prevention Act (some custody decrees entitled to full faith and credit, see p. 99 *infra*);

— § 1738B: Full Faith and Credit for Child Support Orders Act, see p. 73, *infra*;

— § 1738C: The "Respect for Marriage Act," passed by both Houses of Congress late in 2022 repeals the former Defense of Marriage Act (DOMA) which had allowed states to deny recognition to same-sex marriages or civil unions. DOMA had been held unconstitutional (*infra* Chapter V, Section III(A)). The new § 1738C prohibits denial of full faith and credit to a "marriage" on grounds of sex, race, ethnicity or national origin. Religion and same-sex relationships are not mentioned. A new § 7 of U.S.C. Title 1, provides that validity of a "marriage" is determined by the law of the State where it was concluded.

b. Judgments Covered

The Full Faith and Credit Clause refers to "States," and therefore does not extend to judgments of foreign countries, or even to those of federal courts. By statute, Congress has extended the full faith and credit requirement to federal courts in which recognition of a state court judgment is sought. While the constitutional and statutory texts are silent, state courts, in turn, are required to give full faith and credit to federal court judgments. See *Baldwin v. Iowa Traveling Men's Association,* 283 U.S. 522, 51 S. Ct. 517, 75 L. Ed. 1244 (1931).

c. Method of Enforcement

The common law method for the enforcement of a sister-state judgment is to bring suit upon it in the courts of F-2. If the F-1 judgment is entitled to recognition under the Full Faith and Credit Clause, i.e., if it is not subject to the defenses discussed in Section C below, the F-2 court will then enter its own judgment which, of course, is directly enforceable within its state.

2. Registration and Summary Proceedings

a. Federal Judgments in Federal Courts

28 U.S.C.A. § 1963 provides that a final "judgment in an action for the recovery of money or property" entered in one U.S. district court may be registered in any other district and will then have the same effect as a judgment rendered by the federal court in the district of registration.

b. State Court Judgments

Similarly, the Uniform Enforcement of Foreign Judgments Act (Revised 1964 Act) provides for the registration of any state court judgment, decree, or order "which is entitled to full faith and credit" by simple filing in F-2. The quoted language incorporates by reference all the criteria which make an F-1 judgment enforceable in F-2. In addition, the uniform act provides that an F-1 judgment that is filed in F-2 is "subject to the same procedures, defenses and proceedings for reopening, vacating or staying as a judgment" of an F-2 court. In other words, *local* (F-2) *defenses* may be asserted against the F-1 judgment. This is in contrast to a suit on the F-1 judgment that seeks recognition on the basis of the Full Faith and Credit Clause and the federal implementing statute. In the latter case, *only F-1 defenses,* not F-2 defenses, may be asserted in F-2 against the F-1 judgment. This follows from 28 U.S.C.A. § 1738, *supra,* which provides that the effect to be given by F-2 is that which the judgment has in the state "from which [it is] taken."

An interstate judgment creditor thus has the choice between suing on the F-1 judgment under full faith and credit and the implementing legislation, and thereby being protected against F-2 defenses, and using the summary filing procedure, which is faster, but which also exposes him to F-2 defenses.

The 1964 act is now in force in all but a handful of states and the District of Columbia. Missouri adopted parts of the 1964 act and kept parts of the earlier 1948 act.

C. Defenses to the Enforcement of Sister-State Judgments

1. Lack of Jurisdiction of the Rendering Court (F-1)

a. Basic Principle

A judgment rendered by a court without jurisdiction over the parties or the subject matter is not entitled to full faith and credit. The court that is being asked to recognize an interstate judgment (F-2) may therefore inquire whether the F-1 court (a) had jurisdiction under the laws of its own state, and (b) whether the exercise of such jurisdiction complied with the federal constitutional standards for the assertion of state court jurisdiction (*supra* Chapter III).

This is so because the entry of a judgment without jurisdiction violates due process and renders such a judgment void where entered. To give full faith and credit to such a judgment would itself violate due process.

The foregoing, however, remains categorically true only when jurisdiction in F-1 *was not litigated.* If both parties were before the F-1 court and litigated (or *could have* litigated) jurisdiction there, but either failed to do so (i.e., a default judgment in F-1, with the F-1 court having had proper jurisdiction, see (b)(i) below) or lost, **the jurisdictional issue—like any other—becomes *res judicata*** and may no longer be raised collaterally in F-2. See *Baldwin v. Iowa State Traveling Men's Association,* 283 U.S. 522, 51 S. Ct. 517, 75 L. Ed. 1244 (1931).

The foregoing also applies when successive proceedings in different states conclude that the judgment resulting from the respective prior proceeding was entered by a court without jurisdiction. In *Treinies v. Sunshine Mining Co.,* 308 U.S. 66, 60 S. Ct. 44, 84 L. Ed. 85 (1939), there were parallel actions in Washington and Idaho. The Washington court concluded that it had jurisdiction and entered a judgment. That judgment was pleaded in bar in the Idaho proceeding. However, the Idaho court concluded that Washington had lacked jurisdiction, therefore refused to recognize that judgment, and entered its own. The question subsequently before the Washington court was whether the initial Washington judgment or the subsequent Idaho judgment was binding on the parties. The 9th Circuit concluded that the Idaho court had proper jurisdiction and that its judgment was entitled to recognition and enforcement. The U.S. Supreme Court affirmed: "If [the question of jurisdiction in Washington courts was] decided erroneously in the Idaho proceedings, the right to review that error was in those (the Idaho) proceedings." 308 U.S. at 77, 60 S. Ct. at 50. "The principles of res judicata apply to questions of jurisdiction as well as to other issues." Id. at 78, 51 (quoting *American Surety Co. v. Baldwin,* 287 U.S. 156, 166, 53 S. Ct. 98, 101, 77 L. Ed. 231 (1932)).

Thus, when the parties are before the court, objections to the court's jurisdiction must be made and pursued by *appeal,* and *not* collaterally.

b. Particular Problems

i. Default Judgments

When the judgment debtor did *not* appear in the first forum, in person or through counsel (including in a cognovit context), or had no opportunity to litigate jurisdiction there, the jurisdictional issue cannot become res judicata. The party (who has now become a judgment debtor by default) may therefore litigate F-1's jurisdiction in F-2 when enforcement of the F-1 judgment is sought there. By not having appeared in F-1 in the first place, the party of course runs the risk that F-2 will agree with F-1 that F-1 did have jurisdiction after all. Following such a determination in F-2—that the F-1 default judgment was by a court with competent jurisdiction it would be binding on the judgment debtor. Thus, by taking the risk of not appearing, the judgment debtor may have lost the opportunity to litigate the merits. The case for preclusion in a subsequent proceeding is even clearer, of course, if a party participated in the first proceeding but chose not to follow up. For an example, see *Storey, supra* at p. 95. See also No. 4(b), below.

ii. Subject Matter Jurisdiction

The existence of subject matter jurisdiction in the F-1 court may similarly be reviewed by F-2, but as in all the other cases reviewed above, such a review may also be precluded by prior litigation in F-1.

In *Aldrich v. Aldrich,* 378 U.S. 540, 84 S. Ct. 1687, 12 L. Ed. 2d 1020 (1964), a Florida divorce court had made an alimony decree a charge upon the estate of the defendant husband. It did not have such jurisdiction, but upon certification to it from the U.S. Supreme Court, the Florida Supreme Court advised that the decree would not be subject to collateral attack in Florida. Hence, F-2 had to give it the same effect.

In *Durfee v. Duke,* 375 U.S. 106, 84 S. Ct. 242, 11 L. Ed. 2d 186 (1963), the Court's determination as to the location of land for the purpose of awarding a party title to it was binding *upon the parties* in a subsequent collateral proceeding in F-2. See also *Legum v. Brown,* 909 A.2d. 672, 679 (Md. 2006). The first court's decision is of course not binding on non-parties, including affected states. 375 U.S. at 115–16, 84 S. Ct. at 247. See also *Lowe v. Richards,* 763 S.E.2d 64, 65 (W. Va. 2014).

2. Erroneous Judgments

Errors of fact or law committed by the F-1 court in a proceeding with jurisdiction over both parties (or in which they participated without raising the jurisdictional issue) will also become res judicata and cannot be raised collaterally. *Roche v. McDonald,* 275 U.S. 449, 48 S. Ct. 142 (Mem.), 72 L. Ed. 365 (1928). See also *Del Prado v. B.N. Development Co.,* 602 F.3d 660 (5th Cir. 2010).

3. Summary and Review of Previous Sections

Hypotheticals and Their Solutions

a. No appearance in F-l, default judgment brought to F-2: Jurisdiction of F-1 may be questioned in F-2.

   i. If F-2 finds that F-1 did not have jurisdiction, the F-1 judgment is not entitled to recognition under Full Faith and Credit. In fact, recognition would violate the judgment debtor's due process rights. For a federal court's application, see *Kremer v. Chemical Construction Corp.,* 456 U.S. 461, 102 S. Ct. 1883, 72 L. Ed. 2d 262 (1982).

   ii. If F-1 is found to have had jurisdiction (e.g., on the basis of sufficient contacts, *J. McIntyre, supra* at p. 70), the default judgment must be recognized.

   iii. If F-2 found that F-1 had jurisdiction under (ii), then the only additional defenses available in F-2 are those which would be available in F-1 (e.g., vacating or reopening of the default judgment, injunction against enforcement for fraud in the procurement).

b. Appearance in F-1 (special *or* general) with *or without* subsequent litigation of the merits:

   i. F-2 must recognize. The only defenses available in F-2 are those which would be available in F-1 (see No. a(iii) *supra*).

   ii. Assume that F-2 does *not* recognize the F-1 judgment, for instance because it finds (although not allowed to do so) that F-1 lacked jurisdiction, that F-1 was wrong on the merits, that the F-1 judgment is now time-barred, etc. This decision may be *appealed* for purposes of reviewing the (constitutional) question whether Full Faith and Credit was wrongfully withheld.

   iii. Same as (ii), except that no appeal was taken, and that the F-1 judgment is now in issue in F-3: the failure to have appealed in F-2 now means that the F-2 determination is res judicata with respect to the validity of the F-1 judgment and must be recognized in F-3. *Treinies*, *supra*, p. 101. If it is not, appeal in F-3 is the appropriate remedy (same as (ii), *supra*). If not appealed, and F-3's (incorrect) ruling is in issue in F-4, F-3's decision is res judicata for F-4 purposes, and on and on and on. . . .

Rules

a. The judgment of the last court with jurisdiction over the parties must be given the same effect in another state as it has in the state of rendition.

b. Errors of a court with jurisdiction—regardless of whether that court is F-1, F-2, F-3, F-4, etc.—**must be raised by appeal, not collaterally**. Thus, *when the parties participated*, that court's ruling—again, regardless of whether that was F-1, F-2, F-3, F-4, etc.—is res judicata not only with respect to the merits but also with respect to its own and any prior court's jurisdiction.

4. Foreign Judgment Not on the Merits

a. "On the Merits" and Preclusion

According to the Full Faith and Credit Clause and the federal implementing legislation (*supra*), the F-1 judgment is to have the same effect in F-2 as it has in F-1. It is not always easy to determine to what extent the first judgment was "on the merits" and therefore should have preclusive effect in F-2. Thus, under the older law which characterized statutes of limitation as procedural (*infra* Chapter VII, III(D)), a dismissal by F-1 on the basis of its statute would not be "on the merits" and therefore would not bar a subsequent suit on the same claim in F-2.

On the other hand, if F-1 had dismissed on the basis of a statute of limitations, which it regarded as substantive, or by "borrowing" the statute of limitations of the state whose law applied to the main claim, the dismissal might well be "on the merits" and bar subsequent litigation in F-2. It is similarly difficult to determine whether the effect of F-1's two-dismissal or compulsory counterclaim rules should be considered "on the merits," with preclusive effect elsewhere. In contrast, a dismissal "with prejudice" clearly precludes litigation of issues that were or could have been raised in the earlier case. *Storey, supra* at p. 95.

Clear examples of decisions which are *not* "on the merits" include dismissals for *forum non conveniens*, lack of jurisdiction, improper venue, or a party's lack of capacity. For antisuit injunctions, see also *infra* Section II(C-6-d).

The underlying question, in all of these and other cases, is whether F-1's rule is basically **a court closing** rule or *is meant to* **affect the underlying obligation**. In the first case, the effect of the F-1 rule would not be "on the merits" and would therefore not have preclusive effect elsewhere; in the latter case, the F-1 rule would have preclusive effect.

b. "Opportunity to Litigate" and Preclusion

When a party had an *opportunity* to litigate (but did not in fact litigate) an issue, such matters may be treated *as if* they had been litigated, thus precluding re-litigation in F-2. A well-known example is the U.S. Supreme Court's decision in *Angel v. Bullington,* 330 U.S. 183, 67 S. Ct. 657, 91 L. Ed. 832 (1947). In that case, the plaintiff, after the sale of Virginia land, sought to enforce a deficiency in an action in North Carolina state court. The North Carolina Supreme Court ultimately dismissed the plaintiff's complaint on the basis of a North Carolina statute prohibiting actions for deficiencies. The plaintiff sought no further review but refiled his claim in North Carolina federal court. His argument was that the earlier state court proceeding did not preclude the second action because North Carolina had unconstitutionally closed its courts to him. Held, the second action is precluded.

While the constitutionality of the North Carolina statute had not been addressed in any of the North Carolina state court proceedings, it had been *open* to the plaintiff to do so and would have been a natural part of his case/argument. "It is a misconception of res judicata to assume that the doctrine does not come into operation if a court has not passed on the 'merits' in the sense of the ultimate substantive issues of litigation. An adjudication declining to reach such ultimate substantive issues may bar a second attempt in another court of the State." 330 U.S. at 190, 67 S. Ct. at 661.

For recent application, see *Storey, supra* at p. 95; *Phillips v. Metropolitan Transportation Authority,* 2024 WL 4350533, **7–8 (E.D.N.Y.); motion to reopen denied: 2025 WL 2889272 (E.D.N.Y.).

c. Greater Preclusion in F-2 than in F-1

Litigating, or *having the opportunity to litigate,* an issue may, in an appropriate case, conceivably result in *greater preclusive effect in F-2* than in F-1. This may be the case, for instance, when facts or issues were litigated in one kind of proceeding in F-1, and F-2 now denies re-litigation of the same facts or issues, even though F-1 might not have. In other words, the two jurisdictions differ with respect to the extent of collateral estoppel effect which they attach to prior litigation.

In *Harnischfeger Sales Corp. v. Sternberg Dredging Co.,* 191 So. 94 (Miss. 1939), *supra* at 68, the F-1 proceeding, which was *in rem,* sought the foreclosure of a lien on a chattel. The non-resident defendant, over whom F-1 did not have personal jurisdiction, appeared in the *in rem* proceeding and resisted the enforcement of the lien on the ground of breach of warranty, alleging that the machine could not perform as represented. Having lost in F-1, the defendant interposed a defense of fraud and deceit in an F-2 action in which the plaintiff, with personal jurisdiction over the defendant, sought to collect a deficiency on the original contract obligation, which remained after the F-1 foreclosure. Even though the F-1 proceeding had been *in rem*, and therefore could not have established an obligation on the part of the defendant in excess of the chattel, the F-2 court accorded preclusive effect to the F-1 court's findings *with respect to the facts.*

The conclusion to be drawn is this: regardless of how the actions are denominated (e.g., classified as *in rem* or as *in personam*), a defendant who fully litigated the facts (in *Harnischfeger,* the machine's characteristics) in F-1 cannot claim a second opportunity to litigate these facts or issues in F-2. See also Restatement (Second) of Judgments § 30 ("A valid and final judgment in an action based only on jurisdiction to determine interests in a thing: . . . (3) Is conclusive between the parties, in accordance with the rules of issue preclusion, as to any issues actually litigated by them . . . . "). All of this expresses the same "one bite at the apple" idea that also underlies non-mutual offensive collateral estoppel, *supra* at 94. See also *United States v. Black Canyon Irrigation District,* 408 P.3d 52, 58 (Idaho 2017).

d. Defining the Reach of Preclusion: Worker Compensation Awards

There has been some uncertainty about the preclusive effect of an F-1 determination in the area of worker compensation. The essential issue is whether the first determination *is meant to adjudicate all rights and* obligations between the parties *or addresses only a portion of the claim,* therefore not precluding additional relief in another jurisdiction.

In *Magnolia Petroleum Co. v. Hunt,* 320 U.S. 430, 64 S. Ct. 208, 88 L. Ed. 149 (1943) a Louisiana employer sent its employee (the claimant), a Louisiana resident, to perform work in Texas, where he was injured. While in Texas, he accepted benefits under the Texas worker's compensation act, *which made the receipt of benefits exclusive of all other rights.* When he subsequently sought additional benefits under the Louisiana statute (not a second recovery, but the difference between the Texas ceiling and the Louisiana benefits), the claim for such an add-on was denied. "[Plaintiff] was free to pursue his remedy in either state but, having chosen to seek it in Texas, where the award was res judicata, the full faith and credit clause precludes him from again seeking a remedy in Louisiana upon the same grounds." 320 U.S. at 444, 64 S. Ct. at 216.

In *Industrial Commission of Wisconsin v. McCartin,* 330 U.S. 622, 67 S. Ct. 886, 91 L. Ed. 1140 (1947), an Illinois settlement contract had specifically preserved whatever additional rights the claimant might have under Wisconsin law. The Court said, furthermore (possibly in dictum), that the Illinois statute itself did not mean to preclude an add-on recovery elsewhere; it lacked "unmistakable language" making the Illinois recovery the one and only recovery, to the exclusion of all others. 330 U.S. at 628, 67 S. Ct. at 889.

The difference between *Magnolia* and *McCartin* is the extent of the preclusive effect that F-1 meant to attach to its award.

The Supreme Court again considered the matter in *Thomas v. Washington Gas Light Co.,* 448 U.S. 261, 100 S. Ct. 2647, 65 L. Ed. 2d 757 (1980), but was unable to muster a majority for any one position. A plurality of four undertook to balance the interests of Virginia (F-1) and of the District of Columbia (F-2). It concluded that the District of Columbia had an interest in permitting an add-on, and that Virginia did not have an interest in precluding such a result. Three concurring Justices reached the same result, but did so based on *McCartin*: the Virginia statute lacked "unmistakable language" that would preclude an add-on recovery in the District of Columbia. The dissent would have applied *Magnolia,* and like the plurality, favored overruling *McCartin.*

Current law in this area still seems uncertain (but see below). The plurality and the dissent in *Thomas* favored overruling *McCartin* but did not do so for failure to agree on a substitute. Four Justices wished to overrule *Magnolia* but fell short of a majority. The concurring and dissenting Justices, representing a majority, criticized the plurality for its weighing of "interests." Justice Rehnquist noted that "[t]he Full Faith and Credit Clause did not allot to this Court the task of 'balancing' interests . . . It simply directed that [judicial proceedings] be given . . . 'Full Faith and Credit' . . . ." 448 U.S. at 296, 100 S. Ct. at 2668.

Lower courts have followed *Thomas* by pointing to the absence of "unmistakable language" in the first award, or by balancing interest. See, e.g., *Landry v. Carlson Mooring Service,* 643 F.2d 1080 (5th Cir. 1981); *Ansello v. Wisconsin Central, Ltd.,* 900 N.W.2d 167, 172 (Minn. 2017). See also *Kwiecinski v. Medi-Tech International Corp,* 736 Fed.Appx 659, 661 (9th Cir. 2018); Rich, 3 Modern Constitutional Law § 34:62 (3d ed. 2011, updated 2021).

The worker compensation cases demonstrate two things. First, *administrative determinations*, particularly with respect to compensation, will be given the same preclusive effect in other states that is enjoyed by judgments. Thus, whether the administrative determination had first been reduced to judgment in F-1 was not an element in the worker compensation cases. This may become increasingly important as compensation decisions are made by administrative agencies or hearing boards in areas other than worker compensation. But see *Trueblood v. MMIC Ins. Co., Inc.,* 14 N.W. 3rd 163, 171 (Iowa App. 2024): since an administrative agency applies only its own law and, unlike a court, does not make choice of law decisions to determine what law applies, and defines the obligations in issue, a second tribunal, such as a court in another state, is not precluded from applying its or another law.

Second, the cases thus also show that the essential problem—determining just what was "on the merits"—remains. A state interest in affording compensation might influence this determination. However, this state interest is relevant for a *different* reason from the one envisioned by the majority in *Thomas*. The state interest is *not used to weigh* how much or how little faith and credit F-2 must give to the F-1 determination. Its significance lies in what its existence may say about the *intended reach* of the F-1 adjudication. In this light, it may be reasonable to conclude that the F-1 determination was limited to *local* (F-1) effects and compensation, and that it did not mean to address the compensation interests that F-2 might wish to effectuate. See also *Trueblood*, above. It is the *lack* of "unmistakable language" in the F-1 determination (or underlying statutory remedy), precluding an F-2 add-on recovery, which supports the conclusion that such a preclusive effect was not intended. Conversely, it remains true that F-1 *could* preclude an F-2 add-on recovery by using appropriate "unmistakable language" to that effect. It is readily apparent, however, that F-1 is unlikely to do so: why should it? What purpose would be served by precluding F-2 when both states favor compensation and the employer has provided coverage in both?

In a case arising after *Thomas*, the U.S. Supreme Court inquired only into the jurisdiction of F-1, the scope of the litigation there, and concluded that matters determined there were entitled to recognition in F-2. *Underwriters National Assurance Co. v. North Carolina Life & Accident,* 455 U.S. 691, 102 S. Ct. 1357, 71 L. Ed. 2d 558 (1982). See also *Trueblood*, above. The "scope of the litigation" and the "matters to be determined" are of course, at the heart of the *McCartin/Thomas* problem. Since "unmistakable language" is likely to be lacking, as suggested, *Thomas* may be assumed to apply and therefore to permit an add-on.

e. Preclusion in Federal Court

Does a prior state court judgment have issue-preclusive effect, preventing litigation of a federal claim over which the state court lacked subject matter jurisdiction (e.g., in antitrust)? In *Marrese v. American Academy of Orthopaedic Surgeons,* 470 U.S. 373, 105 S. Ct. 1327, 84 L. Ed. 2d 274 (1985), the Supreme Court required the trial court to inquire into the reach of state preclusion law. Ordinarily, state law would not claim preclusive effect on claims within exclusive federal jurisdiction. If, exceptionally, it did, the federal courts would have to determine whether a federal interest required disregard of the state law result, explained on the basis that the congressional grant of exclusive federal jurisdiction represented a partial repeal of the command of § 1738, *supra* at p. 99. See *Advance Products & Systems, Inc. v. CCI Piping Systems, L.L.C.*, No. 2:14-CV-2456, 2018 WL 1542100, at *3 (W.D. La. Mar. 29, 2018) (Louisiana res judicata law does not bar federal claims that could not have been brought in state court).

5. Public Policy, Penal Judgments, Tax Judgments, and Lack of a Competent Court

a. Public Policy

In *Fauntleroy v. Lum,* 210 U.S. 230, 28 S. Ct. 641, 52 L. Ed. 1039 (1908), a Missouri court, with proper jurisdiction over the parties, had entered a judgment enforcing a contract debt. The contract in question was a Mississippi gambling contract, which would have been illegal and void in Mississippi. When the judgment was brought to Mississippi for enforcement, recognition was denied on the ground that the underlying cause of action violated Mississippi public policy. The U.S. Supreme Court held that the nature of the original Mississippi cause of action could not be relied upon as a ground for denying recovery. A later decision, which relies on *Fauntleroy*, sums things up nicely: "[A] judgment shall be accorded the same faith and credit in every court within the United States as it has . . . in the state . . . where it was originally rendered; and this is true, though the cause of action upon which the judgment is based is against the law and public policy of the state . . . in which enforcement is sought." *Hieston v. National City Bank of Chicago*, 280 F. 525, 528 (D.C. Cir. 1922). If, for some reason, Missouri was bound to respect Mississippi's public policy, this should have been raised in Missouri, and not collaterally. In this respect, the decision tracks *Angel v. Bullington, supra* at p. 104. Could a Mississippi court have issued a writ of prohibition before the Missouri court entered its judgment? In a later case, the Mississippi Supreme Court said "no": Mississippi courts are not "superior" to those of a sister state with jurisdiction over the parties and the case. *Binning v. State*, 262 So.3d 1107 (Miss. 2019).

Fauntleroy also demonstrates the common law doctrine that in an action at law, the cause of action "merges" in the judgment, *supra* at 88. Thus, the Missouri judgment—sought to be enforced in Mississippi—is a *money judgment like any other,* and the original cause of action is no longer there. As a judgment for money, and nothing else, the Missouri judgment can no more violate Mississippi public policy than could any other money judgment, for instance, one which compensates for personal injuries. For another application, see *EBF Partners, LLC v. Novabella, Inc.*, 96 N.E.3d 87, 93 (Ind. Ct. App. 2018) (full faith and credit to be given New York money judgment based on cognovit note, even though cognovit notes are prohibited in Indiana; the New York court had proper jurisdiction).

The matter may be different if the F-1 judgment does not award money but does award relief of a different kind. An example is an F-1 decree enjoining a party from proceeding in F-2. Here, the F-1 court might be interfering with the administration of justice in F-2. It follows that F-2 might consider the decree to be violative of its public policy and justifiably deny it recognition. See *James v. Grand Trunk Western R. Co.,* 152 N.E.2d 858 (Ill. 1958). See also *Baker v. General Motors, supra* at 97 and *infra.*

The results of *Fauntleroy* and *James* also follow from the basic *policy of preclusion.* That policy requires that there be an end to litigation once the parties have litigated, or had a fair opportunity to litigate, the merits of a claim or an issue. In *Fauntleroy,* the merits of the claim were (or could have been) litigated in Missouri, and the parties were therefore precluded from relitigating them in Mississippi. Moreover, there was no separate Mississippi public policy concern. In *James,* the anti-suit injunction in F-1 did not address the merits of the case. Instead, it sought to close the courts of F-2 to the parties, something which only F-2 can do.

b. No Competent Court in F-2

A few early decisions held that F-2 was not obliged to provide a remedy or a court to administer a remedy when it itself lacked such a remedy or procedure for intrastate cases. Subsequently, some F-2 courts attempted to invoke the doctrine to exclude foreign judgments based on causes of action which F-2 considered to be against its public policy, or to refuse to entertain foreign statutory causes of action (for instance, a wrongful death claim based on a sister-state statute). As we have seen, the nature of the underlying cause of action does not justify refusal to recognize a foreign judgment *when it is for money. Fauntleroy v. Lum, supra* at 107. Other U.S. Supreme Court decisions have held that so long as the cause of action is one also known to the forum, it may not refuse to entertain a claim, or to enforce a judgment based upon such a claim, just because the cause of action was not created by its own law, but by the law of a sister state. See *Hughes v. Fetter,* 341 U.S. 609, 71 S. Ct. 980, 95 L. Ed. 1212 (1951); *Waranka v. Wadena Ins. Co.,* 832 N.W.2d 133 (Wis. Ct. App. 2013) (applying *Hughes*), *aff'd,* 847 N.W.2d 324 (Wis. 2014). See also *Franchise Tax Bd. of California v. Hyatt,* 578 U.S. 171, 177, 136 S. Ct. 1277, 1281, 194 L. Ed. 2d 431 (2016) (Nevada may not award higher damages against a California agency than it would be allowed to award against a Nevada agency); Pittman v. Rutherford, No. 19-36-DLB-CJS, 2020 WL 6384726, at *5–6, (E.D. Ky. Oct. 30, 2020) (slip op.) (citing *Hyatt*).

c. Tax and Penal Judgments

The historic position of Anglo-American courts has been that F-2 will not enforce the tax and penal laws of another state or country. Recognizing such foreign claims was thought to violate the territorial sovereignty of F-2 and thus its public policy.

In *Milwaukee County v. M.E. White Co.,* 296 U.S. 268, 56 S. Ct. 229, 80 L. Ed. 220 (1935), the Court required recognition and enforcement of a *tax judgment.* This decision is consistent with *Fauntleroy v. Lum, supra* at 107: a judgment for taxes is one for money and must be recognized as such. It is irrelevant what the underlying cause of action was.

Milwaukee County of course does not require the recognition of *unadjudicated tax claims.* Nevertheless, many states do enforce such claims, and more than half so provide by reciprocal statute. In the international context, the "revenue rule" was confirmed in a case that might have called for a departure: the court refused to entertain a claim for lost revenue, brought as part of a damage claim for alleged violations of RICO by defendants' activities in the United States. *Attorney General of Canada v. R.J. Reynolds Tobacco Holdings, Inc.,* 103 F. Supp. 2d 134 (N.D.N.Y. 2000), *aff'd,* 268 F.3d 103 (2d Cir. 2001), *cert denied,* 537 U.S. 1000, 123 S. Ct. 513, 154 L. Ed. 2d 394 (2002); *European Community v. RJR Nabisco, Inc.,* 424 F.3d 175 (2d Cir. 2005), *cert. denied,* 546 U.S. 1092, 126 S. Ct. 1045, 163 L. Ed. 2d 858 (2006). See also *Republic of Colombia v. Diageo North America, Inc.,* 531 F. Supp. 2d 365 (E.D.N.Y. 2007); *Salini Construttori S.p.A. v. Kingdom of Morocco,* 233 F. Supp. 3d 190, 200 (D.D.C. 2017) (claim against foreign government to enforce contractual obligation for repayment of taxes paid is not barred by the revenue rule).

Also, for sovereignty reasons, traditional doctrine provides that a state will not enforce the *penal laws* of another. In *Huntington v. Attrill,* 146 U.S. 657, 13 S. Ct. 224, 36 L. Ed. 1123 (1892), the Court provided a narrow definition of what constitutes a penalty. When the foreign claim or judgment seeks to punish, or through punishment deter conduct for the future, *on behalf and for the sake of the public,* it is a penalty. When, however, *the "penalty" inures to the benefit of a private party* (for instance, an award of punitive damages in addition to compensatory damages for personal injuries), it is regarded as part of the civil remedy and not as a "penalty" in the conflicts sense. In *Huntington,* the F-1 award went to the private party, hence it was not a penalty and was therefore entitled to recognition. Foreign countries, in contrast, normally view American punitive damages as penalties and deny recognition to such awards. For the revenue rule and penalties, see also *Pasquantino v. United States*, 544 U.S. 349, 361, 125 S. Ct. 1766, 161 L. Ed. 2d 619 (2005); *U.S. v. Federative Republic of Brazil*, 748 F.3d 86, 93 (2d Cir. 2014).

The U.S. Supreme Court has not ruled on whether true penalties are entitled to recognition and enforcement, at least when they have been reduced to a money judgment in F-1. The decisions in *Fauntleroy* and *Milwaukee County, supra*, respectively, suggest that *adjudicated* penalties should be entitled to recognition.

The area of *criminal law* furnishes an example of the kind of F-1 penalties that, historically, F-2 will not assist in enforcing. Criminal jurisdiction is thus thought to be *exclusive* at the place where the crime is charged. Even here, however, the widespread practice of interstate extradition alleviates the restrictive effects of the territorial-sovereignty approach of prior law in *interstate* practice. It is here that differences between interstate and international practice properly persist (the latter being a uniquely federal function in this area).

6. Other Defenses

a. Judgment Obtained by Fraud and Equitable Defenses

The older case law made a distinction between *extrinsic* and *intrinsic* fraud. The former was thought to go to the court's jurisdiction (see also *supra* at 93), such as when the defendant had been lured into the jurisdiction by false representations or was prevented from obtaining a fair hearing (such as when judges had been bribed). *Extrinsic* fraud, going to the court's jurisdiction, caused its ensuing judgment to be *void where rendered*, and consequently not entitled to recognition elsewhere. See *Stearns v. Stearns*, 187 N.W.2d 733 *4 (Iowa 1971); *In re Marriage of Shanks,* No. 00-0274, 2001 WL 246358 (Iowa Ct. App. Mar. 14, 2001) (extrinsic vs. intrinsic fraud explained); *Kraus v. Mummau*, No. 16-2034, 912 N.W.2d 856 (Table), 2018 WL 542628 (Iowa Ct. App. Jan. 24, 2018) (no extrinsic fraud).

Intrinsic fraud includes perjury, misrepresentation of evidence and the like, and was thought not to go to the court's jurisdiction. Instead, it might give rise to *equitable defenses* in the state of rendition (F-1). If so, the same defenses would of course be available in F-2 when the F-1 judgment is sought to be enforced there. See *Levin v. Gladstein,* 55 S.E. 371 (N.C. 1906).

The line between extrinsic and intrinsic fraud is of course very fine (see *Shanks, supra*). Nor is the distinction particularly important for practical purposes because all states provide procedures for relief from judgments obtained by fraud. In such a case, the rule in *Levin, supra,* applies: F-2 should grant the same relief that F-1 would grant.

b. Non-Final Judgments

As discussed *supra* at p. 99, the Full Faith and Credit Clause does not require that a judgment be final to be entitled to recognition. Nevertheless, finality has usually been required. However, in several important areas, such as support and custody, non-final or modifiable judgments are increasingly recognized. See *infra* at Chapter VI (Section IV)(A).

Apart from the possibility that an F-1 judgment may be modifiable retrospectively or prospectively, it may not be final in other respects, and it may therefore be proper to deny it recognition. This may be so when the F-1 judgment has been appealed or vacated, or when its execution has been stayed.

c. Inconsistent Judgments

It is possible that two courts (F-1 and F-2) render inconsistent judgments with respect to the same cause of action. This may occur when litigation is pending simultaneously in both jurisdictions, or when F-1 renders a judgment that F-2 refuses to recognize, instead entering its own inconsistent judgment.

In the second example, the validity of the first judgment was adjudicated in the second proceeding. The second judgment is now res judicata and entitled to recognition in F-3. This is the principle of *Treinies, supra* at p. 101.

In the first case the same result is obtained. **As between inconsistent judgments, the later in time controls**. Actually, and while often stated as a simple rule of convenience, this result also follows from *Treinies*: since both F-1 and F-2 had jurisdiction, there was an opportunity to interpose the first judgment before the rendition of the second. The failure to do so then allowed the second judgment to ripen into res judicata with respect to the validity of the first.

Note: This subsection deals with *inconsistent* judgments. The later-in-time-rule *does not apply* in the case of subsequent *consistent* judgments. The later-in-time-rule selects the later inconsistent judgment for recognition because the validity of the first judgment could have been (or was) litigated in the second proceeding. In the case of *consistent* judgments, the validity of the other (previous or contemporaneous) proceeding was not and could not have been an issue. Hence, there is no res judicata effect. Furthermore, the traditional rule is that judgments do not merge. The first judgment thus did not merge into the second; *both judgments are valid,* and the judgment creditor has the *option* of which judgment he will seek to enforce. This may be a particularly important option if enforcement of one of the judgments should now be time-barred, while enforcement of the other one is not.

d. Injunctions Against Enforcement or Prohibiting Action

A judgment creditor may be enjoined from enforcing his judgment. This injunction may be issued either by the court which rendered the original judgment or by a court in a second jurisdiction. In the first case, the second decree (the injunction) of F-1 is to be given the same effect in F-2 as it enjoys in F-1. Thus, the original judgment is not enforceable. In the second case, F-2 entered its own injunction, for whatever reason (including in possible disregard of its duty to recognize and enforce the F-1 judgment under the Full Faith and Credit command). Since we assume, as we must, that F-2 had jurisdiction over the parties, it becomes irrelevant why F-2 entered its injunction; the case is the same as that of *inconsistent judgments,* discussed in the subsection immediately preceding.

Injunctions may also seek to achieve other results, such as to prevent testimony from potential witnesses elsewhere. If all parties are before the court, these equity decrees may bind all parties before it but not absent parties. See *Baker v. General Motors, supra* at p. 97.

Antisuit injunctions may bind parties before the issuing court, but they have no direct preclusive effect on the merits of litigation in the second forum since they do not address those merits. Sanctions for violation of such injunctions are then also imposed by the first and not the second forum. See *Baker v. General Motors Corp., supra* (dictum).

e. Reversal of Prior Judgment

If the original F-1 judgment is reversed prior to the commencement of enforcement proceedings in F-2, F-2 is now faced with inconsistent judgments, and the later-in-time rule applies. In the rare case that F-2 has already entered a judgment recognizing the original F-1 judgment by the time the F-1 reversal occurs, F-2 will either provide equitable defenses, under its law, against the enforcement of its own judgment, or it will treat the F-1 reversal as determining the rights and obligations of the parties. The latter would enable a party possibly injured by the F-2 enforcement to seek restitution relief.

f. Payment

The law of F-1 determines the effect of its judgment and what constitutes satisfaction of it.

If, for instance, F-1 law provides that only complete payment of a judgment will release a joint tortfeasor, then a pro rata payment by one tortfeasor will not discharge him, and F-2 is bound to recognize the F-1 judgment as continuing to be an obligation upon such joint tortfeasor.

g. Statutes of Limitation

A statute of limitations applying to judgments has traditionally been thought to go to the remedy and not the substance of the obligation imposed by the F-1 judgment. Thus, it has been said that the second forum (F-2) may apply its *longer* statute of limitation to a judgment already barred by F-1. For practical purposes, however, this would be the rare result. Normally, states do not wish to entertain stale claims; they therefore will "borrow" the foreign limitation ("borrowing statutes") or will apply their own shorter limitation.

The view has been stated that F-2 may apply its *shorter* statute so long as the limitation provided by it applies equally to domestic and foreign judgments. Restatement (Second) § 118 cmt. *c*. The U.S. Supreme Court has held that F-2's shorter statute may apply in circumstances when the judgment creditor could revive his F-1 judgment. *Watkins v. Conway,* 385 U.S. 188, 87 S. Ct. 357, 17 L. Ed. 2d 286 (1966). When the judgment creditor has revived the judgment in F-1, F-2 must give it the same effect that it has in F-1 (i.e., it is valid and in force). The Supreme Court has *not* addressed the case where F-2's limitation is shorter than F-1's, and F-1 does *not* provide for revival but prolongs the original judgment. In such circumstances, the implementing statute to the Full Faith and Credit Clause ("the same effect" as where rendered) would seem to require F-2 to accord recognition. *Schmierer v. The Tribal Trust,* 427 P.3d 143, 151–52 (N.M. Ct. App.), *cert. denied,* No. S-1-SC-37207, 2018 WL 11277107 (N.M. Sept. 20, 2018) (adopting this view, citing to Hornbook § 24.32 (5th ed. 2010)); *Dawson v. Sonju,* 343 A.3d 1281, 1291 (Pa. Super. 2025). If a foreign judgment has been domesticated (registered), but enforcement was not sought, the forum's five-year limitation does not apply. However, the foreign judgment may be enforced like any other judgment within the limits of the state's dormancy statute. *Taracorp, Ltd. v. Dailey,* 419 P.3d 217 (Okla. 2018); *In re Carpenter,* 2024 WL 4172534 (W.D. Okla. 2024) .

The foregoing may also be affected by the current change in the way statutes of limitation are perceived. As discussed in connection with choice of law (*infra*), limitations are increasingly viewed as part of the *substance of the obligation*. As such, it would seem that full faith and credit requires that the effect given a judgment in F-2 closely track the effect it has in F-1.

III. Recognition of Foreign-Country Judgments

A. Recognition and Enforcement

1. The *Hilton* Doctrine

Foreign country judgments are not entitled to recognition under the Constitution's Full Faith and Credit Clause. Their effect was considered in the U.S. Supreme Court's early decision of *Hilton v. Guyot,* 159 U.S. 113, 16 S. Ct. 139, 40 L. Ed. 95 (1895). At the outset, the Court made it clear that foreign judgments *in rem* (e.g., adjudicating title to property), foreign status determinations (confirming or dissolving a marriage), and foreign judgments in actions between foreigners would ordinarily be entitled to recognition in this country. The narrow issue in *Hilton* was whether a foreign country judgment for money, rendered *against an American,* would be entitled to recognition here.

Invoking the ancient doctrine of *comity,* which calls for cooperation with other members of the international community and the reasonable accommodation of their legitimate interests, the Court said that the foreign country judgment is prima facie evidence of the determination of the merits of the case and should be enforced "unless some special ground is shown for impeaching the judgment." In the case at bar, it appeared that there might have been fraud in the procurement of the judgment, which by itself would have been enough to impeach it.

Nevertheless, the Court also said that a foreign country's personal judgments against Americans *will not be conclusive in the United States* (and therefore not entitled to recognition and enforcement) if the foreign country in question does not treat American judgments as conclusive. *Hilton* thus established *reciprocity* as a precondition to recognition.

2. Modern Recognition Practice

In *Klaxon Co. v. Stentor Electric Mfg. Co.,* 313 U.S. 487, 61 S. Ct. 1020, 85 L. Ed. 1477 (1941), the U.S. Supreme Court decided that the *Erie* doctrine (304 U.S. 64, 58 S. Ct. 817, 82 L. Ed. 1188 (1938)) extends to conflicts law, thus requiring federal courts sitting in diversity to apply the conflicts law of the state in which they sit. After *Klaxon,* it has been thought that *Hilton* no longer binds either state or federal courts. As a result, most state courts have declined to follow the reciprocity requirement of *Hilton.* They essentially accord recognition to foreign-country judgments on the same basis as sister-state judgments. In a few states, reciprocity is required by statute.

To provide for nationwide uniform rules for dealing with foreign country judgments, the American Law Institute has maintained a research project, and in 2005 proposed a draft federal statute on the Recognition and Enforcement of Foreign Judgments. A controversial § 7 of the draft act would have introduced a general reciprocity requirement.

The Uniform Foreign Money-Judgments Recognition Act (1962) was adopted by 32 states. It provides for the recognition and enforcement "in the same manner as the judgment of the sister state which is entitled to full faith and credit" of foreign-country judgments that grant or deny the recovery of money. Prerequisites include that the foreign court had personal and subject matter jurisdiction, that the judgment would not conflict with another judgment, that it was not obtained by fraud, and that it does not violate the public policy of the recognizing forum. With respect to defenses, see also *infra* Section B. As of 2025, a 2005 revision (the Uniform Foreign-Country Money Judgments Recognition Act) is in force in thirty states and the District of Columbia, while the prior Act remains in force in eight states. The revision provides some clarification of the grounds for non-recognition as well as additional procedural rules.

Some uncertainty still exists concerning the preclusive effects of foreign-country judgments. On the one hand, older decisions, as well as the Restatement (Second) (§ 95 cmt. *c*(1)), do not consider the foreign country judgment to merge the underlying cause of action. As a result, the judgment creditor would be free to seek enforcement of his judgment *or* to sue on his original claim, for instance, to obtain a higher recovery. This rule has been severely criticized on the ground that the policy reasons favoring preclusion and an end to litigation in interstate practice are the same in international practice.

On the other hand, res judicata and estoppel effect will be accorded foreign-country determinations that have been finally litigated (in the foreign country) when such a judgment is sought to be enforced in the United States. This is despite the fact that foreign rules with respect to res judicata may differ from American law.

Can preclusive effect be gained by having a foreign-country judgment recognized under the Uniform Foreign Money-Judgments Recognition Act in state A, and then seeking registration of the state A judgment of recognition in state B, under the (interstate) Uniform Enforcement of Foreign Judgments Act (*supra*)? A Texas court said "no," because this would give the foreign country judgment full faith and credit "through the back door". *Reading & Bates Construction Co. v. Baker Energy Resources Corp.*, 976 S.W.2d 702 (Tex. App. 1998). This result is arguably wrong: a foreign country judgment recognized by one of the states, either at common law or under the uniform law, is then a judgment of that state, and as such, entitled to full faith and credit in all other states. For expansive discussion of the conflicting case law, see *Alberta Securities Commission v. Ryckman*, No. N13J–02847, 2015 WL 2265473 (Del. Super. Ct. May 5, 2015) (recognizing the sister state's domestication of the foreign-country judgment). See also *Cargill Financial Services International, Inc. v. Barshchovkij*, 2025 WL 522108 (S.D.N.Y. 2025), followed in .*Drip Capital Inc. v. JY Imports of NY, Inc*, 348 F.R.D. 536, 546 (E.D.N.Y. 2025). For the like result in Canada, see *Girsberger v. Kresz* (1999), 135 Man. R. 2d 34, 1999 CarswellMan 56, para. 30 (Man. Q.B.).

B. Defenses to Foreign-Country Judgments

1. Jurisdiction

To be entitled to recognition in the United States, the foreign-country judgment must have been rendered by a court with jurisdiction, as *tested by American standards*. It is not enough that the foreign court had jurisdiction under its own law; unless the defendant voluntarily submitted to the jurisdiction of the foreign court (by appearance, or on the basis of a valid forum-selection clause), that court's jurisdiction must satisfy American due process standards. Thus, a foreign-country judgment may well be valid where rendered yet not be entitled to recognition in the United States. An example is a French default judgment in which jurisdiction is based on the French nationality or domicile of the plaintiff. It would not be entitled to recognition in the United States because of insufficient connection of the defendant with the rendering forum.

When the defendant has contested the foreign-country's jurisdiction (i.e., did not submit to the jurisdiction of the foreign court), an adverse finding will *not* preclude relitigation of the jurisdictional question when recognition is sought in the United States. In this respect, the recognition of a foreign country judgment differs from the recognition of a sister-state judgment. This is so because, in the interstate setting, the unsuccessful defendant could have appealed the adverse jurisdictional ruling on United States constitutional grounds; in contrast, United States constitutional grounds could not be the basis for an appeal of the foreign court's jurisdictional determination. Hence, that determination cannot be res judicata for purposes of collateral attack.

2. Foreign Judgment for Taxes or Penalties

According to the traditional view, a foreign-country judgment for taxes or penalties will not be recognized in the United States, just as a *claim* for taxes or penalties would not be entertained. As was seen previously (*supra*), the defense that the underlying claim is one for taxes or penalties can no longer justify, *in interstate practice,* the refusal to enforce a sister-state judgment reducing such a claim to money. To the extent that the non-merger rule may be abandoned as to international judgments (*supra*), it would follow that international judgments *for money* should also be enforced regardless of the nature of the original claim underlying them. The trial court in *Attorney General of Canada* (*supra*) expressed some doubt about the continued vitality of the "revenue rule" in the context of judgments.

3. Public Policy

As in interstate practice, the public policy defense will lie only in exceptional cases. The defense is expressly retained in the Uniform Foreign Money-Judgment Recognition Act. An application is *Matusevitch v. Telnikoff*, 877 F. Supp. 1 (D.D.C. 1995), in which an English damage award in a libel action was denied recognition because English libel laws violate U.S. First Amendment guarantees. Cf. *Society of Lloyd's v. Siemon-Netto*, 457 F.3d 94, 100–01 (D.C. Cir. 2006) (it is the cause of action, and not any "particular application" of that cause of action, that justifies the public policy defense). This result is a consequence of the rule that foreign-country judgments do not merge the underlying cause of action. This contrasts with interstate practice. See *Fauntleroy v. Lum*, *supra* at p. 107. In interstate practice, this kind of *révision au fond* is unacceptable if the first court had and properly exercised jurisdiction. All such issues would be res judicata.

The public policy view expressed in *Matusevitch* was codified in the federal SPEECH Act of 2010, at 28 U.S.C.A. § 4102 (West 2022). The Act prohibits recognition of a foreign country judgment for defamation by any U.S. court unless the court determines that the foreign proceedings afforded the judgment debtor essentially the protections guaranteed by the First Amendment, or that the plaintiff would also have prevailed in the United States. For an application, see *Trout Point Lodge, Ltd. v. Handshoe,* 729 F.3d 481 (5th Cir. 2013); *Electronic Frontier Found. v. Global Equity Mgmt. (SA) Pty Ltd.*, 290 F. Supp. 3d 923, 941–48 (N.D. Cal. 2017) (Australian injunction unenforceable in the United States). See also *Harpur v. Bich*, 2024 WL 4930286 (S.D.N.Y. 2024), followed in *Harpur v. Rich*, 87 Misc. 3d 1223(A), 242 N.Y.S.3d 912 (Table) (N.Y.Sup. 2025)., For extensive discussion of the extraterritorial application of the First Amendment, and a determination that plaintiff's defamation claim was not made out under state law, see *Jang v. Trustees of St. Johnsbury Academy*, 331 F. Supp. 3d 312 (D. Vt. 2018), *aff'd*, 771 Fed. App'x 86 (2d Cir. 2019).

A foreign country judgment may also be denied recognition if the foreign legal system does not provide for fair trials (systemic evaluation), or if the particular proceeding did not accord with American concepts of fair trial and due process. However, success with such a claim is often difficult, as such success condemns the legal system of another country, an act which might cross from the legal to the political. A recent pair of cases in New York state court demonstrate the difficulty. At issue was whether U.S. State Department reports could be used as evidence of unfairness in China courts. *Shanghai Yongrun Inv. Mgmt. Co., Ltd. v. Kashi Galazy Venture Capital, Ltd.*, No. 156328/2020, 2021 WL 1716424, at *3 (N.Y. Sup. Ct. Apr. 30th, 2021). The trial court declined to enforce the foreign judgment, finding the foreign court system unfair. Id. at *5–*6. The appellate court reversed, holding that the specific proceeding did provide a fair trial. *Shanghai Yongrun Inv. Mgt. Co., Ltd. v. Xu*, 203 A.D.3d 495 (N.Y. App. Div. 2022).

The Uniform Money-Judgments Recognition Act provides, furthermore, that a foreign judgment is not conclusive, in the first place, if it "was rendered under a system which does not provide impartial tribunals or procedures compatible with the requirements of due process of law" (§ 4(a)(1)). Note that the inquiry is not limited to the proceedings leading to the particular judgment sought to be recognized, but extends to the foreign legal system generally. Thus, in *Society of Lloyd's v. Ashenden*, 233 F.3d 473, 477 (7th Cir. 2000), the Court assumed that the English legal system met the standards of Section 4(a)(1) (as then in effect in Illinois), but suggested that a closer inquiry might be warranted in the case of judgments from the Congo, Cuba, North Korea, Iran, or Iraq. One might question whether a generalized—and not a case-specific—inquiry could improperly invade the executive's foreign affairs power. See *Zschernig v. Miller*, 389 U.S. 429, 88 S. Ct. 664, 19 L. Ed. 2d 683 (1968), and *infra* Chapter XII, at II(B-5).

IV. Arbitral Awards

The Federal Arbitration Act of 1947 provides for the enforcement of arbitration agreements and of resulting awards with respect to matters within the legislative competence of Congress (admiralty, interstate and foreign commerce).

The United States is also a member of the 1958 United Nations Convention on Recognition and Enforcement of Foreign Arbitral Awards (generally referred to as the "New York Convention"), which provides for enforcement of an *agreement* to arbitrate and for recognition, in the United States, of arbitration *awards* rendered in other contracting states. Thus, arbitral awards rendered in nations adhering to the New York Convention will, under the terms of that Convention and its preemptive effect under the Supremacy Clause of the Constitution, be entitled to recognition and enforcement in all the states of the Union. However, in one case, in which the parties and the matter arbitrated lacked any connection with the United States, a motion to "confirm" a foreign arbitral award was dismissed on grounds of *forum non conveniens*, in analogy to arbitration practice under U.S. law. *In re Arbitration between Monegasque de Reassurances S.A.M. v. NAK Naftogaz of Ukraine*, 311 F.3d 488 (2d Cir. 2002). The Second Circuit also dealt with the concept of veil piercing, to hold a successor-in-interest (and non-signatory of the arbitration agreement) liable. Id. at 495. In a New York Convention proceeding for the enforcement of a foreign arbitral award, the veil piercing part of the *Monegasque* decision is discussed extensively. *CBF Industria de Gusa S/A v. AMCI Holdings, Inc.,* 14 F. Supp. 3d 463, 474–78 (S.D.N.Y. 2014), *on remand at* 316 F. Supp. 3d 635, 646 (S.D.N.Y. 2018) (successful veil-piercing under alter-ego theory). The application of remedies of American procedural law to an international obligation is questionable.

V. Review Questions

1. T or F: "Preclusion" means that:

a. A party who has litigated a claim and reduced it to judgment may not sue on the claim again.

b. A defendant may interpose a previous judgment in his or her favor as a defense against renewed litigation, on the same claim, by the plaintiff.

c. A defendant has the same defense as under (b) in subsequent litigation on a different claim, if the plaintiff could or should have raised the issue in the first litigation.

d. "Merger," "bar," and "collateral estoppel" are expressions of different aspects of "preclusion."

e. A plaintiff who sued and recovered against a non-resident defendant, upon a claim arising from an injury within the forum from a defective product manufactured outside the forum by the defendant, may not sue the defendant for breach of a contract unrelated to the tort and to the forum because the contract claim should have been brought together within the tort claim.

f. A creditor who has recovered a judgment in England, but is unhappy with it, may bring a new action on the claim in the United States.

2. Under the Full Faith and Credit Clause of the United States Constitution,

a. T or F: A money judgment of a sister state, entered with valid personal jurisdiction over the defendant, is entitled to recognition in the forum.

b. T or F: The foregoing is also true if the defendant owns property within the forum but has no other contacts with the forum state.

c. T or F: A sister-state support decree is entitled to recognition for past-due and future installments.

d. T or F: The situs state is required to recognize the (non-situs) state's decree quieting title to forum (situs state) land.

e. T or F: A decree ordering the conveyance of forum land, issued in a sister state, must be accorded recognition by the forum.

f. T or F: The forum, as the situs of land, recognizes the adjudication of the equities to local land as between the parties subject to the personal jurisdiction of the non-situs court.

g. T or F: The forum recognizes the judgment of a sister-state court, which lacked personal or subject matter jurisdiction, in a proceeding in which the defendant participated—it is valid.

h. T or F: The forum recognizes a valid personal judgment of a sister-state, and decrees execution against the defendant's local assets, even if the defendant and the cause of action resulting in the foreign judgment have no "minimum contacts" to the forum as required by jurisdictional theory (Chapter III above).

i. T or F: The judgment of a London (England) court, in the circumstances of (a), above, is entitled to recognition by a United States court.

j. T or F: Forum law (F-2) determines whether non-mutual offensive estoppel may be invoked.

k. T or F: F-2 will give effect to an antisuit injunction entered by F-1 and dismiss a local suit brought in violation of it.

3. List and describe the implementing legislation to the Full Faith and Credit Clause.

4. a. T or F: F-2 need not recognize an F-1 judgment based on errors of fact or of substantive law.

b. T or F: F-2 need not recognize an F-1 judgment in circumstances in which F-1, over defendant's strenuous objection, erroneously concluded that it had jurisdiction.

c. T or F: When faced with inconsistent, but otherwise valid judgments from F-1 and F-2, F-3 is free to choose which one, if any, to recognize.

d. T or F: F-2 must recognize an F-1 money judgment despite the fact that the underlying claim (for instance, for interest at a rate regarded as usurious by F-2) violates F-2 public policy.

e. T or F: A had sued B in F-1 on a cause of action to which F-1 would have applied the substantive law of F-2. The Statute of Limitations had run in F-1, and the court therefore dismissed A's suit. A is not precluded from now suing in F-2, assuming that F-2 has jurisdiction and that its statute of limitations has not run.

f. T or F: Registration of a F-1 judgment in F-2 under the Uniform Act, if in force in F-2, may have risks that enforcement relying on the Full Faith and Credit Clause does not have.

g. T or F: A worker compensation award obtained in F-1 settles the matter, and the injured employee is precluded from seeking and obtaining an additional award in F-2, even if F-2 has jurisdiction and its (more generous) award could have been sought in the first place.

Part Three

Domestic Relations

■ ANALYSIS

V. The Creation of Status and Its Consequences
VI. Dissolution of Domestic Relationships and Its Consequences (Support, Custody)

Chapter V

The Creation of Status and Its Consequences

■ ANALYSIS

I. **Introduction**

II. **Traditional Marriage**

- A. Recognition
  - 1. The General Rule
  - 2. Special Problems
    - a. Non-Age
    - b. "Incestuous" Marriages
    - c. Polygamous Marriages
    - d. Remarriage After Divorce
- B. Interspousal Property Rights
  - 1. By Operation of Law
    - a. Common Law and Community Property Systems Described
    - b. What Law Applies?
    - c. Effect of Change of Domicile
      - i. Traditional Approaches
      - ii. Legislative Responses
      - iii. Foreign Country Situations
    - d. Debts
  - 2. By Contract

III. **Contemporary Issues**

- A. Same-Sex Marriage
- B. Non-Marital Partnerships

IV. **Legitimation**

V. **Adoption**

- A. Jurisdiction
- B. Incidents

VI. **Review Questions**

I. Introduction

This chapter deals with a person's status: the status of being married, of being a party to another recognized domestic relationship (such as a civil union or a common law marriage), of having been legitimated, or of being an adopted child. A person's status is seldom in issue by itself. It usually arises as a *preliminary question* to other issues, such as the right to inherit from an adoptive parent, to be considered the "surviving spouse" for inheritance purposes, or to share in pension rights as a former "spouse." In most cases, we inquire into the existence of a status because of the *consequences* which flow from it. These consequences are also called *incidents* of the status. The dissolution of a status (e.g., divorce) will also have consequences; those incidents are discussed in Chapter VI.

Note that most rules summarized in this part (Domestic Relations) are rules of *forum jurisdictional law*. This is because the general rule in common law jurisdictions, like the United States and England, is that the forum applies its law almost exclusively. By contrast, many civil law systems may rely on the law of the nationality of each of the spouses (cumulatively), if that law differs from the forum's law.

II. Traditional Marriage

A. Recognition

1. The General Rule

The traditional statement in the United States is that a marriage that is valid under the law of the state where it took place will be recognized as valid everywhere—the **place-of-celebration rule**. Restatement (Second) § 283(2); *In re May's Estate*, 114 N.E.2d 4 (N.Y. 1953). See also § 7 of U.S.C. Title I. The rule also extends to *common law marriages*. Thus, states that have abolished common law marriages (living as husband and wife, being so regarded by the community, but not having participated in a formal ceremony, civil or religious) will usually recognize such a marriage "formed" in a state still allowing it. See, e.g., *George v. George*, 389 So. 2d 1389, 1390 (Miss. 1980) ("if a valid common-law marriage was celebrated in [another State], it will be recognized in this State."); *Enis v. State,* 408 So. 2d 486, 487 n.1 (Miss. 1981) (favorably citing *George*); *Hawkins v. State*, 377 So.3d 969, 972 (Miss. 2024); Cal. Fam. Code § 308 (West 2024). Very few states still allow (new) common law marriages. See, e.g., N.H. Rev. Stat. Ann. § 457:39 (2024); Utah Code Ann. § 30–1–4.5 (West 2024). For California, see *People v. Barefield*, 283 Cal.Rptr.3rd 742, 752 (Cal.App. 2021); Before the U.S. Supreme Court validated same-sex marriages in *Obergefell* in 2015 (see *infra* at Section III), there could not be common law same-sex marriages. After 2015 and now under the Respect for Marriage Act (*infra* Section III), the common-law nature of a same-sex relationship is to be treated the same as that of a heterosexual relationship. For Colorado, see *LaFleur v. Pyfer*, 479 P.3d 869 (Colo. S.Ct. 2021), reh. den. 479 P.3d 869 (2021). See, e.g., *Ranolls v. Dewling*, 223 F. Supp. 3d 613, 622 (E.D. Tex. 2016) (conferring surviving spouse status by retroactive application of *Obergefell, infra* p.131). The new legislation incorporates the place-of-celebration rule for the validity of a marriage.

The policy in favor of validating a marriage also led to the provision in the *Uniform Marriage and Divorce Act* (in effect in 6 states in 2025) that a marriage should be recognized, even if invalid where first contracted, if it was considered valid by the parties' domicile (i.e., there is an *alternative* reference to either the law of celebration *or* of the domicile).

Nonetheless, there will be situations in which an out-of-state marriage will be met with objections derived from the law of the forum. These will be considered in turn.

Three states (Arizona, Arkansas, Louisiana) provide for a stricter form of marriage, the "covenant marriage." The parties agree to make all efforts to preserve the marriage, to seek dissolution only on fault grounds or after a long waiting period, and to have the law of the state of celebration apply to dissolution. These marriages will of course be recognized by other states, but it has been argued, with regard to dissolution, that forum law applies. See *Hay*, The American "Covenant Marriage" in the Conflict of Laws, 64 La. L. Rev. 43 (2003). Accord *Blackburn v. Blackburn*, 180 So. 3d 16 (Ala. Civ. App. 2015) (declining to enforce Louisiana covenant marriage contract); *Melki v. Melki*, No. 744, Sept. Term, 2019, 2020 WL 5797869, at *4 (Md. Ct. Spec. App. Sept. 29, 2020), *cert. denied*, 243 A.3d 1023 (Md. 2021) (holding that "marriage is not a contract that is constitutionally protected from interference").

2. Special Problems

a. Non-Age

State statutes generally establish a minimum age for marriage. If minors from X, where they lack capacity, get married in Y, where they may legally do so, will X recognize the marriage upon their return? Note that this case is one of those rare situations in which the status may be in issue for its own sake, for instance when the parents or one of the young spouses seek to attack and set aside the out-of-state marriage.

In *State v. Graves,* 307 S.W.2d 545 (Ark. 1957), the domiciliary court recognized the out-of-state marriage in application of the basic place-of-celebration rule and refused to convict the minors' parents for contributing to their "delinquency." This should also be the result under the 2022 Respect for Marriage Act, *infra* Section III. For a far-reaching modern application, see *Stovall v. Preston*, 539 S.W.3d 638 (Ark. Ct. App. 2018).

In *Wilkins v. Zelichowski,* 140 A.2d 65 (N.J. 1958), the court granted the young wife an annulment of the out-of-state marriage when she so petitioned upon reaching age 18. While *Wilkins* differs from *Graves* in result, note that the *Wilkins* court enforced its state's protective policy at the request of one of the persons for whom the protection had been enacted. Under the place-of-celebration rule under the new Respect for Marriage Act, the forum may not apply its standards to a valid sister state marriage.

The general rule in favor of honoring validly contracted out-of-state marriages had an exception in *marriage evasion legislation.* In force in only a handful of states, such legislation provided that if local domiciliaries contracted an out-of-state marriage for which they lacked capacity, or which would otherwise be void by local law (e.g., laws on consanguinity), then such out-of-state marriages "shall be null and void . . . in this state." Unif. Marriage Evasion Act § 1. Under the 2022 legislation (previous paragraph), these exceptions to the place-of-celebration rule may no longer be applied.

b. "Incestuous" Marriages

State statutes forbid marriages between persons of certain degrees of family relationship ("degrees of *consanguinity*"—uncle/niece, cousins, etc.). Such marriages are incestuous and therefore void. Again, assume a conflict between the domiciliary state's law (with narrowly defined degrees of affinity) and the state where the marriage was contracted (with a wider definition). The majority of states would have recognized such a marriage, as the underlying state policies would not really have conflicted, and differences tended to be slight. See *In re May's Estate, supra*. Furthermore, and very importantly, the objection to the marriage in these cases often arose in the context of inheritance, for instance, to deny a person inheritance rights as a "surviving spouse." There is a strong public policy in favor of letting a spouse inherit and be provided for from the assets of the decedent. The Respect for Marriage Act (*supra* previous paragraphs) accepted these results by enaction the place-of-celebration rule.

c. Polygamous Marriages

Polygamy—being married to more than one partner at the same time—is valid in some foreign legal systems but not in the United States. Again, however, much depends on the purpose for which we need to determine the status: is it to allow all spouses to live together or to provide support to a surviving "spouse"? A California court recognized this difference and held that it would not violate California's policy against polygamous marriages (among *living* people) to allow two surviving "spouses" to divide the statutory "widow's" share of a decedent's estate between them. *In re Dalip Singh Bir's Estate,* 188 P.2d 499 (Cal. Dist. Ct. App. 1948).A more recent decision emphasized that Bir was limited to cases of intestate succession, but did not affect California's policy cases when, for instance, a living bigamous "spouse" seeks support: *In re Marriage of Elali & Marchoud,* 294 Cal.Reptr. 3d 804, 817 (Cal.4th Dist.Ct.App. 2022). The Respect for Marriage Act leaves this question open for foreign country marriages: the outcome is left to the "applicable law."

d. Remarriage After Divorce

Two principal problems may arise, usually in the context of inheritance or other property claims (i.e., in the context of the incidents of status). First, whether someone is the "surviving" spouse of a decedent may depend on whether his or her *prior* marriage was validly and effectively dissolved, so that he or she was free to marry the decedent (if not, the marriage to the decedent would be bigamous and void in the state in which it was concluded). When there is some evidence of a valid dissolution of a prior marriage, or even in the absence of evidence to the contrary, there will be a strong presumption in favor of the validity of the last marriage (i.e., the one in issue). See *Headen v. Pope & Talbot, Inc.,* 252 F.2d 739 (3d Cir. 1958).

Second, under the law of the state where a party obtained a divorce, there may be a waiting period between the interlocutory and final decrees. The forum law or the law of the domicile of the divorced or to-be-divorced party may also impose a waiting period before remarriage. Will remarriage before removal of the particular impediment be valid? Under the *majority* view, the second marriage is valid if valid where celebrated (whether in the forum or in a third state). Moreover, the cases which address this problem date to the era of fault divorces. With *no-fault divorces* the rule everywhere today, any objections to the recognition of remarriage upon (an otherwise valid) divorce should now have disappeared.

Some of the above may change as a result of the 2022 Respect for Marriage Act and the new § 7 of U.S.C. Title I (see *supra* p. 99 and *infra* p. 132). For formalized Same-Sex Relationships, see *infra* at Section III.

B. Interspousal Property Rights

1. By Operation of Law

a. Common Law and Community Property Systems Described

The majority of states follow the **common law** approach to interspousal property rights: the property which a spouse brings into the marriage, as well as any property acquired by his or her efforts, thereafter, is the **separate property** of that spouse (unless the spouses themselves put such property into joint ownership). In these states, the law provides protection for divorced or surviving spouses by imposing support obligations and by giving the surviving spouse certain inheritance rights in the property of the other. With inheritance rights, the former common law interests of (a wife's) *dower* and (a husband's) *curtesy* have been replaced by a statutory claim for a *family allowance* and the right to take against the will and to receive a *statutory share,* i.e., a percentage of the estate.

Arizona, California, Idaho, Louisiana, Nevada, New Mexico, Texas, Washington, and Wisconsin have the **community property** system. (Alaska and Tennessee have statutes that allow spouses to select a community property regime.) Property acquired before marriage is *separate property,* but all property acquired thereafter (except by gift or inheritance) is *community property,* i.e., it belongs to the spouses equally when acquired, and it is distributed upon death or divorce. However, there is variation even within these states. See (c)(ii) below.

Note: Since community property states provide for a divorced or surviving spouse through the community property system (i.e., an undivided one-half interest in all property acquired during the marriage, except by gift or inheritance), there is ***no*** additional statutory charge against the estate of the decedent spouse. In other words, the common law system presumes individual ownership and provides for a division (statutory share) at the death of one of the spouses, while the community system presumes joint ownership from the time of acquisition, so there is no need to make another division at the death of one of the spouses.

b. What Law Applies?

The relevant *time* for determining interspousal property interests is the time of *acquisition of the asset.* The relevant *law* is that of the *domicile of the spouses* in the case of *movable property,* and that of the *situs* in the case of *immovable property.*

There have been some departures in favor of a *general* application of the law of domicile. One state, however—Louisiana—provides for the application of its law to *all* assets, movable or immovable, *located in Louisiana,* by spouses regardless of their domicile(s). See, e.g., *Robinson v. Robinson,* 778 So. 2d 1105 (La. 2001) (wife's waiver of Louisiana pension rights not recognized by Louisiana because the chosen law (North Carolina) did not have a "sufficient" link to the parties). But domiciliary states may not give effect to that rule. In *Estate of Crichton,* 228 N.E.2d 799 (N.Y. 1967), the New York domicile of the spouses, with jurisdiction over all parties, applied its law to Louisiana personal property. Louisiana subsequently accorded Full Faith and Credit. *Crichton v. Succession of Crichton,* 232 So. 2d 109, 116 (La. Ct. App.), *cert. denied,* 400 U.S. 919, 91 S. Ct. 172, 27 L. Ed. 2d 159 (1970).

The time-of-acquisition rule is also important for the determination of interspousal property rights in State B with assets originally acquired in State A. Normally, the A assets will be ***traced*** into the B asset.

Example: Spouses domiciled in Iowa, a common law state, take their assets, acquired by the husband, move to New Mexico, a community property state, and buy real property there. Several years later, the spouses divorce. The Iowa assets were the husband's separate property at the time of acquisition, and are traced into the New Mexico real property, so that it is the husband's separate property, and not community property. *Hughes v. Hughes,* 573 P.2d 1194 (N.M. 1978); *Stephens v. Stephens,* 595 P.2d 1196, 1197–1198 (N.M. 1979).

The coming Restatement (Third) focuses on the law of the state of the marital domicile at the time of marriage or at the time of acquisition, respectively, for property owned before or acquired during marriage. See § 7.13. The law of the current marital domicile also applies to the rights of spouses upon divorce or the death of one spouse. See §§ 7.14 and 7.15. The "marital domicile" is the state of the spouses' current or last common domicile or, if they never had one, the state to which both of them had the closest connection. § 7.12.

Income from immovable property should logically be treated the same way as the property which produced it. This is the rule in California: rents and other income from separate immovable property is the owner-spouse's separate property. The rule is contrary in Texas: income received from immovable property is community property. With respect to *movable property,* the law of the spouses' current domicile usually determines the nature of income derived from it.

In same-sex marriages, the rights of the spouses are the same as in traditional heterosexual marriage.

c. Effect of Change of Domicile

i. Traditional Approaches

The rules discussed above (time of acquisition and tracing) may have important consequences when parties change domiciles and one spouse subsequently dies.

Example: H and W move from A (a common law state) to B (a community property state). Assume that all their property was movable and that it was acquired largely by H's efforts. H dies intestate in B. What does W receive? Intestate succession to movables is governed by the law of the domicile at death—here B. B law gives the surviving spouse his or her one-half interest in the community property, but no part of the decedent's separate property. In the example, there was no community property—only separate property. Thus, W takes nothing. *In re Thornton's Estate,* 33 P.2d 1 (Cal. 1934). If the spouses also had immovable property, situs law would determine W's interests in it.

Assume the reverse case: change of domicile from community property state to common law state. What does W take upon H's death? All the movable property was community property; W retains her undivided one-half interest. Succession to the decedent's one-half interest in the community is governed, in the case of intestacy, by the law of domicile at death, here the common law state. It will additionally give W a portion of H's half of the community.

Results similar to the foregoing examples occur when parties *divorce* after a change in domiciles.

As the examples show, the interplay of these rules may have the result that the policies of both states are frustrated. In the first case, W receives less than her home state would have given her, or less than her new domicile gives spouses who acquired their property there. In the second example, W receives more than either state intended.

ii. Legislative Responses

Five community property states have adopted legislation which introduces the **quasi-community property** concept: all property will be considered to be community property which would have been community property had it been acquired by the parties while domiciled in the state. California, Idaho, and Wisconsin apply the concept for property distribution at death or upon divorce, while Arizona and Texas apply the concept only for divorce. Parties, originally from out-of-state, will thus be treated the same, and have the same protection, as local spouses. See, e.g., *Addison v. Addison,* 399 P.2d 897 (Cal. 1965) (en banc).

The *Uniform Disposition of Community Property at Death Act,* which is in force in 25 states, addresses the reverse case, i.e., where the change of domicile occurs from a community property state to a common law state. It provides, for intestate succession, that the surviving spouse is restricted to his or her interest in the community, and receives no share of the decedent's half. A revised version (of 2021) has been enacted in three states and was introduced in a fourth in 2025.

iii. Foreign Country Situations

The problems described under (i) may obviously also arise when the spouses move from a foreign country to the United States or vice versa. In the first case, the result will be the same as discussed above. In the second case, foreign countries that use a "national law" choice-of-law rule may apply the national law of the spouses (i.e., the last U.S. domicile) to issues of succession and marital property. In the European Union, which has now adopted the domicile-at-death approach for the distribution of the estates of decedents who die in an EU state, a person may choose the law of his or her different (non-EU) nationality in his or her testamentary disposition.

d. Debts

Just as there is separate and community *property* in community property states, there are also separate and community *debts.* Separate debts are those incurred before marriage or in the management of separate property thereafter. Again, there can be conflicts between common law and community property states.

Example: W, from a community property state, incurs a debt in a common law state. That debt is her separate debt in the common law state, but W and H own only community property. W defaults on the debt. Does Creditor lose because there is no separate property of W that she can go after? No. By analogy to the quasi-community property concept (*supra* (c)), the property which would have been at risk had the transaction occurred entirely within one state should also be at risk when the transaction crosses state lines. In the example, the community property would have been at risk had W incurred the debt in her home state, and so it should be when she incurs the debt elsewhere. *Not* at risk, i.e., protected, should be H's *separate* property. See *Pacific States Cut Stone Co. v. Goble,* 425 P.2d 631 (Wash. 1967) (en banc), discussed in *Ou Kullasadu Invest v. Kark,* 130 Wash.App. 1008, *3–4 (Wash. Ct.App. 2005).

2. By Contract

Spouses may affect their property rights by the way in which they set up legal ownership to assets (e.g., joint ownership with right to survivorship), by antenuptial agreements, or by contracts entered into after marriage. Agreements may regulate property rights upon death and divorce. Although there is some uncertainty about the validity of these agreements in some states, the trend is toward their recognition if freely adopted by the parties. The *Uniform Marital Property Act* also approves of them. Among community property states, California and Wisconsin recognize these contracts by statute.

The effectiveness of contractual arrangements regarding interspousal property rights is usually governed by the law of the matrimonial domicile. However, courts at the situs have also upheld the parties' intention to vary their property rights.

In *Wyatt v. Fulrath,* 211 N.E.2d 637 (N.Y. 1965), a Spanish couple established a joint account, with rights of survivorship, in New York. Upon H's death, W succeeded to the entire account. Under Spanish law, H's half was not subject to complete disposition by him. New York upheld the choice of its law to govern the couple's property interest. In contrast, *Estate of Clark,* 236 N.E.2d 152 (N.Y. 1968), did not uphold a testamentary disposition selecting New York law and setting up New York trusts, which would have given the widow less than provided by the couple's domicile, Virginia. New York deferred to Virginia law.

Note: *Wyatt* was a *consensual* act by H and W to change their property rights, while *Clark* was a unilateral attempt by H to do so.

III. Contemporary Issues

A. Same-Sex Marriage

Hawaii was the first state to appear willing to recognize formalized same-sex relationships, followed by Vermont, the first state to introduce the concept of a "civil union," and by Massachusetts, the first state to permit same-sex marriage. Most states did not permit it in the first decade of this century. Federal legislation—in the form of an implementing statute under the Full Faith and Credit Clause (28 U.S.C. § 1738C), the "Defense of Marriage Act" (DOMA)—permitted states in its § 2 to refuse recognition to same-sex marriages concluded in sister states; it was a *negative* implementation of the constitutional provision. The Act's § 1 defined marriage as the union between man and woman for federal law purposes (for instance, who qualifies as a surviving "spouse" for social security benefits purposes). In 2013, the U.S. Supreme Court struck down § 1, but did not address the constitutionality of § 2. *United States v. Windsor*, 570 U.S. 744, 133 S. Ct. 2675, 186 L. Ed. 2d 808 (2013). By this time, additional states permitted (and recognized out-of-state) same-sex marriages. Conflict-of-laws problems abounded: whose marriage is recognized where? What are the property and inheritance rights of same-sex partners (depending on the form of their relationship and where asserted)? What about adoption and custody rights?

In 2015, the U.S. Supreme Court addressed same-sex marriage and the constitutionality of § 2 of DOMA in four consolidated cases, decided as *Obergefell v. Hodges*, 576 U.S. 644, 135 S. Ct. 2584, 192 L. Ed. 2d 609 (2015). Writing for the 5–4 majority, Justice Kennedy considered the right to marry ("a keystone of the Nation's social order") and the right to "individual dignity and autonomy" to be "principles and traditions" that inhere in the Due Process Clause of the Fourteenth Amendment, also referring to the Equal Protection Clause. *Id.* at 646, 2590. States therefore may not deny same-sex couples marriage nor refuse to recognize same-sex marriages validly concluded in a sister state. The minority, in separate dissents, shared one common ground: the definition of the Nation's social structure should be left to its elected representatives. Chief Justice Roberts also wondered whether the majority's rationale would not also require acceptance of polygamy.

While these decisions settled the principal legal question—validity and recognition of same-sex marriage—many questions relating to the incidents of a marriage remained undecided. The *Obergefell* decision itself identified many of them in discussing marriage as a "keystone" of the social order: inheritance and property rights, intestate succession, medical decision-making, professional ethics rules, hospital access, visitation rules, and others. The answer to many or most of these questions seems obvious in light of *Obergefell*, but often, the extent to which the decision covers them must still be declared judicially.

Obergefell could have laid to rest social and religious objections held by many. However, such objections gave rise to litigation, and with it, to conflicts issues. One example of resistance was a state agency's refusal to change a death certificate to show the decedent's same-sex married name. That agency was ordered to make the change on the strength of *Obergefell*. *Birchfield v. Armstrong*, No. 4:15–cv–00615, 2017 WL 1319844 (N.D. Fla. Mar. 23, 2017).

Other examples of resistance included free speech and religious belief objections to same-sex marriage. Such objections could have been addressed, but were not, in *Masterpiece Cakeshop v. Colorado Civil Rights Commission*, 584 U.S. 617, 138 S. Ct. 1719, 201 L. Ed. 2d 35 (2018). There, the owner of a bakery refused to create a cake for the celebration of a same-sex marriage. Both the state administrative agency and the Colorado Court of Appeals rejected the bakery owner's First Amendment claims, but the U.S. Supreme Court reversed, citing homophobic sentiment displayed during the administrative procedure. It did not decide whether business considerations, free speech rights, or religious convictions justified the bakeshop's refusal to design and create a wedding cake for a same-sex couple.

In 2022 Congress passed the Respect for Marriage Act. The Act replaces the old § 1738C of 28 U.S.C. The new section prohibits discrimination against a marriage on the basis of sex, race, ethnicity or national origin. Religion is not mentioned but should be covered by the new § 7 of U.S.C. Title 1 which refers to the law of the place of celebration for the determination of a valid marriage. See also *supra* p. 99.

Note that same-sex marriage (or an equivalent) is possible in an increasing number of foreign countries (38 in 2025). A number of Eastern European, African as well as Islamic countries do not recognize it. Some countries provide for some kind of registered domestic partnership. The recognition of foreign-country same-sex marriages in the United States, while not required by the Full Faith and Credit Clause, should pose no problem today (see above). American same-sex marriages, however, may receive differing recognition abroad, depending on the state of domestic legislation on the issue.

B. Non-Marital Partnerships

As mentioned under (A) above, Vermont led the way in providing "civil unions" for same-sex couples as an alternative to marriage. Its 2009 legislation legalizing same-sex marriages (ahead of *Obergefell*) included a provision converting all existing civil unions to marriages on September 1, 2009.

A number of States, cities and communities also recognize "domestic partnerships" of people living together (whether same-sex or heterosexual) in a relationship, short of a common law marriage (which may or not be recognized in the particular State) and not a civil union. Such a partnership may provide insurance rights, health and survivor benefits. It will usually require the partners to register their relationship.

Civil-union legislation or practice also exists in a number of foreign countries. As in the case of foreign-country same-sex marriages (see above), parties to such unions, whether Americans or foreigners, may seek recognition of their relationships in the United States. In this respect the recognition problems do not differ from those discussed above regarding same-sex marriage.

Earlier discussion emphasized that whatever policy view one holds, it may be important to ask for what purpose a recognition question is being raised. See above at p. 131. A New Jersey court followed this approach (before *Obergefell*, while DOMA was still in force) when it held that New Jersey public policy was not offended by recognition of a Vermont civil union for the purpose of a claim for a disabled veteran's property tax exemption. *Hennefeld v. Township of Montclair*, 22 N.J. Tax 166 (N.J. Tax Ct. 2005). The court reached this holding while expressly *not* recognizing the Plaintiffs' Canadian marriage and *not* equating their property rights with those of a married couple. Id. at 202.

The coming Restatement (Third) states in its § 9.03(a) that a state *may* recognize a non-marital relationship that has a legally recognized status where its was formed and—under § 9.04—may also formally dissolve it. The new Restatement's rules regarding matrimonial property rights also apply to non-marital partnerships. § 7.18. These provisions reflect the policy underlying the Respect for Marriage Act as well as 7 U.S.C. § 7. See *supra* at p. 132.

IV. Legitimation

Legitimacy: A child is *"legitimate"* when born after a marriage of its parents. By statute, children of voidable or void marriages are also often considered "legitimate."

Legitimation is the conferral of legitimacy after the child's birth. It may occur as a result of the parents' subsequent marriage or as a result of recognition by the father.

Legitimacy (at birth or through subsequent legitimation) is significant only as it relates to the consequences ("incidents") that flow from it. These nearly always involve inheritance claims.

As a general policy, courts favor legitimacy and its incidents (i.e., equality of all children of the decedent). This finds expression in their choice of a validating law. Thus, when the status of legitimacy is created by another state or nation, the same consequences attach as if legitimation had occurred in the forum. Restatement (Second) § 288 cmt. *b*. As a matter of substantive law, the legitimated child will then be able to inherit.

Courts have even regarded a child as legitimated (and, as such entitled to inherit from a local estate) when the acts of legitimation sufficed under forum law (place of the decedent's domicile at death) but possibly not in the state where they occurred. *In re Estate of Bassi,* 44 Cal. Rptr. 541 (Cal. Dist. Ct. App. 1965). For conclusive presumption of paternity, see *Boettger ex rel. Boettger v. Roberts*, Nos. B156388, B159840, 2003 WL 21084214 (Cal. Ct. App. May 14, 2003).

Illegitimate children inherited from no one at common law, and from the mother by statute. Today, if the father's paternity has been established, the Equal Protection Clause of the Constitution requires that they may inherit the same as legitimate(d) children. State statutes and decisions differ considerably as to how paternity may be established. Some states adhere to the Uniform Parentage Act (1973). Additionally, § 2–109 of the

Uniform Probate Code (in force in whole or in part in 19 states as of 2022) provides that if a state has not adopted the Uniform Parentage Act, a person is a "child" for purposes of interstate succession if paternity was adjudicated before the decedent's death "or is established thereafter by clear and convincing proof. . . ."

V. Adoption

Adoption was unknown to the common law. It is wholly statutory. There are two issues: they relate to a court's *jurisdiction* to grant an adoption and to the *incidents* of adoption. There are no choice-of-law problems; the forum always applies its own law.

A. Jurisdiction

In addition to the case where all parties (natural parents, child, and adoptive parents) are domiciled in the forum state, a court at the *domicile of the child* and with *personal jurisdiction over the child's custodian* will have jurisdiction. Restatement (Second) § 78. In addition, a court at the domicile of the adoptive parents (without more) may have jurisdiction. See *A v. M,* 180 A.2d 541 (N.J. Middlesex Cnty. Ct. 1962). Some decisions have likened jurisdiction for adoption to *in rem* jurisdiction, with the focus on the location of the child. See, e.g., *Lutheran Social Services of New Jersey v. Doe,* 411 A.2d 1183 (N.J. Super. Ct. Law Div. 1979). Note the analogy to the *in rem* idea underlying *ex parte* divorce jurisdiction, *infra.*

The Uniform Adoption Act, in force only in Vermont, has the widest provision: jurisdiction at the place of the petitioner's residence, or of the child's residence, or where the agency that has control over the minor is located.

A parent who stands to lose parental rights (for instance, when an ex-spouse remarries and his or her new spouse wishes to adopt the child) must receive notice and an opportunity to be heard for the adoption decree to be valid. *Armstrong v. Manzo,* 380 U.S. 545, 85 S. Ct. 1187, 14 L. Ed. 2d 62 (1965). However, an unwed father who has not legitimated the child and has not lived in a home situation with the child need not be afforded an opportunity to object. *Lehr v. Robertson,* 463 U.S. 248, 103 S. Ct. 2985, 77 L. Ed. 2d 614 (1983). But see *Heart of Adoptions, Inc. v. J.A.,* 963 So.2d 189, 204 (Fla. 2007) (Lewis, C.J., concurring) (unmarried biological father has a constitutionally protected, inchoate right to develop a relationship with his child, and therefore has a right to notice and to be heard). See also *In re Adoption of S.K.G.,* 257 N.C. App. 540 (N.C. Ct. App. 2018).

State law determines who may adopt whom (e.g., whether singles may adopt children, adults may adopt adults, etc.). This issue has renewed importance as same-sex partners of a marriage or a civil union seek to adopt the child of the other partner. Close to half of the states permit the same-sex partner to adopt the biological child of the other. See, e.g., *In re Jacob,* 660 N.E.2d 397 (N.Y. 1995). Others did or do not. For a decision upholding a state "prohibition on adoption by any 'homosexual' person," see *Lofton v. Secretary of Florida Dept. of Children & Family Services,* 358 F.3d 804 (11th Cir. 2004), *cert. denied,* 543 U.S. 1081, 125 S. Ct. 869, 160 L. Ed. 2d 825 (2005). It would be six more years before the statute in *Lofton* was held to be unconstitutional. *Fla. Dep't of Children & Families v. Adoption of X.X.G.,* 45 So. 3d 79 (Fla. Dist. Ct. App. 2010).

In *V.L. v. E.L.,* 577 U.S. 404, 136 S. Ct. 1017, 194 L. Ed. 2d 92 (2016), the U.S. Supreme Court reversed Alabama's denial of recognition of a Georgia adoption decree in favor of a same-sex couple on full faith and credit grounds. As in *Fauntleroy v. Lum, supra* at p. 107, Alabama was precluded from looking behind the Georgia decree. The Court did not base its decision on *Obergefell,* nor have subsequent state or federal decisions so far. In addition to possibly continuing restrictions on adoption by same-sex couples (expressed in terms of finding the particular family to be unsuitable, considering the best interests of the child), some states, such as Arkansas, also do not allow adoption by unmarried couples by statute.

B. Incidents

An adoption decree entered by a court with competent jurisdiction will generally be recognized everywhere. In the context of same-sex couples, some states recognized an adoptive parent's right (after dissolution of a same-sex relationship) to enforce a custody determination, even if the state would not recognize the underlying relationship. See, e.g., *Giancaspro v. Congleton,* No. 283267, 2009 WL 416301 (Mich. Ct. App. Feb. 19, 2009), *aff'd after remand,* No. 314254, 2013 WL 5663109 (Mich. Ct. App. Oct. 17, 2013).

Occasional contrary decisions refused recognition on the ground that the out-of-state adoption violates local public policy. See, e.g., *Matter of Estate of Griswold,* 354 A.2d 717 (N.J. Morris Cnty. Ct. 1976). These have now been superseded by the U.S. Supreme Court's decision in *V.L. v. E.L.*, *supra* this page.

The effect of the out-of-state decree will be the same as that of a local decree, and the adopted child will usually inherit along with all other children of the adoptive parent. See Restatement (Second) § 290 cmt. *b*.

The effect of the adoption is also in issue when the adopted child claims inheritance rights from its natural parents. The substantive laws of the states are split on this issue. Some states regard adoption as the complete substitution of the new parents for the natural parents, severing all links with the latter. Others permit the child to inherit from both sets of parents.

VI. Review Questions

1. T or F: As a general rule, a marriage valid where contracted will be recognized as valid everywhere.

2. T or F: When a marriage validly contracted in F-1 is contrary to F-2 law with respect to the permitted degrees of consanguinity (marriage between blood relatives) or is bigamous, F-2 may still recognize the marriage for all purposes, in accordance with the general rule (No. 1, above)?

3. a. T or F: Under the community property system, each spouse owns half of what either spouse has acquired after marriage.

b. T or F: Under the common law system, each owns his or her pre-marital property as well as the property he or she acquired after marriage. The other does not share, except for possible inchoate rights, such as dower, or for arrangements entered into by the parties themselves (such as opening and maintaining joint accounts with right of survivorship).

c. T or F: Under either system, the surviving spouse inherits from the decedent.

d. T or F: The nature of immovable property (as common-law or community property) is determined by the law of its situs.

e. T or F: The nature of movable property (as common-law or community property) is determined at the time of its acquisition according to the law of the place where the spouses were married.

f. T or F: When parties move from a state with one type of marital property system to a state with another, the new state's law applies to their property rights after they have become settled there.

g. T or F: When a couple from a community property state moves to a common law property state and reinvests all proceeds from the sale of the property previously held in the first state, the new property will continue to be community property.

h. T or F: When only one spouse owns property and the spouses move from Indiana (a common law state) to California (a community property state) and the spouse owning property dies, now domiciled in the new state, the survivor inherits his or her statutory share unless a will provides for more.

4. T or F: The rights (incidents) accorded children legitimated or adopted elsewhere will generally be the same as those enjoyed by children legitimated or adopted in the forum.

5. Discuss:

a. Same-sex partners from Poland, which does not provide for same-sex marriage, wish to enter into such a marriage in a state of the United States. Having satisfied other requirements (such as length of local residence), will they obtain a license?

b. Some foreign country laws provide for registered same-sex partnerships, but not marriage. How should an American state treat such a relationship if such a couple has now become domiciled here?

Chapter VI

Dissolution of Domestic Relationships and Its Consequences (Support, Custody)

■ ANALYSIS

I. **Introduction and Summary: Issues and Problems Addressed in This Part; Definitions**
   - A. Dissolution of Domestic Relationships
   - B. Support and Custody

II. **Interstate Divorces: *Ex Parte***
   - A. The *Williams* Cases
   - B. The Definition of Domicile for Divorce Jurisdiction
     - 1. State or Federal Law?
     - 2. The *In Rem* Approach and "Minimum Contacts"
   - C. Parties to Collateral Attack
   - D. Is Domicile Really Needed?
   - E. Divisible Divorce

III. **Interstate Divorces: Bilateral**
   - A. The *Sherrer* Doctrine
     - 1. The Parties
     - 2. Third Parties
   - B. Effect of Collateral Determinations of Invalidity

IV. **Incidents of Divorce: Support and Custody**
   - A. Support
   - B. Custody

V. **Annulment**

VI. International Situations
- A. Dissolution of Marriage
  - 1. By Judicial Proceeding
  - 2. Non-Judicial Divorces
- B. Support
- C. Child Custody
- D. Legitimation and Adoption

VII. Review Questions

I. Introduction and Summary: Issues and Problems Addressed in This Part; Definitions

A. Dissolution of Domestic Relationships

A marriage or civil union may be dissolved by *divorce* (or similar decree) or may be declared never to have existed validly at all (*annulment*). In addition, some states may still provide a procedure for a limited divorce (a judicial decree for *separate maintenance*, short of actual dissolution of the marriage). Dissolution by divorce raises no choice-of-law problem. The central question concerns the court's *jurisdiction*, to the end that the change in the parties' status will be recognized elsewhere. In the United States, the court applies forum law. (This may be a problem for recognition abroad of an American divorce of foreigners, see below).

Annulment may raise a choice-of-law problem when jurisdiction is asserted on a basis different from that required for divorce. Separate maintenance raises jurisdictional issues which may or may not be the same as for divorce. Those differences are noted below.

A divorce may be sought by **one** of the spouses in circumstances in which the forum lacks personal jurisdiction over the other (the respondent spouse). This type of divorce is called an *ex parte* divorce. Section II, below, examines the requirements which must be met before a court may issue a decree of divorce, entitled to recognition elsewhere, when only **one** spouse is before it.

Since the divorcing court, in an *ex parte* divorce, lacks jurisdiction over one of the parties, its power to affect the legal relationships of the parties is limited. Section II-E examines this limitation under the heading of "**Divisible Divorce**." See also below (Section B).

When a court does have personal jurisdiction over both parties, its powers to affect the relationship of the parties is broader. Divorces based on personal jurisdiction over both parties are discussed in Section III below under the title "Bilateral Divorces." Section V addresses the extent to which an **annulment** or a decree for separate maintenance raises issues different from those involved in divorce.

The jurisdictional requirements discussed in connection with divorce, separate maintenance, and annulment derive from the U.S. Constitution. If they are satisfied, the resulting decree is entitled to full faith and credit in all states of the Union. A subsequent section of this chapter (Section VI-A) discusses the extent to which divorces decreed in foreign nations—where jurisdiction may be based on criteria other than those constitutionally recognized in the United States—will be given effect in the United States.

B. Support and Custody

A court's jurisdiction to grant a divorce does not necessarily include jurisdiction to deal with other aspects of the post-divorce relationship of the parties, such as support and child custody. To affect these consequences of divorce (the *"incidents"* of divorce), a court traditionally needed *personal jurisdiction* over the respondent. This will naturally be the case when the divorce is *bilateral* (see Section III below). It will not be the case when the divorce is *ex parte* (see Section II below). In the latter case, the court has jurisdiction to grant the divorce, but may lack jurisdiction to affect the incidents of divorce directly. A second proceeding, with personal jurisdiction over the respondent, will then be required to deal with the incidents of divorce. This is the concept of *"divisible divorce."* In a bilateral divorce, unless a court acquires continuing jurisdiction (see above), subsequent modification of a decree dealing with an incident of divorce also requires personal jurisdiction over the respondent. However, with respect to *child custody* and *support,* the adoption of uniform legislation signals a change to the jurisdictional requirements, noted in further detail below. Sections II-E and IV deal with the incidents of divorce.

II. Interstate Divorces: *Ex Parte*

An ex parte divorce is one in which *only the petitioner* is before the divorce court; only the petitioner is subject to its personal jurisdiction.

A. The *Williams* Cases

The early case law was restrictive (and uncertain) concerning a court's power to grant a divorce in the absence of personal jurisdiction (presence or domicile) over both spouses. The landmark decisions in *Williams v. North Carolina* addressed this problem but did not resolve it completely. 317 U.S. 287, 63 S. Ct. 207, 87 L. Ed. 279 (1942) (*Williams I*); 325 U.S. 226, 65 S. Ct. 1092, 89 L. Ed. 1577 (1945) (*Williams II*).

In the *Williams* cases, the husband of one marriage and the wife of another marriage went to Nevada, complied with that state's residence requirement (six weeks), divorced their respective spouses, married each other, and returned to North Carolina. The Nevada court did not have personal jurisdiction over the North Carolina stay-at-home spouses, but they had received notice in North Carolina of the Nevada divorce proceedings. Upon their return to North Carolina, the Nevada newlyweds faced criminal charges for bigamous cohabitation, on the ground that their Nevada divorces were invalid, and that their subsequent marriage to each other was therefore bigamous.

The U.S. Supreme Court held in the first *Williams* decision that the *domicile of the petitioner* is sufficient for divorce jurisdiction. The Court likened an *ex parte* divorce proceeding (i.e., a proceeding in which the petitioner, who is before the court, seeks divorce from a spouse who is not) to a proceeding *in rem.* The *res* before the court is the *marital status* of the parties, and that status is *localized at the domicile of each spouse.* With jurisdiction over the *res,* the court then has power to affect the marital status, for instance, to dissolve the marriage. (Some courts have also used the *in rem* concept to base adoption jurisdiction on the presence of the child.)

Williams I thus established that the state of the petitioner's domicile has jurisdiction to grant a divorce. Whether the state of rendition was the petitioner's domicile, however, is a question of *fact.* Since the absent spouse, by definition, did not have an opportunity to litigate this jurisdictional fact, he or she cannot be precluded by the F-1 decision with respect to this issue. The Supreme Court therefore held in the *Williams II* decision that F-2 may reexamine the existence of the petitioner's domicile in F-1, and with it, F-1's jurisdiction. In *Williams II,* the Supreme Court upheld North Carolina's finding that the parties had not established proper domicile, that their divorces were therefore invalid, and that their subsequent marriage was bigamous.

The *Williams* decisions raise a number of problems. They are outlined in the following subsections.

B. The Definition of Domicile for Divorce Jurisdiction

1. State or Federal Law?

The Supreme Court said in *Williams II* that the definition of domicile for divorce jurisdiction raises a federal question. 325 U.S. at 231 n.7. This is so because *Williams I* involves the Constitution's full faith and credit mandate. If the F-1 court exercised jurisdiction in accordance with constitutional standards, then the Full Faith and Credit Clause applies. *Williams I* held that jurisdiction exists—that due process is satisfied—if the petitioner-spouse has his or her domicile in the forum state. If domicile is required to satisfy due process, it follows that a state cannot define domicile by itself. Otherwise, it could decide for itself whether it has complied with the due process requirement. The Court concluded in *Williams II* that North Carolina's view of the respondents' Nevada domicile was not unreasonable. Thus, rather than provide an independent federal definition of domicile, the Court merely reviewed whether the state court's determination was reasonable. (For the Court's adoption of state law to inform the federal standard, see *infra*.)

Only nine states adopted the *Uniform Divorce Recognition Act* before its withdrawal by the Uniform Law Commission. It contains a presumption that a person, domiciled in an enacting state, who obtains a divorce in another state and returns to the enacting state thereafter, was domiciled in the enacting state at the time of the divorce. Applying the *Williams* decisions, the out-of-state divorce would therefore be invalid. The constitutional validity of the presumption in the Uniform Act, in light of due process considerations, has not been tested.

2. The *In Rem* Approach and "Minimum Contacts"

In *Shaffer v. Heitner,* 433 U.S. 186, 97 S. Ct. 2569, 53 L. Ed. 2d 683 (1977), the U.S. Supreme Court said that all assertions of state court jurisdiction, including those based on *in rem* jurisdiction, must satisfy the "minimum contacts" test of *International Shoe* (*supra*). The question is: are minimum contacts an additional requirement for *ex parte* divorce jurisdiction?

The answer is probably "no" **if** *ex parte* divorce jurisdiction is based on the petitioner's domicile. By definition, domicile is the closest connection a person can have to a state (*supra*); it therefore far exceeds any required "minimum" contacts. The Court also noted in *Shaffer* that its decision is not meant to address traditional bases for jurisdiction in status matters. 433 U.S. at 208 n.30.

May a court assert *ex parte* divorce jurisdiction on a basis *short* of the petitioner's domicile? The answer is less clear; see Section D, below.

For the *in rem* approach to *ex parte* divorce, see *supra*.

C. Parties to Collateral Attack

The respondent spouse may collaterally attack the *ex parte* divorce on jurisdictional grounds. This is so because he or she is not bound by the determination of the underlying jurisdictional facts in an action to which he or she was not a party. Similarly, any other interested party, for instance, an heir, may collaterally attack the F-1 decree. See further below at Section III-A.

D. Is Domicile Really Needed?

Several authorities, including the Restatement (Second) § 72, suggest that a state may exercise *ex parte* divorce jurisdiction when the petitioner has a **close connection** with the state but does not maintain his or her domicile there. To meet the needs of military personnel who may lack the capacity to establish a local domicile (see *supra*), several states have enacted statutes providing for divorce jurisdiction based on specified periods of residence. The court in *Lauterbach v. Lauterbach,* 392 P.2d 24 (Alaska 1964), upheld such a statute on the ground that "domicile is not the sole jurisdictional basis for divorce." Id. at 25. When the durational residence requirement was not met in another Alaska case, the petitioner's one-day presence in Alaska was considered sufficient for her to have become a domiciliary (viz. intent to remain indefinitely). On that basis, exercise of divorce jurisdiction was allowed. *Perito v. Perito,* 756 P.2d 895 (Alaska 1988). See also *Parrott v. Abraham*, 146 S.W.3d 623, 628 (Tenn. Ct. App. 2003). More broadly, Arkansas law bases divorce jurisdiction solely on residence and not on domicile. *Wheat v. Wheat,* 318 S.W.2d 793 (Ark. 1958) (divorce decree not entitled to recognition in a sister state under full faith and credit, because jurisdiction was not based on domicile, would still be valid in the forum state if due process were satisfied). See also *Weaver v. Weaver*, 329 S.W.2d 422, 424 (Ark. 1959) (following *Wheat*). This makes little sense: if full faith and credit requires jurisdiction based on due process, it is hard to see how the due process requirement can be split. Also, is the petitioning spouse served by a divorce that might be valid where rendered but not be recognized elsewhere (for instance, for the purpose of remarriage)?

The *Williams* decisions are not necessarily inconsistent with a wider view of *ex parte* divorce jurisdiction. There, Nevada law itself had equated six weeks of residence in Nevada with Nevada domicile. Nevada law therefore required domicile, and the question before the Supreme Court was only whether domicile was a sufficient basis, not whether it was the *only* basis for *ex parte* divorce jurisdiction. In *Perito*, the divorcing state found that the petitioner had indeed established a local domicile. Would this little change in the facts from the *Williams* cases preclude the stay-at-home respondent and/or his or her state to challenge that conclusion? Would not *Williams II* permit a test of the petitioner's domicile in the divorcing state, on the basis of its own standards?

In *Sosna v. Iowa,* 419 U.S. 393, 95 S. Ct. 553, 42 L. Ed. 2d 532 (1975), the Supreme Court repeated that jurisdiction to divorce is based on domicile. However, the issue in *Sosna* was the validity of a durational (one year) residence requirement *in addition* to domicile. The reference to the domicile requirement in *Sosna* was therefore *dictum*. It is thus possible that *ex parte* divorce jurisdiction on a basis other than domicile will be sanctioned in the future, so long as the absent party receives sufficient notice and an adequate opportunity to be heard. (This is especially the case since, as a consequence of no-fault legislation, substantive differences in state laws have largely disappeared.)

Two further questions remain. First, may a court with proper divorce jurisdiction, either on the basis of domicile or of residence of one or both of the parties, refuse to proceed on *forum non conveniens* grounds? *In re Marriage of Townley & Carraz,* 2014 IL App (4th) 130935-U, answered the first question in the affirmative. The parties had lived in Ireland for many years, and petitioner sought to invoke Illinois divorce jurisdiction because of the state's shorter waiting period. If all relevant evidence (and possibly the respondent) is abroad, application of the *forum non conveniens* doctrine seems appropriate, quite apart from petitioner's motives.

Second, may a court with proper divorce jurisdiction dismiss on the basis of a forum selection clause, adopted by the parties, in favor of another court? *Ofer v. Sirota* answered this second question in the affirmative. 984 N.Y.S.2d 312 (N.Y. App. Div. 2014). The court dismissed in favor of Israel because the parties' antenuptial agreement had so stipulated. The court recognized that New York law specifically sought to facilitate divorce for parties who might be disadvantaged by the husband-orientation of Jewish law (see *infra* at p. 151). However, it gave greater weight to the parties' freedom to enter into a forum selection clause.

E. Divisible Divorce

In an *ex parte* divorce, the granting court's jurisdiction extends only to the status of the parties' marriage. See also *supra*. Absent personal jurisdiction over the respondent, *the court lacks the power to affect the incidents of the marriage*, such as support and custody rights. Its decree will be entitled to recognition in so far as it had jurisdiction (i.e., dissolution of the marriage), but not in so far as it attempted to affect the incidents of marriage without proper jurisdiction to do so. The divorce decree is thus "divisible." *Estin v. Estin,* 334 U.S. 541, 68 S. Ct. 1213, 92 L. Ed. 1561 (1948). When the divorcing court lacks jurisdiction to deal with the incidents of marriage, they must be litigated in a subsequent proceeding in which there is personal jurisdiction over the respondent.

Examples:

1) F-1 grants an *ex parte* divorce to P and awards her alimony. Assuming that P was domiciled in F-1, the divorce is entitled to full faith and credit in F-2 but, absent personal jurisdiction over D, the alimony decree is not.

2) F-1 grants an *ex parte* divorce to P upon a finding that D had committed one of the marital offenses specified in F-1 law. F-2 law provides that a divorced spouse may claim support only if he or she had not been "at fault." Does the F-1 finding preclude D from claiming support in F-2? Not automatically. F-1, assuming that P was domiciled there, did have jurisdiction to dissolve the marriage. However, its finding cannot preclude D absent personal jurisdiction over her, with respect to jurisdictional or *other facts.* She remains free to litigate these in a forum with personal jurisdiction over both parties. The outcome of such litigation, of course, is another matter.

3) Assume that F-2 grants a "wife" or "widow" dower rights in the husband's property. If H obtains an *ex parte* divorce in F-1, what happens to W's dower rights in F-2? They are cut off. This is so *not* because the F-1 decree has an effect in F-2 beyond affecting the *status* of the parties (divorce), but because *F-2 law* conditions her rights on her status as a "wife." F-1 *did* have the power to terminate the status, and F-2 may attach consequences to that status (or lack thereof) with respect to local property. *Simons v. Miami Beach First National Bank,* 381 U.S. 81, 85 S. Ct. 1315, 14 L. Ed. 2d 232 (1965).

III. Interstate Divorces: Bilateral

A. The *Sherrer* Doctrine

1. The Parties

When both parties participate in a divorce, ordinary principles of preclusion apply. Unless raised by appeal, defects underlying the F-1 decree (except perhaps for certain species of fraud) are lost when that decree becomes final; they cannot be raised collaterally. (For discussion of *preclusion* and the *full faith and credit* requirement for the recognition of judgments, see *supra* Chapter IV Section I(B). Thus, even though a party's domicile may be required for the court's jurisdiction to grant a divorce, when both parties participate, the absence of domicile cannot be raised collaterally. Since it could have been raised in the F-1 proceeding, it is *res judicata*. *Sherrer v. Sherrer,* 334 U.S. 343, 68 S. Ct. 1087, 92 L. Ed. 1429 (1948). "Participation" in this context means that the respondent entered an appearance that afforded him or her an opportunity to be heard, *Cook v. Cook,* 342 U.S. 126, 72 S. Ct. 157, 96 L. Ed. 146 (1951), or was subject to personal jurisdiction in the forum state by long-arm statute or otherwise.

2. Third Parties

Parties in privity with a former spouse, such as children, are bound by a decree and will be barred from a collateral attack the same as the spouses themselves. *Johnson v. Muelberger,* 340 U.S. 581, 71 S. Ct. 474, 95 L. Ed. 552 (1951) (daughter). Persons not in privity with the former spouse(s) have sometimes also been barred from a collateral attack. See, e.g., *Cook* (second husband). The Supreme Court has not (again) addressed the question whether the former home state of the parties, such as in the *Williams* cases, may collaterally attack a divorce when it was procured bilaterally and not *ex parte* (as in *Williams*). Since it was not in privity, the home state technically is not precluded. The suggested answer, however, is that the home state is not a "third party to the marriage relationship" and thus has *no standing* to raise jurisdictional defects. Decisions like those in *Williams* must therefore be restricted to their context: the home state protecting the societal interest of the home state in and on behalf of the resident stay-at-home spouse.

B. Effect of Collateral Determinations of Invalidity

Assume that F-1 has granted an *ex parte* divorce and has even done so upon the express jurisdictional finding that the petitioner spouse was domiciled there. Since the absent spouse was not bound by the jurisdictional determination in the *ex parte* proceeding, she collaterally attacked the F-1 decree in F-2 in a proceeding with personal jurisdiction over the F-1 petitioner. F-2 finds that F-1 lacked jurisdiction and holds the F-1 divorce to be invalid. What is the effect of the F-2 determination on the validity of the F-1 decree in F-1? The F-1 decree is invalid *everywhere,* including in F-1.

In *Colby v. Colby,* 369 P.2d 1019 (Nev. 1962), the Nevada court refused to recognize a Maryland determination that a prior Nevada *ex parte* divorce was not valid. It reasoned that the Maryland decree was not entitled to more faith and credit than its own earlier decree. This view is probably erroneous. On the facts of *Colby,* the Maryland decision was the first to determine *conclusively for both parties* the existence or nonexistence of facts requisite to give Nevada divorce jurisdiction. The Nevada court's argument assumes that both decisions are valid, when in fact, the very issue in Maryland was the validity of the Nevada decision. The F-2 decision (here, that of Maryland) is entitled to full faith and credit. By dictum, the Supreme Court has so held. *Sutton v. Leib,* 342 U.S. 402, 72 S. Ct. 398, 96 L. Ed. 448 (1952). Accord *Campion v. State, Dep't of Community & Regional Affairs, Hous. Assistance Div.,* 876 P.2d 1096, 1100 (Alaska 1994); *Winkler v. Stowe,* No. 95 CA 763, 1997 WL 30947, at *5 (Ohio Ct. App. Jan. 21, 1997) (citing an early edition of the *Hornbook*).

IV. Incidents of Divorce: Support and Custody

A. Support

As noted before, a court must have *personal jurisdiction* over the respondent to enter a support decree against him or her. Jurisdiction based upon attachment of the respondent's in-state property (*quasi in rem* jurisdiction) is no longer constitutional. See *Shaffer v. Heitner,* 433 U.S. 186, 97 S. Ct. 2569, 53 L. Ed. 2d 683 (1977).

Except for isolated and unusual statutes permitting the assertion of jurisdiction over an absent respondent when the forum state was the state of the parties' last matrimonial domicile, the usual requirements for personal jurisdiction apply. Thus, **the respondent himself must have brought about a relationship between the forum state and himself;** the *petitioner's* relationship to the forum state is not enough. Even when the absent respondent father permits a change of residence of the parties' children from his state to that of the petitioner mother, the children's move has been held insufficient to establish the necessary nexus between the respondent and the forum state. *Kulko v. Superior Court,* 436 U.S. 84, 98 S. Ct. 1690, 56 L. Ed. 2d 132 (1978).

To alleviate the plight of obligees who cannot satisfy the usual jurisdictional requirements, the **Uniform Interstate Family Support Act (UIFSA)** has now been adopted by all states. It replaces a previous uniform law, the Uniform Reciprocal Enforcement of Support Act (URESA).

The Act provides for interstate judicial assistance for the establishment of support decrees. Once a child support order has issued, the court has continuing, exclusive jurisdiction over the order so long as the obligor, the obligee (generally, the custodial parent), or the child resides in the state, unless each party consents in writing that a court of another state may assume jurisdiction and modify the order. *Hornblower v. Hornblower,* 94 A.3d 1218, 1222 n.5 (Conn. App. Ct. 2014); *Malpeso v. Malpeso,* No. FSTFA010185205S, 2015 WL 1086692 (Conn. Super. Ct. Feb. 17, 2015). The same applies to spousal support orders. But, in responding to a request for enforcement of an order of another state, the requested court may review the support duty and its amount on the basis of "the support guidelines of this state." UIFSA applies to support orders of foreign countries that have substantially similar procedures (for instance, Canada).

The Full Faith and Credit for Child Support Orders Act of 1994 is a further implementation of the "effect" provision of the Full Faith and Credit Clause and appears as 28 U.S.C. § 1738B. It requires F-2 to enforce F-1's child support order "according to its terms" and to interpret it according to F-1 law.

B. Custody

In an early decision, *People ex rel. Halvey v. Halvey,* 330 U.S. 610, 67 S. Ct. 903, 91 L. Ed. 1133 (1947), the U.S. Supreme Court upheld the right of New York to modify a custody decree rendered by Florida. The narrow ground for the decision was that, since custody decrees are never final, F-2 could modify to the same extent that F-1, the original state of rendition, could or would. Additionally, in *Halvey,* New York had acquired jurisdiction over the child before the Florida decree had come down. *Halvey,* therefore, did not address the extent to which an F-1 custody decree is binding:

- when both parents were before the F-1 court (at least with respect to the facts then existing);
- when one parent had wrongfully removed a child from the control of the custodial parent to seek modification in F-2;
- or when F-1—with jurisdiction over *one* parent and a child—intended to adjudicate the custody question as a matter of the child's *status,* very much akin to its exercise of jurisdiction in *ex parte* divorces (*supra* at p. 140).

As a result, courts freely asserted jurisdiction in custody matters to modify, on the (asserted) ground of changed circumstances, the earlier decree of another state, often in express recognition of the possibility that the new decree would similarly be modified subsequently elsewhere. See *Sampsell v. Superior Court,* 197 P.2d 739 (Cal. 1948). Large-scale child snatching ensued when parents, disappointed by the outcome in F-1, sought a modification in F-2 or, worse, used the child custody disagreement as a way to get at the ex-spouse. A few courts stemmed the worst excesses by adopting a "clean hands" requirement, refusing to entertain claims by parents who had removed children in violation of a sister-state's custody decree. See *Ferreira v. Ferreira,* 512 P.2d 304 (Cal. 1973). Nevertheless, the problem acquired national, and even international, dimensions in the 1960s.

The U.S. Supreme Court's decision in *May v. Anderson,* 345 U.S. 528, 73 S. Ct. 840, 97 L. Ed. 1221 (1953), contributed to the confusion about the extent of F-1's jurisdictional reach and the recognition that should be accorded its decrees. On its face, the decision requires personal jurisdiction over *both* parties for custody decisions (a) to be binding where rendered and (b) to be entitled to recognition in other states.

In *May,* the father obtained a custody decree in Wisconsin, incident to a divorce, when the mother and the child were both in Ohio, although the child probably had its domicile in Wisconsin (see "derivative domicile," *supra* at Chapter II, Section II(D)(1).) A plurality of four Justices regarded custody proceedings as involving issues "incident to a divorce," i.e., the same as property rights. As with all rights incident to a divorce (see "divisible divorce," *supra* at p. 143), the binding resolution of such an incident requires personal jurisdiction over the other party.

One Justice took the position that Ohio was free to recognize (or to not recognize) the Wisconsin decree; the lack of finality of a custody decree would justify this freedom. No issue of lack of due process in the Wisconsin proceeding was involved, according to this view. Three Justices, in dissent, regarded custody proceedings as status decisions, very much like *ex parte* divorces (*supra* at p. 140 *et seq.*), with the result that proper jurisdiction over the child (akin to *in rem* jurisdiction) would be the single jurisdictional issue.

The meaning of *May v. Anderson* has been much disputed. One view points to the position of the concurrence—that the narrowest ground on which the plurality and the concurrence agreed should be regarded as the rule of the case. Nevertheless, three dissenting judges understood the plurality as saying that Wisconsin lacked personal jurisdiction over the mother, that its decree was therefore flawed for due process reasons, and that it was not entitled to recognition in Ohio. It is this view with which the dissent disagreed. Thus, seven Justices thought that the rule of *May* was founded on constitutional (due process) concerns.

The **Uniform Child Custody Jurisdiction and Enforcement Act (UCCJEA)**, which replaced the Uniform Child Custody Jurisdiction Act, identifies a "home state" with primary jurisdiction to award or to modify child custody. When F-1 meets the requirement of being the "home state," the Act provides that other states should defer to its jurisdiction. Unlike its predecessor, the UCCJEA provides for *continuing exclusive jurisdiction* in the court making the original order. This is so unless the case no longer has a "significant connection" with the state, or the court considers itself an inconvenient forum (for instance, when the child has moved away).

The **Federal Parental Kidnapping Prevention Act** of 1980, 28 U.S.C. § 1738A, requires that states give full faith and credit to custody decrees rendered by a court with jurisdiction essentially as defined by the Uniform Acts. But see, e.g., *In re L.S.*, 257 P.3d 201, 204 (Colo. 2011) (en banc) (Colorado need not recognize Nevada custody decree because Nevada was not the child's home state and therefore lacked jurisdiction); *In re Marriage of Dedie & Springston*, 255 P.3d 1142 (Colo. 2011) (en banc) (following *In re L.S.*). See also *People In Interest of S.L.S.*, 2025 WL 227376 *2 ¶¶ 13–14 (Colo.Ct.App.2025).

The Federal Act does not confer jurisdiction on federal courts to grant or modify custody. It is a statute mandating full faith and credit to *state* court decisions. Federal courts also do not have jurisdiction to decide which of two or more competing state courts has original jurisdiction. Instead, as in all cases involving a state's duty under the full faith and credit requirement, the *initial jurisdictional decision* also rests with the *state courts,* to be reviewed on constitutional grounds by way of subsequent appeal. "[T]he Full Faith and Credit Clause . . . does not give rise to an [independent] federal cause of action." *Thompson v. Thompson,* 484 U.S. 174, 182, 108 S. Ct. 513, 518, 98 L. Ed. 2d 512 (1988). See also *Kee v. Hines*, No. C 17-3780 SBA, 2018 WL 789586 (N.D. Cal. Feb. 8, 2018).

The U.S. Supreme Court has not yet addressed the constitutionality of the Uniform Acts. The interpretation of *May v. Anderson* suggested above would cast doubt on the validity of custody decisions that are based on personal jurisdiction over the child and one contestant, but not both. Nonetheless, it is widely assumed that the Supreme Court would uphold the validity of the Uniform Acts, perhaps by adopting the rationale of the dissenters in *May*.

The Parental Kidnapping Prevention Act—implementing the Full Faith and Credit Clause—of course does not apply to international situations. They are the subject of the **Hague Convention on the Civil Aspects of International Child Abduction**. The United States ratified the Convention, and it entered into force in 1988. Like the interstate Uniform Acts, the Hague Convention requires deference to valid foreign custody decrees and the return of the child, except in special emergency cases, to the foreign jurisdiction from where it was wrongfully taken. However, in *Golan v. Saada*, the U.S. Supreme Court held that a court need not consider "ameliorative measures" after finding that the return of a child to a foreign country involves a "grave risk" of harm to the child. 596 U.S. 666, 142 S. Ct. 1880 (2022); Yuriiovych v. Hryhorivna, 730 F.Supp.3d 1119, at 1128, 1132 (D.Mont. 2024); *Ciampa v. Nichols*, 2025 WL 521009 (C.D.Cal.2025); *Elkaiat v. Mawashi*, 2025 WL 711949 (D.Ariz. 2025). See also next paragraph.

The Convention was implemented by the **International Child Abduction Remedies Act** (ICARA), 22 U.S.C.A. § 9001–11 (West 2022) (formerly cited as 42 U.S.C.A. § 11601). Illustrative decisions include *Navani v. Shahani*, 496 F.3d 1121 (10th Cir. 2007) and *Crane v. Merriman*, No. CIV-17-849-D, 2017 WL 4079406 (W.D. Okla. Sept. 14, 2017); *Olga Sugey Centano Aguirre v. Hernandez*, 757 F.Supp.3d 1211 (D.Colo.2024). The federal **International Parental Kidnapping Crime Act** of 1993, 18 U.S.C.A. § 1204 (West 2022) proscribes the removal of children from the United States in violation of "parental rights," including those under a custody decree. See, e.g., *United States v. Patel*, No. 20–613 (RMB), 2022 WL 500567 (D.N.J. Feb. 18, 2022) (slip op.) (no violation); *United States v. Helbrans*, No. S3 19-CR-497 (NSR), 2022 WL 562930 (S.D.N.Y. Feb. 22, 2022) (slip op.) (violation). The European Union has adopted Union-wide legislation to the same effect. Council Regulation 2201/2003, Concerning Jurisdiction and the Recognition and Enforcement of Judgments in Matrimonial Matters and the Matters of Parental Responsibility, 2003 O.J. (L 338) 1 (EC).

V. Annulment

An annulment is the judicial determination that the marriage of the parties never existed because of impediments present at the time of the attempted marriage, such as non-age (minority) or the existence of a valid prior marriage. In some states, grounds for annulment—such as bigamy (the existence of a valid prior marriage)—are also grounds for divorce. Though this is illogical, it is explained by the fact that termination of a status by divorce might result in a support obligation, while a finding that the status never existed would not carry with it such an obligation.

As in most domestic relations cases, there is usually no choice-of-law problem. Courts will apply forum law if they have jurisdiction (but see #4, below). That said, the question of when a court has jurisdiction to decree an annulment has not been finally settled.

1) The easiest case involves an annulment proceeding at the common domicile of the parties when that state is also the place of celebration of the purported marriage. There need be no inquiry whether jurisdiction is *in personam* or *in rem*, and since the forum state and the state of celebration are the same, local law will of course be applied.

2) If the forum is the domicile of the petitioner, jurisdiction has been upheld in analogy to the *in rem*-type of jurisdiction in *ex parte* divorce cases (above at p. 140 *et seq.*). Restatement (Second) § 76(a). The analogy is not quite proper: in *ex parte* divorces, the status of the marriage (the *res*) confers jurisdiction, while in annulment, the very object of the proceeding is the determination that there is *no* status, *no* res.

3) If the forum is the place of celebration and has personal jurisdiction over both spouses, jurisdiction has been considered proper. See Restatement (Second) § 76(b).

4) Jurisdiction has also been upheld when the forum merely has personal jurisdiction over both spouses. *Whealton v. Whealton*, 432 P.2d 979 (Cal. 1967). This seems proper for two reasons. First, courts may adjudicate personal claims when they have personal jurisdiction over both parties. Second, even if *in rem*-type jurisdiction were needed, jurisdictional objections are lost if not appealed. *Sherrer, supra* at p. 144. The

only question in cases in which jurisdiction is founded merely upon personal jurisdiction over the parties (see also #3, above) is whether the court is still justified in applying forum law. It seems that annulment cases are no different from others in which the permissibility of applying local law is in issue: whether it applies depends on the relationship of the forum to the parties and to the issue (see Chapter X below). Because of the societal values involved in domestic relations cases, it may be that *mere* personal jurisdiction, without some connection to the purported marital relationship, is not enough. The modern view therefore favors application of the law of the place of celebration. See Restatement (Second) § 286, in connection with § 283(2).

Judicial separation used to be called a "limited divorce," or divorce from bed and board, though it is not really a divorce. It usually regulates support rights while the parties live separately but continue to be married. Jurisdiction exists at the domicile, and with respect to personal rights, in the state where there is personal jurisdiction over the respondent. A decree for separate maintenance (awarding support) will not be affected by a subsequent *ex parte* divorce obtained by the obligor. *Estin v. Estin,* 334 U.S. 541, 68 S. Ct. 1213, 92 L. Ed. 1561 (1948).

VI. International Situations

A. Dissolution of Marriage

1. By Judicial Proceeding

In principle, foreign-country divorces are recognized in the United States on the same basis as sister-state divorces. There may be a problem, however, because many foreign countries do not require domicile of one of the parties as a condition for divorce jurisdiction. Instead, they may base jurisdiction only on residence. However, unlike American law, they will then often apply the substantive law of the parties' home state(s). In an interstate case in the United States, the personal appearance of both parties (bilateral divorce) would mean that the jurisdictional issue (lack of domicile) is lost for purposes of collateral attack for want of appeal. *Sherrer*, above. In the foreign-country case, the *Sherrer* doctrine does not apply because the objection that jurisdiction may need to be based on *domicile* (U.S. law) is not available under the foreign forum's law (where the U.S. Constitution of course does not furnish the standard for review).

At a time when divorce could be obtained only on very limited fault grounds in parts of the U.S., the availability of "quickie" divorces on no-fault grounds in some foreign countries became very attractive. In *Rosenstiel v. Rosenstiel,* 209 N.E.2d 709 (1965), the New York Court of Appeals was asked to recognize a Mexican divorce in which jurisdiction was based on little more than the parties' appearance (although, in *Rosenstiel*, there had been a formal entry in a record of the petitioners Mexican "residence").

The New York court noted that the strict substantive requirements of New York divorce law (at that time) could also be avoided by a divorce in Nevada, so that the only difference between a Nevada divorce (mandated to be recognized under the Full Faith and Credit Clause) and a Mexican divorce (not entitled to the same automatic recognition) was the durational residence requirement (six weeks in Nevada versus virtually none in Mexico). The court, over strong dissent, held—in effect—that bilateral foreign divorces are entitled to recognition, even though domicile was not a jurisdictional requirement in the country of rendition.

Rosenstiel thus also lends support to the suggestion that divorce jurisdiction may be based on something other than domicile (*supra*). The Mexican law that gave rise to *Rosenstiel* has meanwhile been changed. But "quickie" divorces can now be obtained in Haiti and the Dominican Republic, so their validity continues to raise an important question. ("Quickie" divorces can also be obtained in Guam, a U.S. territory, so interstate recognition principles apply.)

In addition to New York, other states have accepted the result in *Rosenstiel,* although on differing grounds. Some simply estop the parties from questioning their foreign divorce. Others recognize, as had New York, that divorce jurisdiction may be based on mere personal jurisdiction. See *Adjei v. Mayorkas,* 59 F.4th 659 (2023). A number of other states have expressly rejected the *Rosenstiel* result. The majority of states have not addressed the issue.

A "quickie" divorce that is really a sham will not be recognized. *Kushnick v. Kushnick,* 763 N.Y.S.2d 889 (N.Y. Sup. Ct. 2003) (petitioner merely filled out an internet form, and never resided in Mexico; respondent had not received notice); *Jiminez v. De La Cruz,* No. FA156058052, 2017 WL 4653025 (Conn. Super. Ct. Sept. 5, 2017) (neither party had appeared, although the Dominican court had set a time for the proceeding and then entered a decree on that date without a hearing).

The validity of an out of state divorce usually is not in issue by itself. It generally arises in a different context, such as a property settlement, a support claim, or a child custody proceeding. Thus, if a state—as part of a different proceeding—recognizes the foreign-country divorce, this issue (the validity of the foreign-country divorce) becomes *res judicata,* and as any other issue decided by a U.S. state court, is thus entitled to full faith and credit in the other states. In effect, a foreign country divorce may be "domesticated" in a proceeding in one of the states of the Union that recognizes such divorces. Recall that in *Kulko v. Superior Court,* 436 U.S. 84, 98 S. Ct. 1690, 56 L. Ed. 2d 132 (1978), the Court observed that Mrs. Horn, formerly Mrs. Kulko, had obtained a Haitian divorce. She had flown there in person, and her husband, Mr. Kulko, had appeared through an attorney. Id. at 87 n.1, 1694 n.1. The California court had assumed the validity of the divorce and of Mr. Kulko's obligation to make child support payments to his former wife. The U.S. Supreme Court did not question this assumption.

Foreign-country divorces based only on personal jurisdiction will generally be recognized. In most cases, the existence of domicile will be assumed, in that the foreign requirement of "residence" will be read to be the equivalent of the American domicile. (In the case of foreign bilateral divorces that are clearly "quickie" divorces, a court willing to accept such a divorce will look for the respondent spouse's actual consent to jurisdiction.)

Mail order divorces and other sham arrangements (for instance, marriages to gain entry into the United States as a "spouse" of a citizen), let alone *unilateral* divorces without domicile of the petitioner, will not be recognized. Some sham divorces will even be open to challenge by public bodies.

It was noted at the beginning of this subsection that foreign countries will often base jurisdiction on less than domicile but then apply the parties' home-state law. Since we do it the other way around, foreign parties who obtain an American divorce may face recognition difficulties in their home state because the American court did not apply home-state law (it applied forum law). If the parties' home state would not recognize the American divorce for this reason, remarriage would be precluded or bigamous.

2. Non-Judicial Divorces

In the United States, divorce requires a judicial decree. Traditionally, it is entered after a spouse has filed a petition for a divorce, the respondent has answered, and there has been a hearing (bilateral divorce), or after the court goes ahead in the absence of the respondent (*ex parte* divorce). More recently, the *Uniform Collaborative Law Act* provides for settlement of disputes through negotiation, such that parties may tailor the outcome of their dispute to their particular needs. A section of the Act applies to family law matters, including divorce. Of some twenty-three jurisdictions in which the Act is in force, six restrict its use to family law matters. The outcome of this collaborative process of negotiation still requires a court decree to give it binding effect. In that respect, it still differs from purely private forms of divorce, such as religious divorces (immediately following) or rituals derived from custom, as in some countries.

Talaq. Under Islamic law, a husband may divorce his wife by three times repeating words of divorce (*talaq*). Indeed, it has been held that a *talaq* by e-mail is effective. See answer provided by IslamQA: http://www.islamqa.info/en/answers/36761/ruling-on-divorce-via-e-mail with reference to 28/Dhu al-Qi'dah/1424 of Jan. 20 (2004) (last visited Jan. 27, 2026). When a divorce by *talaq* occurs abroad and is valid where pronounced, the divorce will often be recognized, in particular, when one of the parties has remarried. However, the fact that the pronouncement of a *talaq* is the unilateral right of the man has caused some courts to deny comity to such a divorce on public policy grounds. *Aleem v. Aleem,* 947 A.2d 489 (Md. 2008); *Tarikonda v. Pinjari,* No. 287403, 2009 WL 930007 (Mich. Ct. App. Apr. 7, 2009). On comity see also *In re Estate of Mehdi Ahmad,* 2023 WL 2607377 *4 (Md. App. 2023). Contra *Ashfaq v. Ashfaq,* 467 S.W.3d 539 (Tex. App. 2015) (adequate notice to wife satisfied due process concerns for recognition of a Pakistani divorce). The continued use of divorce by *talaq* is much debated in the Islamic world: the Supreme Court of India held the practice to be unconstitutional by a 3:2 decision in 2017. Dhananjay Mahapatra, *Supreme Court Declares Triple Talaq Unconstitutional, Strikes It Down By 3:2 Majority*, The Times of India, Aug. 22, 2017, available at https://timesofindia.indiatimes.com/india/supreme-court-bars-triple-talaq-for-6-months-until-parliament-legislates-on-issue/articleshow/60170130.cms (last visited Aug. 21, 2022) (discussing *Bano v. Union of India,* 9 S.C.C. 1 (India)).

Get. Under Jewish religious law, the husband must give the wife a letter of divorcement (*get*); she can force the issuance of a *get* only exceptionally, and with the help of the Rabbinical Court. To counteract this one-sidedness, New York law requires a man to remove all impediments to the remarriage of the spouse (i.e., to issue a *get*) before he can obtain a New York civil divorce. N.Y. Dom. Rel. Law § 253 (McKinney 2022). New York courts have also held husbands in contempt for non-compliance with orders to provide a *get*. *Kaplinsky v. Kaplinsky*, 603 N.Y.S.2d 574 (N.Y. App. Div. 1993); *Schwartz v. Schwartz*, 913

N.Y.S.2d 313 (N.Y. App. Div. 2010); *Satz v. Satz,* 301 A.3d 847 (N.J. Super. A.D. 2023). See also *Ofer v. Sirota,* 984 N.Y.S.2d 312 (N.Y. App. Div. 2014) (enforcing an antenuptial agreement in favor of Israel), *supra* at p. 143. A New Jersey court, in contrast, held that courts lacked power to order husbands to provide a *get*. *Mayer-Kolker v. Kolker,* 819 A.2d 17 (N.J. Super. Ct. App. Div. 2003).

Native American Indian law regulates domestic relations of members of the particular Nation on the reservation. The law of the Navajo Nation permits and will recognize informal marriage, either in the form of a common law marriage or one performed by a medicine man. However, formal dissolution of a marriage and formal certification of divorce is needed for the latter to be valid. *United States v. Jarvison,* 409 F.3d 1221, 1230 (10th Cir. 2005). Again, recognition elsewhere would depend on the validity of the divorce on the Nation's reservation. See *Beller ex rel. Beller v. U.S.,* 221 F.R.D. 679 (D.N.M. 2003) (Navajo common law marriage recognized for purpose of invoking marital privilege when sought to be deposed in civil action). See also *United States v. Murphy,* 2021 WL 646852 (E.D.Okla. 2021) when two different tribes are involved. See generally *Begay v. Miller,* 222 P.2d 624 (Ariz. 1950) (history of jurisdiction of reservations of Indian Nations in domestic matters).

B. Support

Foreign-country *judgments* that reduce a support obligation to a money judgment are recognized in the United States like any other money judgment. The *obligation* established by the foreign decree usually is not so readily recognized, and thus enjoys less force than a comparable sister-state decree for future support or for past installments not yet reduced to judgment. The *Uniform Foreign Money-Judgments Recognition Act* and its successor, the *Uniform Foreign-Country Money Judgments Recognition Act, supra,* also expressly *exclude* foreign-country support decrees. However, the need for international cooperation in support matters has been recognized, just as the need for interstate cooperation led to the Uniform Interstate Family Support Act. Pursuant to the policy of the Act, a number of U.S. jurisdictions have entered into reciprocal arrangements with foreign nations.

C. Child Custody

Section 23 of the *Uniform Child Custody Jurisdiction Act* extended recognition to foreign-country custody decrees rendered pursuant to the principles of the Act. A few states omitted § 23 when adopting the Act, and as a consequence, refused recognition to foreign custody decrees. In contrast, some courts, although not required to do so, deferred to the foreign court, ordering the parties to exhaust their remedies there. See, e.g., *Custody of a Minor (No. 3),* 468 N.E.2d 251 (Mass. 1984) (holding that a father residing in Australia was entitled to enforcement of a child custody order by an Australian court in Massachusetts); *Al-Ajmi v. Turki,* 87 Mass.App.Ct. 1121, No. 14-P-279 (Mass. App. Ct., 2015) (Saudi Arabia). Cf. *Tazziz v. Tazziz,* 533 N.E.2d 202 (Mass. App. Ct. 1988) (Israel). Section 105 of the new *Uniform Child Custody Jurisdiction and Enforcement Act, supra,* provides for the recognition of foreign-country custody determinations "made . . . in substantial conformity with the jurisdictional standards of this . . ." act, but not "if the child custody law of a foreign country violates fundamental principles of human rights."

Since 1988, the United States has been a party to the *Hague Convention on the Civil Aspects of International Child Abduction.* The Convention parallels the Uniform Child Custody Jurisdiction and Enforcement Act in that it requires deference to the court with principal jurisdiction. In particular, this means the return of a child removed in contravention of the decree of a court that had jurisdiction in the matter. The Convention does not purport to define "jurisdiction," thus deferring to national law. In the United States, that law is the Uniform Acts, discussed earlier, as "federalized" by the *Parental Kidnapping Prevention Act*, and supplemented by the *International Child Abduction Remedies Act* (ICARA) (above). The Convention, as a treaty, governs international cases in all states of the Union (under the Supremacy Clause). The Convention (and the implementing American law) do not require the return of the child if doing so would expose the child to a "grave risk of harm." What must a court consider? How extensive must its examination be? While it may consider, in its discretion, that certain facts minimize the threat of harm, the U.S. Supreme Court has held that the trial court need not "consider *all* ameliorative measures," and remanded a case in which that had been required. *Golan v. Saada*, 596 U.S. 666, 142 S. Ct. 1880, 1887 (2022) (emphasis added).

In *Abbott v. Abbott*, 560 U.S. 1, 130 S. Ct. 1983, 176 L. Ed. 2d 789 (2010), the U.S. Supreme Court held that "custody" under the Convention extends to rights of access and *ne exeat* provisions. However, the general exception to the duty to return a child also applies here, when return would pose a danger to the child. See, e.g., *Leonard v. Lentz*, 288 F. Supp. 3d 945 (N.D. Iowa 2018) (after kidney transplant, child should remain close to Iowa hospital and not be returned to Turkey right away). In *Lozano v. Montoya Alvarez*, 572 U.S. 1, 134 S. Ct. 1224, 188 L. Ed. 2d 200 (2014), the U.S. Supreme Court held that "equitable tolling" does not apply to treaties, and therefore also not to the Convention's one-year limitation for seeking the return of a child. For the federal International Parental Kidnapping Crime Act of 1993, see above.

D. Legitimation and Adoption

As discussed in the interstate context, *supra* Chapter V (IV–V), legitimation and adoption issues usually arise when litigation concerns a property claim, such as the right to inherit from the adoptive parent. Since these incidents are usually governed by forum law, the fact that legitimation or adoption occurred abroad, rather than in a sister state, will usually be irrelevant. The international element may be relevant when a U.S. adoption is in issue abroad. Some foreign countries require the application of the adopted child's personal law and may refuse recognition to an adoption based on a different law. The result may then also be denial of incidents (property rights claims).

VII. Review Questions

1. T or F: In an *ex parte* divorce, only the petitioner is before the court.

2. T or F: For an *ex parte* divorce to be entitled to recognition in other states,

a. The *Williams* cases have been interpreted as requiring that the petitioner was domiciled in the state granting the divorce.

b. The *Williams* cases technically leave open whether another close connection to the divorcing state will also confer jurisdiction.

3. T or F: When both spouses were before the F-1 divorcing court in a state of the United States (by participating, appearance, service based upon proper jurisdiction, including under long-arm statute)—i.e., when the divorce is "bilateral"—F-2 must recognize the divorce, even when it is clear that neither of the ex-spouses was domiciled in F-1 at the time.

4. T or F: Question 3 would have the same result if F-1 were a foreign country.

5. T or F: A bilateral divorce also precludes third parties, such as children, from attacking it on jurisdictional grounds.

6. T or F: In any divorce, the divorcing court may determine the parties' support and custody rights along with the divorce itself.

7. T or F: The "divisible divorce" concept arises in connection with *ex parte* divorces.

8. T or F: A divorce by *talaq* pronounced in a foreign country will be recognized in the United States.

9. T or F: When a Jewish husband has delivered a *get* to his Jewish wife in New York, both parties are free to remarry.

10. T or F: A spouse may obtain a decree awarding support (or a judgment modifying an earlier decree) in an action with personal jurisdiction over the respondent or by utilizing the procedures of the Uniform Interstate Family Support Act.

11. T or F: "Child-snatching" by the non-custodial parent can be prevented by making sure that the court awarding custody had jurisdiction over, and therefore could bind, both parents.

12. T or F: Annulment may be granted at the petitioner's domicile or by the court with personal jurisdiction over both parties, following divorce-jurisdiction analogies.

13. T or F: The Uniform Child Custody Jurisdiction and Enforcement Act (with state court decisions under it given full faith and credit effect by the Federal Parental Kidnapping Prevention Act) should be an effective solution to custody battles and resulting "child-snatching." Why?

14. T or F: *"Incidents"* in family law cases refer to the *personal consequences* (rights and obligations)—such as support, custody, inheritance rights—which flow from the *status* of "spouse," "parent," "adopted child," and so forth.

15. T or F: F-2 must give full faith and credit to a modifiable F-1 child support decree.

16. T or F: Under the Uniform Child Custody Jurisdiction and Enforcement Act, just as under the UCCJA before it, the F-2 court may assume jurisdiction and may modify the original order when the child has lawfully lived in F-1 such that F-1 has become the child's home state.

Part Four

Choice of Law: Basic Considerations

■ ANALYSIS

VII. Pervasive Problems
VIII. Approaches to Choice of Law: Theory

Chapter VII

Pervasive Problems

■ ANALYSIS

I. **Introduction**
- A. Jurisdiction and Choice of Law
- B. Sources for the Choice-of-Law Decision
- C. Pervasive Problems

II. **Characterization: Subject Matter**

III. **Characterization: Substance or Procedure**
- A. In General
- B. What Law Determines How an Issue Should Be Characterized?
- C. Statute of Frauds
- D. Statute of Limitations
  - 1. The Traditional Approach
  - 2. Modern Approaches
    - a. Case Law
    - b. The Uniform Conflict of Laws Limitations Act
    - c. Restatement (Second) and (Third)
    - d. Dépeçage

IV. **Renvoi**
- A. In General: Statutory and Restatement Directives
- B. Conflicting Choice-of-Law Rules: The *Renvoi* Problem

V. **Public Policy**

VI. **Proof of Foreign Law**

VII. **Review Questions**

I. Introduction

A. Jurisdiction and Choice of Law

What law should a court apply when the case before it involves out-of-state parties occurrences or problems? The law of its own state, or that of a perhaps more closely connected foreign jurisdiction? This is the **choice-of-law problem**.

The court will be guided in its choice either by statutory direction of its state (see B, below) or by the rules or approach to choice-of-law adopted and followed by the case law of its state (Chapter VIII and Part Five, below). **Just because a court has jurisdiction to hear the case, it does not follow—and the United States Supreme Court has often stated—that the court should, or even may, apply local law (the law of the forum).**

Chapter III detailed the constitutional limitations upon the exercise of judicial *jurisdiction*: unless a court has *general jurisdiction* over the defendant, the forum state may exercise *specific jurisdiction* when the defendant had minimum contacts with the state and the claim arose from or was related to these contacts or activities. Chapter X will detail the constitutional limitations that a court must observe in *choice of law*. The contacts necessary to exercise jurisdiction and to apply forum law will often be the same if the case is one of specific jurisdiction. However, this will not always be the case when general jurisdiction is involved (for instance, when jurisdiction is based on transient service).

Caveat: As you study the various approaches to choice of law used by the courts, you must keep in mind that choice of law does not automatically follow from jurisdiction, nor the other way around. You must analyze jurisdiction and choice of law ***separately***.

B. Sources for the Choice-of-Law Decision

Choice-of-law rules are rarely contained in *statutes*. One exception, however, is the Uniform Commercial Code, which contains specific choice-of-law rules with respect to secured transactions. For instance, § 9–301(1) (revised), which deals with the effect of perfection or non-perfection of a security interest, refers to the local law of the jurisdiction (not its conflicts law) where the debtor was at the time.

Section 1–301 of the UCC, formerly § 1–105 (and still designated as such by states that have not revised Article 1), requires, for the validity of the parties' choice, that the chosen law be related to the transaction. In the absence of a choice (or an effective choice), the section provides that the applicable law shall be forum law if it has an "appropriate" relationship to the transaction. UCC § 1–301 sounds inward looking (the law of "this state" absent a party choice) but has usually been interpreted as calling for the "most significantly related" law. The Restatement (Second) and the Draft Restatement (Third) likewise permit some choice of law by party agreement (see *infra*), otherwise suggest some rules, and call for the law of the "most significant relationship," "the most appropriate law," or the law of the state with the "dominant interest" (see *infra*). These tests, of course, leave room for different interpretations.

Occasionally, *treaties* of the United States will provide for the application of a particular law. In such a case, state conflicts law is displaced under the Supremacy Clause of the Constitution. Finally, as discussed in Chapter X, the United States Constitution places some *limits* on the choice of law that a state may make.

Most choice-of-law rules or approaches, however, have their source in the *case law* of the several states. (Exceptions are Louisiana, Oregon, and Puerto Rico, which have codified their choice-of-law rules.) The uniformity displayed by the case law some fifty or sixty years ago, and reflected in the First Restatement, has been replaced by a number of new approaches. They are the subject of Chapters VIII and IX.

C. Pervasive Problems

The remainder of this chapter deals with a number of problems that are *pervasive to the entire choice-of-law process*. How relevant they are to a particular matter will depend in part on the approach to choice of law used by a particular jurisdiction. As an example: the public policy of the forum state (discussed below at V) plays a different role, analytically, in jurisdictions following one of the traditional approaches than in jurisdictions engaged in interest analysis. In the former, public policy functions as a corrective force at the end of the analysis; in the latter, it is a part of the analysis. It is important that you are acquainted with these pervasive problems; their respective weight will be mentioned again in connection with the individual approaches to choice of law.

II. Characterization: Subject Matter

Before a court can apply a choice-of-law rule to a problem or undertake the type of analysis advocated by modern choice-of-law approaches, it must first identify the area of the law that is involved. It must ***characterize*** the legal issue or case as arising in a particular substantive area of the law, such as tort, contract, or family law. In states that still adhere to the *traditional approach* to choice of law, characterization of the legal issue may have a decisive effect on the outcome of the case. In states following one of the modern approaches, policy considerations may differ depending on how the case or particular issue is characterized.

In fact, if a court seeks to determine the law of the place of the "most significant relationship" to an issue (*infra* at p. 181 *et seq.*), or to determine "governmental interests" (*infra* at p. 177 *et seq.*), **subject-matter characterization becomes less important: the *issue* counts, not its fitting into a particular cubbyhole**.

Illustration (traditional approach): In *Reeves v. Schulmeier*, 303 F.2d 802 (5th Cir. 1962), a married woman sued for personal injuries sustained in a car accident in Texas. The question was whether her husband should have joined in the action because Texas, the place of the tort, considered claims for personal injuries to be part of the community property of the spouses. To decide, the court had to characterize: if it was a *tort* issue, Texas law, as the place where the tort occurred, might apply. In contrast, if the issue of who owned the personal injury claim related to the area of *interspousal property rights*, then the law of the spouses' domicile might apply. The court characterized the issue as relating to property, looked to the spouses' state of domicile (Oklahoma), and found that under that law, the personal injury claim was the wife's separate property, so the husband was not required to join in the action. A court following one of the modern approaches would have asked which state (and its law) had the most significant relationship to this issue (perhaps the state where the proceeding took place?), or which state had the greater (policy) interest in having its law applied (perhaps the state of the matrimonial domicile, since the procedural issue involved a question of marital property?). For other examples see *Grant v. McAuliffe*, 264 P.2d 944 (Cal. 1953), and *Haumschild v. Continental Casualty Co.*, *infra* p. 203.

III. Characterization: Substance or Procedure

A. In General

When a forum state's choice of law calls for application of the law of another jurisdiction, the question arises how much of the other state's law the court will use. Will it sit and decide as if it were a court of that other jurisdiction, or will it function within its own framework, seeking answers to some *issues* in the other state's law?

As a general rule, the forum will use only the other jurisdiction's **substantive** law; it will use its *own* **procedure**. The characterization of some matters as procedural is relatively easy because they are so obviously local housekeeping rules and are unlikely to affect the outcome of the case. This will be true, for instance, with respect to rules for the service of process, rules defining time periods for filing various pleadings, and the like. Other matters are more difficult to characterize because they may have an effect on the outcome of the case.

Example: The burden of proof and rules of evidence have generally been regarded as procedural. Traditionally, the same has been true for testimonial privileges. More recently, the Restatement (Second) calls for application of the law of the state with the most significant relationship to the communication. This is less mechanical than a characterization as procedural (calling for forum law no matter what) and may affect the outcome of the case.

The ***types*** of damages that can be awarded, traditionally, were considered to be substantive. However, restrictive foreign law has, at times, been disregarded on public policy grounds (*infra* at V), for example, as in *Kilberg v. Northeast Airlines, Inc.*, 172 N.E.2d 526 (N.Y. 1961). ***Quantification*** of damages, in contrast, has traditionally been characterized as procedural, although some decisions are to the contrary. See, e.g., *Karim v. Finch Shipping Co.*, 265 F.3d 258 (5th Cir. 2001) (law of Bangladesh used to determine amount of damages for pain and suffering). Under modern choice-of-law approaches, the law applicable to these issues may be determined separately from the underlying claim, on the basis of the "most-significant-relationship" test, or through "interest analysis." Indeed, much current commentary urges damage quantification to be characterized by the law applicable to liability in damages in the first place. See Russell J. Weintraub, *Commentary on the Conflict of Laws*, 85, 432 (6th ed. 2010).

B. What Law Determines How an Issue Should Be Characterized?

Assume that the question is whether the statute of frauds is substantive or procedural (Subsection C, below): does the forum state use its own or the other state's concept as to the proper characterization?

Illustration: In *Marie v. Garrison*, 13 Abb. N. Cas. 210 (N.Y. Super. Ct. 1883), the court in state A concluded that an oral contract was governed by the substantive law of state B. In characterizing the statute of frauds to determine whether A's or B's statute applied, the court concluded that A's statute was "substantive" and B's "procedural." Since the forum (A) does not apply its substantive law to a claim governed by another state's law, and since A does not apply another state's procedure, **neither** statute applied, and the contract was therefore enforceable.

Had the contract in *Marie* been an *intrastate* case, A would have applied its own statute. In a reverse situation, B would have applied its statute. Either way, the contract would not have been enforceable. By looking at conflicting characterizations, the *Marie* court gave *interstate* validity to a contract that neither state would have upheld in a purely intrastate setting.

To avoid results such as in *Marie,* courts generally characterize only according to forum law. The coming Restatement (Third) also so provides (§ 5.05, T.D., # 3, 2022)), but subject to exceptions (see below). Had the *Marie* court said that statutes of frauds are substantive *for all purposes,* it would have regarded B's statute as substantive and applied it. Conversely, had the *Marie* court said that statutes of frauds are always procedural, it would have applied its own. Switch the courts and apply the same approach: B would have applied either A law or its own. In both cases, the contract would have been unenforceable; the fact of interstate litigation would not have affected what both states would otherwise have done.—The coming Restatement (Third) provision (above) refers to its § 5.06 as an exception. That provision (subsection (1), T.D. # 3, 2022) provides for the application of the "internal law" of the another state when the forum's choice-of-law rules "direct it to apply" the other states law. "Internal law" is the law, other than conflicts law, that a state applies when it applies its "own law as the rule of decision for one or more issues." § 1.03(1).

C. Statute of Frauds

Early cases adopted characterizations for the statute of frauds depending on the particular language of the statute. If it said "no action shall be brought," the characterization was procedural; if language such as "no contract shall be valid . . . " was used, a substantive characterization was applied. Modern cases will either characterize the statute of frauds as substantive, or they will apply the law of the state that has the most significant relationship to the issue of a contract's validity (which, most usually, will amount to the same thing). The latter will often lead to a law *upholding* the contract.

D. Statute of Limitations

1. The Traditional Approach

Until recently, *general* statutes of limitations were uniformly characterized as ***procedural.*** Courts took the view that a limitation *does not affect the right but only the remedy.* Thus, the application of the forum state's shorter limitation would leave the plaintiff free to sue elsewhere on his claim, while application of the forum state's longer limitation was not thought to impose any new obligation upon the defendant. There were, however, two *exceptions* to the rule.

First, since a procedural characterization would call for application of the forum's longer limitation as well as its shorter limitation, plaintiffs would be encouraged to engage in forum shopping. The result would be to overburden some courts with suits and claims that are stale where they arose. Many states therefore adopted "**borrowing statutes**," calling for application of the shorter limitation in effect in the state where the action "arose."

There are a number of problems with borrowing statutes. Their reference to the state where the claim "arose" dates to the era where fixed choice-of-law rules assigned a definite location to a claim. With modern approaches to choice of law (Chapters VIII and IX), a great many factors may be involved in determining the applicable law. As a result, borrowing statutes are far from uniform in their application. Additionally, there is some uncertainty whether a borrowing statute also borrows the other jurisdiction's *tolling statute*. Such a statute suspends the running of the limitation for the time that the defendant is not subject to service in the state. In some circumstances, tolling statutes are today unconstitutional. *Bendix Autolite Corp. v. Midwesco Enter., Inc.*, 486 U.S. 888, 108 S. Ct. 2218, 100 L. Ed. 2d 896 (1988), discussed *infra* p. 240.

The second exception to the traditional rule are so-called "**built-in**" limitations: when a foreign claim was created by statute (i.e., it does not arise from the common law), and the statute provides a limitation specifically for this claim, then this "built-in" limitation was thought to bar the right, and not just the remedy, and would be applied by the forum state.

There was some earlier authority for the view that the forum state could not constitutionally apply its longer statute of limitations when it had no connection with the case other than being the place of trial. The argument was that, just as the forum state may not apply its substantive law to an unrelated claim, it may also not affect the outcome of a case by applying its procedural law. However, the U.S. Supreme Court in 1988 expressly held that the forum *may* apply its longer limitation in these circumstances. *Sun Oil Co. v. Wortman,* 486 U.S. 717, 108 S. Ct. 2117, 100 L. Ed. 2d 743 (1988). There was strong dissent. More recently, in a 5–4 decision, the Court held that "toll," in a federal statute, means that the time limitation applicable to the claim is held in abeyance ("stop-the-clock") while the claim is being litigated, and it restarts when the claim is dismissed for reasons other than on the merits. *Artis v. District of Columbia,* 583 U.S. 71, 138 S. Ct. 594, 199 L. Ed. 2d 473 (2018).

2. Modern Approaches

a. Case Law

One court, *Heavner v. Uniroyal, Inc.,* 305 A.2d 412 (N.J. 1973), expressly adopted a *substantive* characterization: the limitation was governed by the same law that applied to the claim itself. Subsequent New Jersey decisions construed *Heavner* narrowly, and in 2017, New Jersey adopted the approach of the Restatement (Second). *McCarrell v. Hoffman-La Roche, Inc.,* 153 A.3d 207, 210 (N.J. 2017). Most courts continued to use the "procedural" label. However, they also tended to determine the law applicable to the limitation according to their general approach to choice of law. Thus, courts following "interest analysis" (Chapter VIII and Part Five, below), would inquire what state had the greatest "interest" in having its limitation applied, while states adopting the "most significant relationship" approach would apply that approach to the limitation issue as well. Add to this the widespread existence of borrowing statutes, and for practical purposes, if not in name, limitations are treated as substantive.

b. The Uniform Conflict of Laws Limitations Act

This Uniform Act adopts a substantive characterization for statutes of limitations and is in force in Colorado, Delaware, Idaho, Minnesota, Montana, Nebraska, North Dakota, Oregon, and Washington. See also the revision of Louisiana's statutory conflicts law. La. Civ. Code Ann. art. 3549 (2022).

c. Restatement (Second) and (Third)

Section 142 of the Restatement (Second) originally characterized limitations as procedural. It was revised in 1988, and directs the court to choose the applicable statute of limitations on the basis of the general principles for choice of law in the Restatement (Second). These are generally designed to lead to the application of the law of the most significant relationship (*infra* Chapter VIII and Part Five). However, the revised § 142 does not expressly refer to the law of the most significant relationship, and moreover contains two subsections, which state that "in general," the forum will apply **both** *its shorter and its longer limitation.* The shorter limitation is not to apply if "exceptional circumstances of the case" make it unreasonable to do so, and the longer limitation is not to apply if a more significantly related state would bar the claim *and* application of the forum's statute would further no forum interest. For similar provisions in the forthcoming Restatemen (Third) see its § 5.31(a).

d. Dépeçage

The discussion of the modern case law and of the Restatement (Second) revision addresses the statute of limitations that is to be applied to the *limitation issue.* While the *Heavner* decision and the Uniform Act treat the limitation as part of the claim, other decisions, the Restatement (Second), and the coming Restatement (Third) take an *issue-by-issue* approach. This may result in application of a law to the limitation issue that is different from the law that applies to the claim itself. The issue-by-issue approach is known as ***dépeçage***, and will be discussed further in connection with the modern approaches.

IV. Renvoi

A. In General: Statutory and Restatement Directives

The question of how much of the other jurisdiction's law the forum should use (encountered in connection with the substance/procedure characterization above) also extends to the question of whether the forum's reference includes the other jurisdiction's choice-of-law rules. When the reference includes the foreign conflicts law, the reference may be to the **whole law**, not just to the **local** (internal) law of the other jurisdiction. The Uniform Commercial Code (revised) contains a number of references to the "whole law" of another jurisdiction, for instance, in § 8–110 (investment securities) and in § 9–301 (secured transactions).

The reference in the Federal Tort Claims Act to the law of the "place where the act or omission occurred" has been held to include the choice of law rules of that state. *Richards v. United States*, 369 U.S. 1, 82 S. Ct. 585, 7 L. Ed. 2d 492 (1962). See also *McKinley v. United States,* No. 5:15-CV-101, 2015 WL 5842626 (M.D. Ga. Oct. 6, 2015).

The Restatement (Second) also provides for application of the foreign conflicts law in the specific cases addressed by its § 223 (validity and effect of a transfer of an interest in land), § 245 (validity and effect of a transfer of an interest in a chattel), and §§ 260, 263 (succession to interest in movables). The Restatement (Second) suggests *generally* that use of the foreign conflicts law should be considered when this would lead all concerned states to reach a uniform result. Id. at § 8(2). The coming Restatement (Third) expressly rejects consideration of the other state's conflicts law, but also permits an exception if all involved states' laws seek to reach the same result. § 5.06 (T.D. 3, 2022). The latter may require the forum to interpret the other state's law and policies, which may be a difficult task (some would consider it inappropriate). For discussion of the role of another state's choice-of-law rules in the forum state's determination whether different laws present a "true" or a "false" conflict, see *infra* at B (Illustration IV).

B. Conflicting Choice-of-Law Rules: The *Renvoi* Problem

Except in cases where everyone's conflicts law is the same (as in the UCC examples discussed above), use of the other jurisdiction's conflicts law will have one of the following results.

Remission: Assume that the conflicts law of A refers to B, and that B's conflicts law refers to A. This is the **renvoi** problem. If both jurisdictions include the other's conflicts law in their reference, a never ending circle, a ping-pong game, ensues. For that reason, the majority view in the United States is to **reject the *renvoi***, i.e., not to consider the other state's conflicts law at all, but only its internal (substantive) law.

Another possibility would be for the forum to **accept the *renvoi***, that is, to accept the other state's reference to its law and to cut off the otherwise circular reference at that point. This is the practice in many European countries (except in contract, where there is no renvoi). It has the advantage of allowing the court to apply forum law, which it will know better than the foreign law. However, this approach is not usually followed in the United States.

Note that if **both** states involved use the **same** approach—either they both reject or they both accept the *renvoi*—there will be no uniformity of result. Instead, the outcome will depend entirely on where suit is brought. See the illustration below.

Transmission: Uniformity of result may sometimes be achieved in cases of transmission. Assume that A refers to B, and B refers to C, and C refers to itself. Here, use of the conflicts law of all the states involved will lead to a uniform result: the ultimate application of the law of C, regardless of where suit was brought.

Foreign Court Theory: English courts use a variation of the approaches discussed under "remission" above. It is known as the "foreign court theory." When the English conflicts rule refers to another country, the English court will sit as if it were a court of the other country and do what that court would do: accept or reject the renvoi, or partially accept it by cutting off the reference when it comes back. *In re Annesley,* [1926] Ch. 692. Note that if both England and the other state apply the foreign court theory, there will be no uniformity, and the outcome of the case will again depend on where suit was brought.

Illustrations:

Remission

I. If either F-1 or F-2 were the forum in a given case, and under their conflicts rules, both would apply the substantive law of the respective other state but would not apply that state's conflicts rules, forum shopping may result:

Suit begun in:	Law applied:
F-1	F-2
F-2	F-1

II. *Variation of No. I*: Both F-1 and F-2 *do* consider the other's conflicts rules and avoid potential ping-pong games by cutting off the other state's reference when it first comes back. Forum shopping may result again:

Suit begun in:	Reference to:	Reference back to, accepted (cut off at this point) by:	Law applied:
F-1	F-2	F-1	F-1
F-2	F-1	F-2	F-2

III. Therefore, remission avoids forum shopping *only* if (a) F-1 considers the other's conflicts law, *and* (b) F-2 does not:

Suit begun in:	Reference to:	Further reference:	Law applied:
F-1	F-2	F-1	F-1
F-2	F-1	none	F-1

If F-1 does not consider F-2's conflicts law, it's a case of No. I, above.

IV. Remission may be useful in Case II to demonstrate to the forum that the other state has no interest (as demonstrated by its conflicts rule) in having its substantive law applied. The forum may then treat the case as presenting a false conflict and apply forum law. At this point, the result is the same as in Case III. For "false conflicts," see *infra* p. 148.

Many foreign legal systems, including the Succession Regulation of the European Union, accept remission in succession cases. The Restatements (Second) and Draft (Third) do not expressly address this, but § 8(2) of the Restatement (Second) and the similar provision of the Draft Restatement (Third) (discussed *supra* under A) might support such a use.

V. *In re Annesley* is a hybrid ("foreign court theory"): F-1 sits *as if it were* the F-2 court and then applies the process described under II and III, above.

Transmission

Occasionally, F-2's conflicts rule will not point back to F-1, but to F-3, and the latter, to itself. In these circumstances, F-1 can achieve the same result as F-2 would by looking at F-2's conflicts law and honoring its reference. For example, a Spanish citizen died domiciled in France, having personal property in a U.S. state. He had no will. For intestate succession to personal property, most U.S. states ("F-1," below) look to the law of the decedent's domicile at death. Both French and Spanish law ("F-2" and "F-3," respectively, below) would look to Spanish law ("F-3").

Suit begun in:	**Reference to:**	**Further reference:**	**Law applied:**
F-1	F-2	F-3	F-3*
F-2	F-3	none	F-3*
F-3	none	none	F-3*

**Assume that F-3 would apply its own law.*

Note that F-3 may, of course, refer to F-4 or back to F-2, and in the former case, F-4 may refer back to F-3 or whatever; transmission and remission situations can thus occur in combination. Too much chasing around is not helpful. In such a case, F-1 might properly wish to refer only to F-2 and *not* go on from there.

United States Law

I. Traditionally: no *renvoi* (see *supra,* Remission Case I).

II. Restatement (Second) § 8 favors its use when doing so might bring about uniformity of result. Some cases follow the suggestion, especially for purposes of Remission Case IV, above. Here, *renvoi* becomes part of the policy analysis that leads initially (and not just by way of a reference back or forward) to the application of a particular law, usually forum law: because the other state's conflicts law would refer to the forum, the forum could conclude that there is a "false conflict" (i.e., none at all) and apply its own law. For an example, see *American Motorists Ins. Co. v. ARTRA Group, Inc.*, 659 A.2d 1295 (Md. 1995), discussed below at pp. 179, 211. The coming Restatement (Third) rejects this. See above Section A. For policy analysis in choice of law, see below.

V. Public Policy

Under the traditional approach to choice of law (Chapters VIII and IX), the forum's conflicts rules direct it to the law of a particular state, initially without regard to the content of that law. Upon examination of the other state's law, the forum might then discover that the other law offends its local public policy. For example, a claim, valid under the law of the state where it arose, involves a gambling debt, yet gambling is prohibited in the forum state. In these circumstances, the forum would not entertain the foreign claim. A contemporary example from international practice is that European courts will not entertain claims for exemplary (punitive) or treble damages under American law. *Public policy thus serves as a defense* against unpalatable results under the otherwise applicable foreign law.

The public policy defense is construed narrowly. Mere differences in law are usually not regarded as offensive to local public policy. The formulation in *Loucks v. Standard Oil Co. of New York,* 120 N.E. 198 (N.Y. 1918), is still the standard statement. Courts should not refuse to entertain a claim unless application of forum law would "violate some fundamental principle of justice, some prevalent conception of good morals, some deep-rooted tradition of the common weal." Id. at 202. For an application of *Standard Oil*, see *Galeotti v. Cianbro Corp.*, No. 5:12–cv–00900, 2013 WL 3207312, at *16 (N.D.N.Y. June 24, 2013). See also *EMA Financial, LLC v. Nfusz, Inc.*, 444 F. Supp. 3d 530 542 (S.D.N.Y. 2020) (applying *Galeotti*); *Monroe Staffing Services, LLC v. Whitaker*, 2023 WL 4285292

(S.D.N.Y. 2023). The coming Restatement (Third) takes a slightly less restrictive view: application of foreign law "*may be declined*" if it "would offend a deep-rooted forum public policy." § 5.04.

In the context of modern approaches to choice of law (Chapter VIII and Part Five, below), the interests of the forum and of the other concerned state(s) are often considered as part of the initial choice. The issue-by-issue approach of the Restatement (Second) and the coming Restatement (Third) *(dépeçage)* also encourages weighing interests and policy considerations. Thus, a foreign law selected for application in this fashion is unlikely to offend local public policy on other grounds.

Whatever the choice-of-law approach, the public policy of the forum will generally continue to bar claims based on foreign criminal law, claims based on punitive provisions of foreign private law, and claims of foreign governments (for instance, for taxes, for which see *supra*). However, the definition of what is penal tends to be narrow.

As the U.S. Supreme Court said, whether a claim is to be called penal "depends on the question whether its purpose is to punish an offense against the public justice of the State, or to afford a private remedy to a person injured by the wrongful act." *Huntington v. Attrill,* 146 U.S. 657, 673–74, 13 S. Ct. 224, 230, 36 L. Ed. 1123 (1892).

Note that a state *may not* decline to accord Full Faith and Credit to the *judgment* of a sister-state, which reduces a claim to a money judgment, on the ground that the underlying claim violates its public policy. See Chapter IV.

VI. Proof of Foreign Law

At common law, a court would recognize as "law" only the law of its own state. The law of all other states and countries was only a *fact*. As a result, when choice-of-law rules referred to the law of another state or country, that law had to be pleaded and proved like any other fact. Its determination was for the trier of facts and the decision on it was not appealable.

Statutory changes in the United States have modified the common law rule. The *Uniform Judicial Notice of Foreign Law Act*, adopted by 28 states, provides for judicial notice of *sister state law*. Its section 5 excludes foreign country law but some states will recognize the law of a common law-oriented foreign country.

The *Uniform Interstate and International Procedure Act* (1962) requires that a party intending to rely on foreign law (here meaning foreign-country law) give reasonable written notice. It provides that the issue of foreign law is one for the court and not for the jury, and permits the court to consider any relevant materials without being bound by the usual rules of evidence. It also requires that the party intending to rely on foreign law assist the court in the determination of the foreign law, and makes the court's decision subject to review on appeal.

Federal Rule of Civil Procedure 44.1 is modeled after the Uniform Act Interstate and International Procedure Act; it is essentially identical with the provisions of the Act.

The coming Restatement (Third) is modeled after the Federal Rule, but states in addition that the forum should generally follow the interpretation of a foreign law given by the courts of that jurisdiction. § 5.08(b). However, the United States Supreme Court has taken a different view. In *Animal Science Products v. Hebei Welcome Pharmaceutical Co.*, 585 U.S. 33, 138 S. Ct. 1865, 201 L. Ed. 225 (2018), the Second Circuit had held that a federal court is "bound to defer" to an official statement of a foreign country interpreting its law, but the Supreme Court reversed. Id. at 1869. Finding that the Second Circuit ruling did not comport with Rule 44.1, the Court held that "[a] federal court should accord respectful consideration to a foreign government's [interpretation] but is not bound to accord [it] conclusive effect." Id. For a recent application, see *Trower v. Blinken*, No. 4:22-CV-00077-JAR, 2022 WL 1908914, at *9 (E.D. Mo. June 3, 2022) (denying motion to dismiss; need for "additional presentation" on foreign law precludes its dismissal); *Shen v. Garland*, 198 F.4th 1144, 1154 (9th Cir. 2024). The coming Restatement (Third) acknowledges the *Animal Science* decision (§ 5.07, comment *e*) with respect to a foreign government's "views" about its own country's law but calls for "respectful consideration." Other than that, the court is to determine foreign law in the way that it is "authoritatively interpreted and applied in the foreign state." § 5.08(a).

When judicial notice is not applicable (see above), and when proof of foreign law fails, courts at times *presume the foreign law to be identical with that of the forum*, or may dismiss the suit.

In *Walton v. Arabian American Oil Co.*, 233 F.2d 541 (2d Cir. 1956), the plaintiff had sued on a tort committed by defendant in Saudi Arabia. Plaintiff failed to prove Saudi law. The court was unwilling to assume that Saudi law was identical with New York law. It was also unwilling to assume that Saudi Arabia was "uncivilized" and had no law, thus leaving New York as the only possible law to apply. As a consequence, the suit was dismissed. See also *Bonsu v. Holder*, 646 F.Supp.2d 273, 276 (D.Conn. 2009). As an alternative to *Walton*, a court may simply apply forum law when foreign law has not been proved. See *Salesky v. CRMNEXT, Inc.*, 2024 WL 2932346 at *11 (Cal. App. 2024).

Another presumption that can help is that with the content of the foreign law not shown, the parties are taken to have *acquiesced* in the application of forum law. *Leary v. Gledhill*, 84 A.2d 725 (N.J. 1951). What if a party objects (does *not* acquiesce)? Absent a statutory solution, it is then back to the common law approach represented by *Walton*.

VII. Review Questions

1. T or F: Choice of Law,

   a. follows jurisdiction: i.e., the court with jurisdiction generally applies its own law;

   b. often involves considerations which track the jurisdictional decision;

   c. is predominantly a matter of (forum) state law.

2. "Subject matter characterization" means deciding what field of law the case involves and may have important consequences for the choice of the applicable law.

3. Substance/Procedure Characterization

   a. T or F: Assuming that the forum state's choice-of-law rule or analysis would apply the law of another state to the case pending before the forum court, the forum court will only apply the other state's substantive law. It will continue to apply its own procedural law.

   b. T or F: The forum court should make the substance/procedural characterization,

      i. according to its *and* the other state's concepts,

      ii. according to its own conception alone.

   c. T or F: The statute of frauds is generally characterized as substantive.

d. T or F: The statute of limitations under traditional (see (e)) approaches is,

i. substantive if "built-in,"

ii. substantive, as a result of borrowing statutes,

iii. otherwise procedural in most states.

e. T or F: Modern approaches (Uniform Act, Restatement (Second), Louisiana conflicts statute revision) modify the general procedural characterization.

4. T or F: Dépeçage is the issue-by-issue approach to choice of law. And what does this mean?

5. T or F:

a. *Renvoi* means the consideration of the conflicts (choice-of-law) rules along with the rules of substantive law of the state to which the choice-of-law rules of the forum refer the forum court.

b. American courts generally do not engage in renvoi.

c. *Renvoi* could help to resolve conflicts by disclosing "false conflicts."

6. T or F: The Federal Rules of Civil Procedure and the Uniform Interstate and International Procedure Act modify the common law approach to foreign law, which was to regard it as a *fact*, which would then require its proof and make the trial court's determination not appealable.

7. T or F: The "public policy defense" (also: "public policy exception") is important,

a. in interstate recognition practice of litigated (non-default) judgments;

b. in the recognition of foreign-country judgments;

c. in choice-of-law decisions in states following traditional (First Restatement-type) territorial orientations;

d. in choice-of-law decisions in states following one of the modern policy-oriented approaches;

e. in choice-of-law decisions involving foreign-country cases.

Chapter VIII

Approaches to Choice of Law: Theory

■ ANALYSIS

I. **Introduction**

II. **The Traditional Approach**

- A. The Territorial Focus: Vested Rights
- B. Application
- C. Illustration

III. **Interest Analysis**

- A. Introduction
- B. "False" Versus "True" Conflicts
  1. Currie's Methodology
  2. Criticism
  3. Application
  4. Interest Analysis and "Pervasive Problems"
- C. "Comparative Impairment"

IV. **Restatement (Second): Most Significant Relationship**

- A. Overview
- B. Determining the State of the Most Significant Relationship: Applying the Restatement (Second)
- C. Application
- D. Restatement (Second) and Pervasive Problems
- E. Narrow Rules: New York's Tort Approach
  1. From *Babcock* to *Neumeier*
  2. From *Neumeier* to *Schultz* to *Edwards*

V. **Restatement (Third): Some Rules and the Search for the "Most Appropriate Law"**

- A. Overview
- B. Rules and General Approach

VI. **Leflar's Choice-Influencing Considerations, Particularly Also the "Better Rule of Law"**

- A. In General
- B. The "Better Rule of Law"

VII. Other Approaches
- A. Functional Analysis
- B. "Lex Fori"
- C. "Principles of Preference"

VIII. Conclusion: The Choice-of-Law Continuum
IX. The Future: The Coming Restatement (Third)
X. Overview
XI. Review Questions

I. Introduction

Suppose A sues his neighbor B for a tort committed locally. Ordinarily, there will not be any question as to what law applies. It will be the tort law of the forum state. However, change the facts so that either or both parties are from out of state, or that the tort occurred in another state, or that neither the parties nor the tort has any connection with the forum, and the answers will often be different. In the last case, when there is no connection with the forum state, it may not even be constitutional to apply local law. Due Process under the Federal Constitution requires that the forum have significant contacts with the parties or the occurrence to be able to apply its own law. Constitutional limitations on choice of law are discussed *infra* in Chapter X.

If the forum does have some contact with the parties, the occurrence, or both, its own basic approach to choice of law will determine whether local law or the law of another state will apply. Thus, if the forum adheres to the traditional choice-of-law approach in a tort conflicts case, it will focus on the state where the tort occurred. More modern approaches may focus on other or additional factors, such as the state of the parties' domicile, or where the negligent conduct occurred, or where the tort had a financial or other impact.

Assume that the forum is free to use either its own law or that of another state. Why should it not always apply its own law? Those adhering to the traditional approach answer that the application of forum law in all instances will encourage forum shopping, as well as may disappoint the justified expectations of the parties. Fixed rules provide a kind of predictability of result that automatic application of forum law does not (since it is the plaintiff who chooses the forum). Fixed rules thus prevent forum shopping by contributing to uniformity of decisions.

The modern approaches also do not favor forum shopping. However, they accept that it may occur as the result of their methodology, which may assign greater weight to other considerations than to uniformity of result. Among those considerations are party expectations, a state's interest in regulating conduct, a state's interest in providing compensation, and other policy reasons. Part of the difference between the traditional approach and modern approaches is that the former seeks to identify a *single law* to apply to the entire case, while the latter ask which law should apply to various *issues* of the case. The issue-by-issue approach is known as ***dépeçage***. A translation of the French in this context might be "splitting."

The following presents an overview of the various approaches to choice of law. Chapter IX deals with choice of law by subject matter.

II. The Traditional Approach

A. The Territorial Focus: Vested Rights

The First Restatement of Conflict of Laws (1934) embodies the traditional approach. It had a *territorial* focus: its rules sought to identify the state where rights and obligations were created, where they **vested**. "[A]s the only source of this obligation is the law of the place of the act, it follows that that law determines not merely the existence of the obligation . . . but equally determines its extent." *Slater v. Mexican National Railroad Co.,* 194 U.S. 120, 126, 24 S. Ct. 581, 583, 48 L. Ed. 900, 903 (1904) (Holmes, J.). Today, the new Restatement (Third) also calls for the determination of the other law's "scope," though for a somewhat different purpose: if the other law is intended to address only local issue, then the forum can disregard it (there is no conflict, it's a "false conflict") and forum law will apply. See below at III(B).

The **vested rights** approach sought to specify the act or occurrence which causes a right to vest. The court would look for that element (act, occurrence) in order to *localize* the case within a jurisdiction; that state's law would then apply.

Examples: In tort, suffering the injury is the last element necessary to give the plaintiff a cause of action. Thus, his or her rights vested where the injury was suffered, and the law of that state governed the tort. In contract, the place of the making of the contract governed its validity (i.e., were rights created?), while the place of performance might govern the question whether there was a breach (i.e., did claims for damages arise, "vest"?).

Almost without exception, the vested rights approach looks to a *single* substantive law. It is *jurisdiction selective*. In this way, it differs from approaches proceeding issue by issue, i.e., engaging in *dépeçage* (for which see above). The vested rights approach also selects the applicable law *without regard to its content*. Policy-centered modern approaches are very much concerned about the content of the potentially applicable laws and will select a law by taking account of policies and policy differences.

Pros and cons: The vested rights approach provides predictability and certainty. If widely followed, there would be little or no forum shopping, as everyone's conflicts rule would point to the same substantive law. Policy-centered approaches are much less certain and predictable because policy analysis requires evaluating different potential results and that involves making judgment calls. To the extent that policy analysis may favor forum law, forum shopping may occur.

On the other hand, the vested rights approach is unduly rigid and mechanical. In tort, for example, it makes the place of injury the decisive factor, even when that place was wholly fortuitous. The modern approaches permit consideration of additional factors and arrive at results that more nearly address the particular (not hypothetical or general) circumstances of the parties and of the case.

B. Application

The choice of the applicable law under the <u>vested rights approach</u> begins with

(1) **the characterization of the subject matter**. After the determination that the case involves a certain area of law (e.g. torts),

(2) **the choice-of-law rule for that area of law** is applied (e.g., place of injury in tort), and the state of the applicable law is identified.

(3) The **substance/procedure characterization** tells us at this point how much of that state's law to apply. For example, that state's law applies to rules regarding liability (substantive), but not to the manner of proof (procedural); forum law applies to the latter.

(4) A court can deal with unpalatable results by rejecting the foreign law as violative of the **public policy** of the forum. Occasionally, a court may also

(5) **re-characterize** the subject matter, since a different area of the law would result in the applicability of different choice-of-law rules (see *Reeves v. Schulmeier*, 303 F.2d 802 (5th Cir. 1962), and *supra*).

(6) At step #3, the court may also consider whether to follow the other jurisdiction's conflicts rules **(renvoi)**. As mentioned earlier, this has been done rarely in

American conflicts law. *Renvoi* may have a greater role in policy-oriented approaches.

Note: The foregoing does not consider additional problems raised by the *Erie* doctrine, for which see *infra* at p. 246 *et seq.*

C. Illustration

P, a resident of state X, was employed by a state X railroad company and worked on trains as they travelled from state X to state Y. He suffered an injury in Y as the result of another employee's negligence. X had a statute making employers liable for injuries suffered by employees in the course of employment. Y still followed the common law, whereby an employer is not liable to an employee for acts of a "fellow servant." Suit against the employer in X.

Held, that this is a **tort** claim. Torts are governed by the substantive law of the state where the last act occurred to give the plaintiff a claim ("the place of wrong"), i.e., the injury. Here, the injury occurred in Y, therefore Y law applied, and the plaintiff does not recover. *Alabama Great Southern R.R. Co. v. Carroll,* 11 So. 803 (Ala. 1892).

Notes:

1) The choice-of-law rule employed (place of wrong) is certain, predictable, and—if used by both state X and state Y—prevents forum-shopping. But it is rigid, and the outcome of a case like *Carroll* may be troublesome.
2) Even under the traditional approach, the X court could have reached a different result by characterizing the problem as one pertaining to the employment relationship of the parties. In that case, X law would have applied. (In the court's view, the local statute did not cover out-of-state accidents.) A finding that Y law offends X's public policy also would not have helped: the suit would then have been dismissed, and Y certainly would have applied its rule had P sued all over again there. Note that courts have at times **re-characterized** a case (in the manner suggested above) to avoid results they did not like. Such a use of characterization as an "**escape device**" has been much criticized.
3) Modern approaches would not regard the place of injury as decisive. They would focus additionally on the parties' residence (or place of business), on the relationship of the parties, and on the interests of the states involved.
4) The traditional approach has been rejected—as to tort—by most courts that have considered it. As to contract, it is followed only by a small number of states. See *Hornbook,* at §§ 17.7 and 18.21, respectively. Most states now follow a flexible approach to choice of law.

III. Interest Analysis

A. Introduction

The traditional approach (*supra* at p. 173) stresses predictability and achieves it by adopting general rules for the selection of the applicable law without regard to the content of that law. Interest analysis (also called **governmental interest analysis**) seeks to find a solution *to the particular case, including to particular issues raised by the case.* To do this, the court must look at the potentially applicable laws, ask what purposes (*policies*) they seek to further, and then determine how these policies would be advanced by the application of one state's law over that of another.

Interest analysis was first developed by the late Professor Brainerd *Currie* and is often associated with his name. In further development and in the case law, it has since been modified, as will be seen. One modification, the **comparative impairment** approach developed by Professor *Baxter*, was adopted in California. It is now also reflected in Louisiana's codification of conflicts law. The interest analysis approach also influences the ongoing work on the Restatement (Third) of Conflict of Laws (see further below at p. 194).

B. "False" Versus "True" Conflicts

1. Currie's Methodology

Currie's distinction between "false" and "true" conflicts is *now part of all approaches to choice of law except the traditional (vested rights) approach.* A conflict is "false" when the potentially applicable laws do not differ or when one law—by its own terms *or policies*—is not intended to apply to the case situation. A false conflict on the basis of *policy* is present when application of one law would advance that law's policies (goals) while non-application of the other law would not detract from that state's policies.

Example: In *Alabama Great Southern Railroad Co. v. Carroll,* above at p. 175 there was a false conflict (if we assume that there was no problem of statutory interpretation). The policies of the law of X would be furthered by its application (holding employers liable for the negligence of employees, compensation of tort victims for their injuries, private compensation vs. public aid), while non-application of the law of Y would not detract from its (Y's) policy (immunity of employers), since neither the employer nor the employee was a Y resident, and since Y's *immunity rule* does not regulate conduct (in the way that a *liability rule* does).

Whenever there is a false conflict between the law of the forum and of another state, no choice has to be made: the law of the interested state applies (state X in the example).

When the laws of two states conflict, there *may* be a true conflict. *Currie* stresses the "may": before calling it a true conflict, he would ask whether a "*restrained*" interpretation of the law of one of the states would avoid the conflict.

Example: Assume that Carroll had sued Alabama Great Southern Railroad in state Y and not in state X. The laws conflict. Although it is now the forum, state Y really has no greater interest than in the case of the false conflict discussed above. True, its policy is to shield employers, but does that policy extend to out-of-state employers who are not so immunized in their home state? This ("restrained") view of Y law shows that no real conflict exists; X law should apply.

What if there is an unavoidable **true conflict**? Consider the following case. Kaufman, an Oregon resident, went to California and there executed two promissory notes in favor of Lilienthal, a California resident. When Kaufman defaulted, Lilienthal sued in Oregon. Kaufman had previously been adjudged a spendthrift, and his guardian had used his statutory powers to avoid payment. Under California law, Kaufman had capacity, and the obligation could not be avoided. What law applies? *Lilienthal v. Kaufman,* 395 P.2d 543 (Or. 1964) (en banc).

The policies of California and Oregon presented a *true conflict.* California favors holding people to their bargains and protecting the expectation of parties who deal with each other in California against the background of California law. Oregon, while not insensitive to the expectations of Lilienthal, seeks to protect (Oregon) spendthrifts and their families. How to resolve the conflict? *Currie* answered that courts are not legislatures and therefore should not engage in balancing or evaluating policies. The only policy they should follow is that of the forum (so long as it is constitutionally permissible to do so). This is precisely what the court in *Lilienthal* did: it applied Oregon law.

Notes:

1) The traditional approach would have applied California law (place of execution *and* of performance of the contract), as would have the Restatement (Second) (most-significant-relationship test, *infra*) and the new Restatement (Third) would now (see *infra* at 194 *et seq.*).
2) The *Lilienthal* result, as well as the resolution of all true conflicts in *Currie's* methodology, will depend on the place of suit, leading to forum shopping.
3) *Currie* also envisioned the (rare) case in which the forum is a "disinterested" state. Since the court should not weigh the relative policies of other interested states any more than it should when the forum state itself is involved, *Currie* suggested that such a case be dismissed on *forum non conveniens* grounds (see at p. 80). If this could not be done (e.g., because the statute of limitations has run in the other state(s)), the law of the state most nearly analogous to that of the forum should be applied.

Finally, there may be "*unprovided for*" cases, i.e., when no state has an interest in applying its law. *Currie* favored application of forum law, since—by definition—it was not displaced by the law of another (interested) state. Query whether there might be a constitutional problem in cases where the forum is also a non-connected state. See Chapter X.

2. Criticism

Interest analysis, especially in the methodology developed by *Currie,* has been the subject of severe criticism. *Currie's* reference to "**governmental interests**" suggested, perhaps unintentionally, that governments (administering *public law*) have an interest in *private-law* relationships. Under the traditional approach, this is true only when the forum's **public policy** is violated by the content of the law selected by its choice-of-law rule. This, however, cannot happen under interest analysis because the forum's public policy ("governmental interest") already enters into the decision of what law to choose in the *first place.*

"Governmental interests" therefore must really mean *"policies underlying the laws of the states whose laws could potentially apply to the case (or issue)."* But how can these policies be identified? They are often unarticulated. For example, what is the purpose of a guest statute (which immunizes the host/driver against guest/passenger suits)? Is it freedom from collusive suits, protection of insurers, discouragement of ingratitude, or protection of assets for the benefit of third parties? If policies are unarticulated, or if multiple policies underlie a rule of law, it may then become a subjective decision to assign controlling weight to one policy over another.

Even if there are discernible state policies, they will usually not have been developed for *multi-state* cases. Yet, to take a domestic (intrastate) policy and apply it to a foreign (interstate or international) case may be quite a leap—it may not have been at all in the minds of those who initially formulated the policy and the rule flowing from it.

Currie's insistence on forum law for the adjudication of true conflicts encourages forum shopping as between two "interested" states. Critics have thus faulted *Currie's* approach for what they perceived as a **forum-bias** that does not ask whether the forum has a legitimate (policy) interest in the application of its law. Indeed, it is a fair question whether forum law (expressive of its policy) should ever be applied in a conflicts (interstate) case when the forum has no legitimate *intrastate* regulatory, compensatory, or other interest in that case. See, e.g., Brilmayer, Interest Analysis and the Myth of Legislative Intent, 78 Mich. L. Rev. 392 (1980).

The strong criticism of *Currie's* approach has caused contemporary commentators and courts who use interest analysis to advocate a change: in *true conflicts*, courts **should balance** (weigh) the interests (policies) of the connected states. In true conflicts cases, such weighing will often tip the balance in favor of the forum, but at least the mechanical law-of-wrong rule (First Restatement) will not necessarily have been replaced by an equally mechanical, forum-oriented rule.

The new Restatement (Third) echoes *Currie's* question whether a conflict exists as between laws that are relevant. It has a court determine whether "a material difference [exists] among relevant laws" (§ 5.02(a), step one), and if so, then decide which law should be given priority (step two). For the latter, the court should refer to "a local statute that identifies the law to be given priority," or absent such a statute, then to Restatement rules. Such rules allow for application of a "manifestly more appropriate law" under "exceptional" circumstances. § 5.03. See further at p. 194 *et seq.*, below. To simplify the foregoing: The Draft follows Currie's "true/false" conflict analysis, but if a true conflict exists, it either applies formulaic rules or has the court undertake a weighing for the "appropriateness" of applying one law or another, always keeping in mind that we are considering issues (*dépeçage*), not necessarily the whole case. In determining whether a conflict exists, the new Restatement (Third) stresses the need to determine the "scope" of the various laws: if they are limited to territorial application or only to certain persons or circumstances, they are not in conflict with another law (see *comments* A–C to § 5.02).

3. Application

Few states follow "pure" interest analysis, but many use policy analysis as part of their resolution of true conflicts, for instance, as a factor in the determination of the law of the "place of the most significant relationship" (Restatement (Second), below). New York, which once embraced it, has retreated to a more rule-oriented approach (below at p. 184). California, by case law, and Louisiana, by statute, have adopted a variant, the "comparative impairment" approach (above at p. 176 and below at p. 180).

In its modified form, i.e., as weighing policies of legal rules, *interest analysis has influenced much of modern American conflicts law*. It is also part of choice-of-law analysis under the Restatement (Second) (below at p. 181) and the Draft Restatement (Third), below at p. 194 *et seq*.

4. Interest Analysis and "Pervasive Problems"

Interest analysis tends to be *forum-oriented*. Given this orientation, what is the role of the traditional "pervasive problems" (above Chapter VII)?

Subject matter characterization may favor the "interested state," i.e., the forum in true conflicts and in many or most false conflicts cases.

Procedural characterization of the traditional kind becomes unimportant if forum law is the starting point for most cases. Note that both subject matter and procedural/substantive characterization are made by the forum (see § 5.05 of the Draft Restatement (Third)).

Renvoi is not an issue if forum law is selected for application. But note that the other state's conflicts rules will say something about its "interest," especially if they point *away* from it, perhaps even to the forum. In other words, *the other state's conflicts rules may disclose the existence of a "false conflict."* The Draft Restatement (Third) will reject renvoi, except when the objective of the forum's conflicts law is to reach the same result as the courts of the other state would—and then only if it is practical and feasible. § 5.06(2). Given the two "ifs" in the provision, a court might well decline to deal with the other state's conflicts law.

In *American Motorist Insurance Co. v. ARTRA Group, Inc.*, 659 A.2d 1295 (Md. 1995), plaintiff had urged that Maryland abandon the *lex loci contractus* rule (application of the law of the place where a contract was made to questions relating to its validity and construction). Instead, plaintiff suggested adoption of the "most significant relationship" test. The Maryland court was not prepared to jettison the traditional rule. Instead, it adopted a limited *renvoi* exception to that rule (referring to the *Hornbook*): when the conflicts rule of the state where the contract was made would lead to the conclusion that Maryland has the most significant relationship to the issue and would not apply its own law for that reason, Maryland should indeed apply its own law. By identifying a "false conflict," the court applied forum law as the law of the state of the most significant relationship, while formally retaining the traditional rule. See also *Macsherry v. Sparrows Point, LLC*, No. ELH-15-22, 2017 WL 3315262, at *17 (D. Md. Aug. 3, 2017); *Gourdine v. Karl Storz Endoscopy-America, Inc.*, 223 F. Supp. 3d 475, 494 (D.S.C. 2016).

The Draft Restatement (Third) formulation, discussed above, does not use renvoi to determine whether there might be a "false" conflict. Instead, it requires that the objective of the forum's choice-of-law rule is to bring about uniformity ("reach the same result as would the courts of the other state"). See cmt. *h*. It might seem that the latter follows from the former, but this is not necessarily so. A false conflict leads to forum law, but the search for the same result that the other court would reach might lead to yet another law (transmission). However, to determine what the result the other court would want to reach in a case like the one at hand would seem to require a look at that state's choice-of-law rules. Are we not in a circle? But even if a look at the other state's choice-of law rule might provide an answer, the "subject to practicability and feasibility" limitation, still gives the forum court another escape. § 5.06(2).

Public policy will rarely be an issue because it will have been part of the determination of the "governmental interest" of the forum in the *initial* choice of law.

C. "Comparative Impairment"

One variation of interest analysis is a **weighing approach** first adopted by California: in true conflicts cases the court should apply *the law of the jurisdiction whose policies would be more impaired than those of the other jurisdiction if its law were not applied.* The Louisiana conflicts codification generally adopts the comparative impairment test for choice of law in tort. La. Civ. Code Ann. art. 3515 (2022). Other provisions, however, particularize with respect to issues of conduct, loss allocation, and products liability. La. Civ. Code Ann. arts. 3543–3545 (2022).

Illustrations:

1) Under California law, taverns are liable for injuries caused by patrons who were served while intoxicated. Nevada law does not provide for such civil liability. Held, that California law applied to an action by a California plaintiff against a Nevada tavern. California's policies (in favor of compensation) would be more impaired by non-application of its laws than would Nevada's (no liability) when the tavern regulated solicited business from California. *Bernhard v. Harrah's Club,* 546 P.2d 719 (Cal. 1976) (en banc). (Two years later, California abrogated *Bernhard* by statute. Cal. Civ. Code § 1714(b) (West 2022) (absolving tavern owners from civil liability).)

2) An Ontario plaintiff was injured there as a result of a defect in a machine manufactured in California. He had received worker compensation benefits in Ontario. In a suit against the California manufacturer, held, that Ontario law (barring claims against third parties) applies; its policies "would be fully served," while California's interests would be "far less significantly impaired if its law were not applied." *Paulo v. Bepex Corp.,* 792 F.2d 894, 896 (9th Cir. 1986). But see *McCormack v. Medcor, Inc.*, No. 14 CV 3551, 2014 WL 5622172 (N.D. Ill. Nov. 4, 2014) (Illinois law would be more impaired).

The "comparative impairment" approach assumes that the strength of competing policies can be readily ascertained. In fact, the determination of greater or lesser impairment will often be nothing more than a judgment call.

Example: In *Offshore Rental Co. v. Continental Oil Co.,* 583 P.2d 721 (Cal. 1978) (en banc), the court applied Louisiana law, which it found to be more in the "main stream" than California's more archaic law. See also the discussion of the "better law" approach, below Section V(B).

The Draft Restatement (Third) will also depart from an express forum orientation, just as the comparative impairment approach does. Nor does it adopt the Second Restatement's "most significant relationship" test (described below), but—when laws conflict—calls for the application of the "most appropriate relevant law." § 5.01(ii). More on this below.

IV. Restatement (Second): Most Significant Relationship

A. Overview

The Restatement (Second) (1971) also rejects the rigidity of the First Restatement's territorially-focused rule approach. At the same time, it also does not engage in open-ended interest analysis, nor, for the most part, does it share the forum-bias of that approach. Its goals, like that of the traditional approach (First Restatement) are predictability, uniformity of result, and the prevention of forum shopping.

It seeks to achieve these goals through an approach which retains some of the traditional rules (for instance, in the area of property law), but in the main, provides criteria and an approach designed to lead to the formulation of *narrow, **issue-oriented** rules.* See further *infra* Chapter IX.

In the areas in which it has abandoned the traditional rules, the Restatement (Second) calls for the identification of the "**place of the most significant relationship**" with respect to the particular issue and for the application of that state's law to that issue.

B. Determining the State of the Most Significant Relationship: Applying the Restatement (Second)

In the areas for which it does not suggest specific rules but provides a more flexible approach, the Restatement (Second):

(1) calls for the application of the law of the state which has the *most significant relationship* to (for instance) the occurrence (tort) or transaction (contract) *and* the parties;

(2) provides that this determination is to be done "under the principles stated in § 6" (see below);

(3) lists a *non-exclusive* number of "contacts," which are to be taken into account in making the determination under #1 and #2;

(4) makes clear that the contacts under #3 are to be evaluated "in accordance with their relative importance to the particular issue" (meaning both *dépeçage* and no priority among the contacts cited illustratively); and

(5) establishes some presumptions as to the applicable law, but provides that these may be displaced by another more significantly related law.

Examples: Section 145 calls for application of the law of the most significant relationship to tort issues. Section 146 calls for application of the law of the place of the tort in personal injury cases, unless another state has a more significant relationship to the issue. Section 188(3) provides that when the place of negotiating a contract and the place of its performance are in the same state, that state's law will "usually" be applied. This is so because that state will probably ("usually") be the state of the most significant relationship.

The reference to the general principles of § 6 provides the court with a list of considerations to guide it in determining the state with the most significant relationship to the issue. These principles are: (a) the needs of the interstate and international legal systems; (b) the forum's policies; (c) the policies of other states and those states' interest in the application of their law to the issue; (d) protection of party expectations; (e) the policy underlying the particular field of law; (f) certainty, predictability, and uniformity of result; (g) the relative ease of determining and applying a law.

Note: The principles are *not listed in any order of priority.* Section 6 thus permits courts to emphasize *different* principles as they shape rules for determining the law of the state of the most significant relationship. For instance, more traditionally-oriented courts may emphasize (a), (d), and (f). Courts with a policy or interest-analysis orientation may focus more on (b), (c), and (e), and courts adopting the "better law" approach (Section V, below) will work with (e) and (g).

The principles also overlap, and depending on the case, may express the same policy in different ways. For instance, the protection of party expectations (d) is also a basic policy underlying the law of contract and trusts (e), while it is a need of the interstate and international legal systems (a) to have a fair degree of predictability, certainty and uniformity of result (f).

C. Application

Recall the facts of *Alabama Great Southern Railroad Co.,* above at p. 175. Under the Restatement (Second), a court would first need to characterize the subject matter of the issue, just as it would under the traditional approach. Assume that it decides that what is involved are "rights and liabilities . . . with respect to an issue in tort," and that the tort chapter therefore applies. § 145(1). For personal injuries, § 146 calls for the law of the place of the wrong, unless another state has a more significant relationship to the occurrence and to the parties. Section 145, establishing general principles for tort choice of law, lists a number of "contacts" for determining the law of the state of the most significant relationship: (a) place of injury, (b) place of conduct, (c) domicile or place of business of parties, and (d) the place where the relationship of the parties was centered.

Illustrations: 1) In *Alabama Great Southern Railroad Co.,* contacts (a) and (b) point to Y law, while contacts (c) and (d) point to X law. Does this split mean that § 146 (place of wrong) does not get displaced by a more significantly related (other) law? Not necessarily, because the § 145 contacts are to be evaluated in the light of the general principles of § 6 (above at p. 181). Of these, (b) (viz. the forum's policy in favor of compensation and of holding local companies liable for torts of their employees), (e) (viz. a policy of tort law is compensation), and (g) (ease of applying forum law) all point to state X. In addition, the policies and interests of the other state—state Y—will not be frustrated (principle (c)), since it has no connection with the parties and the consequences of the injuries, being only the fortuitous place of the accident. Finally, if the parties had any expectation at all (d) as to what law would apply to tort claims between them, they would probably have expected home state law (X) to apply. Thus, while the § 145 contacts are *numerically* evenly divided, evaluating them in the light of § 6 leads to the conclusion that the contacts pointing to state

X are relatively more important. Thus, the law of a state other than that of the place of injury (§ 146) is more significantly related to the occurrence and the parties (§ 145), and displaces the law of the state of the wrong: X law applies.

2) The early leading decision in *Babcock v. Jackson,* 191 N.E.2d 279 (N.Y. 1963), antedates the Restatement (Second). New York residents take a trip by car. The trip is to start and terminate in New York, but takes them through Canada, where they have an accident not involving any other parties. Canada barred suits, in ordinary negligence, by guest/passengers against their host/drivers; New York did not. Apply the above analytic illustration to *Babcock* to test your understanding of why the New York court decided to apply New York law.

Note that in the analytic illustration above, the *policies* of the two states (X and Y) play an important role. Courts inclined toward policy or interest analysis can engage in it to a significant degree while working within the general framework of the Restatement (Second). As a practical matter, policy analysis underlies much of the Restatement (Second) case law.

The Restatement (Second) approach has had significant effect on the case law. The great majority of states have departed from the traditional approach, especially with respect to tort.

Note: It is very hard—indeed risky—to classify states as "Restatement (Second) states" or as interest-analysis states. A very few states stick with the traditional approach entirely. Most will make a total break, but may do so only for tort and not yet entirely for contract, or they may apply policy analysis to some particular issues while generally keeping a traditional orientation. An annual survey in the *American Journal of Comparative Law* provides state-by-state information. See, e.g., Symeonides, Choice of Law in the American Courts in 2020, 69 Am. J. Comp. L. 177 (2021); Coyle, Dodge & Simowitz, Choice of Law in American Courts in 2024, 73 Am. J. Comp. L. 485 (2025).

D. Restatement (Second) and Pervasive Problems

The Second Restatement expressly uses an **issue-by-issue** approach: the task is to choose the law applicable to a particular issue, not the whole case. This approach (*dépeçage,* see *supra* p. 173) may result to the application of several laws to different issues of a case.

Subject matter characterization continues to be part of the Restatement (Second) approach. This is so both when the Restatement retains express rules derived from the traditional approach and when it calls for the application of the most significant law in other areas. In the latter case, characterization of the subject matter continues to be important because the Restatement lists different connecting factors and establishes different presumptions (see above) depending on whether the issue is one of—say—tort or contract.

Similarly, the Restatement (Second), in its Chapter VI, retains the ***substance/procedure*** dichotomy, identifying those areas that, because they are "procedural," will be governed by the law of the forum. This is, and also has been traditionally, a case of *dépeçage*. These include the form of the action (§ 124), service (§ 126), pleadings (§ 127), some aspects of the burden of proof (§§ 133–34), the sufficiency of the evidence (§ 135), and competency of witnesses (§ 137).

The question of which **statute of frauds** applies (§ 141) is governed by the law selected by application of §§ 187–88, the choice of law rules for contract: either the law chosen by the parties or, absent a choice, the law of the most significant relationship.

Traditionally, statutes of limitations were characterized as *procedural* (i.e., forum law applies). In 1988, § 142 was revised as follows: select the law applicable to the limitation *issue* (note: *dépeçage*!) in accordance with the general principles of § 6 (above), but "in general," and absent special circumstances, forum law governs. See also above and *Erickson v. Pharmacia LLC*, 578 P.3d 306 (Wash. 2025)

Renvoi: Restatement (Second) § 8 advocates the limited use of another state's conflicts law. To summarize, when the objective is to reach the same result as another state, apply that state's conflicts rules. When the forum has little or no connection with the parties or case, and other interested states would select a particular state's law, do as they would do. Note that the second of these, in essence, describes a *false conflict* situation (see also above at p. 176 *et seq.*).

The **public policy** of the forum—as a reason for not applying an otherwise applicable law—is not expressly mentioned by the Restatement (Second). Note, however, that the relevant policies of the forum and of other interested states will be considered as part of the initial **choice of law**. Therefore, there is no reason to engage in a second inquiry at the end of the choice-of-law process.

E. Narrow Rules: New York's Tort Approach

1. From *Babcock* to *Neumeier*

The development of the case law in New York illustrates well one state's search for meaningful alternatives to the mechanical place-of-wrong rule for tort choice of law under the vested rights approach.

In the early leading decision of *Babcock v. Jackson* (above at p. 183), New York disregarded the place of the accident as "fortuitous" and applied forum law when all contacts were with New York: the parties' domicile, the formation of their relationship, and the place where the car was garaged and insured. In subsequent cases, New York increasingly tended toward interest analysis. In *Neumeier v. Kuehner,* 286 N.E.2d 454 (N.Y. 1972), the New York Court of Appeals adopted more narrowly-drawn rules. While they do not represent a return to the vested rights approach, they were written against the background of competing state policies and different party expectations. As such, they differ from interest analysis and the Restatement (Second) in that they establish *rules,* not merely a method for choice of law.

In *Neumeier,* a guest/passenger from Ontario (which had a guest-statute immunizing the host/driver) was injured in Ontario while a guest in the New York (no guest statute) defendant's car. The Court of Appeals adopted these rules:

(1) When both parties are domiciled in the same state and the car is registered there, that state's law determines the standard of care;

(2) When the defendant acts at his or her domicile and incurs no liability under its law, no liability results; but if he or she acts at the plaintiff's domicile and that law provides for liability, liability results in the absence of special circumstances;

(3) In other situations, when the parties are from different states, the law of the place of the accident will "normally" apply unless displacing that law "will advance the relevant substantive law purposes [of another state] without impairing the smooth working of the multi-state system or producing great uncertainty for litigants." Id. at 458.

On the facts of the case, Rule 3 applied; the defendant was not liable. Note that the two aspects common to all three *Neumeier* rules are the interests of the states involved and party expectations. In the second and third *Neumeier* rules, place of acting and party expectation (or absence of unfair surprise to a party) normally coincide. Of the two elements, the *parties' common domicile* displaces the place of the occurrence. Rule 1; see also the proviso of Rule 3.

Note: Actually, Rule 2, like the first part of Rule 3, is place-of-tort-oriented. So—is there much difference between Rule 2 and Rule 3's first part? Note further that Rule 3 provides for an escape, while Rule 2 (at least in its first part) does not.

2. From *Neumeier* to *Schultz* to *Edwards*

The Court of Appeals applied *Neumeier,* and reemphasized the criteria underlying its three rules, in *Schultz v. Boy Scouts of America, Inc.,* 480 N.E.2d 679 (N.Y. 1985). "[T]he significant contacts are, almost exclusively, the parties' domiciles and the locus of the tort." Id. at 684. In *Schultz,* the Court declared that the *Neumeier* rules apply in all cases, not just those involving guest statutes, in which the conflicting rule of law is a "**loss-allocating**" rule. However, if conflicting rules of law address the appropriate standards of conduct (e.g., rules of the road), then the law of the place of the tort will have "a predominant, if not exclusive, concern." Id. *Schultz* observed that "the relative interests of the domicile and locus jurisdictions in having their laws apply will depend on the particular tort issue in conflict in the case." Id.

The issue in *Schultz* was whether the defendant was immune under New Jersey's charitable immunity rule, or could be held liable for wrongful death under New York law, which did not have a charitable immunity rule. The Court held that a charitable immunity rule was loss allocating (i.e., from the tortfeasor to the public, in consideration of the former's charitable work), that *Neumeier* therefore applied, and since plaintiff and defendant had the same New Jersey domicile, *Neumeier* # 1 called for application of New Jersey law, immunizing the defendant. *Schultz,* in turn, was followed in *Cooney v. Osgood Machinery, Inc.,* 612 N.E.2d 277 (N.Y. 1993).

The question might be asked, as did the dissent in *Schultz,* whether the absence of a rule in New York law immunizing charities did not in fact regulate the conduct of charities, namely, to hold them liable—like everyone else—for wrongful conduct. In the absence of an immunity rule, New York law as the law of the place of the tort should have applied. The New Jersey Supreme Court arrived at such a result when it declined to apply the New Jersey charitable immunity rule in an action by a New Jersey domiciliary against a New Jersey charity for injuries sustained in Pennsylvania, which does not immunize charities. The New Jersey immunity rule had no extraterritorial effect *P.V. ex rel. T.V. v. Camp Jaycee*, 962 A.2d 453 (N.J. 2008). The court arrived at this result by applying an interest analysis approach, concluding that the law of the parties' common domicile did not outweigh Pennsylvania's interest in applying its law to torts committed in Pennsylvania. Maybe the plaintiffs in *Schultz* would have been better off if they had sued at home? In terms of the Draft Restatement (Third), see below, the question was the "scope" of the New Jersey immunity rule. The New York court that decided *Schultz* did not ask that question.

Returning to New York, in *Edwards v. Erie Coach Lines Co.*, 952 N.E.2d 1033 (N.Y. 2011), the issue concerned the applicability of Ontario's cap on damages (considered to be a loss-allocating rule) when the accident occurred in the New York forum state. The plaintiffs and one defendant shared an Ontario domicile, so that the *Neumeier* # 1 rule applied: damages were capped by Ontario law. The other defendants were Pennsylvania domiciliaries. They claimed the benefit of the Ontario cap, just as the Franciscan Brothers (Ohio domiciliaries) had claimed and received the benefit of New Jersey's immunity rule in *Schultz* (above). But, as the Court noted, the Franciscans were actively involved in charity work in *Schultz*, so that treating them the same as the defendant Boy Scouts was justified under the exception to *Neumeier* # 3. In the present case, the Pennsylvania defendants had had no contact with Ontario, so *Neumeier* # 3 therefore applied: New York law, as the law of the place of the accident. For an application of *Edwards*, see *In re Air Crash Near Clarence Center*, 983 F. Supp. 2d 249, 253 (W.D.N.Y. 2013). For a brief overview of the New York approach to choice-of-law in tort, see *In re Terrorist Attacks on September 11, 2001*, 2023 WL 5207985 **2–3 (S.D.N.Y. 2023). See also *Bordes v. Deveaux*, 2025 WL 1042323 (S.D.N.Y. 2025).

V. Restatement (Third): Some Rules and the Search for the "Most Appropriate Law"

A. Overview

Work on the Restatement (Third) began on 2014. By now, the membership of the American Law Institute has approved a number provisions proposed by the Reporters and then approved and submitted to the membership by the Council. The some parts still need to be finished. When they are done, the Restatement (Third) will be promulgated as such.

The introduction to choice of law rephrases, but mainly repeats what is familiar. First, the "relevant law" must be identified because the task will be to apply the "most appropriate relevant law to govern particular issues." § 5.01 (Tentative Draft No. 3, approved 2022). Apart from substance, relevance also means that the "scope" of the other law extends to a case like the present one (for instance, is not restricted to local matters).

Possibly relevant laws must be examined to determine whether they are materially different. One of the relevant rules might be one presented by the Restatement (Third) itself. But such a rule should be disregarded if another law is "manifestly more appropriate." § 5.03.

A law that may be relevant other than the forum's own is the other state's (or country's) "internal law." Consideration of another jurisdiction's choice-of-law rules is more restricted than it is under § 8 of the Restatement (Second): the other state's rules should only be considered if both they and the forum's rules would reach the same result. § 5.6(2), discussed above at p. 164.

This limited consideration of the other state's conflicts rules precludes examination whether there might be a "false conflict" (for instance, because the other state would refer to this forum's law). Here, the choice-of-law rule of the other state and the "scope" of its internal law (see above) seem to intertwine.

B. Rules and General Approach

The Restatement (Third) provides definite rules in a number of areas. They are based upon, derived from a particular policy approach for that subject matter and, as already stated above, the underlying policy may require disregard of the rule in favor of a "manifestly more appropriate" other law (§ 5.03). Some of these rules will be stated in the context of the particular subject matter.

An example are the provisions relating to torts (see also below at p. 203 *et seq.* Underlying the provisions is the objective to apply the law of the state with the "dominant interest" (unless the parties had made a choice). § 6.01. For personal torts, the Restatement (Third) adopts the distinction between "loss-allocating" and "conduct-regulating" rules of law and provides lists of such rules in §§ 6.03–6.09 (for instance, that the "contributory negligence" rule is loss-allocating, Section 6.05(g)), seeks application of the law "appropriate to the type of issue" when no rule exists, and of course permits displacement by a most appropriate other law.

The Restatement (Third) of course also needs to provide guidance when no particular law or none of its rules applies. When laws identified to be "relevant" to a torts issue "conflict," the Restatement (Third) provides for the selection of the law "most appropriate relevant law to govern particular issues." § 5.01. Comment E to § 5.02 explains that "most appropriate law is not intended to replicate any major pre-existing approach to choice of law," in particular mentioning "most significant relationship" and "more impaired." Thus, for instance, it is said that the Restatement (Second) approach should not be commingled with what the Restatement (Third) seeks to provide. For instance, in the tort chapter, the beginning reference is to the "dominant interest." The Restatement (Second) provided guidance in its § 145 to determine the law of the "most significant relationship" to the issue and provided relatively few rules (for instance, § 146).

In building on the "dominant interest" in the torts chapter, the Restatement (Third) adopts the distinction between "loss-allocating" and "conduct-regulating" rules of law and provides lists of such rules in §§ 6.03–6.09 (for instance, that the "contributory negligence" rule is loss-allocating, Section 6.05(g)), seeks application of the law "appropriate to the type of issue" when no rule exists, and of course permits displacement by a most appropriate other law.

While the Comments of the Restatement (Third) counsel against interpreting its rules and approach on the basis of prior approaches or key words or phrase, its approach derives more directly from interest-analysis (both in establishing specific rules and providing an approach when rules are lacking) than does the more quantitative approach followed by its predecessor.

VI. Leflar's Choice-Influencing Considerations, Particularly Also the "Better Rule of Law"

Whenever an applicable law needs to be determined or chosen, concrete rules may be lacking, approaches suggested by Restatements or even laws may often require giving preference to one or another consideration or hypothetical outcome. During the times of the desired departure from fixed, even rigid, traditional rules (see above), scholars and some decisions suggested or advocated approaches or considerations that never became dominant (like Professor Currie's interest analysis) nor were (directly) picked up in the Restatements but probably did influence decisions when alternatives were in issue.

The following two sections describe important early suggestions. The first (Part A) obviously had great influence on the general considerations of provisions like § 145 of the Restatement (Second).

A. In General

The late Professor Robert Leflar reduced the policy considerations that underlie interest analysis and most other modern approaches, including that of the Restatement (Second), to five *"choice-influencing considerations."* They are:

1) *Predictability of Results:* Forum shopping should be discouraged, parties should be protected in their expectations (applicable mainly in consensual and other planned transactions, as distinguished from torts).
2) *Maintenance of Interstate and International Order:* To facilitate interstate and international movement of goods and people, states should recognize that another state may have a superior interest in the matter, should therefore exercise restraint in the assertion of their own sovereignty and application of their own law, and when appropriate, apply the law of the other state.
3) *Simplification of the Judicial Task:* States will apply their own procedural law in the interest of the smooth administration of justice, but when another state's rules (for instance, with respect to the measure of damages or the statute of frauds) are outcome-determinative, the forum may also apply another state's procedural law if this can be done with relative ease.
4) *Advancement of the Forum's Governmental Interest:* The forum should apply local law when the forum state has a genuine governmental interest. To Leflar, this is more than an interest in the advancement of a policy with respect to a particular issue; it represents the "total governmental concerns of a justice-dispensing court in a modern American state."
5) *Application of the Better Rule of Law:* The courts' choice is not between the law of one state over the law of another, but should have for its purpose the selection of the "better rule of law" for the solution of the problem at hand in view of present day conditions.

Leflar's choice-influencing considerations differ from interest analysis in that they do not seem to focus on the advancement of forum policy (or, if lacking, that of another interested state) with respect to particular issues. Rather, the approach seems more *problem oriented.* If so, it would also differ from that of the Restatement (Second). Consistent with its more free-flowing problem orientation, it does not identify relevant contacts in advance, let alone suggest a law which should be presumptively applicable in particular circumstances (such as the law of the state where the contract was both negotiated and to be performed).

Yet, the considerations contained in Leflar's enumeration are very much the same ones a court will review in interest analysis. Similarly, Leflar's list has a striking similarity with the general principles of § 6 of the Restatement (Second) (above at pp. 181–182). However, his list lacks the further elaboration which the Restatement (Second) provides in its subject matter provisions. Note also, that like interest analysis, Leflar's approach does contain a *forum bias* in the third and fourth of his considerations. That bias has become particularly pronounced in those states that have focused primarily on the fifth consideration, the application of the "better rule of law."

B. The "Better Rule of Law"

Leflar's choice-influencing considerations are not stated in any priority order. Nonetheless, *courts utilizing his approach have looked primarily to the "better rule of law" consideration.* Almost invariably, when presented with a conflict between the policies of forum law and those of another state, *the court concluded that forum law and policy reflected the "better rule of law."*

Illustration: A resident of Wisconsin (who happened to be employed in Minnesota and who therefore commuted daily to Minnesota) was killed in Wisconsin in a traffic accident caused by an uninsured motorist who is also a resident of Wisconsin. Subsequent to his death, his widow moved to Minnesota and there sued the decedent's own insurance carrier under his policy's uninsured motorist coverage. The decedent had maintained three policies on three different vehicles, and the question was whether the uninsured motorist coverage of these policies could be cumulated ("stacking"), or whether there would be but one recovery. Minnesota law permitted stacking, Wisconsin law did not. The Minnesota court concluded that Minnesota had an interest in the application of its law: the decedent had been a member of the Minnesota work force (although the accident had happened in Wisconsin at a time when the decedent was not commuting to or from work), the widow had changed her domicile to Minnesota (although she had done so after the accident), the estate (the present claim) was a Minnesota estate, and the insurance carrier, doing business in Minnesota, could not claim unfair surprise. Stacking was allowed. The U.S. Supreme Court confirmed the constitutionality of the application of Minnesota law under the circumstances. *Allstate Insurance Co. v. Hague,* 449 U.S. 302, 101 S. Ct. 633, 66 L. Ed. 2d 521 (1981). Constitutional limitations on choice of law are discussed below in Chapter X.

In *Jepson v. General Casualty Co. of Wisconsin,* 513 N.W.2d 467 (1994), the Supreme Court of Minnesota departed from the "better law approach," emphasizing "predictability and maintenance of the interstate order," and yielding, on that kind of interest analysis, to the law of another state. Id. at 472. "Sometimes different laws are neither better nor worse in an objective way, just different." Id. at 473. How true.

As they evolved, Leflar's choice-influencing considerations came down to the application of the "better rule of law," which in turn, often amounted to the application of forum law. The goals of the first and second "considerations" (predictability of result by prevention of forum shopping and promotion of interstate and international order through deference to other states' interests) are then lost. Arkansas, Minnesota, New Hampshire, Rhode Island, and Wisconsin adopted the "better rule of law" approach in torts. Minnesota retreated somewhat from that rule in 1994 (*Jepson*) and adopted policy analysis instead (see immediately preceding paragraph). For further discussion of *Jepson*, see *Nodak Mutual Ins. Co. v. American Family Mutual Ins. Co.*, 604 N.W.2d 91 (Minn. 2000).

VII. Other Approaches

The following describes other approaches suggested during the search for a more flexible way to determine the law—one's own or that of another jurisdiction and, if the latter, which one. These many other ideas and suggestions have been mentioned here and there but decisions are not expressly based on them. Quite obviously, however, many modern approaches and even rules echo them. See, for instance, immediately following, the reference to "predominantly concerned states" or the preference of the lex fori. Do these thoughts not echo Currie, aspects the new Restatement (Third) and the *Allstate v. Hague* decision (above)?

A. Functional Analysis

Two approaches of **functional analysis** have been offered, which, in effect, have interest analysis as their starting point but seek to refine it.

Professors von Mehren and Trautman speak of "**concerned states**" (instead of "interested states") and seek to identify the "**predominantly concerned**" state whose law would then be applied. When there is no "predominantly concerned state"—i.e., when there is a "false conflict"—the forum is to weigh the "status" of the potentially applicable laws. It is to determine the strength of the policy underlying the law, whether the law is anachronistic or represents a modern trend, and whether it serves to address "multistate" concerns. If this inquiry and weighing of policy does not lead to a resolution, the forum is to apply the law of "effective control" (e.g., the law of the situs in the case of immovables), or is to apply forum law, so long as it itself is one of the concerned jurisdictions.

Professor Weintraub similarly engaged in interest analysis, but identifies specific policy goals and values, which then enable him to formulate broad policy-based rules.

Illustration: In tort, the modern trend of the law is toward loss distribution through insurance; anachronistic laws inconsistent with a modern trend should not be applied, unfair surprise should be avoided, and choice-of-law rules should be examined since they may reveal the existence of a "false conflict" (see also above at p. 176). On the basis of these considerations, Weintraub once formulated the following choice-of-law rule for torts: "An actor is liable for his conduct if he is liable under the law of any state whose interests would be advanced significantly by imposing liability, unless imposition of liability would unfairly surprise the actor." For his later, more differentiated, "consequences-based" approach, see Weintraub, *Commentary on the Conflict of Laws* § 6.2 *et seq.* (6th ed. 2010).

For contract, Weintraub starts with a rebuttable presumption that the contract is valid, but also gives consideration to the possibility of anachronistic law, the possibility that the contract was the result of unequal bargaining power (adhesion contract), the policies of the interested states, unfair surprise, the "false conflict" disclosed by a choice-of-law rule, and the nature of the contract as commercial or non-commercial. He derives as a rule that contracts should be upheld if valid under the law of a connected state unless the law of another state, which would invalidate the contract, would be significantly advanced as a result of the foregoing policy considerations.

The Weintraub approach, more than the general *"comparative impairment"* approach (above at p. 180), identifies relevant policies in advance in order to state a broad rule. The breadth of the rules, however, still offers less guidance than do the sections of the Restatement (Second), which particularize the general principles of its § 6.

B. "Lex Fori"

The approach of the late Professor Ehrenzweig, the **lex fori** approach, urged the *application of forum law in most cases* even more directly than Currie's interest analysis.

In its own complicated vocabulary, the approach provides, first, that the forum court apply existing *"true rules"* of choice of law.

These may be "formulated rules of choice," either by statute or by settled rules of common law (for instance, that the law of the situs applies to immovable property). Additionally, there might be *"non-formulated, inchoate"* rules, for instance, principles recognized by judicial precedent.

In the absence of "true rules," the approach calls for an examination of the law of the forum to determine whether, by its own terms, it is not perhaps applicable to the case. If there is no reason to displace forum law, then it applies. Finally, if there is neither a true rule pointing to another law nor policy reasons for the application of forum law, forum law nonetheless applies as the "residual law."

The theory underlying Ehrenzweig's approach is that there is no "super law" (a federal mandate for a particular choice of law), so the starting point must therefore be forum law and the basic question whether there is any reason why it should be displaced. Ehrenzweig's goal was that the "proper law" should be applied "in the proper forum." The end result is nonetheless that forum law will apply for precisely the same reason that it does under the pure interest analysis urged by Currie: in the absence of a (legislative or other) directive to the contrary, courts are not to weigh competing policies, and forum law is therefore not displaced.

The *lex fori* approach has found very little independent following in the case law. But interest analysis may lead to the same result, as may the forum-oriented "General Principles" of § 6 of the Restatement (Second), above p. 182.

C. "Principles of Preference"

Professor David Cavers thought that the smooth working of the federal system (combined with fairness to the parties) required that the policies underlying interest analysis be developed into rules, beyond presenting only an approach or framework for analysis. Like Professor Weintraub (above at p. 190), he used interest analysis to isolate true conflicts from false conflicts. Unlike Professor Weintraub, he assigned priorities to different *policies—"principles of preference"*—which then permitted him to make a specific, territorially-based choice of law.

Tort:

1) When the state of injury provides a higher standard of conduct or of financial protection against injury as compared with the state where the act occurred or where the defendant was domiciled, the law of the state of injury provides the standard of conduct and the measure of financial protection

(except, perhaps, when there is a particularly close relationship between plaintiff and defendant, in which case a law related to their relationship might apply).

2) When the state where the act *and* injury occurred provides a lower standard of conduct and of financial protection than the law of the plaintiff's domicile, the law of the place of injury (lower standard) governs.

3) When the state where the defendant acts imposes special regulatory controls on his conduct, this law should apply (and benefit the plaintiff), even though the law of the state of injury imposes no similar controls. For example, when the state in which the defendant tavern does business imposes dram shop liability (permitting recovery against the tavern for injuries caused by someone who was served by the tavern despite being intoxicated), a plaintiff injured in a non-dram shop act state by a patron of defendant's tavern should be able to invoke the defendant's dram shop liability.

4) When the law of the state in which a relationship between the parties, relevant to the tort, was centered imposes a higher standard of conduct or of financial protection than the state of injury, the first state's law governs. See *Babcock v. Jackson,* 191 N.E.2d 279 (N.Y. 1963), in which New York law applied: the parties formed the guest/host relationship in New York (where the host enjoys no guest-statute immunity), the trip began and was to terminate in New York, and an accident occurred en route in Canada, which provides for immunity for the host.

5) When the state where the relationship was centered imposes a lower standard of conduct or of financial protection than the state of the injury, the lower standard applies (protecting the defendant). This is the reverse of *Babcock v. Jackson,* above: Canadian parties (guest-statute immunity) travel to New York (no immunity), where the accident occurs. Under the principle of preference just stated, the Canadian guest statute should immunize the defendant. Cf. *Neumeier v. Kuehner,* 286 N.E.2d 454 (N.Y. 1972).

Note: Cavers' "principles of preference" are in many cases quite similar to the narrow policy-based rules adopted by the New York Court of Appeals in *Neumeier v. Kuehner,* which are discussed above at p. 184. How about if a state followed §§ 145, 146 of the Restatement (Second), above at p. 181. What about the Restatement (Third), above at p. 186?

Contract: Cavers favors the law that would validate the parties' contract, thereby protecting their expectations. His major principle of preference in this area deals with the role of protective legislation: when the law of a state accords protection to the defendant (immunizes him from liability for whatever reasons), that law will apply *if* the defendant had a home in that state *and* the affected transaction or property interest was centered there.

Illustration: An Oregon resident, who has been declared a spendthrift there and therefore lacks capacity to contract, goes to California and there enters into a contract with a California resident; the contract is also to be performed in California. Under Cavers' principle of preference, the protection of the Oregon law does not apply—and the contract obligation is to be governed by California law—because, while the defendant had a home in the state with the protective legislation, the transaction was not centered there. For the contrary result in the actual case see *Lilienthal v. Kaufman,* 395 P.2d 543 (Or. 1964). For additional discussion of this case see p. 212 below.

Cavers' principles are territorially oriented, as are the rules of the New York Court of Appeals (above at p. 184 *et seq.*). They are relatively narrow. For that reason, they may be more likely to reintroduce the rigidity of the First Restatement than may the somewhat more open-ended approach of the Restatement (Second), although Cavers' principles also look toward the elaboration of rules rather than to ad hoc adjudication.

VIII. Conclusion: The Choice-of-Law Continuum

Try to envision the various approaches summarized in this chapter as located somewhere on a continuum between two extremes. Then ask yourself where each approach fits and where, today, the majority of American jurisdictions stand.

Keep in mind, as stated above at p. 183, that generalizations are *dangerous:* some states have adopted one approach for one area of the law and not, or not yet, for another. In some states, the issue whether, and for what cases, there should be a change has not (or not recently) arisen. Therefore, be familiar with the principal approaches, but examine carefully the posture of the particular state in which you are interested. The principal approaches are the First Restatement (still followed in some states), the Restatement (Second) (with various views influencing which of the "General Principles" of § 6 dominate in determining the "most significant relationship"), modified interest analysis, the coming Restatement (Third) (also echoing interest analysis in parts), and the California and New York approaches. As to the Restatement (Third): see the summary above at p. 186 and below p. 194.

At one end of the continuum is the traditional approach of the First Restatement: fixed rules, often criticized as too mechanical and not responsive to various policy concerns. *At the other end* stands the "better rule of law" approach: it is *result-selective*; it seeks justice in the individual case. It may be criticized for its ad hoc approach and its encouragement of forum shopping.

The *principles of preference* inject policy considerations in the determination of territorially-oriented rules. So do the *Neumeier* rules of the New York Court of Appeals, as refined by *Schultz* and *Edwards.*

Switching back to the other side of the continuum, *"pure" interest analysis,* as advocated by Currie, proceeds from entirely different premises than the "better rule of law" approach, but its effect will often be the same. Because no weighing of policies is involved, there is a very decided forum bias. This in turn permits and encourages forum shopping. The *comparative impairment* approach admits of weighing and thus moves away from the "pure" interest analysis. The concept of "comparative impairment," however, is stated in terms so general that a court with a forum bias can easily reach the desired result.

The *functional approaches* seek to give greater definition to the interests to be weighed, especially as developed by Weintraub, than the statement of some general rules.

The *Restatement (Second)* provides more flexibility—in terms of permitting consideration of a number of factors and policies depending on the varying fact patterns of cases—than do the modifications of the territorial approach as represented by the "principles of preference" and the *Neumeier* rules. At the same time, the Restatement (Second) gives more guidance, even territorially-oriented guidance for the selection of a law applicable to a particular issue, than do the functional approaches. The general principles of § 6, in contrast, present considerations permitting a variety of choices. They can accommodate all approaches and for that reason provide justification for a given choice, but little guidance for how to get there.

The coming Restatement (Third) introduces new approaches. Many of them are very welcome because they clarify matters so far left unanswered but they also introduce some question that still need to be resolved. Whether and when state courts will adopt its approaches is of course uncertain. A Restatement rule or approach becomes that state's conflicts rule only when adopted by its highest court, and that will take awhile. The Second Restatement and other approaches will therefore continue for some times or (like rules of the First Restatement in some states) for a long time. Also, how parts or provisions of the Restatement (Third) will be applied may differ among states that adopt it. See *Erickson v. Pharmacia LLC*, 578 P.3d 306 (Wash. 2025) and the conflicting amici briefs submitted to the court.

At the present time, most courts will still invoke the Restatement (Second) and interest analysis. A few will undertake careful and articulated analysis. A great many, however, speak in both "most-significant-relationship" and interest-analysis terms. Since § 6 of the Restatement (Second) contains an amalgam of policies, interest analysis can also be an important (or even the principal) element in a decision purporting to apply the Restatement (Second).

In the middle of our continuum, the approach of the Restatement (Second)—to the extent that it has not led to the development of narrowly defined rules—overlaps with functional interest analysis. Despite its repeated nods to territorialism ("state of the most significant relationship," presumption in favor of the state where the contract was negotiated and was to be performed, and the like), its issue-by-issue approach (*dépeçage*) demonstrates that it seeks to combine the approaches.

IX. The Future: The Coming Restatement (Third)

Many proposed provisions of the new Restatement (Third) have already been approved by the membership of the American Law Institute. Some aspects have already been described in Part V above. Overall, the new Restatement expressly continues the issue-by-issue approach of the Restatement (Second). The sections so far presented include a new definition of domicile (Chapter II, Section II(B)(2)), a major and welcome change regarding the law applicable to succession (*infra* at p. 220), and reformulations of public policy (p. 166) and *renvoi* (p. 159). The Restatement (Third) directs a court to determine first whether the relevant laws conflict (that is Currie's false conflict inquiry). This specifically includes the question about the "scope" of a possibly conflicting law, i.e., whether it is limited to that state's territory or to specific persons. The latter is illustrated by the *P.V. ex rel. T.V.* decision (above at p. 186). In the case of a conflict, the court should give "priority" to the "most appropriate law." Specific Restatement rules will provide the answer.

In tort, the specific rules for the determination of the most appropriate law (or the inquiry to be used if there is no specific rule) focus on the distinction between issues that are conduct-regulating or loss-allocating—a distinction that goes back to *Babcock, Neumeier,* and *Schultz.* This distinction is not always easy or clear: does the contributory negligence rule distribute the loss or does it seek to regulate the now-plaintiff's conduct? See also *P.V. ex rel. T.V, supra* p. 186. What about vicarious liability?

For contract issues, for which no specific rules have been so far provided, the court should again seek to apply the most appropriate law, also described as the law of the state with the "dominant interest." To determine the latter, the Draft provides guidance with a list that resembles a short version of § 6 of the Restatement (Second) (*supra* at p. 181). The choice of law by agreement of the parties (party autonomy) will be enforced only if the parties could have stipulated themselves what the other law provides. That would not be the case if the other law is restricted in its scope (see above) because parties cannot extend a state's law (so the reason for the restriction). However, if the parties meant to incorporate the content of the foreign law as their own, they could do so: the court needs to interpret whether this is what they intended. These provisions limit party autonomy to a greater degree than other legal systems and may not be helpful in business contracts. It will be remembered that the UCC is also restrictive in this matter.

X. Overview

Do the various approaches as well as the Restatements Second and Third provide ways to reach objective conclusions?

Unlike some foreign conflicts laws, including that of the European Union, the various approaches, including the Restatement (Second), provide just that: approaches. These suggest various factors that should be considered. Those factors are not in any priority order and therefore can be selected/relied upon as one wishes. The result can be homeward-trending. The Restatement (Third) now does provide some rules. But these can also be replaced by overriding policy-oriented factors or such factors are decisive when there are no rules to begin with. Interest analysis influenced the Restatement (Third). When decisions must be made on the basis of a number of factors and considerations, homeward trending becomes possible: The *Ehrenzweig* considerations remind us that one's thinking always starts first with the *lex fori*.

XI. Review Questions

During a stopover in state A, Plaintiff's private airplane is negligently maintained by Defendant. As a result, the engine quits while Plaintiff is flying over state B. The plane crashes in state C. Plaintiff is taken to a hospital in state D, where he dies. Under the First Restatement,

1. T or F: A wrongful death action against Defendant will be governed by the law of state C;

2. T or F: An action for the loss of the airplane will be governed by the law of state C;

3. T or F: The results would always be the same, even if Defendant had acted intentionally;

4. T or F: An action for breach of contract will be governed by the law of state B.

Assume that Plaintiff was a resident of A, that litigation is in A, and that A law, contrary to the law of C and D, contains no limitation on damages for wrongful death.

5. T or F: In states following the First Restatement, these additional facts would not change the law applicable to the wrongful death action.

6. T or F: All modern approaches would apply the law of A.

Assume that Plaintiff was a resident of C, which does not limit liability, that the law of A is the same, but that both B and D do limit liability. In addition to the individual defendant, Plaintiff's estate also sues the plane's manufacturer (X) in products liability.

X is incorporated and has its principal place of business in B. Assuming that there are no constitutional problems with the choice of the law of any of these states and that suit is brought in C (if C has jurisdiction under the jurisdictional rules in effect according to *Ford v. Montana, supra* at p. 71),

7. T or F: Under the First Restatement, same result as (5);

8. T or F: Pure interest analysis would lead to the law of C with respect to *both* tort claims (against Defendant No. 1 and X);

9. T or F: A "better law" state would apply C's law;

10. T or F: New York would apply the law of D;

11. T or F: The Restatement (Second) would also apply the law of D;

12. T or F: A "comparative impairment" approach would lead to the law of C.

Now, assume jurisdiction over all parties can only be obtained in A.

13. Which of the above (7 through 12) might change?

14. T or F: "Public policy" continues to be an important check, in all approaches, to test whether another state's law may offend the policy of the forum and therefore should not be applied.

15. T or F: The Restatement (Second) retains fixed choice-of-law rules for some areas of the law and calls for the application of the law of the most significant relationship in others.

16. T or F: *Renvoi* can help to identify false conflicts.

The Restatement (Third) is still in preparation, but some sections have been adopted and others have been proposed. How will new Restatement (Third) improve the present Restatement (Second)? See Section VIII above and consider the following questions.

17. T or F: The proposed focus of the proposed Restatement (Third) for determining the law applicable to a tort issue (loss-allocation or conduct-regulation is preferable to §§ 145 and 146 of the Restatement (Second).

18. T or F: The forum's determination of the "scope" of another possibly relevant/ applicable law may result in renvoi, despite the Draft's general rejection of renvoi.

19. T or F: There should be a presumption that the parties to a contract with a choice-of-law clause intended to incorporate the substance of the relevant foreign law, even if it would not have been applicable under that law's definition of its own "scope."

20. T or F: The new Restatement (Third) provides some rules. For many tort cases they derive in part from New York cases like *Neumeier* and *Schultz.*

21. T or F: "Dominant interest" in the coming Restatement (Third) replicates the Second Restatement's most-significant-relationship test of its § 145.

22. T or F: Analysis of another law's "scope," as the Restatement (Third) should be done at the beginning of a choice-of-law decision and will determine whether the conflicts law of the other relevant state or country refers to its own substantive law or to that of another state (perhaps the forum) in a case like the one in issue.

Part Five

Particular Choice-of-Law Problems

■ ANALYSIS

IX. Choice of Law by Subject Matter
X. Constitutional Limitations on State Choice of Law

Chapter IX

Choice of Law by Subject Matter

■ ANALYSIS

I. **Introduction**
II. **Torts**
    A. Introduction: Overview, Answering Exam Questions
    B. The Traditional Approach
    C. Modern Approaches
    D. Particular Problems and Issues
        1. Multistate Torts
        2. Fraud and Misrepresentation
        3. Common Law Tort of Unfair Competition
        4. Worker Compensation
        5. No-Fault Insurance
        6. Admiralty
III. **Contract**
    A. Introduction
    B. The Traditional Approach
        1. Validity
            a. Express Choice by the Parties
            b. Applicable Law Absent Party Stipulation
            c. Exceptions: Special Problems
        2. Performance
        3. Current Practice
    C. Modern Approaches
        1. Express Choice by the Parties
            a. Restatement (Second)
            b. The Forthcoming Restatement (Third)
        2. The Applicable Law in the Absence of an Express Choice
            a. False Conflicts
            b. True Conflicts: Pure Interest Analysis
            c. True Conflicts: Comparative Impairment
            d. Restatement (Second): Most Significant Relationship
            e. The Forthcoming Restatement (Third)

- D. Particular Contracts and Contract Issues
  - 1. Interest in Land
  - 2. Sale of Goods
  - 3. Insurance
  - 4. Surety
  - 5. Loans, Negotiable Instruments
  - 6. Services, Including Employment Contracts
  - 7. Other Contracts and Issues

IV. Property
- A. Introduction
- B. Interests in Land (Immovables)
- C. Tangible Movable Property
- D. Intangibles

V. Succession
- A. Introduction
- B. Intestate Succession
  - 1. Immovables
  - 2. Movables
- C. Testate Succession
  - 1. Immovables
    - a. Formal Validity
    - b. Equitable Conversion
  - 2. Movables
    - a. Formal Validity
    - b. Substantive Validity
    - c. Testator's Choice
  - 3. Forced Shares
  - 4. Family Allowance

VI. Trusts
- A. Validity
- B. Other Issues

VII. Probate and Administration of Estates
- A. Probate
- B. Administration
- C. Creditors' Rights
- D. Distribution

VIII. Corporations
- A. Existence and Internal Affairs
- B. Other Issues
- C. Regulation by the Forum

IX. Review Questions

I. Introduction

This chapter summarizes choice-of-law *rules* (where they exist) or *approaches* to choice of law with respect to specific areas of substantive law.

Note that a number of specific examples, particularly with respect to choice of law in tort cases, served as illustrations in Chapter VIII (dealing with theoretical approaches to choice of law). The tort section below therefore incorporates these illustrations by reference and directs your attention to the earlier treatment. Similarly, you will recall that domestic relations issues are generally decided in accordance with the law of the forum. The subsequent discussion therefore excludes domestic relations issues. For them, you should consult the treatment in Part Three above.

II. Torts

A. Introduction: Overview, Answering Exam Questions

The "revolution" in choice-of-law approaches had its principal origin in tort conflicts cases, and secondarily in contract cases. Tort cases were an early area of concern because the traditional (First Restatement) rules were thought to be too *mechanical,* often leading to unjust results.

Remember that negligent torts just happen; thus, there is no "party expectation" that a particular law will apply (as there may often be in contract). At most, parties may expect home law and be *surprised* that some other law is applied.

Modern approaches to choice of law in tort therefore seek to *achieve reasonable (just) results,* taking account of both *party interests* (e.g., compensation) and *societal concerns* (e.g., deterrence, compensation from private rather than public funds), while shielding the defendant from *unfair surprise.* "**Unfair surprise**" (in tort) is the flipside of **party expectation** (in contract).

Chapter VIII reviewed the various approaches to choice of law, mainly by utilizing illustrations from tort. Careful review of Chapter VIII will help you understand how to analyze tort cases and tort issues. The present chapter summarizes rules and approaches; but choice-of-law analysis *must be practiced,* and for that **repeated review of Chapter VIII is essential**.

Courts that have abandoned the traditional approach have not necessarily embraced in full one of the competing approaches. In fact, few jurisdictions are entirely consistent in their approach. For instance, many Restatement (Second) decisions will contain a good dose of interest analysis, and interest-analysis states (especially California, with its "comparative impairment" approach) will render decisions which would not be different in "most-significant-relationship test" (Restatement (Second)) states. The coming Restatement (Third) provides a number of rules (derived from its adoption of the distinction between loss-allocation and conduct-regulation in tort conflicts law that New York cases had developed. When there is no rule, the new Restatement seeks to determine which is the state with the "dominant interest" and to apply its law. **In answering exam questions when there is no rule that tells you what law to apply, you should *draw on and evaluate all contacts,*** in terms of their relevance to the parties and to the policies of involved or interested states. Doing this seems less appropriate, at first blush, when a jurisdiction still follows the traditional approach of the First Restatement—or *says* that it does. Remember: *characterization, false-conflict-analysis,* and *renvoi* also have policy elements. The way in which the *American Motorist*-court, above at p. 179 and below at p. 211, used *renvoi* to identify a false conflict, applied forum law as the most significantly related law—all the while claiming that it was not really giving up the traditional rule—is an illustration. For *characterization,* see above at p. 160 *et seq*. For definition and illustration of *false conflicts*, see above at p. 176.

Even in the volatile field of torts, many choice-of-law problems are settled. For instance, whether the defendant's conduct was "tortious" at all will be determined by the law of the place of acting or of the place where the plaintiff's injury occurred, if that state imposes liability and if application of that law was foreseeable for the defendant. See *Reese,* Choice of Law in Torts and Contracts and Directions for the Future, 16 Colum. J. Transnat'l. L. 1, 13 (1977). And, as detailed in Chapter VIII, new "rules"—albeit more flexible than those of the First Restatement—emerged in some states, e.g., the *Neumeier* rules (further refined above at p. 184), and are now part of the Restatement (Third).

With respect to all of the above, remember that choice-of-law analysis focuses on the *particular issue*, not the whole case. Thus, selecting a law that should be applied to issue A does not mean that other issues of the case (issues B, C, and so forth) are therefore also governed by that law. The issue-by-issue approach is specifically used in the tort and contract provisions of the Restatement (Second) and the forthcoming Restatement (Third). The result may therefore be that different laws apply to different issues of the same case: *dépeçage* (see also *supra* at p. 163). Note that this has also been true, to some extent, under the traditional or more specific choice-of-law approaches. For instance, the characterization of an issue as "procedural" has led to the application of forum law when another law applied to other issues of the case (see also below, immediately following).

B. The Traditional Approach

The traditional approach (First Restatement § 377) applies the law of the "**place of the wrong**," the place where the tortious act took place ("lex loci delicti commissi"). Where is the place of wrong? Where the last act occurred to give the plaintiff a cause of action. Note that this is not necessarily the place where the negligent act occurred, but ***where the injury was suffered*** (the rationale is that there is no action for damages—actual or nominal—without injury). See *Alabama Great Southern Railroad v. Carroll,* above at p. 176. For summary of criticism of the traditional approach (as mechanical, making results depend on the fortuitous place of injury), see above.

Alternatives to "Place of Injury." Even the traditional—vested rights—approach recognized that the "place of injury" was insufficient to address the interest of the forum state in *regulating conduct within its borders.* Therefore, the law of the **place of acting** (i.e., the place where the tortious conduct took place)—when this is the *forum state*—will govern the tort, even if the ultimate injury was suffered elsewhere.

A number of early cases held that in actions for alienation of affection, the law of the forum—where the adulterous *conduct* occurred—provided the applicable law (liability), rather than the law where the plaintiff and spouse were domiciled and where the effect of the "alienation" presumably was felt (even if the defendant would have no liability under the law of that state). *Gordon v. Parker,* 83 F. Supp. 40 (D. Mass. 1949); *Marra v. Bushee,* 317 F. Supp. 972 (D. Vt. 1970), rev'd on other grounds, 447 F.2d 1282 (2d Cir. 1971). The rationale of these cases (regulation of conduct) *holds true for all intentional torts,* as well as for those cases in which the law imposes *strict liability* (e.g., products liability, dram shop liability). The coming Restatement

(Third) also distinguishing between rules of law that are conduct-regulating and those that are loss-allocating.

Characterization (of an issue as "procedural" or as *not presenting a tort* problem) permits courts to choose a law other than that of the place of injury or conduct. A ***procedural*** characterization allows the court to apply forum law. For characterization, see above at p. 160 *et seq.*

Example: In *Kilberg v. Northeast Airlines, Inc.*, 172 N.E.2d 526 (N.Y. 1961), the court said that damage limitations on wrongful death recoveries are procedural. Massachusetts law—applicable to the merits—therefore did not limit the damage recovery; New York (forum) law applied, containing no limitation.

Subject matter characterization also will circumvent—let the court escape from—the traditional tort choice-of-law rule.

For instance, a married woman was injured in an accident in which the driver-husband was arguably negligent. There was interspousal immunity from suit (spouses may not sue each other) in the state of the accident, but not in the state of the parties' matrimonial domicile. Held, that capacity of spouses to sue each other is not a concern of the (fortuitous) state of the tort. Rather, it is a *domestic relations* issue and therefore should be decided by the *law applicable to the domestic relations of the parties* (i.e., **the law of their marital domicile**), and not by the law applicable to the tort. *Haumschild v. Continental Casualty Co.,* 95 N.W.2d 814 (Wis. 1959). See also *Nelson v. Hix,* 522 N.E.2d 1214 (Ill. 1988).

C. Modern Approaches

Chapter VIII, which provides a comprehensive analysis of approaches to choice of law in substitution for the vested rights approach of the First Restatement, **is built around the "revolution" in tort choice of law. Please consult that chapter again at this point**. Note that the Restatement (Second), while generally adopting the most-significant-relationship test for torts (§ 145), provides in § 146 that the law of the place of injury will apply in actions for personal injuries unless another state has a "more significant relationship" to the issue. The *place of injury thus remains the starting point, subject to displacement.* The place of acting (and injury) also remains important in the Second and Third *Neumeier* rules (above at p. 184), and in the New York decisions in *Schultz* and *Edwards*, above at p. 185 *et seq*.

The new Restatement (Third) provides that tort issues are "governed by the law of the state with the dominant interest in the issue." § 6.01. It establishes some particular "tort- and issues-specific rules" in §§ 6.11–6.12 (on product liability and punitive damages). In its §§ 6.03–6.05 it focuses on the distinction of the New York decisions (see above) between loss-allocating and conduct-regulating rules for tort claims. For instance, "issues relating to conduct include, but are not limited to" the required standard of conduct, whether a duty was owed to the plaintiff, whether a defense might "negate wrongfulness." § 6.04(b, d, f). Examples of issues that relate to loss-allocation "include" vicarious liability, joint and several liability, and comparative and contributory negligence. § 6.05 (c, e, g). As briefly mentioned earlier, opinions might differ about how issues are defined: does contributory negligence law allocate the loss (by denying or reducing recovery) or does it mean to regulate conduct for the sake of safety? Or both and, if so, which should come first?

What law applies? If the parties have the same domicile, that law applies to loss allocation; if their domiciles differ, but conduct and injury occurred in the same state, that state's law applies. In cross-border torts with conduct and injury in different states, the law of the state of conduct applies, but the injured person may request application of the law of the state of injury (i.e., may select the more favorable law).

A case may not fit into any of the above situations, i.e., no rule that would apply to it. The court should then examine whether the particular issue should be regarded as conduct-regulating or loss-allocation: see the use of "include but . . . not limited to" in the provisions quoted above. If that also does not help, a court a is left with the direction underlying all of the foregoing: application of the law of the state with the "dominant interest." To determine which state that is, the court should consider the "relevant policies of the forum and other interested states . . . And the reasonable expectations of the parties." § 6.01. With this residual rule for not-provided-for issues, the Restatement (Third) resembles §§ 6 and 145 of the Restatement (Second).

D. Particular Problems and Issues

1. Multistate Torts

A libel may be disseminated in a national publication and cause reputational injury in a number of states. A product put into the stream of commerce in A may cause harm in B, C, and other states. An airplane may crash in A, carrying passengers who bought tickets, boarded the plane, and were destined to different states. What law applies?

a. Traditionally, the laws of the *individual places* of injury applied. See, e.g., *O'Reilly v. Curtis Pub. Co.,* 31 F. Supp. 364 (D. Mass. 1940) (39 states where publication occurred). In airplane accidents, the estates of decedents sitting next to each other might be treated quite differently with respect to wrongful death and punitive damage claims. The applicable law might be that of the place of the injury, of where the ticket was bought, of where the trip began or was to end, or of the forum (procedural characterization). Such different treatment of similar claims is a very real possibility, particularly when suits filed in federal courts in different states are transferred for consolidation to one court. That court must apply the conflicts principles followed by each of the transferor courts (on choice of law upon transfer, see below at p. 222). In products liability, the "place of wrong" is defined as the place of injury, or also as the place of manufacture or sale. The alternative reference often expresses the regulatory interest of the particular state.

b. Modern Approaches: For *reputational torts* (libel, defamation), the *Uniform Single Publications Act* (in force in a number of states, its principle adopted in others by case law) provides that there is but ***one*** cause of action in which the plaintiff (must) claim all damages. The Act does not specify which law applies to the plaintiff's *one cause of action.* The forum therefore determines that *one* law, according to its own tort choice-of-law rules.

For *products liability,* the Restatement (Second) also applies its most-significant-relationship approach (with initial emphasis on the place of injury, above at p. 180). The case law follows this approach, but some decisions apply plaintiff-favoring law, e.g., the law of his or her domicile. This may be especially important in a case, for instance, in which the consumer contracted and was injured outside of her state of domicile but used her domicile address and credit card for the purchase. The Restatement (Third) would have the court apply the law of the place of the product's delivery to the end user, of the plaintiff's central link, of the place of manufacture, or of the defendant's central link, so long as the one chosen was also in combination with one of the other contacts and the product was obtained through ordinary commercial channels. If none of this applied, ordinary tort rules apply. See § 6.11 with Comments and Reporters' Notes.

In Louisiana, local law applies if the injury was sustained there by a domiciliary or resident, or if the defective product was manufactured, produced or acquired there *and* caused injury there *or* caused injury elsewhere to a Louisiana domiciliary or resident *unless* the defendant can show that the product was not available in Louisiana through ordinary commercial channels. For detailed discussion, see *Hornbook* § 17.64 *et seq.*

Mass tort cases are often consolidated for trial in federal court under 28 U.S.C. § 1407. That court, under *Erie,* applies the law of the transferor jurisdictions. The ALI Complex Litigation Proposal (1994) envisions the choice of a single law for mass tort cases.

2. Fraud and Misrepresentation

The case law focuses mainly on the protection of the plaintiff's interests and thus applies the law of the place where he or she acted in reliance on the fraud or misrepresentation. The Restatement (Third) adopts this.

3. Common Law Tort of Unfair Competition

Restatement (Second) § 145 cmt. *f* suggests that the place of the defendant's *conduct* is the place of the most significant relationship. A number of decisions apply the law of the place where the defendant was injured in his or her business. The Restatement (Third) refers to the law of the affected market.

4. Worker Compensation

Worker compensation is statutory. The applicable law to an employee's claims for compensation for injuries may be that of the state of the injury, of the employment relationship, or of the employer's place of business. If none of these purports to make the remedy exclusive, the worker can seek an award in any of them. Whether a claim to exclusivity must be honored by a second state and whether a second state may permit a common law recovery instead of, or in addition to, a worker compensation award is discussed above in Chapter IV, at II(C-4-d).

5. No-Fault Insurance

No-fault legislation provides automobile accident victims with compensation for their injuries. The actor's fault is not a precondition to recovery; on the other hand, the victim's recovery is limited to economic losses, and tort claims are excluded (except when they exceed a certain threshold). No-fault statutes regulate their own applicability. Some are *territorial* in focus: they provide benefits for in-state accidents regardless of the victim's domicile. Other states award benefits to in-state *domiciliaries* regardless of the place of the accident. A few states follow a mixed approach: out-of-state victims may recover if the insurer does business in-state; if the insurer does not, only domiciliaries may recover.

6. Admiralty

The Federal Jones Act provides a remedy to "any seaman who suffers injury in the course of his employment." The case law has restricted the applicability of the Act to cases involving American seamen or having American contacts.

In *Lauritzen v. Larsen,* 345 U.S. 571, 73 S. Ct. 921, 97 L. Ed. 1254 (1953), the Court applied Danish law to the injury sustained by a Danish seaman on a Danish vessel in Cuban waters. In *Hellenic Lines Ltd. v. Rhoditis,* 398 U.S. 306, 90 S. Ct. 1731, 26 L. Ed. 2d 252 (1970), the Court affirmed the application of the Jones Act to the injury sustained by a Greek seaman in an American port. In 1995, the Third Circuit decided that the applicable law in Jones Act cases should be determined on the basis of the approach of the Restatement (Third) of the Foreign Relations Law of the United States, not the Conflicts Restatement. The former does not look for the state of the most significant relationship. Instead, it applies forum law when doing so is reasonable and would advance forum policies. *Neely v. Club Med Management Services, Inc.*, 63 F.3d 166 (3d Cir. 1995). See also *Ellerton v. Ellerton,* 745 F. Supp. 2d 458, 466 (D. Vt. 2010) (weighing United States versus Canadian interests with respect to application of Canadian cap on damages).

III. Contract

A. Introduction

In tort, as discussed above, parties do not have actual "expectations." Instead, their "expectation" is really to be protected against *unfair surprise*: an "unexpected" law should not be applied to create liability. In contract, on the other hand, parties do have expectations. The fundamental expectation is that, having bargained in good faith (which the law will assume, almost as an irrebuttable presumption), they will be protected in their bargain. They expect the contract to be upheld and their rights to be vindicated if there should be a breach. **The protection of party interests is therefore a fundamental policy that must guide a court in the choice of the applicable law in contract**.

Society also has an interest in upholding contractual commitments. The "marketplace" is best served when transactions validly concluded in a state will be upheld everywhere. Both party expectations and the security of commercial transactions in the forum will be served; this aids the forum as a place where people like to do business.

Example: See, for instance, New York's statute providing that courts should not dismiss for *forum non conveniens* when a contract provides for New York courts and New York law and exceeds $1 million in value, even though there are no New York connections. New York is promoting its position as a center of commercial activity through this statute.

Party expectations and the concern of the forum for the security of commercial transactions concluded in the forum state thus coincide more often than not. Occasionally, however, party expectations and the concern of the forum may not align. The forum may have other interests to protect or to provide for as well. If the latter are *regulatory* interests, perhaps serving a particular public (consumer) good, they will override party expectations.

Example: Provisions invalidating short claim periods in insurance contracts; state statutes regulating the interest rates that may be charged to in-state consumers in small loan and installment sales transactions (*Hornbook* § 18.28).

UCC and CISG

The following deals with choice-of-law in contract cases that are not governed by Art. 2 of the Uniform Commercial Code (UCC)—in force in all States except Louisiana—or by the Convention on the International Sale of Goods (CISG)—ratified by the United States and thus in force as federal law. If a contract involves both the sale of goods and rendition of services, a court may conclude that it is primarily a contract for services and that Art. 2 of the UCC therefore does not apply, so that aspects relating to goods will be subject to common law contract law. For an example, see *Bonebrake v. Cox*, 499 F.2d 951, 960 (8th Cir.1974); *Z-Modular, LLC v. MCN Build, Inc*, 729 F.Supp.3d 1 (D.D.C.2024).

When applicable, the UCC and CISG provide rules about the applicable law in interstate or international cases. They also provide rules for choice-of-law agreements by the parties. Such agreements may then refer to a State's common law provisions or to another country's law, including the CISG, if adopted by that country. See CISG Art. 1(1)(a).

B. The Traditional Approach

1. Validity

a. Express Choice by the Parties

The extent to which the parties may stipulate the applicable law is discussed below at p. 209 *et seq.*

b. Applicable Law Absent Party Stipulation

The vested rights-approach of the First Restatement, above Chapter VIII, Section II(A), proceeded on the premise that rights and obligations of parties "vested" at a particular time and location, and that the law of that place would therefore necessarily govern those rights and obligations. Thus, a contract was **valid if valid according to the law of the place *where it was made***. First Restatement § 332. The uniform rule of substantive contract law in the United States is that a contract is "made" when the offer is "accepted," upon dispatch of the acceptance ("mailbox rule") (exception: Louisiana), or upon its receipt when the "mailbox rule" does not apply.

Example: In *Milliken v. Pratt,* 125 Mass. 374 (1878), the court upheld the contract of a Massachusetts married woman under the law of the state where it was "made" (where the acceptance occurred—Maine), even though she lacked capacity under the law of the Massachusetts forum. In modern terms, the expectations of the Maine contracting parties were upheld, the integrity of the Maine marketplace was preserved, but the public policy of Massachusetts—according to which married women lacked capacity—was subordinated to these other values. Explanations may be that (a) rights "vested" in Maine should be disregarded only if forum policy is most seriously offended, or (b) that the change in Massachusetts policy, which was occurring at the same time, reduced the matter to a "false conflict" (see above Chapter VIII, Section III(B)). For the older case law, however, *Milliken v. Pratt* is the classic statement of the vested rights theory: if valid where entered, then the contract is also valid at the forum.

Assume, however, that a multi-state transaction involves a contract that is not valid where concluded but is valid under the law of the place of the intended performance. This was the case in another famous older decision, *Pritchard v. Norton,* 106 U.S. (16 Otto) 124, 1 S. Ct. 102, 27 L. Ed. 104 (1882). The contract of surety was not valid under the law of New York, where made, for lack of consideration. It would have been valid under the law of Louisiana, where the surety was to indemnify the other party. The court presumed that (1) the parties had meant to enter into a valid contract, and that (2) since the contract looked for performance in Louisiana, the parties had *intended* that the law of that state apply. The Court upheld the validity of the contract under the law that the parties had chosen *by implication.* On express stipulation of the applicable law by the parties, see below p. 209 *et seq.*

c. Exceptions: Special Problems

At times, the reference to the place of making, or alternatively, to the place of intended performance still will not validate the contract. Conversely, there may be policy reasons why the forum would *not* wish to apply a validating law to which its conflicts rule refers.

Characterization and **public policy** serve as the traditional "escape devices." The **substance-procedure characterization** may affect the result.

Example: If the place-of-making of the contract validates it, but the forum's Statute of Frauds would hold it unenforceable, all will depend on how the statute is characterized. If considered *procedural,* the forum's statute will apply, and the contract will be unenforceable. If a *substantive* characterization is used, the forum's statute will apply only to contracts made in the forum state, not to contracts made elsewhere; the out-of-state contract will be enforced. *Lams v. F.H. Smith Co.,* 178 A. 651 (Del. Super. Ct. 1935). Conversely, the policy underlying the statutory requirement that agreements to make a will must be in writing may be so strong as to lead a forum to characterize the statute as procedural. The statute will then render all oral contracts unenforceable in the forum, even if validly concluded out of state. *Emery v. Burbank,* 39 N.E. 1026 (Mass. 1895). In the reverse type of case (invalidity under the law of the place of making, but valid under forum law), a court upheld the contract. *Woll v. Dugas,* 250 A.2d 775 (N.J. Super. Ct. Ch. Div. 1969).

The **public policy** of the forum may *override* contracts that are valid according to the choice-of-law rules which the forum would ordinarily apply.

Example: Regulation of interest charged in consumer loan and installment purchase agreements. *Hornbook* § 18.28; *Emery v. Burbank,* above.

2. Performance

The traditional approach called for application of the **law of the place of performance** to determine questions of how performance was to be effected, excuse for nonperformance, breach, and damages. First Restatement § 358. Note that questions of contract *interpretation* are considered to relate to *validity*, even though they may have a direct effect on the question whether a party breached its obligation.

3. Current Practice

Most states have abandoned the traditional approach in contract as they have in tort choice of law. They have adopted the significant-relationship approach of the Restatement (Second), whatever that means in terms of objective weighing of contract-elements or policy analysis, including forum-favoring interest analysis. In a few states, the current position seems unsettled. A small number of states continue to adhere to **the traditional approach**. *Hornbook* § 18.21 (state by state).

C. Modern Approaches

1. Express Choice by the Parties

All current approaches permit the parties, within limits, to choose the applicable law ("party autonomy").

Restatement (Second) § 187 and forthcoming Restatement (Third) § 8.02 (the latter really closely following the former) differentiate between issues that the parties could have "resolved by an explicit provision" in their contract (for instance, how a particular term should be construed) and those that they could not have resolved themselves (e.g., capacity to contract, necessary formalities).

When the parties stipulate the applicable law with respect to the first kind of these issues, *they really incorporate the stipulated law by reference.* It becomes a contract term. When they stipulate the applicable law with respect to the second type of issues, they are making a choice-of-law decision.

A choice-of-law provision is subject to limitations, **Restatement (Second)** § 187(2) and Restatement (Third) § 802(1) and (2):

a. The chosen state must have a substantial relationship to the parties or the transaction, *or*

b. there must be some other reasonable basis for the choice (e.g., the choice of a law which is particularly well developed in the subject matter relevant to the contract), *and*

c. the chosen law must not offend fundamental policies of the forum (e.g., limitations on interest rates in installment purchase agreements concluded with local residents). Restatement (Second) § 187(2)(b) also invalidates a choice that offends the public policy of the state that has the most significant relationship to the parties or the transaction.

The ***Uniform Commercial Code*** (§ 1–301, revised; formerly § 1–105) permits the parties to choose the applicable law (including foreign-country law in the case of international contracts), but requires that the transaction bear a relation to the state or country whose law has been selected. A proposed revision (also to be styled on § 1–301) would have dropped the requirement of a related law and would have made special provisions for consumer transactions. The proposal was withdrawn in 2008 for lack of adoptions.

Art. 9 (secured transactions) has been revised. The revised Article is in force in all states. Its provisions uniformly refer to the *local* law of the state whose law applies (no longer picking up that state's conflicts law).

If the parties chose a law which will *invalidate* their contract, the stipulation may be treated as a *mutual mistake* and disregarded. This is the result of the basic assumption that the parties, acting in good faith, wanted a valid contract. The European rule is otherwise: you get the law you stipulated, including its defenses against liability. Which rule do you prefer?

The future Restatement (Third) will honor the parties' choice of law with respect to matters that they could have resolved by stipulation but did not) but not when the chosen law was limited in its scope to intrastate matters or parties. A stated reason is that parties cannot alter a state's law. However, if the parties intended to stipulate (in the sense of incorporate in their contract) what the chosen law would have provided, their intention will be honored, and the chosen law applied. The court therefore needs to determine the parties' intent in these types of cases. Unless an intent to incorporate is presumed, their intent then becomes a question of the court's judgement and on this issue opinions might differ.

The coming ***Restatement (Third)*** states expressly that the "reference to the 'law' . . . of a particular state . . . is *presumed* to select only the internal law," i.e., to exclude that state's conflicts law. § 8.03 (2)(c), italics added, and the Section's Comment f (stating that this presumption is followed "almost universally"). The presumption can be rebutted "by clear language in the agreement." § 8.03(3). This exclusion of the chosen state's conflicts law makes good sense because the parties must have intended to select a particular outcome, rather than a possible reference onward. However, the rejection of renvoi whenever it is the forum's conflicts law rather than the parties' choice that refers to another state's law may not make sense, as discussed above at p. 164.

2. The Applicable Law in the Absence of an Express Choice

a. False Conflicts

As in other areas, a court employing a modern choice-of-law approach will ordinarily inquire whether a true or a false conflict exists. If the case presents a false conflict, no choice need be made: only one law, by definition, claims applicability. This will often be the law of the forum but could also be the law of the other state. Note that except for the limitation imposed by local public policy, the false conflicts analysis will be influenced by the basic policy of honoring party expectations.

Illustration: Nevada parties made an oral contract to make a will. Such a contract was valid under Nevada law, where made, but not under the statute of frauds of California, the decedent's state of domicile at death. Held, that both states have a basic policy of upholding contracts. Parties should be able to rely on the law of the place where they act; they were not bound to anticipate that the testator would ultimately move to and die domiciled in a state requiring the contract to be in writing. No conflict existed between Nevada and California law and policy; the contract was given effect. *Bernkrant v. Fowler,* 360 P.2d 906 (Cal. 1961) (en banc). Compare also *The Pep Boys Manny Moe & Jack of California v. Old Republic Ins. Co.*, 98 Cal.App.5th 329, 349 (2023).

Note: The *Bernkrant* Court found a false conflict because it took a *restrained view of forum law.* It could also have concluded that a true conflict existed because the California statute was designed to protect California estates against false claims, as well as California heirs against diminution of their shares as a result of claims derived from oral contracts. Compare *Bernkrant* with *Lilienthal,* immediately following.

The court in *American Motorists Ins. Co. v. ARTRA Group, Inc.,* 659 A.2d 1295 (Md. 1995), looked at the conflicts law of the state in which the insurance contract was concluded and found that it would refer to the forum state (where the insured risk was located). The court concluded that it made no sense to apply the other state's law if that state wouldn't apply its own law: it accepted the *renvoi* to forum law, citing § 3.13 of the *Hornbook* (2d ed. 1992). The forthcoming Restatement (Third) also provides that a court must determine in the first place whether a true conflict exists, which needs to be resolved, but it rejects consideration of another state's conflicts law and the possibility of a resulting renvoi. In the new Restatement's view, another state's conflicts law should only be considered for a possible *renvoi* if the policies of both the forum and the other state agree that the same law should govern the issue. Question: since the remission type of *renvoi* is a merry-go-round that the forum usually cuts off by application of its own law, will the restricted approach of the new Restatement then limit consideration of another state's conflicts law to remission cases? For renvoi, see *supra* at p. 163.

b. True Conflicts: Pure Interest Analysis

Interest analysis, as advocated by Currie (above), *resolves true conflicts in favor of the forum when doing so is constitutionally permissible.*

Illustration: An Oregon defendant executed and delivered promissory notes to the California plaintiff in California. They were also payable there. The defendant had been declared a spendthrift in Oregon, a fact of which the plaintiff had been unaware. When the plaintiff sought to collect in Oregon, the defendant's guardian declared the obligation void. Held, that both California and Oregon favor holding parties to their obligations. Also, all significant contacts are with California. Nevertheless, courts are "instruments of state policy" and must apply forum law; they may not balance policies. Oregon law applied. *Lilienthal v. Kaufman,* 395 P.2d 543 (Or. 1964).

Notes:

1) The decision did not just close Oregon courts to the plaintiff; it was "on the merits" (above Chapter IV) and voided the defendant's obligation to the plaintiff. From a policy point of view, that is objectionable. Arguably, the application of Oregon law to a claim with which it had no contact was also unconstitutional. See below at Chapter X (Sections II–III) .
2) Oregon legislation now provides that a party may assert his or her incapacity under the law of the state of his or her residence "against a party that knew or should have known of the incapacity. . . ." Or. Rev. Stat. Ann. § 15.330(2) (West 2025).
3) The traditional (First Restatement) approach, the comparative impairment test, as well as the Restatement (Second) would have applied California law in *Lilienthal.*

c. True Conflicts: Comparative Impairment

Most states that have adopted interest analysis (as well as those in which policy analysis is part of the basic approach, e.g., those following the Restatement (Second)) will **weigh interests** in true conflicts cases. The particular approach adopted by **California** and **Louisiana** is the **comparative impairment test**. It asks which state's policy and interests *would be more impaired,* as between two competing states, if its law were *not* applied. For additional discussion see above at p. 180 *et seq.*

Illustrations: 1) *Bernkrant v. Fowler,* above at p. 211, could also have been decided the way it was by use of the comparative impairment approach. Nevada's policy in favor of having its (validating) law applied to contracts made in Nevada by Nevada residents was greater than California's in the application of its law when the testator had moved there after the fact. Stated differently, Nevada's policy would have been more impaired by not applying its law than California's interests would have been.

2) The comparative impairment test would have resulted in the application of California law in *Lilienthal,* above at p. 212, upholding local transactions.

3) California permits extrinsic evidence to resolve the question of whether a contract is ambiguous, even if it is facially unambiguous. Hawaii applies the parole evidence rule strictly. When a California partnership was organized for the purpose of acquiring real property in Hawaii, retained counsel in Hawaii, litigation occurred in Hawaii, and the California party subsequently sued the Hawaiian law firm for legal malpractice, it was held that Hawaii's interests would be more impaired than California's if its law were not applied. *KL Group v. Case, Kay & Lynch,* 829 F.2d 909, 915–16 (9th Cir. 1987). Note that the most-significant-relationship test and the traditional approach (the documents were executed in Hawaii) would have led to the same result, while pure interest analysis would not have.

For discussion of the difficulties with the comparative impairment test, see *Weintraub,* Commentary on the Conflict of Laws § 6.26 (6th ed. 2010).

d. Restatement (Second): Most Significant Relationship

Parallel to its treatment of choice of law in tort, the Restatement (Second)—in § 188—incorporates by reference the "general principles" of § 6 to determine, with respect to a particular contract *issue,* the state of the most significant relationship.

Cross reference: For discussion of the *structure* of the Restatement's "most significant relationship" provisions, see above at p. 181. For the Restatement's *issue-by-issue approach,* see *dépeçage,* above at p. 163.

Subsection 3 of § 188 declares that when the contract was negotiated and was to be performed in the same state, that state's law will "usually" be applied. Exceptions relate to contracts for interests in land (§§ 189–90) and to certain usurious contracts (§ 203).

Subsection 2 provides guidance for determining the state of the most significant relationship in all other cases.

Remember the incorporation by reference of the "general principles" of § 6. These are discussed above at p. 182.

The relevant **contacts** are the place of contracting, the place of negotiation, the place of performance, the location of the contract's subject matter, and the residence (or place of business) of the parties. Note that, except for the last of these contacts, the traditional approach and the policy-centered approaches also consider these elements.

Illustration: Refer to *KL Group v. Case, Kay & Lynch,* above at p. 213. California was the forum, but the defendant was to perform (provide legal services) in Hawaii, the defendant had its place of business there, and the subject matter of the contract was the provision of services in Hawaii with respect to Hawaiian real property. The general principles of § 6 reinforce the importance of these contacts: protection of the expectations of the (Hawaiian) party, as well as Hawaii's interest in the application of its law to its party. For a decision discussing *KL Group,* but concluding that New York law and not California's applied, see *Liberty Synergistics, Inc. v. Microflo Ltd.,* No. CV 11–0523, 2011 WL 4974832, at *8 (E.D.N.Y. Oct. 9, 2011).

Practice: The great majority of states now follows the flexible approach of the Restatement (Second) or one of the other approaches (such as "comparative impairment"). For a list, see *Hornbook* § 18.21.

e. The Restatement (Third): Most Appropriate Law

The new Restatement (Third) provides "subject-specific" rules (for instance, for insurance contracts, service contracts, and the like) and "contracting-specific" rules (for instance dealing with the relevance of the place of contracting and/or place of performance), with the former taking precedence over the latter. What if there is no rule of either kind for a specific issue or problem? In such a case, the court should apply the "most appropriate law" on the basis of non-exclusive lists of contacts, as well as based on the policies of the forum and of other states. § 811(1). Subsection (2) then presents a non-inclusive list of relevant contacts for evaluating "a state's interest in having its law applied." This default rule very much mirrors §§ 188 and 6 of the Restatement (Second), discussed *supra* at p. 181. The previous discussions of interest analysis and of contacts and policies thus remain relevant. See Restatement (Third) § 8.11(3) which mirrors § 6 of the Restatement (Second).

D. Particular Contracts and Contract Issues

The Restatement (Second) and the case law retain some fairly concrete choice-of-law rules for a number of contracts and contract issues. The Restatement (Third) also provides a number of concrete rules and gives priority to "subject-specific rules" (e.g., relating to service and insurance contracts) over "contract-behavior-specific rules (e.g., negotiating, performing a contract). All are displaced by a "manifestly more appropriate" law or if an otherwise appliable rule would be "deeply offensive to forum public policy" or be injurious to "fundamental forum policy." § 8.05. Strong forum interests thus provide an escape while they are already part the basic determination of the applicable law under § 6 of the Restatement (Second). Nevertheless, a court's view of forum policies is important and provides a way out.

1. Interest in Land

Issues concerning transfers of land by deed (e.g., its validity, compliance with recording requirements) are governed by the law of the situs. Restatement (Third) §§ 7.04,7.05.

Contracts for interests in land are usually governed by the law of the situs, while other issues, for instance liability for damages for breach of a personal covenant or capacity to contract, may be governed by a different law, e.g., the parties' common domicile. § 190.

The Restatement (Third) combines these issues and in an early proposal referred first to the law stipulated by the parties, if enforceable under § 8.02, then to the law of the state of "the parties' common link" (for instance, their common domicile), and only as a third (a follow-up) to the law of the situs of the property. Preliminary Draft No. 5, § 8.09A.

For *equitable conversion*, see below at p. 221.

For the effect of equity decrees, see above at pp. 97, 112.

2. Sale of Goods

UCC § 1–103(d) (revised) provides for the application of the law selected on the basis of the forum's choice-of-law principles.

3. Insurance

The applicable law for *life insurance* contracts is almost always the law of the insured's domicile. Restatement (Second) § 192. The Restatement (Third) § 8.07 refers to the "central link" of a natural person taking out a policy or of the entity that takes out a group insurance policy.

Under the Restatement (Second) the law of the place of the principal location of the insured risk usually applies to *casualty insurance*. Restatement (Second) § 193. Contracts for *liability insurance* are governed by the law applicable to the tort liability, but compliance with contract terms is governed by general contract choice-of-law principles.

The Restatement (Third) combines "contracts for liability and property insurance" in its § 8.08 and provides that issues related to these are "presumed" to be determined by the law that is the "central link" of the entity or natural person that purchased the policy. For references to cases that focus on location of the insured risk (especially when in the forum), see the Reporters' Notes to § 8.08.

4. Surety

Suretyship agreements are governed by the law applicable to the underlying obligation. Restatement (Second) § 194. The Restatement (Third) contains no specific rule on suretyship contracts. See therefore the Introductory Note to this Section.

5. Loans, Negotiable Instruments

The case law and Restatement (Second) § 195 apply the law of the place where the loan is repayable. This will ordinarily be the place of contracting and where the lender is located. Legislation provides consumers with protection against the economically stronger lender, e.g., with respect to interest rates in small loan or installment purchase agreements.

The law of the place of payment also applies to negotiable instruments when the issue relates to performance. Restatement (Second) § 214. Issues relating to negotiability, in contrast, are governed by the law of the place of original execution. Restatement (Second) § 216. As to Restatement (Third), see comment in No 4 above.

6. Services, Including Employment Contracts

Restatement (Second) § 196 selects the law of the place where the services are to be rendered. The case law adopts this reference or refers to the place of contracting or the contract's center of gravity.

For *transportation contracts,* Restatement (Second) § 196 selects the law of departure. The case law reflects this approach, but in most cases the place of departure was also the place of contract formation.

Agency: The contract between *principal and agent* is governed by whatever approach the forum follows with respect to choice of law in contract generally. Thus, Restatement (Second) § 291 cross-references to § 188 (adopting the "most-significant-relationship" test).

A different law may apply to the contract between the *agent* and a *third party.* This is so because the concern now is the protection of the third party's expectation. Thus, whether the agent had actual or apparent authority should be determined by the law of the place where the agent acted. Restatement (Second) § 292.

The Restatement (Third) refers to the law of the state "where the preponderance of the services occurs;" it does not distinguish between different service contracts.

7. Other Contracts and Issues

The Restatement (Second) provides rules for additional specific contracts or contract issues; They are described below. The Restatement (Third) offers a provision for Leases (see (a), immediately following), but not for the other items addressed in this subsection. For them, consult its § 8.10 which addresses "Choice of Law Based on Negotiation, Making, and Performing a Contract." This provision would apply the law of the common place of negotiation and performance of the contract or, if not applicable the law of the common place of making and performance of the contract. If the latter also does not help, § 8.11 directs us to the most "appropriate law." See above Subsection C(e).

a. *Leases:* situs law applies for immovable property (Restatement (Third) § 7.09(2)) and for security interests relating to real property (Restatement (Third) § 7.10(2), unless the parties had chosen a different law according to § 8.2 (above). For movable property, Art. 2A of the UCC contains extensive substantive provisions. Restatement (Third) § 809B. UCC § 2A–106 limits the parties to a "consumer lease" in their freedom to stipulate the applicable law and to select a forum.

b. *Assignments:* assignability is governed by the law applicable to the contract itself, for instance, by the law of the place of the most significant relationship. Restatement (Second) § 208. The rights of an assignee are governed by the law of the place where the assignment took place or by the law of the state of the most significant relationship to the issue. Restatement (Second) § 209. Successive assignments are governed by the law of the place where performance was due. Restatement (Second) § 211.

c. *Releases, Accords:* There is uncertainty in the case law, and the Restatement (Second) reaches inconsistent results. In general, releases are governed by the law applicable to the tort claim, Restatement (Second) § 170, while an accord and satisfaction *should* be governed by the same law as the underlying contract. *Hornbook* § 18.37; *Eldon Industries v. Paradies & Co.,* 397 F. Supp. 535 (N.D. Ga. 1975).

d. *Statute of Frauds, Parole Evidence Rule:* The traditional approach characterized the *statute of frauds* as procedural (forum law) or substantive (law applicable to the contract) depending on whether it provided that the contract was "voidable" (or that no "suit shall be brought") or "void," respectively. Modern approaches apply the law applicable to the contract, in essence, adopting a *substantive* view of statutes of frauds. Restatement (Second) §§ 141, 199. Note that the Convention on the International Sale of Goods (CISG) applies, as a matter of federal law, to contracts within its scope; it does not require a writing, and therefore changes, for contracts to which it applies, both the common law and the UCC.

   Similarly, whether a contract is integrated in a writing is also governed by the law applicable to the contract itself. Restatement (Second) § 140 cmt. *c.* For an illustration, see *KL Group v. Case, Kay & Lynch,* above at p. 213.

e. *Quasi-Contract:* Law of the place where the benefit was conferred by the plaintiff, where the defendant (through tortious conduct) received a benefit at the plaintiff's expense, or the law which applies to the underlying obligation will be chosen. Restatement (Second) § 221; *Hornbook* §§ 18.42–18.48.

IV. Property

A. Introduction

This section treats choice-of-law with respect to property generally. Property rights as between spouses are discussed above in Chapter V, at II(B), while succession, trust, and administration-of-estates issues are treated below at p. 219 *et seq.*

B. Interests in Land (Immovables)

"Immovable" property is a concept which *goes beyond land itself.* It may include, in addition to the land transaction (conveyance), other interests such as leaseholds, covenants running with the land, servitudes, and encumbrances. Therefore, **think of "immovable property" as *interests in land*.** For contracts with respect to land see above at p. 215.

The **general rule** is that the validity and effect of the creation or conveyance of an interest in land (and the definition of what is such an interest) are governed by the **law that the situs would apply**, and the situs usually applies its own law. Restatement (Second) § 222 retains this traditional rule.

Illustration: In *Clarke v. Clarke,* 178 U.S. 186, 20 S. Ct. 873, 44 L. Ed. 1028 (1900), South Carolina purported to determine succession to Connecticut land. Held, that full faith and credit was not due the South Carolina decision since the South Carolina court lacked *jurisdiction* with respect to Connecticut land.

Note that the Court in *Clarke* denied the South Carolina decision direct *in rem* effect in Connecticut. Remember, however, that if all the parties are before the court, even a non-situs court can settle the rights and obligations as *between and among the parties* in a proceeding *in personam*. *Durfee v. Duke,* below p. 220. Such a judgment (for its *in personam* effects) is entitled to full faith and credit.

The justification of the situs rule, both for jurisdiction and for choice of law, is the need to protect third parties who rely on the recording system of the situs. This concern explains why the *non-situs* court cannot affect title to situs land (i.e., its decision cannot have an *in rem* effect). This is what was involved in *Fall v. Eastin,* 215 U.S. 1, 30 S. Ct. 3, 54 L. Ed. 65 (1909).

In another matter, a Washington court, as part of a divorce decree, purported to give title to Nebraska land to the wife. The husband did not himself convey to the wife, but instead conveyed to a third party who was not a bona fide purchaser. Held, that Nebraska need not give full faith and credit to the Washington decree. See *Clarke,* above. It is furthermore a question of *Nebraska* law whether a non-situs decree raises equities against third parties in Nebraska (and Nebraska need not provide for such equities).

Assume that the Washington court had ordered the husband to convey, and that the wife had sought to enforce that order in Nebraska (no third party being involved). Or assume that there had been personal jurisdiction over the third party in Washington, and a decree to convey had issued against the third party. In both situations, the Washington defendant would have been bound *personally,* and the decree would have been entitled to full faith and credit in Nebraska. See *Durfee v. Duke,* below p. 220.

For the extra-state enforcement of equity decrees, mainly injunctions, see *Baker v. General Motors* (mainly dictum), above at pp. 97, 112.

Security in interests in real property (for instance, mortgages) are governed by the law of the situs, unless the parties stipulated another law according to § 8.02 of the Restatement (Third) and this was permitted by the law of the situs: § 7.10,

C. Tangible Movable Property

Restatement (Second) § 244 adopts the most-significant-relationship test for the validity and effect of the transfer of a movable. This will ordinarily make the *place of transfer* the applicable law. The 1998 revision of Art. 9 of the Uniform Commercial Code provides uniform rules for movables to which it applies. The choice-of-law rules for the perfection, the effect of perfection or non-perfection, and for priority in security interests are found in §§ 9–301 through 9–307. See also § 9–316. In all cases, the reference is to the "local law" of the state designated (excluding its conflicts rules). The Article applies the same choice-of-law rules to all debtors, both foreign and domestic. § 9–301, cmt. 8. With respect to consumer leases, UCC § 2A–106 limits the parties in their choice of law and forum.

D. Intangibles

The *assignability* of a claim is governed by the law that applies to the original transaction. Restatement (Second) § 208 calls for application of the law of the place of the most significant relationship to the issue (of assignability); this, however, will be the law applicable to the claim itself.

The Uniform Commercial Code provides in § 9–103(3) that *perfection of a security interest* in accounts receivable is governed by the law of the place where the debtor is located (the debtor's place of business, the debtor's main office if there are more than one place of business, otherwise, the debtor's residence). These rules are found in §§ 9–301, 9–307 (1998 revision).

With respect to *investment securities*, the UCC distinguishes between direct and indirect holding of securities. In direct holding, the investor is registered on the books of the corporation or holds the certificate. The applicable law is the law of the corporation's state of incorporation or of the certificate's location. See UCC § 8–110 (as amended in 1999) and Official Comment 1. If the investor holds a claim against a securities intermediary (rather than an interest in securities themselves), the applicable law is that of the "securities intermediary's jurisdiction," as determined by the rules of UCC § 8–110(e) (in order of priority, parties' choice, location where the account is to be maintained, where it is maintained in fact, location of the intermediary's chief executive).

V. Succession

A. Introduction

The law of all states distinguishes strictly between succession to immovable and to movable property. **As a general rule, the law of the situs of the immovable property applies to succession to it; the law of the decedent's domicile at death applies to succession to movable property.** The Draft Restatement (Third) proposes adoption of the civil law approach that regards the decedent's estate as a unit and applies the law of the decedent's domicile at death to all property. It is important to emphasize that such a change concerning the law applicable to succession to immovables represents quite a change from the traditional (common law) approach, It will require acceptance by the courts of the states of the situs of immovable property when the decedent had been domiciled elsewhere. Whether or until this happens, states may apply different laws.

B. Intestate Succession

1. Immovables

"[T]he law of a state in which land is situated controls and governs . . .its passage in case of intestacy." *Clarke v. Clarke*, 178 U.S. 186, 190, 20 S. Ct. 873, 874, 44 L. Ed. 1028 (1900). Situs law therefore controls who succeeds in the case of intestacy and to how much. *But see* Draft Restatement (Third), Introductory Note above.

The pervasive *situs rule* (see also above at p. 218) derives from the situs' interest in the protection of third parties and from its interest in the regulation of the use and occupancy of land. These concerns are more important in the case of inter vivos transactions than in the case of succession. In the latter, the domicile of the decedent also has an important interest in providing for family members.

It has therefore been suggested that the use of situs law for the determination of shares of family members is outmoded. The situs is of course free to make another choice of law. See above subsection A (at the end).

Note that the situs must give full faith and credit, as to the same parties, to prior determinations by a court of a (non-situs) sister state with personal jurisdiction over the parties. *Durfee v. Duke,* 375 U.S. 106, 84 S. Ct. 242, 11 L. Ed. 2d 186 (1963).

2. Movables

The state where movable property is located of course has control over its disposition. However, almost all states have adopted the choice-of-law rule which applies the **law of the decedent's domicile at death** to the succession to his or her movable property. This achieves the desirable result of having the decedent's estate treated as a unit, even though the assets are located in different states. It also effectuates the domicile's interest in making provision for surviving family members.

Note: When assets are in different states, separate estate administrations may need to be conducted. See below p. 224 *et seq*.

When there are no heirs, the assets may go as *bona vacantia* (unclaimed "vacant" goods) to the situs state, or the situs state may choose to apply domiciliary law. In the case of intangibles, the state of the last known address of the owner of the claim (decedent's domicile) has jurisdiction to escheat it. *Western Union Tel. Co. v. Pennsylvania,* 368 U.S. 71, 82 S. Ct. 199, 7 L. Ed. 2d 139 (1961).

C. Testate Succession

1. Immovables

a. Formal Validity

Since the will operates as a transfer of the land, its validity is governed by *situs law.* Since different laws may have different formal requirements (e.g., number of witnesses), a will may be valid to devise land in one state but not in another. Many states have therefore modified the traditional rule and have adopted *alternative validating references.* Thus, situs law may provide that a will is valid if valid under situs law *or* the law of the place of execution *or* the law of the testator's domicile at death *or* the law of the testator's nationality. See Uniform Probate Code § 2–506.

Validating statutes usually deal only with validating the *execution* of the will; they generally are silent as to the law applicable to *revocation* (partial or in full) of a will. Consequently, a revocation could be effective at the domicile but not at the situs. Since the alternative references for execution are designed to validate and effectuate the testator's intent, they should apply equally to revocation. See *In re Traversi's Estate,* 64 N.Y.S.2d 453 (N.Y. Sur. Ct. 1946).

Situs law has also been applied to the validity of a *testamentary trust in land.* Again, alternative references should be employed to validate the testator's intent.

b. Equitable Conversion

Assume that a will directs the executor to sell land located in A and to distribute the proceeds as directed by the will to named heirs at the testator's last domicile, B. Does this provision of the will deal with immovable property (so that situs law applies to the question of whether a designated heir may take as against other persons), or does the will deal with movable property, the proceeds of the sale, to which domiciliary law applies? This involves the doctrine of **equitable conversion:** "equity regards as done that which ought to be done," i.e., the testator had wanted to "convert" the land into money, and this will therefore be considered as having occurred. A number of decisions flatly hold, in line with the First Restatement, that equitable conversion has "no place in the Conflict of Laws." As a result, situs law applies. *Toledo Society for Crippled Children v. Hickok,* 261 S.W.2d 692 (Tex. 1953). In contrast to these decisions, and in keeping with the policy discussed above, equitable conversion should be adopted as another means for *validating* the testator's intent, but not when it would invalidate it. *Hornbook* § 20.7.

In this light, *Toledo Society* was right in rejecting the doctrine, since acceptance would have invalidated the testator's intent. But see *Ford v. Ford,* 44 N.W. 1057 (Mich. 1890). There, a Wisconsin testator in his will instructed that a part of his estate, consisting of Michigan real property, be sold and the proceeds from the sale be invested in real property in Missouri. The subsequent disposition by the will of that Missouri real property violated Michigan's rule against perpetuities. Held, that Michigan does not apply its rule against perpetuities to a trust of Missouri land acquired with the proceeds from the sale of Michigan land. The will "converted" Michigan land into Missouri land, to which Michigan's rule against perpetuities has no applicability. The testator's intent was effectuated by selling the Michigan land, and the policy underlying the Michigan rule (not to suspend alienation of Michigan land beyond the limit of the rule) was not impaired, as the land *was* to be sold. This decision is an early example of thoughtful policy analysis.

Other examples of decisions effectuating the testator's intent through recourse to "equitable conversion" include *Duckwall v. Lease,* 20 N.E.2d 204 (Ind. App. 1939), and *Moore v. Livingston,* 265 N.E.2d 251 (Ind. App. 1970) (follow situs rule equitably converting immovable into personalty, then apply the lex fori as decedent's domiciliary law and distribute proceeds accordingly).

For cases of contracts for the sale of real property, the coming Restatement (Third) provides for the application of situs law to determine whether the contract results in an equitable conversion of the parties' interests. § 7.06.

2. Movables

a. Formal Validity

The traditional rule refers to the **law of the testator's domicile at death** as governing questions of **formal** and **substantive** validity. With respect to formal validity, statutes providing for **alternative validating references** (above at p. 220) apply also to movables.

For *revocation,* courts usually follow the same rules as for the *validity of execution.* Note, additionally, that *revocation by operation of law* may occur (e.g., upon divorce). Courts apply the decedent's last domicile, even though the domicile at the time the event occurred might have the greater interest. *Hornbook* § 20.12.

Testamentary trusts of movables benefit from a particularly great concern for *validating the testator's intent.* Assets included in such a trust may be scattered all over, as may be beneficiaries. The settlor's preferences should be (and usually are) accommodated to the greatest extent possible. *Hornbook* § 20.14.

b. Substantive Validity

The domicile at death, from a policy point of view, has the greatest interest in such questions as the forced share of the surviving spouse and children, the statutory allowance for surviving family members pending probate, and the like. In recognition of this interest, *domiciliary law* is the law generally applicable.

c. Testator's Choice

New York permits the non-domiciliary testator to choose its law for local assets. See *Estate of Renard,* 437 N.Y.S.2d 860 (N.Y. Sur. Ct.), *aff'd,* 447 N.Y.S.2d 573 (N.Y. App. Div. 1981) (mem.), *aff'd,* 439 N.E.2d 341 (N.Y. 1982); *Wyatt v. Fulrath,* above at p. 102; *In re Chappell,* 883 N.Y.S.2d 857, 862 (N.Y. Sur. Ct. 2009) (trust). By statute, New York also allows the non-domiciliary testator to choose domiciliary law to govern the will's validity with respect to New York immovables. *In re Estate of Rhoades,* 607 N.Y.S.2d 893 (N.Y. Sup. Ct. 1994).

3. Forced Shares

The right of the surviving spouse to take a statutory share (i.e., to take against the will) is determined by the law of the decedent's domicile at death for movable property and by situs law for immovable property. The domicile has the greatest interest in making provision for the surviving spouse; for this reason, the situs may also refer to that law.

In *Colvin v. Hutchison,* 92 S.W.2d 667 (Mo. 1936), the widow renounced the will at the Illinois domicile. Under Illinois law, she was then entitled to an absolute interest in the deceased husband's land, subject to debts. Under Missouri (situs) law, she received a life estate free from debts in the absence of an affirmative election of an absolute interest. Having failed to make such a choice before her own death, she was held—under situs law—to have had only a life estate. Her heirs therefore took nothing. Arguably, application of situs law defeated policy interests of the domicile without advancing situs interests.

In *Estate of Clark,* 236 N.E.2d 152 (N.Y. 1968), the Virginia testator chose New York law to govern a testamentary trust for the benefit of his mother. The New York court disregarded the choice, although ordinarily valid, in favor of Virginia (domiciliary) law, which permitted the widow to renounce the will **and** take a statutory share (one half).

The combination of the New York statute and the testator's choice of Florida law after moving there enabled the testator in the *Rhoades* case (above p. 222) to prevent his second wife from taking against the will with respect to New York immovables; Florida law gave her such a right only with respect to Florida immovables.

4. Family Allowance

Statutes provide the surviving spouse and minor children of the decedent with temporary support for the time immediately following the decedent's death. The general rule is that a family allowance can be sought only in the domiciliary state and under its law. *Jaeglin v. Moakley,* 151 S.W.2d 524 (Mo. Ct. App. 1941). Under some statutes, however, non-residents may claim the allowance in the state of ancillary administration, or if assets are insufficient at the domicile, seek to satisfy the domiciliary allowance out of assets in the ancillary estate. In re *Estate of Plazza,* 526 P.2d 155 (Colo. App. 1974).

VI. Trusts

A. Validity

Testamentary trusts depend for their formal validity on the validity of the will that establishes them *(situs law* or *alternative references* for *immovable* property and the law of the *decedent's domicile at death* for *movable* property). For testamentary trusts and the surviving spouse's right to take against the will, see above Chapter IV.

Inter vivos trusts with respect to land are a form of gratuitous transfer; *situs law* governs validity. As in the case of testamentary trusts, it will often provide for alternative references. Transfers of movables are valid if valid where made. Additionally, a settlor's designation of the (validating) governing law will be given controlling weight.

Examples: A transfer of securities located in New York to a New York trust was valid under New York law, but not under the law of the settlor's domicile: trust upheld. *Hutchison v. Ross,* 187 N.E. 65 (N.Y. 1933).

A New Jersey domiciliary established a New York trust of New York securities, designating New Jersey law as the governing law. The trust was valid under New Jersey law but not under New York law: trust upheld. *Shannon v. Irving Trust Co.,* 285 N.Y.S. 478 (N.Y. App. Div. 1936), *aff'd,* 9 N.E.2d 792 (N.Y. 1937). See *Hornbook* § 21.3 at 1280.

B. Other Issues

Powers of appointment also raise important choice-of-law issues. Their *validity* is generally governed by the law applicable to the instrument creating them. Their *nature and extent* are a matter of the *donor's intent,* of the law of his or her domicile, or of the *location of the property* in an inter vivos trust. Their *exercise* is governed by situs law in the case of immovables, by the donor's domicile in the case of movables, or as to the latter, by the law identified as most relevant to the particular power or issue. The law applicable to the *rule against perpetuities* has been held to be the law governing the original trust, but in more recent cases, the law of the donee's domicile. *Hornbook* §§ 21.8–21.13.

Trust administration with respect to land usually takes place where it is located, but movables may be located at quite different places from the place of administration. This raises questions of the law applicable to the administration and to the right of foreign (out-of-state) trustees to receive local assets. The trend as to the latter is to permit foreign trustees to receive local assets without first qualifying to do business in-state. The law applicable to the administration as well as the permissibility of changing places of administration are largely matters of the settlor's intent (e.g., express choice of the governing law); failing that, the law of the place where the management of trust assets takes place may be applied.

VII. Probate and Administration of Estates

A. Probate

"Probate" means the establishment, before the appropriate court, of a document as being the valid last will of the decedent. "Probating the estate" means the process of winding up an estate according to the directions contained in the will. "Probate" is also often used in a more general, less technical sense: the winding up of an estate regardless of whether the decedent died testate or intestate.

The principal place of probate of the will (or of the administration of an intestate decedent's estate) is at the decedent's domicile at death. *A will admitted to probate at the domicile will be regarded as valid everywhere with respect to movable property.* The law of the *situs of land* determines whether local probate of the will is required. Nearly all states require probate or some form of registration. See also *supra* Section V(A) with respect to the Restatement (Third).

B. Administration

Administration (collecting assets, paying debts, accounting to the court, ultimate distribution to heirs and distributees) can take place *wherever there are assets.* Principal (or "domiciliary") administration takes place at the decedent's domicile, ancillary administration in all other states where there are assets.

The personal representative (executor of the will, administrator of an intestate decedent's estate) is—technically—an officer of the appointing court and therefore traditionally without power in other states. To lessen the expense to the estate of a number of independent administrations, many states permit a foreign domiciliary personal representative, upon compliance with certain filing requirements, to exercise the powers of a local representative with respect to local assets when there is no competing request for local ancillary administration. See Uniform Probate Code §§ 4–204, 4–205.

Assume that a local debtor makes a payment to a foreign domiciliary personal representative who has *not* qualified as a local ancillary administrator and has *not* complied with any applicable filing requirement. Must the debtor pay again when presented with a claim by a subsequently appointed local administrator?

In *Wilkins v. Ellett,* 108 U.S. 256, 2 S. Ct. 641, 27 L. Ed. 718 (1883), the Supreme Court immunized the debtor who had paid in good faith. This *pre-Erie* decision is probably no longer binding on the states but it expresses an important policy. As a result, most states, by statute or decisional law, protect a debtor who paid before the issuance of local letters of administration and without notice of local creditors. Some states, by statute, also protect the debtor after the establishment of local administration.

C. Creditors' Rights

Assume that administration takes place in several different states where assets are located, and that the *overall estate is insolvent.*

1) *May* State A, where there is ancillary administration, use all assets locally available to satisfy the claims of creditors who filed in A, leaving little or nothing to transmit to the domicile (State B), so that creditors who claimed there will receive less than full satisfaction? (The question is the same if the estate is insolvent in *both* states, but to different degrees).

   A state may distribute all locally available assets to creditors who have filed in the local proceeding so long as it does so in a nondiscriminatory manner.

   The Supreme Court held in *Blake v. McClung,* 172 U.S. 239, 19 S. Ct. 165, 43 L. Ed. 432 (1898), that a state may not restrict *filing* to in-state creditors.

2) *Should* State A, in the example, distribute all locally available assets to creditors who filed locally? The response to the previous question forces creditors to file in all states where assets are being administered to maximize their chances of having their claims satisfied to the greatest degree possible. This is expensive and burdensome. State A therefore should **ascertain the value of the *total*** estate, establish an **overall percentage rate of satisfaction** (estate divided by claims), pay local claims to the extent of that percentage, and **remit the balance to the domicile (State B).**

   See *In re Hirsch's Estate,* 66 N.E.2d 636 (Ohio 1946), which represents the preferred resolution of the problem.

D. Distribution

Final distribution to heirs generally occurs at the conclusion of the domiciliary administration. However, where the overall estate is solvent, a court of ancillary administration may also distribute an heir's *proportionate* share out of local assets before remitting the balance to the domicile. *In re Meier's Estate,* 226 N.Y.S.2d 733 (N.Y. Sur. Ct. 1962).

VIII. Corporations

A. Existence and Internal Affairs

The existence and dissolution of a corporation are governed by the law of the state of its incorporation. Restatement (Second) §§ 297–99. That law also applies to the corporation's **internal affairs**. Restatement (Second) §§ 303–04. A corporation's "internal affairs" include the validity of stock issues and of corporate bylaws, voting rights, other stockholder rights, the selection of directors and management, the declaration of dividends, and questions of management.

In *CTS Corp. v. Dynamics Corp. of America,* 481 U.S. 69, 107 S. Ct. 1637, 95 L. Ed. 2d 67 (1987), the Supreme Court upheld Indiana's anti-takeover statute. "No principle of corporation law and practice is more firmly established than a State's authority to regulate domestic corporations, including the authority to define the voting rights of shareholders." Id. at 89, 1649 (citing Restatement (Second) § 304). See also *Delaware v. New York,* 507 U.S. 490, 113 S. Ct. 1550, 123 L. Ed. 2d 211 (1993) (state of incorporation of brokerage house entitled to escheat unclaimed stock dividends).

B. Other Issues

For purposes of **diversity jurisdiction**, a corporation is a citizen of the state of incorporation *and* of the state where it has its *principal place of business.* 28 U.S.C.A. § 1332(c) (West 2022).

The Restatement (Third) provides that *domicile of a corporation* for choice of law purposes is "presumed" to be where it has its *principal place of business.* The latter is decided with respect to the "particular choice-of-law issue" that is involved. § 2.08(2). See also above at p. 163 with regard to dépeçage.

General choice-of-law rules apply to a corporation's **transactions with third parties**. See Restatement (Second) § 301–02.

Investment securities (including corporate stock) are governed by UCC Art. 8. As to the applicable law, see § 8–110. For the transfer of securities, see § 8–301 *et seq.*

C. Regulation by the Forum

Many states require foreign corporations to *"qualify"* before doing business in the state. This requires filing a copy of the articles of incorporation with the secretary of state and designating an agent for receipt of service of process. See *Denicola*, Note, A Proposed Minimum Threshold Analysis for the Imposition of State Door-Closing Statutes, 51 Fordham L. Rev. 1360 (1983). Sanctions include penalties and denial of access to the courts to maintain actions for transactions done *within the state.* **Note** that qualification statutes apply only to ***intrastate*** business done by a foreign corporation.

It was "clearly erroneous" to apply New York's qualification statute to a Bermuda company when the transaction had international as well as intrastate aspects. For the application of the New York qualification statute, the company must have substantial intrastate business activity. *Netherlands Shipmortgage Corp. v. Madias,* 717 F.2d 731 (2d Cir. 1983). For discussion and application, see *Gustavia Home, LLC v. Rutty*, 221 F. Supp. 3d 304 (E.D.N.Y. 2016) (also analogizing the requirement to the U.S. Supreme Court's test—"at home"—in *Daimler, supra* at p. 56).

"Pseudo-Foreign Corporation" statutes were designed to subject a foreign corporation to regulation under forum law when it has its principal or a major place of business in the state. California's statute applies when both local stock ownership and the amount of local business exceed 50%, except when the corporation's stock is listed on a national exchange. *To the extent that these statutes are invoked to apply forum law to the internal affairs of a foreign corporation, they may now be unconstitutional.*

In upholding the Indiana anti-takeover statute, the U.S. Supreme Court in *CTS Corp. v. Dynamics Corp. of America,* 481 U.S. 69, 107 S. Ct. 1637, 95 L. Ed. 2d 67 (1987), cited with approval both the "internal affairs" rule of Restatement (Second) § 304 and its earlier decision in *Edgar v. MITE Corp.,* 457 U.S. 624, 102 S. Ct. 2629, 73 L. Ed. 2d 269 (1982). There, the Court said that "Illinois has no interest in regulating the internal affairs of foreign corporations." Id. at 645–46, 2642. The Court "constitutionalized," as it were, the law of the state of incorporation as the law applicable to a corporation's internal affairs. The Supreme Court of Delaware took the same approach in *Draper v. Gardner Defined Plan Trust,* 625 A.2d 859, 867 (Del. 1993). See also *VantagePoint Venture Partners 1996 v. Examen, Inc.*, 871 A.2d 1108 (Del. 2005) (applying Delaware law, as state of incorporation); *Juul Labs v. Grove,* 238 A.3d 904, 914–18 (Del. Ch. 2020); *Scianella v. AstraZeneca UK Ltd.*, 2024 WL

3327765 *15 (Del. Ch. 2024); *Rein v. ESS Group, Inc.*, 184 A.3d 695 (R.I. 2018) (applying the reasoning of *VantagePoint Partners*). Cf. Uniform Limited Liability Company Act art. 10 (not adopted as such, but similar provisions adopted in most states, e.g., Del. Code Ann. tit. 6, § 18–901(a) (West 2024)). But see below.

The exception in the California statute in favor of corporations whose stock is traded on a national exchange addresses possible Commerce Clause concerns. However, the Supreme Court's rationale in *CTS Corp.*, in favor of according exclusive regulatory power to the state of incorporation, is much broader. 481 U.S. at 89–91, 107 S. Ct. at 1650–51. It would also extend to foreign corporations *not* traded on national exchanges and to issues beyond acquisition of shares, e.g., to a corporation's powers, the manner of amending its charter, and other issues of governance. See *Hornbook* § 23.9.

IX. Review Questions

Note: For choice of law in tort, consult the Review Questions for Chapter VIII.

1. T or F: The "place of wrong," for purposes of the First Restatement is,

a. where the defendant's negligence occurred,

b. where the injury was suffered.

2. Plaintiff, from State A, is injured in B as a result of Defendant's conduct. Under A law, the Defendant would not have acted negligently, under B law it would enjoy charitable immunity (although its conduct would have been considered negligent). C is the place of suit and does not provide charitable immunity. What law applies?

3. P in state A wrote to D in state B offering D to join in a venture in state C. D accepted, by letter sent from state B, to P in state A.

T or F: Under the First Restatement,

a. the validity of the contract is governed by the law of state A;

b. the law of state C governs the remedy for breach of the contract;

c. under no circumstances would a court find that the validity of the contract is also governed by the law of state C.

4. a. T or F: The parties may stipulate that their contract, made and to be performed in the same state, shall be governed by the law of England.

b. T or F: In the absence of a choice by the parties, courts that have abandoned the First Restatement in tort cases will carry the new approach (Restatement (Second), Restatement (Third), interest analysis, whatever) over to contract choice of law.

c. T or F: The UCC provides for the application of the most closely connected law in the absence of choice by the parties.

d. T or F: Contracts for an interest in land are usually governed by the law of the situs.

e. T or F: Modern approaches treat the Statute of Frauds and the Parole Evidence Rule as procedural, and therefore apply the law of the forum.

f. T or F: A court with personal jurisdiction over the parties has no jurisdiction to adjudicate their rights, as between themselves, to land situated elsewhere.

g. T or F: The perfection of a security interest in accounts receivable is governed by the law where the debtor is located.

5. Testator, domiciled in A makes a will, formally valid under A law. The will directs the sale of all assets and provides for the distribution of the proceeds among named beneficiaries. The assets include personal property in several jurisdictions, as well as claims and land in B. The laws of A and B differ with respect to the surviving spouse's statutory share (in the event of an election to take against the will), and B law, moreover, requires three witnesses for a valid will, while Testator used only two (the minimum required in A).

a. T or F: The law of the domicile at death applies to testate (and intestate) succession to movables and the law of the situs to succession to immovables. Testator's will directed the sale of all assets, including the B land. The latter worked an "equitable conversion" into personal property (money), A law applies, the will is valid.

b. T or F: If for some reason the will cannot be validated under A law as a result of equitable conversion, it will fail as to the B land, and the land will pass by way of intestate succession.

c. T or F: The surviving spouse's statutory share will be governed by the law of the decedent's domicile at death with respect to movable property wherever situated (as the uniformly followed choice-of-law rule provides), but by the law of the situs of the land.

d. T or F: The domicile controls probate: the executor (personal representative, administrator) is entitled to collect assets, including claims (receive payment, sue to collect) everywhere.

e. T or F: If the overall estate is insolvent, creditors filing in the state with the most assets have a chance of a proportionately higher rate of satisfaction than if they had filed in a state with fewer assets.

6. a. T or F: The "internal affairs" of a corporation are governed by the law of the state of its incorporation.

b. T or F: A state, through its "qualification statute," may require all corporations, doing any amount of intrastate business, to comply with filing and other requirements, such as appointing an agent to receive service of process.

c. T or F: "Pseudo-foreign corporation" statutes undertake to subject a foreign corporation, doing a stated amount of in-state business, or being owned (to a stated extent) by resident shareholders, to local (corporate) regulatory law.

d. T or F: In circumstances of "c," the forum's interests are such as to allow it to reach the internal affairs of a corporation incorporated elsewhere.

Chapter X

Constitutional Limitations on State Choice of Law

■ ANALYSIS

I. **Introduction**
- A. Overview
- B. Function of Due Process and Full Faith and Credit in Choice of Law

II. **Due Process and Full Faith and Credit: The Early Cases**
- A. Due Process
- B. Full Faith and Credit
- C. Conclusion

III. ***Hague*, *Shutts*, and *Wortman***
- A. The Test
- B. *Hague*
- C. *Shutts*
- D. *Wortman*
  1. Constitutional Limitations on Choice of Law and Characterization: Statutes of Limitations
  2. *Wortman's* Choice of the Applicable Substantive Law

IV. **Court Closing**

V. **Other Constitutional Provisions**
- A. Privileges and Immunities; Equal Protection
- B. Commerce Clause: *Bendix*

VI. **Conclusions**

VII. **Review Questions**

I. Introduction

A. Overview

Chapter VIII showed the wide range of approaches to choice of law employed by most jurisdictions that have abandoned or modified the traditional approach. Chapter IX summarized the particular choice-of-law rules, which have been developed in the case law by application of the modern approaches. You have seen that in many instances, courts will display or even pursue a forum bias in the course of their analysis. The question therefore arises whether state courts are entirely free in their choice of the applicable law, or whether the U.S. Constitution either mandates certain results or imposes limits on the freedom of state courts. Almost invariably, the question arises in the context of *whether the forum may apply its own law* when it has few or no contacts with the case.

In a few early decisions, the U.S. Supreme Court mandated certain results, or so severely limited a state court's choice as to be tantamount to mandating a result. Beginning in the mid-1930s, the Court no longer mandated a particular choice of law, and has given a narrow definition to limitations on a state court's freedom. *As a result, only in exceptional and extreme cases is a state court limited in its choice of the applicable law today.*

However, the Court has continued to address the topic. To understand the status of current law, and to appreciate future developments, a review of the Court's past decisions as well as its current practice will be helpful. The following comments analyze constitutional limitations upon choice of law in the context of the constitutional provisions in which a question is most likely to arise: Due Process, Full Faith and Credit, Privileges and Immunities, and the Commerce Clause.

B. Function of Due Process and Full Faith and Credit in Choice of Law

Of the constitutional provisions discussed in the following sections, the Due Process and Full Faith and Credit Clauses are by far the most important. As a conceptual matter, the two provisions address *different* concerns.

First, the **Due Process Clause** protects the ***defendant*** against the *unfair and arbitrary application of a law unrelated to him or her or the cause of action.* Remember that the U.S. Supreme Court said that—in *jurisdiction*—the Due Process Clause protects the defendant's "individual liberty interest." *Insurance Corp. of Ireland,* above at p. 57. Just as the defendant has an "individual liberty interest" in the *place of suit* (i.e., not to be haled into a forum with which he or she or the claim has no contact), so does the defendant have such an interest *with respect to the law to be selected* for the determination of liability.

Second, "The **Full Faith and Credit Clause** is one of several provisions . . . designed to transform the several States from independent sovereignties into a single, unified Nation." *Allstate Ins. Co. v. Hague,* 449 U.S. 302, 322, 101 S. Ct. 633, 645, 66 L. Ed. 2d 521, 536–37 (1981) (Stevens, J., concurring). The Full Faith and Credit Clause thus addresses the *interests of other states*, and could, theoretically, serve as a limitation upon choice of law that is separate from the due process limitation. See Hay, Full Faith and Credit and Federalism in Choice of Law, 34 Mercer L. Rev. 709 (1983).

The early decisions of the U.S. Supreme Court treated the two provisions separately. The modern cases, while occasionally acknowledging the theoretical distinction, treat them **as co-extensive in practice**.

II. Due Process and Full Faith and Credit: The Early Cases

A. Due Process

In *New York Life Insurance Co. v. Dodge,* 246 U.S. 357, 38 S. Ct. 337, 62 L. Ed. 772 (1918), a Missouri insured exercised a loan privilege under the policy. The loan was approved by the company in New York, and the loan agreement provided for the forfeiture of the policy if the loan should not be repaid. The U.S. Supreme Court held that New York law applied to the loan agreement because it was "made" there, and that it would therefore violate the insurance carrier's due process rights to permit Missouri to apply its non-forfeiture statute, which would have prevented cancellation of the policy. Note that the company had dealt with the Missouri resident, and thus had "contacts" with him. At the time of the decision, this was not a relevant consideration. By precluding Missouri from applying its law, the Court in effect approved, even constitutionalized, the vested rights approach (above at pp. 145, 177). See also *Mutual Life Insurance Co. v. Liebing,* 259 U.S. 209, 42 S. Ct. 467, 66 L. Ed. 900 (1922). *Dodge,* as we will see, is no longer the law.

Home Insurance Co. v. Dick, 281 U.S. 397, 50 S. Ct. 338, 74 L. Ed. 926 (1930), was an important decision, and the U.S. Supreme Court has *frequently and consistently reaffirmed its continued validity.*

The plaintiff had contracted, in Mexico, with the defendant, a Mexican insurance company, for insurance coverage for a vessel located in Mexico. The policy covered the vessel only in Mexican waters, contained a choice-of-law clause in favor of Mexican law, and provided that all claims for loss had to be brought within one year. This provision was valid under the chosen law but not under Texas law. The U.S. Supreme Court disapproved of application of Texas law. The *only* contact that Texas had with the case was that it was the forum.

In *John Hancock Mutual Life Ins. Co. v. Yates,* 299 U.S. 178, 57 S. Ct. 129, 81 L. Ed. 106 (1936), the insured's widow sued on a life insurance policy in Georgia, where she had moved after the insured's death. The Georgia court dealt with the issue whether the allegation that the insured had procured the policy by fraud in New York should be characterized as procedural and be decided by the jury. The U.S. Supreme Court reversed: a procedural characterization does not overcome the prohibition of *Dick* against applying forum law to an unrelated case. There was "no occurrence, nothing done [in Georgia] to which the law of Georgia could apply." Id. at 182, 131. But see Section III(D) at page 236 below.

Note that in *Dick,* there were ***no*** contacts with the forum, other than that it was the place of suit. In *Dodge* and in *Yates,* on the other hand, there were contacts, but the Court perceived an unfairness in applying forum law. (Compare with "unfairness" in the modern jurisdictional context: *Asahi, J. McIntyre,* and *Ford,* above Chapter III, at III(D)). This perceived unfairness was due to the Court's acceptance of the traditional approach to choice of law: rights and obligations of the parties had "vested" at a particular time, in a particular state. But emphasis on preventing unfairness and arbitrariness—on protecting a party's "individual liberty interest"—may at times require subjecting a defendant to a law favoring the plaintiff, which is different from the law of the place where the defendant acted. The U.S. Supreme Court expressed this view in subsequent cases.

In *Watson v. Employers Liability Assurance Corp.,* 348 U.S. 66, 75 S. Ct. 166, 99 L. Ed. 74 (1954), a Louisiana resident was injured using a home hair permanent solution, which was manufactured by the Illinois subsidiary of a Massachusetts firm. The plaintiff brought suit against the manufacturer's insurance carrier under a Louisiana law permitting a "direct action" against a tortfeasor's insurance carrier. The defendant invoked the "no action" clause of the insurance contract made in Massachusetts with the Massachusetts parent corporation, providing that no action shall be brought until after the insured has been found liable. The U.S. Supreme Court held that the manufacturer, having shipped the product to Louisiana where it caused injury, was subject to suit there: the insurer could foresee that injury would result wherever a defective product was shipped and had insured against that risk. The insurance carrier, the same as the insured, was subject to the law of Louisiana. It could not invoke the "no action clause" of the contract, even though that clause was valid and in force under the law of the state where the policy was contracted.

In *Clay v. Sun Insurance Office, Ltd.,* 377 U.S. 179, 84 S. Ct. 1197, 12 L. Ed. 2d 229 (1964), an Illinois resident had purchased a personal property floater insurance policy covering his boat. The policy provided for "world-wide coverage" and stipulated that claims must be brought within twelve months from the date of loss. Subsequently, the plaintiff moved to Florida, where the loss occurred. He brought suit after twelve months had passed by invoking a Florida law permitting suit within five years from loss, overriding contrary contractual stipulations. Again, the U.S. Supreme Court held that the occurrence of a loss in Florida (or anywhere else where the plaintiff might take the boat) was foreseeable by the defendant ("world-wide" coverage had been provided, and the defendant knew of the location of the boat); the application of Florida law was not unfair or arbitrary.

In both *Watson* and *Clay,* the principal emphasis was on the foreseeability, as well as on the fairness vs. unfairness, of applying forum law. The question whether the forum should not have applied the other state's law, under full faith and credit principles, was not asked. According to more modern cases, summarized in the next subsection, the answer today would be "no" because the forum, in both cases, had an *interest* in the application of its law (compensation of a resident) and did not have to subordinate that interest to that of another state.

Today, the answer to the question whether the forum may apply its law consistent with the requirements of due process therefore depends mainly on its ***contacts*** with the case. See particularly Section III below. *Dodge* would not be followed today, *Yates* might not be either, but *Dick* remains valid.

B. Full Faith and Credit

The development of the case law under the Full Faith and Credit Clause parallels that under the Due Process Clause. Thus, in the early decision of *Bradford Electric Light Co. v. Clapper,* 286 U.S. 145, 52 S. Ct. 571, 76 L. Ed. 1026 (1932), the Court disapproved of the application of forum law despite the existence of contacts of the case with the forum.

In *Bradford Electric Light,* the employee of a Vermont company was killed in New Hampshire in the course of his employment. Vermont, where the contract of employment had been formed, made worker compensation the exclusive remedy, while New Hampshire permitted an action for wrongful death. The Court held that the law of Vermont governed the employment relationship between the deceased and the defendant. New Hampshire had to accord it recognition. The Court noted in passing that there was nothing in the decisional law of New Hampshire to the effect that application of Vermont law would be contrary to New Hampshire public policy.

Subsequent decisions have invoked this passing comment from *Bradford Electric Light*. California did not have to apply the worker compensation law of another jurisdiction (where it was the exclusive remedy for an injured worker) when doing so would be *"obnoxious"* to its policy *and* it had contact with the case (place of injury or place where the employment relationship was formed). *Alaska Packers Association v. Industrial Accident Commission,* 294 U.S. 532, 55 S. Ct. 518, 79 L. Ed. 1044 (1935); *Pacific Employers Insurance Co. v. Industrial Accident Commission,* 306 U.S. 493, 59 S. Ct. 629, 83 L. Ed. 940 (1939). Note that there had not been a finding of "obnoxiousness" by the California court in either case. California law was simply *different*, and California had an *interest* in the application of its law, which was considered legitimate in view of its *contacts* with the case.

The foregoing interpretation is borne out by the Court's decision in yet another worker compensation case, *Carroll v. Lanza,* 349 U.S. 408, 75 S. Ct. 804, 99 L. Ed. 1183 (1955). The law of the forum, Arkansas, permitted a common law claim against a general contractor, even after receipt of worker compensation through a subcontractor, while the law of Missouri, the place of employment, did not. The forum, as the place of injury, had contact with the case. Thus, the Court said, "Arkansas [the forum] can adopt Missouri's policy if she likes. Or . . . she may supplement it or displace it with another." Id. at 413–14, 807. The Court no longer relies on an "obnoxiousness" test that must be met before the forum may prefer its law over that of another interested state. The Court therefore **no longer weighed interests**. Instead, it **permitted the forum to apply its law whenever it had sufficient contacts with the case**.

Except for very few areas, e.g., the "internal affairs rule" for corporate law (above at p. 225 and immediately following), the Court permits the states to follow whatever approaches to choice of law they select, subject to the limitations expressed in *Allstate Ins. Co. v. Hague* (below at p. 234). See also *Franchise Tax Board of California v. Hyatt,* 538 U.S. 488, 498, 123 S. Ct. 1683, 1689–90, 155 L. Ed. 2d 702 (2003) (California may apply its no-immunity rule as against Nevada's immunity rule. California's interest and contacts suffice; the Supreme Court will not engage in a "balancing [of] States' competing sovereign interests"). For applications, see *In re Senior Health Ins. Company of Pennsylvania,* 310 A.3d 26, 40, 55 (Pa. 2024); *Promenade D'Iberville, LLC v. Jacksonville Electric Authority,* 411 So.3d 1050, 1065 (Miss. 2025).

There are, however, two possible *exceptions*. First, in *Order of United Commercial Travelers of America v. Wolfe,* 331 U.S. 586, 67 S. Ct. 1355, 91 L. Ed. 1687 (1947), the Court required South Dakota to honor a six-months claim limitation in the constitution of an Ohio fraternal benefit society, valid under Ohio law but not under South Dakota's. The rationale was that all members of the society should be governed by the law of the state that granted the charter. *Wolfe* and other fraternal benefit society cases are unique. They have been thought by some to have lost their authority in light of the more recent worker compensation cases, above.

Second, in *CTS Corp. v. Dynamics Corp. of America,* 481 U.S. 69, 107 S. Ct. 1637, 95 L. Ed. 2d 67 (1987), the Court upheld the constitutionality of Indiana's anti-takeover statute against a Commerce Clause attack. It stated that "no principle of corporation law and practice is more firmly established than a State's authority to regulate domestic corporations [i.e., corporations incorporated under its law], including the authority to define the voting rights of shareholders." Id. at 89, 1649. This statement seems to give *constitutional sanction* to the "internal affairs" rule in choice of law with respect to corporations. If so, it may be broad enough to give renewed authority to *Wolfe.* The Class Action Fairness Act contains an "internal affairs" exception: 28 U.S.C. § 1332(d)(9). No class action may be brought in a federal court when it concerns "governance of corporate enterprises.: Such an action belongs in the courts of the state of incorporation. *Sudholt v. County Mutual Ins. Co.*, 83 F.4th 621, 626 (7th Cir. 2023); applied in *Benes v. Luis de la Aguilera et al.*, 2023 WL 6985498 * 5 (S.D. Fla. 2023).

C. Conclusion

The tests for the satisfaction of the due process and full faith and credit requirements seem to have merged. In any event, they are treated in the case law as being coextensive. The remaining question is what constitutes sufficient contacts for the satisfaction of these constitutional requirements.

III. *Hague*, *Shutts*, and *Wortman*

A. The Test

Analysis of the due process cases (Section II(A)) and of the full faith and credit cases (Section II(B)) showed that a state may **not** apply its law when it has **no** contacts with a case, but that it may do so when it does have contacts. What must be the quality of these contacts?

Beginning with its decision in *Allstate Insurance Co. v. Hague,* 449 U.S. 302, 101 S. Ct. 633, 66 L. Ed. 2d 521 (1981), the U.S. Supreme Court has stated the test as follows: "[F]or a state's substantive law to be selected in a constitutionally permissible manner, that State must have a *significant contact or significant aggregation of contacts, creating state interests, such that choice of its law is neither arbitrary nor fundamentally unfair."* Id. at 312–13, 640 (emphasis added).

Note that there are really two requirements: (1) a *single* significant contact, or a *number* of contacts that *together*, are "significant," and (2) that this contact or these contacts create a "state interest." *Note how due process and full faith and credit concerns are both addressed in this statement:* (a) it addresses the defendant's due process concerns, and (b) it speaks to the competing state interests under full faith and credit. The last clause of this statement ("such that . . .") brings it all back to due process: the focus is on the defendant. The assumption is that if the significant contact(s) and state-interest requirements are met, the application of forum law will not be arbitrary or fundamentally unfair. This stated assumption raises the question whether the state-interest part of the test is perhaps secondary to the significant-contact element of the test.

The "significant" contact(s) requirement is qualitatively different from the "minimum" contacts requirement for judicial jurisdiction. Like the latter, the "significant" contact(s) requirement has been difficult to apply in practice. *There are no bright lines.*

B. *Hague*

Allstate Insurance Co. v. Hague, 449 U.S. 302, 101 S. Ct. 633, 66 L. Ed. 2d 521 (1981) (also discussed above), involved the question whether Minnesota could constitutionally apply its law in an action against the insured's insurance carrier under his uninsured motorist coverage. Minnesota law would permit "stacking" (cumulating) insurance benefits under the insured's three insurance policies. "Stacking" was not permitted by the law of Wisconsin, the state where the insured lived, where the insurance policy was taken out, where the insured's cars were registered and garaged, and where the fatal accident had happened.

All members of the Court participating in the decision (eight) agreed on the test as quoted above (at II(A)). A plurality of four made no distinction between the due process and full faith and credit requirements and found them satisfied. Justice Stevens distinguished between the two, but found full faith and credit to be an obstacle—beyond due process—*only* when a state's application of its own law threatens "national unity." Since it is difficult to imagine a situation in which a private law suit will threaten national unity, five members of the court may be said to have considered the "significant contact(s)" test satisfied on the facts of *Hague,* resulting in the conclusion that the application of Minnesota law was permissible. Three members of the Court dissented; they agreed with the statement of the basic test, but thought that the contacts in *Hague* were "trivial" and therefore did not permit the application of Minnesota law.

The plurality (majority) did not find the "significant contact(s)" test satisfied by any single contact. Instead, it permitted the application of Minnesota law on the *"aggregation" segment of the test.*

(A) Mr. Hague had been employed in Minnesota, and Minnesota has an interest in protecting its work force. *Counter argument by the dissent:* Granted, but how will "stacking" of insurance benefits after death advance this goal? Furthermore, stacking of insurance benefits (i.e., liability on the part of the *victim's* insurer) obviously has no deterrent effect on the *uninsured* tortfeasor.

(B) The plaintiff (decedent's widow) was a Minnesota resident. She had moved there after the accident but before instituting suit, and the Court discounted forum shopping under the circumstances. *Critique:* post-accident changes of domicile by the *plaintiff* have not been relevant before, nor should they be relevant. Such a change obviously has nothing to do with the occurrence (or transaction). Note that the *state interest* (compensation in favor of a current resident), *standing alone,* is not enough. See the analysis of the "Test" in subsection A, above.

(C) The administration, in part, of a Minnesota "estate" is also involved. Underlying this point is that administration of a decedent's estate may be undertaken wherever there is tangible or intangible property. Jurisdiction over the debtor (Allstate) existed in Minnesota. *Critique:* Mrs. Hague, by suing Allstate, can locate the "administration of the estate" of Mr. Hague (with respect to the insurance claim) at any place where she can get jurisdiction over Allstate—presumably, in several states, even within the limits of today's tests for general or specific jurisdiction.

(D) Allstate did business in Minnesota and therefore should not be surprised by the application of Minnesota law. *Critique:* Allstate also does business in most other states of the Union. Had Mrs. Hague been able to assert jurisdiction and bring suit in one of them, the same argument could be made, but obviously would not.

> This argument makes sense only if in addition to doing business in Minnesota, that contact becomes relevant because of other contacts, or in turn, lends strength to them. If the other contacts are found lacking, this contact will not add anything.

Hague has been hotly debated in the legal literature. Those in support of interest analysis have praised it, while those favoring greater predictability of result and fearing forum shopping have criticized the decision. But preference of one choice-of-law approach over another is not the point. Instead, the basic question is how far a forum may favor application of its own law. (Remember that Minnesota was then a forum-favoring, "better rule of law" state. Minnesota has now adopted a policy-analysis approach, which may lead to the law of another state).

The statement of the test is important. It suggests that the contacts needed for the application of forum law *("significant* contact or *significant aggregation* of contacts") are not coextensive with the *minimum* contacts needed for jurisdiction. In practice, the two will often overlap as a factual matter.

On "state interest" and the Supreme Court's disinclination to weigh one state's interest against that of another, see *Franchise Tax Board of California v. Hyatt*, above at p. 233.

C. *Shutts*

The *Hague* test was applied in *Phillips Petroleum Co. v. Shutts,* 472 U.S. 797, 105 S. Ct. 2965, 86 L. Ed. 2d 628 (1985). In this class action, 97% of the members of the plaintiff class had no connection with the Kansas forum, and 99% of the gas leases giving rise to the claims involved were located in states other than Kansas. "Given Kansas' lack of 'interest' in claims unrelated to that State, and the substantive conflict with jurisdictions such as Texas [where some leases were located and some claimants resided], . . . application of Kansas law to every claim in this case is sufficiently arbitrary and unfair as to exceed constitutional limits." Id. at 822, 2979. See also *Parker v. Perdue Foods, LLC*, 2024 WL 3993855 (M.D. Ga. 2024). Note, however, that Kansas had not considered whether and, if so, to what extent the laws of the other states did differ from that of Kansas (the Supreme Court referred to "substantive conflict[s]"). When all also relevant other state laws are the same, the forum may apply its law: *Republic Technologies (NA), LLC v. BBK Tobacco & Foods, LLP*, 135 F.4th 572, 590 (7th Cir. 2025).

D. *Wortman*

The decision in *Sun Oil Co. v. Wortman,* 486 U.S. 717, 108 S. Ct. 2117, 100 L. Ed. 2d 743 (1988) is difficult and potentially far-reaching.

Wortman was a companion case to *Shutts*. The U.S. Supreme Court affirmed a decision of the Kansas Supreme Court, which had (a) applied Kansas' *longer* statute of limitations to claims that were time-barred under the laws of other states, and (b) arrived at a construction of the substantive law of the other states by injecting its own prediction and relying on general principles of contract law. The statute-of-limitations issue can be explained to involve its characterization as involving procedure, not substance. See *id.* at 726 and discussion further below. The second point is more problematical, as Justice O'Connor explained in her partial dissent when she showed that the laws of some of the involved states was clear and needed no construction or resort to general principles (see also further below in subsection (2)).

1. Constitutional Limitations on Choice of Law and Characterization: Statutes of Limitations

Recall that in *John Hancock Mutual Life Ins. Co. v. Yates,* 299 U.S. 178, 57 S. Ct. 129, 81 L. Ed. 106 (1936), above at p. 201, Georgia was not permitted to apply its law, as it had no contact with the transaction at issue. Under that inapplicable Georgia law, the question of whether an insurance policy had been obtained by fraud was, procedurally, a question for the jury.

In the context of statutes of limitations, it has long been held that the forum may apply its *shorter* statute. *Wells v. Simonds Abrasive Co.,* 345 U.S. 514, 73 S. Ct. 856, 97 L. Ed. 1211 (1953). In *Wells,* the forum did have some contact with the case (defendant's place of business). Also, a dismissal because a statute of limitations has run is usually not "on the merits," i.e., it does not affect rights and liabilities for purposes of litigation elsewhere.

Application of the forum's *longer* statute to a claim that is time-barred under the law which governs liability obviously *may affect the outcome.*

Recall *Keeton v. Hustler Magazine, Inc.,* 465 U.S. 770, 104 S. Ct. 1473, 79 L. Ed. 2d 790 (1984). There, a multistate libel was time-barred in all states except New Hampshire. Suit in New Hampshire resulted in a $2 million verdict, part of which was obviously compensating plaintiff for injury in other states. Note that the only issue before the Supreme Court at the time was whether New Hampshire had jurisdiction.

In *Wortman* (above), the Supreme Court permitted the application of the forum's longer statute of limitations. It cited the historical view that statutes of limitations only deal with the remedy and do not affect the underlying right. As a matter of "tradition," they are characterized as *"procedural,"* and states may constitutionally apply their own procedural law. Justice Brennan concurred because he found that Kansas had a "procedural *interest"* in the application of its statute. He was troubled, however, that the majority reached the result on the basis of "tradition," because practice of a conflicts rule over an extended time does not necessarily make it constitutional. Justice O'Connor and Chief Justice Rehnquist also concurred, but expressly left open the question whether the result should be different if the other state considered its statute of limitations to be substantive.

2. *Wortman*'s Choice of the Applicable Substantive Law

Wortman involved a disagreement over royalty payments for gas that petitioner extracted from properties that it leased from respondents. Respondents sought interest on royalty payments that were not timely made. The Kansas courts had found that the laws of Texas, Oklahoma, and Louisiana, which governed most of the claims, provided specific interest rates, but that such rates could be varied by the parties. They then found that as a matter of "industry practice," a higher interest rate, approved by the Federal Power Commission (which regulated the price of the extracted gas in interstate commerce), would be considered an implied agreement to vary the statutory rates provided by those states. Reference was also made to equitable principles. The result then was the same as under Kansas law.

On review, The Supreme Court made clear that a mistaken interpretation of the law of another state was not enough to reverse. "To constitute a violation of the Full Faith and Credit Clause or the Due Process Clause, it is not enough that a state court misconstrue the law of another State. Rather, our cases make plain that the misconstruction must contradict law of the other State that is clearly established and that has been brought to the court's attention." 486 U.S. at 730–31, 108 S. Ct. at 2126 (citations omitted). The Court affirmed the Kansas Supreme Court because petitioner had not presented any decision, from any of the three states, that convinced the Court that the Kansas construction of the law of these states was wrong.

The dissenting justices in *Wortman* (O'Connor, J., and Rehnquist, C.J.), on the other had, regarded the Kansas court's interpretation as a failure to give the required full faith and credit to the *statutory* law of other states (in addition to their decisional law). They thought that the majority's affirmance diminished the authority of *Shutts* (above at p. 236). Justice O'Connor wrote:

> First, invent a legal theory so novel or strange that the other State has never had an opportunity to reject it; then, on the basis of nothing but unsupported speculation, "predict" that the other State would adopt that theory if it had the chance. To call this giving full faith and credit to the law of another State ignores the language of the Constitution.

486 U.S. at 749, 108 S. Ct. at 2136 (dissenting). Upon remand of the *Shutts* case, Kansas applied the same substantive law as it had in *Wortman*. The Supreme Court denied certiorari. 487 U.S. 1223, 108 S. Ct. 2883 (mem.), 101 L. Ed. 2d 918 (1988). The coming Restatement (Third) also provides that a State shall apply the law of another State as construed by that State. In absence of decisional law of that State, the majority opinion of *Wortman* continues to apply. Note that in international cases, the Supreme Court requires less, viz. only "respectful consideration" to the foreign state's interpretation of its law, rather than giving that interpretation conclusive effect.

IV. Court Closing

A state may not *discriminate* against claims arising under the law of another state by closing its courts to those claims.

Illustration: The Wisconsin wrongful death act, which by its terms applied only to a death occurring in Wisconsin, had been interpreted as precluding suit in Wisconsin on a claim arising under the act of another state. The Supreme Court held that the statute violated the Full Faith and Credit Clause. When "*all* elements of the wrong" occurred in a sister state, the forum may not refuse to recognize a cause of action provided by the law of that state. *Hughes v. Fetter,* 341 U.S. 609, 71 S. Ct. 980, 95 L. Ed. 1212 (1951).

However, the *forum* may apply its own procedural law to a foreign claim even if the result is to exclude that claim—so long as it does so in a *non-discriminatory* manner.

Illustration: The forum may apply its shorter statute of limitations to a claim that is not barred where it arose. *Wells v. Simonds Abrasive Co.,* 345 U.S. 514, 73 S. Ct. 856, 97 L. Ed. 1211 (1953).

The forum may also refuse to entertain a claim based on sister-state law that violates its public policy. In *Hughes v. Fetter,* above, Wisconsin could not invoke the public-policy justification, however, since its own law provided a remedy for wrongful death.

Similarly, if the forum is unable to grant the relief provided for by the foreign law, it is not obligated to create a new remedy. *Slater v. Mexican National Railroad Co.,* 194 U.S. 120, 24 S. Ct. 581, 48 L. Ed. 900 (1904). This case involved Mexico. The problem is unlikely to arise in the interstate context.

In reverse, the law of a state creating the cause of action might contain a restriction that suit may be brought only in the courts of that state. If the forum has an interest in permitting the plaintiff to proceed, then it may disregard such a restriction.

Illustration: Consistent with the Full Faith and Credit Clause, Alabama could entertain a worker compensation claim under Georgia law by an Alabama worker, even though Georgia law purported to restrict such claims to be heard by Georgia compensation boards. *Crider v. Zurich Insurance Co.,* 380 U.S. 39, 85 S. Ct. 769, 13 L. Ed. 2d 641 (1965). See also *Albright v. Vining Sparks Securities, Inc.*, 2019 WL 7371810 *57 (N.C.Super. 2019).

Court-closing provisions are different from statutory rules ***conditioning access*** to the courts on the satisfaction of prerequisites, for instance that a plaintiff in a medical malpractice suit first seek redress from a state arbitration panel. These conditions do not raise constitutional problems. See, e.g., *Edelson v. Soricelli,* 610 F.2d 131 (3d Cir. 1979).

When, as a matter of choice of law, another state's substantive law applies to the medical malpractice claim, the forum may consider "substantive law" to include that other state's pre-litigation arbitration requirement and stay the local action as well. *Bledsoe v. Crowley,* 849 F.2d 639 (D.C. Cir. 1988).

V. Other Constitutional Provisions

A. Privileges and Immunities; Equal Protection

Both the Privileges and Immunities and the Equal Protection Clauses guard against the application of forum law when that law *discriminates against an out-of-state party* unless the distinction exists for a legitimate purpose.

Illustration: New Hampshire may not require members of the New Hampshire bar to be New Hampshire residents. *Supreme Court of New Hampshire v. Piper,* 470 U.S. 274, 105 S. Ct. 1272, 84 L. Ed. 2d 205 (1985). Alaska may not require employers in a pipeline project to prefer resident over nonresident employees. *Hicklin v. Orbeck,* 437 U.S. 518, 98 S. Ct. 2482, 57 L. Ed. 2d 397 (1978) (both Privileges and Immunities). The Equal Protection Clause is not violated if there are important reasons for treating non-residents differently. *Sarasota Wine Market, LLC v. Schmitt,* 987 F.3d 1171, 1185 (8th Cir. 2021); *Day v.* Henry, 129 F.4th 1197, 1208 (9th Cir. 2025).The Equal Protection Clause (since it applies to "persons") may be invoked by corporations in circumstances where the Privileges and Immunities Clause ("citizens") would not otherwise provide relief.

Dismissal of a nonresident's suit for reasons of *forum non conveniens* does disadvantage the nonresident but is not a violation of the Privileges and Immunities

Clause; it advances a legitimate forum interest in the efficient operation of its courts. *Douglas v. New York, New Haven & Hartford Railroad Co.,* 279 U.S. 377, 49 S. Ct. 355, 73 L. Ed. 747 (1929). See also *Piper*, above at p. 80. But see *Lubbe, supra* at p. 81, and comments thereto.

B. Commerce Clause: *Bendix*

When state law discriminates against a nonresident by imposing a disadvantageous rule that does not apply to residents, the law may constitute an impermissible burden on interstate commerce and may be unconstitutional for that reason.

In *Bendix Autolite Corp. v. Midwesco Enterprises,* 486 U.S. 888, 108 S. Ct. 2218, 100 L. Ed. 2d 896 (1988), the Illinois defendant had agreed to deliver and install a boiler in the Ohio plaintiff's plant. When sued for breach of contract and fraud, the defendant interposed the Ohio statute of limitations. The plaintiff considered the statute tolled because the defendant had not been "present" in Ohio. To be present, a foreign corporation must appoint an agent for service, which is construed as consent to Ohio's *general* jurisdiction. The U.S. Supreme Court agreed with the trial and appellate courts, that the statute violated the Commerce Clause, because it made foreign corporations choose between submitting to Ohio's general jurisdiction or foregoing the protection of the (tolled) statute of limitations "in perpetuity."

Note the narrow ground of the decision. The defendant *was* subject to Ohio's *specific jurisdiction* for the contract claim (which bore the required relationship to Ohio). When the limitation period had expired, the plaintiff claimed that Ohio's *general jurisdiction* (which would also encompass the contract claim) was not time-barred because tolled. The tolling statute thus sought to give Ohio *general* jurisdiction in the absence of contacts which otherwise make for general jurisdiction (see *Goodyear*, above at p. 55). The focus of the decision was on the construction and effect of the state's tolling provision. The Commerce Clause consideration was but an element in the Court's decision on that issue, and the case might have come out the same way without it.

Limitations on choice of law derived from the Commerce Clause will be rare, especially since the facts giving rise to this defense ordinarily will also raise Due Process and Equal Protection concerns.

In *Bendix,* the defendant had invoked both the Commerce and the Due Process Clauses. The Court dealt only with the former. It did not address due process, perhaps because, as it said in passing, "statute of limitations defenses are not a fundamental right." 486 U.S. at 893. However, not to be subjected to general jurisdiction is a fundamental right. The tolling statute in *Bendix* would have had the effect of giving Ohio general jurisdiction. It seems that due process therefore was, in fact, implicated. This aspect of the case may now need to be considered in light of *Daimler, supra* at pp. 52, 56. Can a state's requirement for the appointment of an agent be construed as consent to general jurisdiction? Can such an appointment amount to a declaration that the company considers itself to be "at home" there? See the discussion in Chapter III. In *Bendix,* the Court said in dictum that asserting general jurisdiction on the basis of registration to do business when there were no minimum contacts would impose "a significant burden." 488 U.S. at 893. Note that in *Mallory, supra* at 56, which upheld general jurisdiction on the basis of compliance with required registration, there were minimum contacts with the State, although they were not related to the cause of action.

VI. Conclusions

1. Throughout this chapter, the focus has been on constitutional *limitations* on choice of law. This is so because apart from the early decisions of the U.S. Supreme Court, which mandated the application of a *specific* law, *modern U.S. Supreme Court case law sets only outer limits.* Within these limits, the states are free in their choice of the applicable law. The context of the issue is usually whether a state may apply its own law.

Generally, then, **there are no constitutionally mandated choice-of-law rules, only (outer) constitutional limits.**

Note: In *CTS Corp. v. Dynamics Corp. of America,* above at pp. 225, 233, the Court upheld the Indiana anti-takeover statute, and seemed to make the "internal affairs" rule for choice of law, with respect to corporations, constitutionally required. The context of this case was whether the forum (Indiana) could apply its own law. Not before the court was the question of whether and for what purpose another state could regulate an Indiana corporation or would be constitutionally required to apply Indiana law. This question remains unanswered. The Delaware Court of Chancery (its highest court) has held that the California "pseudo-foreign corporation" statute violates the internal affairs rule. The coming Restatement (Third) arguably would permit application of the law of the corporation's principal place of business which is determined with respect to the "particular issue." Delaware would hardly accept this in the case of a corporation incorporated there.

2. Due process and full faith and credit address different concerns. Due process protects a party against the application of a law unrelated to the claim, while full faith and credit addresses federalism concerns (the interests of the various states as they interact within our federal system). **The case law now treats due process and full faith and credit limitations as coextensive.**

3. Due Process

   a. Application of forum law (even if the result of a choice of law clause in a standard form contract) may **violate** due process if the claim and the parties have ***no*** contact *with the forum. Home Ins. Co. v. Dick,* above at p. 231.

   b. Choice of forum law will **not** violate due process when there is a significant contact or an aggregation of significant contacts with the forum, creating state interests, so that application of forum law would not be arbitrary or fundamentally unfair. *Allstate Ins. Co. v. Hague,* above at pp. 234, 235; *Phillips Petroleum Co. v. Shutts,* above at p. 236; *Franchise Tax Board of California v. Hyatt,* above at p. 233.

   c. There is **uncertainty** about what the test in *Hague* and *Shutts* requires: what quality of contacts? See *Sun Oil v. Wortman,* above and *Hague* itself, above at pp. 234–236.

   d. A state is **free**—is not subject to constitutional limitations—**in the application of its own procedural law**. The Supreme Court so held with respect to a state's use of its **statute of limitations**, regardless of whether that statute is shorter or longer than that of the state whose law applies to the claim. *Sun Oil Co. v. Wortman,* above at p. 236. **Caveat**: That decision *does not address the question of when a state may legitimately characterize an issue as procedural* to permit the application of forum law. In the state-federal context, see *Shady Grove, infra* Chapter XI.

4. Other constitutional provisions (Privileges and Immunities, Equal Protection, Commerce Clause) have occasionally been invoked, for instance in *Bendix, supra* at pp. 240–240. At best, these provisions support limitations at the margin.

5. This chapter dealt with the choice of **state law**, usually forum law, as the applicable law. Another limitation in this context is that state law **may be displaced by federal law**. The interaction between state and federal courts and the question of whether state law is (or is not) applicable in diversity actions in federal court are the subject of the next chapter.

VII. Review Questions

1. T or F: States are free in their choice of law, including the choice of forum law, so long as constitutional limits are observed.

2. T or F: A state may apply its (regulatory) law to the local business activities of a foreign corporation.

3. T or F: A state may apply its law to the issues affecting the internal affairs of a corporation over which it has specific jurisdiction, that has its principal place of business—with regard to the issue at stake—in this state.

4. T or F: Application of the forum's tolling statute to a foreign defendant, without previous contacts sufficient for general jurisdiction may violate,

   a. the Commerce Clause,

   b. due process,

   c. both.

5. T or F: The U.S. Supreme Court requires that a state have minimum contacts with the parties or the transaction to apply forum law.

6. T or F: The defendant is a domiciliary of the forum state. The plaintiff, a nonresident, seeks damages for defendant's conduct in another state. Defendant's conduct is not actionable under the law of the place where she acted, but would be under forum law. Since the court has general jurisdiction (defendant's domicile), it may apply forum law.

7. T or F: Even if a court has only specific jurisdiction, and not general jurisdiction, it may apply forum law.

Part Six

Issues of Federalism

■ ANALYSIS

XI. State Law in Federal Court
XII. Federal Common Law as the Rule of Decision

Chapter XI

State Law in Federal Court

■ ANALYSIS

I. **The *Erie* Doctrine**
  - A. The Rationale for *Erie R.R. v. Tompkins*
  - B. When Does *Erie* Apply? Substance Versus Procedure
  - C. "Countervailing Considerations": *Byrd*

II. ***Erie* and the Federal Rules of Civil Procedure**
  - A. *Hanna*
  - B. *Walker*
  - C. *Semtek*
  - D. Summary
  - E. *Forum Non Conveniens*
  - F. The Federal Rules in International Cases

III. ***Erie* and Choice of Law**
  - A. *Klaxon* and *Challoner*
  - B. Special *Erie* Problems
    - 1. Interstate Forum Shopping
      - a. Interpleader
      - b. The 100-Mile Bulge Rule
      - c. Supplemental Jurisdiction
      - d. Federal Transfer
      - e. Complex Litigation
    - 2. When Federal Law Is Applicable

IV. **Determining State Decisional Law**

V. **Review Questions**

I. The *Erie* Doctrine

A. The Rationale for *Erie R.R. v. Tompkins*

The Rules of Decision Act provides: "The *laws* of the several states, except where the Constitution or treaties of the United States or Acts of Congress otherwise require or provide, shall be regarded as rules of decision in civil actions in the courts of the United States, in cases where they apply." 28 U.S.C.A. § 1652 (West 2024) (emphasis added). In *Swift v. Tyson,* 41 U.S. (16 Pet.) 1, 10 L. Ed. 865 (1842), the Supreme Court interpreted the word "laws" to encompass only state statutory law and not case law. In the absence of state statutory law, the federal courts were therefore free to make their own common law. When this conflicted with state common law, a plaintiff in a diversity suit was able to shop for the more favorable law by selecting either the state or the federal court.

In *Erie R.R. Co. v. Tompkins,* 304 U.S. 64, 58 S. Ct. 817, 82 L. Ed. 1188 (1938), the Supreme Court overruled *Swift v. Tyson.* Tompkins was injured in Pennsylvania by a train while walking parallel to the tracks. Both train and tracks were owned by the defendant railroad. He could not recover under Pennsylvania common law, but could under federal common law. He therefore brought a diversity suit in New York. He recovered a verdict of $30,000. New York's highest court affirmed. The U.S. Supreme Court reversed.

The *Erie* decision rests on three grounds. First, historical scholarship has shown that the word "laws" in the Rules of Decision Act was probably intended to encompass both state statutory and common law. The concurrence in *Erie* rests on this ground. The other two reasons for the decision are far more significant, especially in light of the pervasive influence they have had on the subsequent definition of when state law, rather than federal law, and vice versa, applies in diversity cases.

Historical interpretation apart, the Court found, secondly, that the result of *Swift* was *unconstitutional.* By freely creating rules of federal common law, the federal courts had in effect made federal law in areas where Congress lacked constitutional authority to legislate (i.e., when it lacked delegated powers, with non-delegated powers reserved to the states by the Tenth Amendment). In other words, the federal courts had asserted federal lawmaking authority where there was none.

Third, *Swift* had favored the non-resident plaintiff by giving him or her the choice of a state or federal court (and, with it, often a choice of different substantive law), while a resident plaintiff, also suing a resident defendant, did not have such a choice. *Intrastate uniformity,* a policy goal, thus requires that both state and federal courts sitting in the same state apply the same law. Whenever there is no federal lawmaking power, this "same law" *has to be* state law. Even when there is federal lawmaking power, there is still the policy question of whether state law nevertheless *should* apply, in order to further intrastate uniformity. This latter question is addressed in Chapter XII.

Erie thus held that for constitutional and policy reasons, **federal courts sitting in diversity must apply the law of the state in which they sit in the absence of applicable federal law** or federal lawmaking authority (which a federal court may decide to exercise for reasons of national uniformity—over intrastate uniformity—as discussed in Chapter XII). The often invoked **"twin aims" of *Erie*** are the avoidance of forum shopping and the uniform application of law (which, really, comes to the same thing).

Federal courts sitting in the District of Columbia are not required to follow the *Erie* doctrine but nevertheless do so analogously to promote uniformity and in deference to the District's laws and policies.

The result in the *Erie* case was that Pennsylvania law was applied and the plaintiff lost. Note, however, that the suit had been brought in New York, not in Pennsylvania. There is therefore the unspoken assumption in the *Erie* decision that New York state courts would apply Pennsylvania law as that of the place of injury *(Erie* arose during the time of the "vested rights" approach of the First Restatement). Perhaps also implicit in the decision was that *Erie* principles may extend to choice of law rules, not just to the substantive rules of liability, a proposition which the Court did not make explicit until its decision in *Klaxon* in 1941 (*infra* p. 253).

B. When Does *Erie* Apply? Substance Versus Procedure

A federal court will not apply state law to every aspect of a case pending before it. It will characterize each issue as being *substantive* or *procedural* **for "*Erie* purposes."** It will decide substantive issues under state law; those which are "procedural" will not be decided under state law.

Note that characterization for *Erie* purposes is NOT the same as the substance/procedural characterization discussed in Chapter IV. Rather, the Supreme Court has cast the *Erie* characterization in terms of whether the issue is "**outcome determinative**." That is, "does it significantly affect the result of a litigation for a federal court to disregard a law of a State that would be controlling in an action upon the same claim by the same parties in a State court?" *Guaranty Trust Co. v. York,* 326 U.S. 99, 109, 65 S. Ct. 1464, 1470, 89 L. Ed. 2079 (1945). Under this test, it is easy to see that some issues will be substantive ("outcome determinative") for *Erie* purposes, and at the same time, will be regarded as "procedural" for choice-of-law purposes. Thus, for instance, the federal court must use the forum state's statute of limitations *(York,* above) as well as the state rule that contributory negligence be pleaded as an affirmative defense. *Palmer v. Hoffman,* 318 U.S. 109, 63 S. Ct. 477, 87 L. Ed. 645 (1943). See also *Gasperini*, below at p. 248.

In *Angel v. Bullington,* 330 U.S. 183, 67 S. Ct. 657, 91 L. Ed. 832 (1947), North Carolina state courts had dismissed plaintiff's action to enforce a deficiency after foreclosure on land upon the buyer's default; a North Carolina statutory provision proscribed such a claim. When the plaintiff then sought and obtained a judgment in a North Carolina federal court, the U.S. Supreme Court reversed, on the ground that the constitutionality of North Carolina's forum-closing rule was *res judicata*. The plaintiff had failed to seek further review of the state court decision, so the issue could no longer be reopened collaterally. "A federal court in North Carolina [sitting in diversity] cannot give that which North Carolina has [constitutionally] withheld." 330 U.S. at 192, 67 S. Ct. at 662. It would be possible to say that a forum-closing rule is not technically a "rule of decision" to which the federal Rules of Decision Act speaks. Such an insistence on technical differences in language would overlook the *policy* of *Erie*. As the Court said, the North Carolina statute was "expressive of North Carolina policy. The essence of diversity jurisdiction is that a federal court enforces State law and State policy." 330 U.S. at 191, 67 S. Ct. at 662.

A literal application of the "outcome determinative" test can lead to an ever-expanding coverage of issues by the *Erie* doctrine. There are few issues that do not affect, in some way, the outcome of litigation. It is therefore important to ask, "when does state law *not* apply, and federal law apply instead?"

C. "Countervailing Considerations": *Byrd*

In *Byrd v. Blue Ridge Rural Electric Cooperative,* 356 U.S. 525, 78 S. Ct. 893, 2 L. Ed. 2d 953 (1958), the issue was whether the plaintiff was the defendant's statutory employee for purposes of the state worker compensation act. Under state law, this question was to be decided by the court, but the Supreme Court held that as a matter of federal law, the issue should be decided by the jury. Although doing so might affect the "outcome" of the case, the Court said that "there are affirmative countervailing considerations at work here. The federal system is an independent system for administering justice to litigants. . . . An essential characteristic of that system is the manner in which, in civil common-law actions, it distributes trial functions between judge and jury. . ." 356 U.S. at 537, 78 S. Ct. at 901.

The specific issue in *Byrd* was further addressed in *Simler v. Conner,* 372 U.S. 221, 83 S. Ct. 609, 9 L. Ed. 2d 691 (1963), in which the Court held that the right to a jury trial in federal courts, both in diversity and in other actions, is a matter of federal law under the Seventh Amendment.

The "countervailing considerations" notion envisions a balancing of **state** and **federal interests**. Note, however, that since *Erie* rests on constitutional as well as policy grounds, "countervailing considerations" cannot overcome the constitutional objection when there is no federal lawmaking authority. Thus, "countervailing considerations" inquire whether, as a matter of *policy,* federal or state law should apply in circumstances in which it is permissible to apply either. The Court has shown considerable restraint in expanding the area of "federal law" (see Chapter XII).

The substance/procedural characterization (for *Erie*-purposes) and the Seventh Amendment were also at issue in *Gasperini v. Center for Humanities, Inc.*, 518 U.S. 415, 116 S. Ct. 2211, 135 L. Ed. 2d 659 (1996).

New York law instructs the (New York) Appellate Division to review a trial court jury's award for excessiveness or inadequacy, measured by what would be "reasonable compensation." The state-law provision is clearly "outcome-determinative." Can it be applied in federal court in the face of the of the Seventh Amendment, which provides that "no fact tried by a jury. . . shall be otherwise re-examined in any Court of the United States, than according to the rules of the common law"? The *Gasperini* Court achieved an accommodation. The federal trial court, as the counterpart of a New York state trial court, must follow the New York ("outcome-determinative") procedure. The U.S. Court of Appeals, functioning on the same level as the New York Appellate Division for these purposes, may not undertake another *review* of the jury verdict for Seventh Amendment reasons. It may, however, review the federal trial court's determination for abuse of discretion, as appellate review for abuse of discretion does not offend the Seventh Amendment. The judgment was vacated because the trial court had not undertaken an analysis of whether and how the jury verdict "deviate[d] materially" from New York practice, as required by New York law. Note that the Court interprets the Reexamination Clause to prohibit only *appellate* review, i.e., a narrow reading of the language "*any* Court of the United States." Compare the Court's reasoning and analysis in *Gasperini* (and also in *Walker, infra* at p. 250), with "false conflicts" analysis in the general choice-of-law inquiry.

The decision raises questions. The Seventh Amendment governs the availability of jury trial in federal court (*Byrd*), but *Hanna's* (see below) "twin aims standard" applies to the federal court's review of the jury verdict.

(a) Might there be forum-shopping if federal and state court review follow different standards? Probably not more than usual, when courts apply discretionary standards.

(b) Damages have generally been characterized as "procedural" in U.S. conflicts law (in contrast to Europe). Might the decision inspire a shift?

(c) What if state courts of the forum state would apply another state's law to the questions of whether and in what amount damages for pain and suffering or punitive damages may be awarded? Must the federal court do likewise because of *Klaxon*, below at p. 253? If the forum is New York, does *Gasperini* then require (permit?) review of the foreign measure of damages, based on local standards? See also *Wortman*, above at p. 236.

II. *Erie* and the Federal Rules of Civil Procedure

A. *Hanna*

In its constitutional aspect, *Erie* addressed a situation in which federal lawmaking power was lacking. Therefore, the reference to "laws" in the Rules of Decision Act had to mean *state law*.

The Federal Rules of Procedure derive their authority from another statute, the Rules Enabling Act, 28 U.S.C.A. § 2072 (West 2024). That statute, in turn, is based on federal lawmaking authority.

> [T]he constitutional provision for a federal court system (augmented by the Necessary and Proper Clause) carries with it congressional power to make rules governing the practice and pleading in those courts, which in turn includes a power to regulate matters which, though falling within the uncertain area between substance and procedure, are rationally capable of classification as either.

Hanna v. Plumer, 380 U.S. 460, 472, 85 S. Ct. 1136, 1144, 14 L. Ed. 2d 8 (1965). The Rules Enabling Act permits the promulgation of Federal Rules of Procedure so long as they do not "abridge, enlarge or modify any substantive right." 28 U.S.C.A. § 2072(b) (West 2024). Note the echoes of *Erie,* but note also the point that the *rule*—as such—must not modify substantive rights, even though its *application* might bring about a different result in federal court than in state court.

Hanna involved a difference between state law, which required service in hand, and Federal Rule of Civil Procedure 4(d)(1), which permits service by delivery to a person residing at the defendant's home. In its decision, the Supreme Court presents the analysis summarized above. Unlike in *Erie* itself, there is federal lawmaking power for the Rules Enabling Act. That Act thus becomes the standard against which a Federal Rule must be reviewed. In *Hanna,* application of the Federal Rule (and upholding the validity of service) might deprive the defendant of a defense, but it did not affect any substantive right within the language of the Act. Instead, the Rule related to the manner of proceeding in federal court.

When they apply (see *Walker,* immediately following), **the Federal Rules of Civil Procedure take precedence over inconsistent rules of state law in diversity cases.**

The Federal Rules of Evidence also apply to civil actions and proceedings in federal courts and before federal magistrates. Fed. R. Evid. 1101(b). Even so, it is often more difficult in this area to determine whether an inconsistent rule of state law is one of "evidence" or state substantive law. Compare *Reed v. General Motors Corp.*, 773 F.2d 660 (5th Cir. 1985) (federal rules govern admissibility of evidence in diversity action), with *In re Air Crash Disaster Near Chicago, Illinois on May 25, 1979*, 526 F. Supp. 226, 232 (N.D. Ill. 1981) (citing *Hanna*, and resolving admissibility of evidence question under state law). Some of the Federal Rules expressly refer to state law if a claim or defense under state law is at issue. See, e.g., Fed. R. Evid. 302 (presumptions), 501 (testimonial privileges), 601 (witness competency).

In *Shady Grove Orthopedic Associates v. Allstate Ins. Co.*, 559 U.S. 393, 130 S. Ct. 1431, 176 L. Ed. 2d 311 (2010), the Court allowed a class action under Rule 23, even though New York state law did not allow the particular claim to be brought as a class action. It characterized Rule 23 as procedural, therefore overriding state law. The dissent disagreed with this characterization because a class action exposes the defendant to far greater liability than even a series of single actions. The Court confirmed *Shady Grove* in *Berk v. Choy*, 607 U.S. ___, 146 S.Ct. 546 (2026), 2026 WL 136974 (2026). *China Agritech, Inc. v. Resh*, 584 U.S. 732, 138 S. Ct. 1800, 201 L. Ed. 2d 123 (2018), declined to extend *Shady Grove*. There, a putative plaintiff of a class action was not allowed to bring a new class action under Rule 23 when the statute of limitations on the first action had run. See also *Williams v. Tech Mahindra (Americas) Inc.*, 70 F.4th 646 (3rd Cir. 2023) and, on wrong-forum tolling, 2024 WL 5055834 (3rd Cir. 2024).

B. *Walker*

In *Ragan v. Merchants Transfer & Warehouse Co.*, 337 U.S. 530, 69 S. Ct. 1233, 93 L. Ed. 1520 (1949), the Supreme Court held that the manner in which a statute of limitations is tolled (for instance, by service on the defendant rather than by filing with the clerk of the court) is substantive for *Erie* purposes. After *Hanna* (above), however, it was widely believed that Federal Rule of Civil Procedure 3, which provides that an action commences upon the "filing [of] a complaint with the court," would now take precedence over inconsistent state law and toll the forum state's statute of limitations. However, in *Walker v. Armco Steel Corp.*, 446 U.S. 740, 100 S. Ct. 1978, 64 L. Ed. 2d 659 (1980), the Supreme Court decided otherwise; it adhered to its previous decision in *Ragan*.

The Court emphasized that in *Hanna*, it had addressed the situation in which a Federal Rule *"clashed"* with a rule of state law. As a first step, it is therefore necessary to determine whether a "clash" exists. Through a process of interpretation, the Court found that there was no clash in *Walker*. The Federal Rule was *not* meant "to toll a state statute of limitations, much less . . . to displace state tolling rules. . . . Rule 3 governs the date from which various timing requirements of the *Federal* Rules begin to run, but does not affect state statutes of limitations." 446 U.S. at 751, 100 S. Ct. at 1985 (emphasis added).

The Court thus undertook a functional analysis that is not all that different from "false conflicts" analysis in traditional choice of law. On the one hand, the state's statute of limitations exists to cut off stale claims, and the service requirement is an integral part of defining when that occurs. Importing a tolling provision, in the form of a different service provision from another system of law, might defeat the state statute of limitations. On the other hand, Federal Rule 3 can be read as not affecting limitation periods, but rather to serve as the starting point for the timetable of events in federal court (such as when the defendant's answer must be filed).

The Supreme Court said in *Walker* that it was not reading Rule 3 narrowly. It did, however, examine the functions of both the state law and the Federal Rule that were in issue, with a view to following the mandate of the Rules Enabling Act not to abridge the defendant's substantive rights. In *York* (above at p. 247), these had been held to include limitation periods. In *Gasperini* (above at p. 248), the court also undertook to strike a balance between the application of federal law and policy reasons favoring state law. In *Feeney v. Dunham*, No. 3:06cv310, 2007 WL 1186046, at *6 (D. Conn. Apr. 18, 2007), the court applied *Walker* to a statute of limitations and also held that Rule 3 does not toll the state statute. See also *Makaeff v. Trump University, LLC*, 715 F.3d 254 (9th Cir. 2013) (application of California's anti-SLAPP statute); Id. at 272, 274 (Kozinski, C.J., concurring, and urging reconsideration of certain 9th Circuit authority for having mischaracterized California's anti-SLAPP statute as substantive).

C. *Semtek*

Federal Rule of Civil Procedure 41 addresses dismissal of actions. Its subsection (b)—with exceptions not applicable here—"operates as an adjudication upon the merits." *Semtek International Inc. v. Lockheed Martin Corp.*, 531 U.S. 497, 121 S. Ct. 1021, 149 L. Ed. 2d 32 (2001), raised the question whether Rule 41(b) had claim-preclusive effect in F-2 state court. The dismissal at issue (statute of limitations) would not have had claim-preclusive effect had it been entered by an F-1 state court. Based on textual analysis, the Court concluded that "on the merits" did not necessarily mean the same thing as "claim-preclusive." Therefore, the effect of the Rule still had to be determined by the Court on the basis of federal law.

"[F]ederal common law governs the claim-preclusive effect of a dismissal by a federal court sitting in diversity." Id. at 508, 1028. Since state law gave rise to the claim, "there is no need for a uniform federal rule." Id. Rather, *Erie* policy concerns favored in-state uniformity, absent a conflict with a federal interest. The Court thus "adopt[ed], as the federally prescribed rule of decision, the law that would be applied by the state courts in the State in which the federal diversity court sits." Id. In the instant case, the (even express) dismissal "on the merits" did not have claim-preclusive effect as a matter of federal law. As in *Walker* and *Gasperini*, the decision explores the reach of a concededly applicable Federal Rule, in light of both federal and state policies, to give meaning to *Hanna's* focus on a "*clash*" between a Federal Rule and state procedure.

D. Summary

The following are the principal points detailed in Parts I and II:

1. In the absence of applicable federal law or a federal lawmaking power, *Erie* requires that in a diversity case, the federal court apply the law of the state in which it sits.

2. When there is federal lawmaking power, the policy underlying *Erie* may still favor the application of state law, so that intrastate uniformity will be furthered and a state's interests in the application of its own law will be preserved. Nevertheless, there may be "countervailing considerations" (*Byrd*), which may argue in favor of a uniform national rule. The various issues addressed in Chapter XII in the context of "federal common law" also fall into this category.

3. There is no balancing to be undertaken—in the sense of a policy favoring the application of state law, on the one hand, and "countervailing considerations,"

on the other—when there is an applicable Federal Rule. Such a Rule derives its authority from the Rules Enabling Act, which in turn, is based on federal lawmaking power. If the Federal Rule is within the scope authorized by the Act, then it is valid and displaces state law (*Hanna*). However, the displacement of state law takes place only when the Federal Rule is indeed "applicable." That is the case when there is a direct clash between a Federal Rule and state law. Whether there is such a clash must be determined by interpretation, taking into account the intended function of the Federal Rule (*Walker*). See the discussion of *Gasperini*, above at p. 248.

4. In the process of interpretation, the federal court may conclude that the applicable law is federal, but that for policy reasons, its content should be derived from state law (*Semtek, supra*).

E. *Forum Non Conveniens*

What should a federal court do when federal concepts of *forum non conveniens* (as expressed in *Gilbert* and *Piper,* above at p. 80) differ from those of the state in which it sits? Note that *forum non conveniens* issues no longer arise in cases to which the federal transfer statute applies. In federal practice, the doctrine today is relevant principally in international cases. Does the federal court apply federal or forum state law standards? According to one Court of Appeals, "the *forum non conveniens* doctrine is a rule of venue, not a rule of decision," so that federal and not state law applies. *Sibaja v. Dow Chemical Co.,* 757 F.2d 1215, 1219, (11th Cir.), *cert. denied,* 474 U.S. 948, 106 S. Ct. 347 (mem.), 88 L. Ed. 2d 294 (1985). And the venue may be proper but inconvenient." *Lee Memorial Health System v.* Martinez, 338 So.3d 350, 356 n.4 (Fla.App. 2022), citing *Sibaja* (above).The Second, Fifth, and Ninth circuits also apply federal law, and the Sixth and Tenth circuits are leaning that way. See *ADT Security Services, Inc. v. Apex Alarm, LLC,* 430 F. Supp. 2d 1199 (D. Colo. 2006) (reviewing the circuit decisions).

F. The Federal Rules in International Cases

The Federal Rules take precedence over inconsistent state rules when there is a direct clash (*Hanna* and *Walker,* above). But the argument was made that the Hague Convention on the Taking of Evidence Abroad provides the exclusive means for obtaining evidence located abroad, even though the foreign defendant is subject to the federal court's jurisdiction. In particular, it was argued that American procedures for trial discovery have been replaced by the Convention procedures when the foreign defendant is a national of a Convention country.

The U.S. Supreme Court has held that the Convention does not displace the Federal Rules. It also does not establish a "first resort" rule. Application of the Convention or of an applicable Federal Rule is left to the determination of the court, which is to "demonstrate due respect for any special problem confronted by the foreign litigant." *Societe Nationale Industrielle Aerospatiale v. U.S. District Court,* 482 U.S. 522, 546, 107 S. Ct. 2542, 2557, 96 L. Ed. 2d 461 (1987). For granting discovery requests (in application of *Aerospatiale* see *Areelik A.S. v. E.I. DuPont der Nemours and Co.,* 856 Fed. Appx. 392, 397 (3rd Cir. 2021); *United States v. Van Averment,* 2024 WL 3835320 *2 (D.D.C. 2024).With respect to the Hague Convention on the Service of Documents Abroad, see above at p. 64.

III. *Erie* and Choice of Law

A. *Klaxon* and *Challoner*

It was already implicit in the *Erie* decision that the state law to be applied by the federal court includes the forum state's choice of law rules. The Supreme Court expressly so held in *Klaxon Co. v. Stentor Electric Mfg. Co.,* 313 U.S. 487, 61 S. Ct. 1020, 85 L. Ed. 1477 (1941).

In a suit heard in Delaware federal court, the New York plaintiff recovered a judgment from a Delaware defendant for breach of a contract entered into in New York. The question was whether the plaintiff was entitled to prejudgment interest. The application of Delaware choice of law rules would lead to a denial of prejudgment interest, while a federal common law choice of law rule would have resulted in its award. The Court emphasized the desirability of uniformity in choice of law as between state and federal courts sitting in the same state.

It can be argued that *Klaxon* is neither constitutionally required nor follows from *Erie* as a matter of policy. Choice of law defines the boundaries of one legal system (state) to another, just as state lines define the physical boundaries. Defining state lines is a federal function, and it could be argued that choice of law, by analogy, is also a federal function. On the same day that it decided *Erie,* the Supreme Court apportioned an interstate stream on the basis of "federal common law." *Hinderlider v. La Plata River & Cherry Creek Ditch Co.,* 304 U.S. 92, 58 S. Ct. 803, 82 L. Ed. 1202 (1938).

Furthermore, if there is federal authority to make choice-of-law rules, they would then take precedence over state law and provide uniformity on the *national* (and not only intrastate) level.

Nevertheless, the Supreme Court confirmed forcefully in 1975 that the *Erie* requirement, to apply state law in diversity cases, includes the choice-of-law rules of the forum state. *Day & Zimmermann, Inc. v. Challoner,* 423 U.S. 3, 96 S. Ct. 167, 46 L. Ed. 2d 3 (1975). The decision required the federal court in Texas to apply that state's place-of-tort rule, which referred to Cambodia, where ammunition had exploded and caused injury, despite the federal court's finding that Cambodia was a disinterested state.

Note that adherence to *Klaxon* also means that changes in choice-of-law rules and approaches can only come from state courts. The federal court is not free to embrace a new methodology; it must wait for the courts of the forum state to take the lead. *Zimmerman* is explained and applied in *Garcia v. Chiquita Brands International, Inc.*, 48 F.4th 1202, 1209 (11th Cir. 2022), followed in 2023 WL 9029693 (S.D.Fla. 2023).

B. Special *Erie* Problems

1. Interstate Forum Shopping

a. Interpleader

The Federal Interpleader Act permits a stakeholder to interplead whenever presented with a demand by one of two or more potential claimants of the same debt, and to require the other claimants to pursue their claims and to protect their interests in that forum. 28 U.S.C.A. § 1335 (West 2022). A federal court's jurisdictional reach for interpleader is nationwide; the jurisdiction of state courts of course does not reach that far. Nevertheless, the decision in *Griffin v. McCoach,* 313 U.S. 498, 61 S. Ct. 1023, 85 L. Ed. 1481 (1941), extended the principles of *Erie* and *Klaxon* to interpleader actions: the federal court hearing the interpleader action is to apply the law of the state in which it sits.

This may increase forum shopping since the stakeholder will file the bill of interpleader as a reaction to the first claimant's demand. The latter may thus trigger the interpleader and thereby influence the choice of law. It is unclear at this point what implications the Supreme Court's decision in *Shutts* (above p. 236) may hold for *Griffin*. (The "plaintiff" stakeholder bringing interpleader *as a reaction* to the first claim (above) is—functionally—in the same position as the defendant in the class action in *Shutts*.)

Returning to *Griffin*: what if the state in which the interpleader is heard follows the issue-by-issue approach in conflicts cases and the resolution of the issue in question (who is the "beneficiary") is not clear? *Ministri Family, LLC v. Bell* is illustrative. No. 6:14-cv-473-Orl-22TBS, 2015 WL 6445954, at *8 (M.D. Fla. Oct. 23, 2015), *appeal dismissed*, No. 15-15182, 2015 WL 6445954 (11th Cir. Apr. 27, 2016). "This court must construe [Florida state law] in the way it believes the Florida Supreme Court would were this case before it." Id. Here, the magistrate examined the matter in the way the state's highest court would, and reached the latter's predicted resolution, which was approved by the district court. This is the correct and usual practice when a federal court must apply state law but the state's highest court has not ruled on the issue in question: the latter's view must be predicted. When the state's law to be applied is that of another state (as decreed by the forum state's conflicts rules), such predicting can encourage a homeward trend. See *Wortman, supra* at p. 236.

b. The 100-Mile Bulge Rule

Federal Rule of Civil Procedure 4(k)(1)(B) permits service on third-party defendants (and specified additional third parties to a pending suit or counterclaim) within a one-hundred-mile radius of the place of suit. Depending on the location of the federal court, this radius might reach into a neighboring state. The state courts of the state in which the federal court sits would not have a similarly wide jurisdictional reach. Again, intrastate uniformity is not furthered by application of the *Erie* and *Klaxon* decisions; rather, forum shopping may result in this situation.

c. Supplemental Jurisdiction

Federal courts may adjudicate state law claims supplemental to a federal claim before them. 28 U.S.C.A. § 1367 (West 2022). If the federal law gives a federal court nationwide jurisdiction, the application of the law of the forum state to the pendent claim could not have been undertaken by a state court (for lack of jurisdiction). See Fed. R. Civ. P. 4(k)(2). Again, intrastate uniformity is not promoted by requiring the use of forum state law; *Klaxon* should not (but does) apply. See *Hornbook* § 3.45.

d. Federal Transfer

When the defendant seeks a transfer under 28 U.S.C. § 1404(a), the transferee court is to apply the same law as the transferor court would have applied. Thus, the transfer effects a change of the courthouse, but not of the applicable law. *Van Dusen v. Barrack,* 376 U.S. 612, 84 S. Ct. 805, 11 L. Ed. 2d 945 (1964).

There used to be much question whether transferor or transferee state law should apply when the transfer was sought by the *plaintiff.* In *Ferens v. John Deere Co.,* 494 U.S. 516, 110 S. Ct. 1274, 108 L. Ed. 2d 443 (1990), the U.S. Supreme Court held that *transferor* law applies, even if this results from blatant forum-shopping by the plaintiff. This result, the Court reasoned, does not flow from *Erie* principles, but from the legal diversity in our federal system.

For a special situation, in which the result of *Ferens* was avoided, see *In re TMI,* 89 F.3d 1106 (3d Cir. 1996), *cert. denied,* 519 U.S. 1077, 117 S. Ct. 739 (mem.), 136 L. Ed. 2d 678 (1997). There, federal legislation called for application of the substantive law of the state in which a nuclear accident occurred. Pennsylvania's limitation was held to be "substantive" for these purposes when the case was transferred there from Mississippi.

In yet another type of case—when the transferor court lacked jurisdiction or when there was improper venue—courts do *not* regard *Van Dusen* as applicable. The law of the transferee court will apply to substantive as well as to choice of law issues. *Hornbook* § 3.46.

e. Complex Litigation

Many plaintiffs may sue a defendant for claims arising out of a single occurrence, for instance, an airline crash. Many plaintiffs may also seek to join together to sue multiple defendants, for instance, in the case of tobacco litigation. The federal court, in the first case, applies the law the forum state would apply. The same also holds true in the second type of case. If various such cases should get consolidated for trial by the Judicial Panel on Multidistrict Litigation, the applicable law remains that of the various transferor courts. This would not be the case if plaintiffs were to join in a class action and a single law, as determined by forum state law, were to govern the claim. Certification of a class, however, requires common questions of law and fact. In *Castano v. American Tobacco Co.,* 84 F.3d 734 (5th Cir. 1996), the court decertified a class because "in a multistate class action, variations in state law may swamp any common issues. . . ." Id. at 741. For this reason, "certification of mass tort claims is now exceedingly rare." *Zuniga v. Bernalillo County,* 319 F.R.D. 640, 673 (D.N.M. 2016). See, e.g., *Hernandez v. Grisham,* 494 F. Supp. 3d 1044, 1139 (D.N.M. 2020) (plaintiff did not show that potential class members had suffered the same injury); similarly, *Golden v. Quality Life Services, LLC,* 2023 WL 3182645 *8 (D.N.M. 2023).

2. When Federal Law Is Applicable

The discussion in this chapter focused on the principles and policies that flow from the *Erie* decision. When *Erie* principles are applicable, federal courts sitting in diversity must ordinarily apply state law (unless there are "countervailing considerations"). When *Erie* principles do not require the application of state law, federal law may displace state law; a good example is the Federal Rules of Civil Procedure, discussed above.

When a federal court does not sit in diversity but entertains a claim arising under *federal law,* it will look to federal law unless a rule of federal law in turn refers to a state law.

A claim under federal law (a "federal question" case) may arise under the United States Constitution, a federal statute, a treaty with (a) foreign nation(s) entered into by the United States, or even federal common law. See Chapter XII for a discussion of federal common law.

An example of a reference to state law in a federal statute is the provision of the Federal Tort Claims Act that refers to the law of the state where the injury occurred. 28 U.S.C.A. § 1346(b)(1) (West 2022). This reference has been interpreted to include the choice of law rules of the state of the injury. *Richards v. United States,* 369 U.S. 1, 82 S. Ct. 585, 7 L. Ed. 2d 492 (1962). Examples of federal common law adopting the law of the state in which the federal court sits include *Semtek, supra* p. 251, and *Williams II* in Chapter VI.

In federal question cases, federal common law rules for choice of law apply. See *Corporacion Venezolana de Fomento v. Vintero Sales Corp.,* 629 F.2d 786 (2d Cir. 1980), *cert. denied,* 449 U.S. 1080, 101 S. Ct. 863, 66 L. Ed. 2d 804 (1981). For extensive discussion of the sources of the applicable law in federal litigation, see *Sky Cable, LLC v. Coley,* No. 5:11cv00048, 2016 WL 3926492, at *12 n.10 (W.D. Va. July 18, 2016).

IV. Determining State Decisional Law

As of 2020, 49 states, the district of Columbia, and three territories had adopted procedures for certifying questions of state law to the particular state's supreme court. Twenty-three of them and the District of Columbia have adopted the *Uniform Certification of Questions of Law Act.* The only state without such a procedure was North Carolina. Where such procedures exist, federal courts (and, under one option, also state courts of sister states) can direct ("certify") questions concerning the applicable state rule of decision to the state supreme court. In the absence of such a provision, federal courts must rely on their own reading of the state's decisional law (that of the forum state or that of another state to which it is directed by the choice of law rules of the forum). The object is to apply the decisional law as the supreme court of the forum state would do.

Intermediate state appellate decisions are regarded as authoritative in the absence of state supreme court decisions. *McKay v. Novartis Pharmaceutical Corp.,* 751 F.3d 694, 707 (5th Cir. 2014). When a state is subdivided into several appellate districts, the federal court's task once again is to select the available precedent that it considers to best represent the most likely view of the state supreme court. See, e.g., *Galvan v. NCO Financial Systems, Inc.,* Nos. 11 C 3918, 11 C 4651, 2013 WL 1628190, at *6 (N.D. Ill. Apr. 15, 2013), rev'd on other grounds, 794 F.3d 716 (7th Cir. 2015).

V. Review Questions

1. a. T or F: *Erie* requires that a federal court apply the law of the state in which it sits whenever not doing so would affect the outcome of the case.

b. T or F: The federal court applies the law of a third state, to which the choice of law rule of the forum state refers, whenever the third state is deemed to be an "interested" state.

c. T or F: The Federal Rules of Civil Procedure are derived from federal lawmaking authority, while the federal rule of tort liability in *Erie* was not.

d. T or F: Whenever there is a Federal Rule of Civil Procedure that can be used, it displaces inconsistent state law.

e. T or F: A federal court exercising interpleader jurisdiction, or hearing a claim based on state law that is pendent to a federal claim for which the court has nationwide jurisdiction, applies the law of the state in which it sits.

f. T or F: The Hague Evidence Convention, which the United States has ratified, displaces the FRCivP for discovery of evidence in international cases involving another Contracting State.

2. If you are in a state that follows the First Restatement—for instance, in tort choice of law—but think that your case presents facts and issues sure to convince a court to adopt a more flexible approach, would you bring your case in state or in federal court (assuming proper diversity jurisdiction)?

3. Federal Rule of Appellate Procedure 38 gives Courts of Appeal discretion to assess "just damages" in order to penalize an appellant for bringing a frivolous appeal. If, in contrast, the penalty under state law is mandatory affirmance, which rule applies?

Chapter XII

Federal Common Law as the Rule of Decision

■ ANALYSIS

I. **Introduction: Sources of Federal Law**

II. **Federal Common Law**

- A. Introduction: Definition; Source of Federal Common Law
- B. Federal Common Law: The Prerequisite of a Federal Interest
  - 1. Government Obligations
  - 2. Contractual Relations with the Government
  - 3. Tort-Related Issues
  - 4. Private Disputes over Government-Created Rights
  - 5. Foreign Relations
- C. Intermediate Summary: When Is Federal Common Law Appropriate?
- D. When Does Federal Legislation Displace Federal Common Law?

III. **Review Questions**

I. Introduction: Sources of Federal Law

Federal law consists of the Constitution, federal statutes, federal treaties concluded with other nations, and federal decisional law. The first three are expressly mentioned in the Constitution as being the *"supreme law of the land"* by which all courts are bound. Federal decisional law consists of the authoritative construction of the three kinds of written law and of federal common law (discussed separately below).

In a number of areas (for instance, International Sales, Child Abduction, Intercountry Adoption), the United State maintains treaties with other nations. Additional treaties are under consideration or pending (for instance, on choice of court agreements). With respect to international cases to which they apply, these treaties supersede the rules of state conflicts law.

Federal law may govern exclusively or concurrently with state law. It will govern exclusively when only Congress has power to legislate (for instance, with respect to bankruptcy) or when Congress, in the exercise of one of its delegated powers, exercises that power and adopts legislation *preempting* state law. In some areas (for instance, consumer protection), remedies may exist under both federal and state law. Finally, federal law may combine a uniform federal scheme with deference to aspects of state law. Examples are the reference to the law of the state where the injury occurred in the Federal Tort Claims Act, and the several references to state law standards in the Federal Rules of Evidence. Decisional law, for instance, with respect to the Federal Rules of Civil Procedure, may also incorporate state law standards. See *Semtek, supra* at p. 251. *Williams II, supra* at Chapter VI (Nevada's jurisdiction to grant *ex parte* divorces raised a federal question, but the Court permitted the use of North Carolina state law standards to answer it).

For purposes of the federal/state law problems in conflicts, a remaining important topic is the scope and effect of **federal common law**.

II. Federal Common Law

A. Introduction: Definition; Source of Federal Common Law

This section deals with federal decisional law by which a court *creates* a rule of law, as distinguished from federal decisional law by which a court interprets, applies, and perhaps further develops a rule of law contained in the Constitution, a statute, or a treaty. "**Federal common law**" describes the first of these.

The decision in *Erie R.R. Co. v. Tompkins,* 304 U.S. 64, 58 S. Ct. 817, 82 L. Ed. 1188 (1938), discussed in Chapter XI, held that there is no *general* federal common law because (apart from policy reasons) there is no *general* federal lawmaking power. As a result, the courts cannot do that (i.e., create federal common law) which Congress cannot do (by legislation). Note that *Erie* involved the question of whether there could be a federal (common) law of tort liability, and to that, the answer was "no."

The emphasis of *Erie* was that there cannot be **general** federal common law. However, in contrast to the issue in *Erie*, when there is federal lawmaking power, the federal courts *may* declare federal common law.

In *Hinderlider v. La Plata River & Cherry Creek Ditch Co.,* 304 U.S. 92, 58 S. Ct. 803, 82 L. Ed. 1202 (1938), decided the same day as *Erie*, the Court apportioned an interstate stream on the basis of "federal common law." In *Byrd*, above at p. 248, the Court invoked the power to regulate procedure in the federal courts to hold that, on the basis of "countervailing considerations" of policy, federal law determines which issues are decided by the court, and which go to the jury.

The question of whether the federal courts *may* (constitutionally) declare federal common law is different from whether it would be *appropriate* to do so in light of the *policy considerations* which are also central to the *Erie* doctrine. Both the scope and the appropriateness of federal common law are summarized below. A third question then relates to the interplay between federal common law and subsequent congressional legislation. For further details, see *Hornbook* § 3.50 *et seq.*

Note: When a claim arises under federal common law, it arises under the federal court's **federal question jurisdiction** (*not* its diversity jurisdiction), the same as if it had arisen under a federal statute. See *Texas v. Pankey*, 441 F.2d 236, 241 (10th Cir. 1971); *Illinois v. City of Milwaukee*, 406 U.S. 91, 99–103, 92 S. Ct. 1385, 1390–92, 31 L. Ed. 2d 712 (1972); *McGinnes Indus. Maint. Corp. v. Phoenix Ins. Co.*, 477 S.W.3d 786, 787 n.5 (Tex. 2015).

B. Federal Common Law: The Prerequisite of a Federal Interest

Assuming that there is federal lawmaking power, which Congress has not yet exercised and which would permit the creation of federal common law, the Supreme Court has required that doing so would further a federal interest. The following summarizes the case categories in which the Supreme Court has found the existence of federal lawmaking power *and* a federal interest in having courts exercise it by making federal common law.

1. Government Obligations

The Supreme Court has applied rules of federal common law over inconsistent state law to define the federal government's liability when dealing in commercial paper. *Clearfield Trust Co. v. United States*, 318 U.S. 363, 63 S. Ct. 573, 87 L. Ed. 838 (1943); *D'Oench, Duhme & Co. v. FDIC*, 315 U.S. 447, 62 S. Ct. 676, 86 L. Ed. 956 (1942). There is a split among the Circuits concerning the continued authority of *D'Oench.* The Eleventh Circuit followed *D'Oench* in *Murphy v. F.D.I.C.*, 208 F.3d 959 (11th Cir. 2000). The U.S. Supreme Court, after first granting certiorari, dismissed the writ the following year. *Murphy v. Beck*, 531 U.S. 1107, 121 S. Ct. 849 (mem.), 148 L. Ed. 2d 733 (2001). The Fourth Circuit followed *D'Oench* in *Young v. F.D.I.C.*, 103 F.3d 1180 (4th Cir.), *cert denied*, 522 U.S. 928, 118 S. Ct. 329 (mem.), 139 L. Ed. 2d 255 (1997). Continued application in the First and Fifth Circuits suggests the continued availability of the doctrine there as well. See, e.g., *F.D.I.C. v. Estrada-Rivera*, 722 F.3d 50, 53 (1st Cir. 2013) and *Marina de Ponce, Inc. v. Federal Deposit Insurance Corporation*, 2018 WL 1061441 *9 (D. Puerto Rico 2018); *C&C Inv. Props., L.L.C. v. Trustmark Nat'l Bank*, 838 F.3d 655, 658 (5th Cir. 2016) and *BY Equities, LLC v. Carver Theater Productions, LLC,* 2024 WL 4216026 E.D. La. 2024). The Third, Eighth, Ninth, and D.C. Circuits no longer follow *D'Oench*. See, e.g., *F.D.I.C. v. Deglau*, 207 F.3d 153, 171 (3d Cir. 2000) ("We agree with the Eighth, Ninth and D.C. Circuits that *D'Oench* is not applicable federal common law. . ."); see also *Schettler v. RalRon Capital Corp.*, 275 P.3d 933, 941 fn. 8 (Nev. 2012).

Compare *D'Oench* with an earlier Supreme Court case, which involved the respective rights of two banks in United States commercial paper. The government's liability was not involved, and there was therefore no federal interest to protect; state law applied. *Bank of Am. Nat'l Trust & Savings Ass'n v. Parnell,* 352 U.S. 29, 77 S. Ct. 119, 1 L. Ed. 2d 93 (1956). The Court acknowledged that even in suits between private parties, federal interests and policies might be involved, calling for the application of federal common law. 352 U.S. at 34. For brief discussion and references, see *National Security Counselors v. C.I.A.*, 960 F. Supp. 2d 101, 142 n.17 (D.D.C. 2013), *aff'd*, 969 F.3d 406 (D.C. Cir. 2020). For an FDIC "policy statement" on when it intends to rely on federal common law invoking *D'Oench*, see Statement of Policy Regarding Federal Common Law, 62 Fed. Reg. 5984 (Feb. 10, 1997).

2. Contractual Relations with the Government

Federal courts have frequently held that state law is not applicable for contracts to which the federal government is a party. The cases include leases and liquidated damage clauses. But contractual liens (because of the parties' expectation interests) are governed by state law. *United States v. Kimbell Foods, Inc.,* 440 U.S. 715, 99 S. Ct. 1448, 59 L. Ed. 2d 711 (1979). As in the commercial paper cases, the courts do not create federal common law when an issue arises only between or among private parties, such as sublessees. *Wallis v. Pan Am. Petroleum Corp.*, 384 U.S. 63, 86 S. Ct. 1301, 16 L. Ed. 2d 369 (1966); see also *Sabal Trail Transmission, LLC v. Real Estate*, No. 1:16-cv-063-MW-GRJ, 2017 WL 2783995, at *2–3 (N.D. Fla. June 27, 2017).

3. Tort-Related Issues

Similar to the commercial paper cases, federal courts have sought to define the federal interest (and to create federal common law to give it uniform definition) in tort claims by or against the federal government.

Example: The government seeks reimbursement for medical expenses for a soldier injured by the defendant. See *United States v. Standard Oil Co.*, 332 U.S. 301, 67 S. Ct. 1604, 91 L. Ed. 2067 (1947). Restrictions apply to the usual right to implead the government as a third-party defendant. *Stencel Aero Eng'g Corp. v. United States*, 431 U.S. 666, 97 S. Ct. 2054, 52 L. Ed. 2d 665 (1977). But see *Boyle v. United Tech. Corp.*, 487 U.S. 500, 108 S. Ct. 2510, 101 L. Ed. 2d 442 (1988) (federal common law defense in favor of military contractors, who had manufactured equipment according to government specifications, against private claimant, to avoid divergent results under state law and conflicts with military policy), declined to be extended by *Badilla v. Midwest Air Traffic Control Serv., Inc.*, 8 F.4th 105 (2d Cir. 2021) (when government official did not direct the activity causing injury), in turn followed by *Hondros v. Hewlett Packard Enterprises*, No. H-21-1982, 2021 WL 5087144, at *3 (S.D. Tex. Nov. 2, 2021) (slip op.). Does federal common law or state law apply for determining the remedy (e.g., "just compensation" under the federal Natural Gas Act)? There is somewhat of a split. *McManaway v. KRB, Inc.*, No. 4:10–cv–1044, 2015 WL 13310061, at *9–10 (S.D. Tex. Aug. 9, 2015), *aff'd*, 852 F.3d 444 (5th Cir. 2017), held that the state tort law remedy was adequate and similar to federal law, so there was no need to displace state law. In *Tennessee Gas Pipeline Co., LLC v. Permanent Easement for 7.053 Acres*, 931 F.3d 237 (3d Cir. 2019), the court looked to state law to be incorporated as the federal common law standard. Since the resulting federal common law will not be uniform across the United States, both approaches come to the same result: state law. See also *Sabal Trail Transmissions, LLC v. 3.921 Acres of Land in Lake County Florida*, 947 F.3d 1362, 1370 (11th Cir. 2020).

4. Private Disputes over Government-Created Rights

The fact that *Clearfield Trust* (above at p. 261) directly involved the rights and obligations of the federal government does not preclude "the application of 'federal common law' to all matters involving only the rights of private citizens. . . . there may be situations where the rights and obligations of private parties are . . . dependent on a specific exercise of congressional regulatory power. . . . [When that power has not been exercised by legislation,] 'the inevitable incompleteness presented by all legislation means that interstitial federal lawmaking is a basic responsibility of the federal courts.' " *Miree v. DeKalb Cnty.*, 433 U.S. 25, 34–35, 97 S. Ct. 2490, 2496, 53 L. Ed. 2d 557 (1977) (Burger, C.J., concurring) (citations omitted).

One example of "interstitial federal lawmaking" for defining the rights of private citizens is the decision that the competence of an insured, under a national service life insurance policy, to change his beneficiary raises a federal and not a state-law question. Another is the definition of the term "children," under the Jones Act, as extending (or not) to illegitimate offspring. *Dyke v. Dyke,* 227 F.2d 461 (6th Cir. 1955), *cert. denied,* 352 U.S. 850, 77 S. Ct. 70 (mem.), 1 L. Ed. 2d 61 (1956); *In re Risdal & Anderson, Inc.,* 266 F. Supp. 157 (D. Mass. 1967). See also *Boyle,* above under No. 3.

More far-reaching are decisions like *Texas v. Pankey,* 441 F.2d 236 (10th Cir. 1971), which declared a federal common law of nuisance in a case involving the pollution of an interstate stream. "[T]he ecological controversy involved is one which is entitled to the application of federal common law as a basis for the existence and determination of the rights in the situation." Id. at 242. The Clean Air Act now displaces the federal common law with regard to domestic pollution, but does not apply to emissions abroad. However, foreign policy precludes the application of federal common law to such emissions. See *City of New York v. Chevron Corp.*, 993 F.3d 81 (2d Cir. 2021).

However, the courts have displayed an even greater restraint than in the areas already noted to declare federal common law when only private rights are involved. Thus, in *Miree* itself, in which Chief Justice Burger made the general statement quoted above in his concurrence, the Court rejected a claim, by survivors of airplane crash victims, that they and their decedents were third-party beneficiaries under a contract between the county owning the airport and the federal government, which required the county to maintain the airport in a manner permitting normal and safe operations. See also *Badilla,* declining to extend *Boyle,* both above under No. 3.

Any federal interest—for instance, to advance federal aviation policy by promoting compliance with federal safety regulations—is " 'far too speculative, far too remote a possibility to justify the application of federal law to transactions essentially of local concern.' " *Miree,* 433 U.S. at 32, 97 S. Ct. at 2495 (quoting *Parnell,* 352 U.S. at 33–344, 77 S. Ct. at 121).

The extent to which federal common law will do more than merely "interstitially" complete the legislative scheme has been restricted further by decisions such as *City of Milwaukee* and *Ouellette*. Both decisions are summarized below at p. 267.

5. Foreign Relations

The Constitution commits the conduct of foreign relations to the President (in some matters, such as the conclusion of treaties, with the advice and consent of the Senate). Many questions that can arise in litigation will be answered by express provision of federal law. Thus, the Foreign Sovereign Immunities Act will determine whether, and in what circumstances, a foreign government or government agency may be sued in United States courts; a treaty with a foreign country will speak to the right of that country's nationals to inherit from a United States decedent; the Warsaw Convention (a treaty) specifies where suit may be brought and defines the carrier's liability in the event of an airplane accident in international travel, causing injury to passengers or property.

At times, however, federal statutory or treaty law will not contain an express provision. When there is no applicable treaty, may a state require reciprocity as a condition to allowing a foreign heir to share in an American estate? May a state, applying state law principles of conversion of property, hold that a foreign government's acts of expropriation are illegal, so that the party to whom the expropriated property passed is not entitled to it, and therefore must make restitution to the previous owner? Both of these questions were actual cases. To both, and consistent with a long line of cases, the Supreme Court answered "no." *When a case implicates the foreign relations of the United States, states and state law may not intrude.* In the second of the examples given above (conversion), the Court went further: there was no *jurisdiction* to question the foreign country's "act of state."

In *Zschernig v. Miller,* 389 U.S. 429, 88 S. Ct. 664, 19 L. Ed. 2d 683 (1968), the Court struck down, as an impermissible interference by a state with the federal foreign relations power, Oregon's "Iron Curtain Statute." It conditioned the right of an East-bloc country's heir to inherit on a review of his home state's law, to determine whether it would assure him the receipt of the benefit of the inheritance or be confiscatory, and whether Americans enjoyed equivalent (reciprocal) rights there.

The majority in *American Insurance Association v. Garamendi*, 539 U.S. 396, 123 S. Ct. 2374, 156 L. Ed. 2d 376 (2003), took a less categorical view of preemption based on the federal foreign relations power. At issue was a California statute requiring insurance companies doing business in California to disclose information about any Holocaust-era policy sold in Europe. The state law was preempted because it "interfere[d] with the National Government's conduct of foreign relations." Id. at 401. See also *Hornbook* § 3.56 *et seq.*

In *Breard v. Greene*, 523 U.S. 371, 118 S. Ct. 1352, 140 L. Ed. 2d 529 (1998), the U.S. Supreme Court denied certiorari to a decision ordering an execution (which took place), despite the (undisputed) claim that the Vienna Consular Convention (notification requirements) had been violated, a declaratory judgment of the International Court of Justice had called for a stay for the same reasons, and despite the U.S. Secretary of State's request to the state governor to suspend the execution. The outcome of the case is quite clearly inconsistent with *Zschernig*.

In the *LaGrand Case* (Germany v. U.S.), Judgment, 2001 I.C.J. 466 (June 27) (available at 40 I.L.M. 1069, and online at https://www.icj-cij.org/en/case/104 (last visited Sept. 3, 2022)), the International Court of Justice held that the United States had breached its treaty commitment to Germany, and also the ICJ's order barring execution until final determination of Germany's action, by "failing to take all measures . . . to ensure" a stay of execution of convicted Germans who had not been advised of their treaty rights to consult consular officials. Similarly, see the ICJ's decision in *Avena and Other Mexican Nationals* (Mexico v. U.S.), Judgment, 2004 I.C.J. 12 (March 31) (available at 2004 WL 2450913, and online at https://www.icj-cij.org/en/case/128 (last visited Sept. 3, 2022)), requiring review of death sentences of Mexicans convicted and sentenced without being afforded their treaty rights.

A shocking repetition of *Breard* is *Medellin v. Texas*, 552 U.S. 491, 128 S. Ct. 1346, 170 L. Ed. 2d 190 (2008). In a prior case (*Avena*), the International Court of Justice found that the United States had violated the U.S.-Mexican treaty rights of defendants to have contact with and assistance of their country's consulate and ordered the United States to suspend executions pending a retrial. (The defendants had been prosecuted, convicted and condemned to death in Texas.) President George W. Bush had made an earlier declaration that the United States would abide by the ICJ's rulings. In *Medellin*, the Supreme Court ruled that neither the *Avena* ruling nor the President's declaration were binding (self-executing) in the United States in the absence of Congressional implementation. Medellin was executed.

Contrary to *Zschernig, supra*, or at least inconsistent with it, *Medellin* not only permits state action but also seemingly limits federal preemption to cases where it is expressly asserted; statements of federal policy were not enough. Reconciling the cases is difficult because both *Zschernig* and *Medellin* involved areas of law traditionally within the purview of the states—succession and state criminal law. However, application of state law in both cases touched upon the foreign affairs of the United States. The only difference—perhaps—lies in the fact that Oregon's statute in *Zschernig* called upon its courts to make evaluations about foreign legal systems, while in Medellin, Texas courts were "only" permitted to be insular, i.e., to look at only Texas law. For applications of *Medellin* see, inter alia, *Cardenas v. Stephens*, 820 F.3d 197, 200 (5th Cir. 2016); *Mitchell v. Lumpkin*, 2022 WL 17550819 *1 (5th Cir. 2022).

Banco Nacional de Cuba v. Sabbatino, 376 U.S. 398, 84 S. Ct. 923, 11 L. Ed. 2d 804 (1964), recognized the "act of state doctrine" and held that its "scope . . . must be determined according to federal law." Id. at 427, 940.

Previously, the Court had held that state law and policy had to yield to the President's conduct of foreign relations, including his agreement to a settlement of claims. *United States v. Pink*, 315 U.S. 203, 62 S. Ct. 552, 86 L. Ed. 796 (1942). In *Pink*, the Court invoked the President's express constitutional authority to extend recognition to new foreign governments, and as part of that, to settle claims. In *Sabbatino*, it drew on the "*constitutional underpinnings*" of the relationship—*not* between the states and the federal government, but between the federal *courts* and the federal *executive*, holding that the conduct of foreign relations belongs exclusively to the latter.

Note: The "Hickenlooper Amendment," 22 U.S.C.A. § 2370(e)(2) (West 2022), substantially reduced the effect of the *Sabbatino* decision, but its

> rationale—the analysis of "constitutional underpinnings"—remains important. See also *Federal Republic of Germany v. Philipp*, 592 U.S. 169, 141 S. Ct. 703, 711 (2021) (the Court's approach in *Sabbatino* prompted passage of the Amendment); *Sierra Estate of Romagosa v. Trafigura Trading LLC*, 2024 WL 4104130 *14 fn. 20 (D.Del. 2024).

The Cuban Liberty and Democratic Solidarity (Libertad) Act of 1996 ("Helms-Burton Act"), 110 Stat. 785, 22 U.S.C.A. § 6021 (West 2024), allows any U.S. "national" to sue anyone "trafficking" in private property, nationalized by Cuba and now in the hands of the defendant, for its return or for compensation. The President has authority to suspend implementation of the Act and third has been done several times. Former President Biden exercised this power on January 14, 2025, but President Trump's omnibus executive order revoked it later that month.

Note that the decisions summarized above *limit* the states, and in *Sabbatino,* the federal courts. These cases raised *foreign policy* concerns. However, even if there is no particular foreign policy concern, it may still be that an *international* case makes a *nationally uniform approach* desirable (it being assumed that usually, there will be federal lawmaking authority under the—interstate and international—Commerce Clause of the Constitution). Thus, federal courts have held that the validity and effect of forum selection clauses in international transactions are matters of federal law. *Manetti-Farrow, Inc. v. Gucci Am., Inc.*, 858 F.2d 509 (9th Cir. 1988); *Crescent Int'l, Inc. v. Avatar Cmty., Inc.*, 857 F.2d 943 (3d Cir. 1988). For the U.S. Supreme Court's decision in *Stewart Organization, Inc. v. Ricoh Corp.*, 487 U.S. 22, 108 S. Ct. 2239, 101 L. Ed. 2d 22 (1988), dealing with forum-selection clauses in the interstate context (and leaving open what happens in international cases), see above at p. 78. See also *Atlantic Marine*, above at p. 55, for remedies for choice-of-court clauses.

The Foreign Sovereign Immunity Act

The Foreign Sovereign Immunity Act provides the ground rules for when U.S. courts may exercise jurisdiction over foreign sovereigns. A foreign state is presumed be immune unless one of the exceptions to the rule applies. The "domestic taking rule" means that when a country takes something from its own citizens, the act is not a "violation of international law" which would be an exception to the sovereign immunity rule. *Sabbatino, supra* p. 265, prohibits the review of a foreign sovereign's public acts on its own territory. The prohibition does not apply when a state takes assets from persons who are not its nationals. This issue is important in litigation concerning the seizure of arts objects by the German Nazi government. See, e.g., *Philipp v. Fed. Republic of Germany*, 894 F.3d 406 (D.C. Cir. 2018) (defendant not immune from suit), *vacated*, 592 U.S. 169, 141 S. Ct. 703 (2021) (defendant immune from suit under FSIA), *on remand sub nom. Philipp v. Stiftung Preussischer Kulturbesitz*, 628 F. Supp. 3d 10 (D.D.C.2022), affirmed 77 F.4th 707 (D.C.Cir. 2023) (dismissing the case; plaintiffs had failed to preserve the argument that the domestic takings rule did not apply because predecessors in interest were not German nationals at the time of the taking). Litigation on such takings continues in both countries. *Philipp* was confirmed again in *Republic of Hungary v. Simon*, 604 U.S. 115

(2025) and applied in *Csepel v. Republic of Hungary*, 2026 WL 179952 (D.C. Cir. 2026).

Warsaw Convention

In *El Al Israel Airlines Ltd. v. Tseng*, 525 U.S. 155, 119 S. Ct. 662, 142 L. Ed. 2d 576 (1999), the plaintiff allegedly suffered emotional harm at the hands of airline personnel. The Warsaw Convention provides a cause of action for "death . . . or . . . bodily injury," but the plaintiff alternatively sought relief on theories of assault and false imprisonment under state law. Held, that the Convention's remedies are exclusive (and preempt state law), even if this leaves the plaintiff without a remedy. Id. at 176, 675.

What law applies to the calculation of damages in a wrongful death case in an air accident for which the Warsaw Convention does not establish a standard? In *Harris v. Polskie Linie Lotnicze*, 820 F.2d 1000 (9th Cir. 1987), the defendant was the Polish government-owned airline, jurisdiction was thus based on federal law, and the court easily concluded that the "federal common law . . . [of] choice-of-law" applied. Id. at 1003 (the court then used Restatement (Second) principles and analytic approaches); see also *In re Sterba*, 852 F.3d 1175, 1179 (9th Cir. 2017) (same); *Boing Co. v. KB Yuzhnoye*, No. CV 13-00730, 2014 WL 12601330 (C.D. Cal. Feb. 20, 2014) (same). It is an open question whether these courts would not have reached the same decision if jurisdiction over the defendant had not been based on federal law but on diversity. Consider the implications of *Gasperini*, above at p. 248.

C. Intermediate Summary: When Is Federal Common Law Appropriate?

As a matter of *law*, federal common law may be created when there is federal lawmaking authority. This is always the case when there is federal-question jurisdiction to begin with (a claim arising from the Constitution, federal statutes, or federal treaties). In diversity cases, the Supreme Court has required that there be not only federal lawmaking authority but also: (a) that there exists a *significant conflict between state and federal law*, and that (b) there exists a *substantial federal interest in having a nationally uniform rule*. As a matter of *policy*, federal courts may nevertheless defer to state law or adopt it as the federal standard. See also immediately following.

D. When Does Federal Legislation Displace Federal Common Law?

In *City of Milwaukee v. Illinois*, 451 U.S. 304, 101 S. Ct. 1784, 68 L. Ed. 2d 114 (1981), the Supreme Court held that "when Congress addresses a question previously governed by a decision rested on federal common law the need for such an unusual exercise of lawmaking by federal courts disappears." Id. at 314, 1791. Note that the Court speaks of the "unusual" exercise of judicial lawmaking. Its restraint, the dissent criticized, seems to consider federal common law displaced *whenever* Congress acts. However, to the extent that legislation is incomplete, the need for "interstitial" federal common law may persist. For a more recent application, see *City of New York v. BP P.L.C.*, 325 F. Supp. 3d 466 (S.D.N.Y. 2018), aff'd sub nom., *City of New York v. Chevron Corp.*, 993 F.3d 81 (2d Cir. 2021). The foregoing may have been severely limited by the U.S. Supreme Court's decision in *West Virginia v. E.P.A.*, 597 U.S. 697, 142 S. Ct. 2587, 213 L. Ed. 2d 896 (2022) (unless specifically so directed by Congress, the EPA may not develop rules under the Clean Air Act). For applications see *Alliance for Fair Board Recruitment v. Securities and Exchange Commission*, 125 F.4th 159, 181 (5th Cir. 2024); *Kansas v. Kennedy*, 787 F.Supp.3d 906, 926 (N.D. Iowa 2025).

City of Milwaukee was also applied in *International Paper Co. v. Ouellette*, 479 U.S. 481, 107 S. Ct. 805, 93 L. Ed. 2d 883 (1987). In *Ouellette,* the question was when federal law displaces state common law; the Federal Clean Water Act preempts all common law. In this case, Vermont had jurisdiction over a New York defendant that was causing water-pollution in Vermont. However, application of Vermont law was preempted by the Act, lest the federal scheme for uniform regulation through federal agencies be frustrated. However, there were no applicable federal standards, leaving only New York law applicable—the law of the point source. *Oulette v. Int'l Paper Co.*, 666 F. Supp. 58, 60 (D.Vt. 1987). Note two other (arguably preferable) ways to resolve this case: (1) absent a standard in the federal act, federal common law should have furnished the standard "interstitially," or should have made its own choice of the applicable state law (i.e., a federal common law rule of choice of law); and (2) if federal common law is not to be created, application of the rule in *Klaxon,* above at 253, should have resulted in application of the choice of law rule of the state in which the federal court sits, here, Vermont.

A restrictive view of the appropriateness of federal common law—even in the absence of federal legislation—has also been taken in several of the mass-tort products liability cases, notably those involving asbestos and "Agent Orange" personal injury claims. For example, in *Jackson v. Johns-Manville Sales Corp.,* 750 F.2d 1314 (5th Cir. 1985), defendants in numerous asbestos cases sought a national solution through development of federal common law. The Fifth Circuit said that it would not be appropriate to do so because of the lack of a federal interest and "the practical problems that would attend the displacement of state law." Id. at 1327. For the suggestion that a federal court could determine and apply "a form of national consensus law," see *In re Agent Orange Product Liability Litigation,* 580 F. Supp. 690, 698 (E.D.N.Y. 1984). A settlement was subsequently ordered and reached.

III. Review Questions

1. T or F: "Federal common law" describes the case law that interprets federal constitutional and statutory law.

2. T or F: The federal courts will create "federal common law" whenever there is a "federal interest" in doing so.

3. T or F: The *Erie* decision does not bar the creation of "federal common law" when there is federal lawmaking authority under the Constitution.

4. T or F: When the liability of the federal government is in issue, for instance in connection with commercial paper issued by it or in relation to its contractors, federal common law will define that liability in the absence of statutory provisions.

5. T or F: Products liability is an appropriate area for federal common law because of the need for nationally uniform standards.

Appendix A

Answers to Review Questions

I. OVERVIEW AND GENERAL BACKGROUND

1. The "forum" is the place where the case is pending. The reference is to the "forum state," to the "court of the forum," or simply to the "forum." The "lex fori" is the law of the forum state.

2. (c) "Foreign" refers to *all* parties and events outside the forum.

3. (c) Technically, the subject of conflict of laws encompasses everything under (b), but "conflicts" is also used as shorthand for "choice of law."

4. (a) ***True.***

   (b) ***False.*** (Only sister-state judgments).

   (c) ***False.***

   (d) ***True.***

   (e) ***True.***

   (f) ***False.*** The Restatement (Second) purports to be value-neutral in its call for the application of the law of the "place of the most significant relationship" (in contrast to the "better law-approach," see text *supra*). This "neutrality" cannot be, and is not always, maintained in practice. See Chapter VIII, IV (B–C).

5. (a) & (b) Federal law generally does **not** provide conflicts rules. With respect to jurisdiction, federal law sets limits to state court assertion of jurisdiction. With respect to choice of law, it also sets limits and rarely provides which law applies.

   (c) The Convention on the International Sale of Goods (CISG) applies. As a treaty, it is federal law; the supremacy clause of the Constitution therefore applies.

II. DOMICILE AND HABITUAL RESIDENCE

1. (a) ***True.***

   (b) ***False.*** Intent alone (for instance, to be domiciled in a neighboring state) is not enough. Intent must be accompanied by physical facts (see No. 2, below).

   (c) ***True.***

   (d) ***False.*** This may be, but need not be so; see (c).

   (e) ***True.***

   (f) ***True.***

2. Domicile of origin is simply derivative from the custodial parent; this is the domicile with which one is born. A domicile of choice is obtained by abandoning the previous

domicile (of origin or choice), and arriving at the new, with no present intent to leave it (i.e., intent to stay indefinitely).

3. Domicile of origin is the domicile with which a person is born. Derivative domicile is the domicile of a minor (either the minor's domicile of origin or a subsequent new domicile of choice of the custodial parent). Domicile of choice is the domicile acquired by a person with capacity to do so.

4. The state of incorporation and the state where it has its principal place of business.

5. (a) ***False.*** Whether state B became her new domicile depends on whether she intended to make it her permanent home. The fact that she only went to school there does not necessarily preclude this, for she might have originally planned to remain in the state after graduation.

(b) ***True.*** Intent alone is not sufficient; physical presence must coincide with it to establish a new domicile.

(c) ***False.*** A person can have only one domicile at a time. Acquisition of a new one inevitably means loss of the old one.

(d) ***True.*** A person can be a resident of more than one state at a time. But note that oftentimes statutes and courts use the term "residence" when they really mean domicile.

III. JURISDICTION TO ADJUDICATE

1. (a) ***False.***

(b) ***True.***

(c) ***True.***

(d) ***False.*** But if the injury was caused in the forum state, jurisdiction may be based on the state's long arm statute, if it has one.

(e) ***True.***

(f) ***False.*** (*Burnham*).

(g) ***False.*** See also (d), above.

(h) ***True.***

(i) ***False,* in the broad formulation of the question.** Convenience is a factor, but the conditions of the transfer statute must be met.

(j) ***True,*** only insofar as the case will be tried in a newer, convenient court. ***False,*** insofar as transfer does not affect the applicable law, while a *forum non conveniens* dismissal may have that effect.

(k) ***True.***

(*l*) ***True.***

(m) ***True.***

(n) ***False.*** Only the Federal Interpleader Act provides for nationwide service of process. For "rule interpleader," ordinary rules of jurisdiction apply.

(o) ***True.***

2. (a) ***False.***

(b) ***False,*** insofar as the validity of the assertion of specific jurisdiction on stream-of-commerce grounds is still unclear. A plurality of the U.S. Supreme Court has rejected it and requires direct defendant contact (see *Asahi, J. McIntyre*), but lower courts have found such contact on sometimes very weak facts.

(c) ***False.*** Not foreseeability of injury, but of litigation *(World-Wide Volkswagen).* Even if litigation was foreseeable, *J. McIntyre* now requires more. See (b) above.

(d) ***False.*** *Goodyear* and *Baumann v. Daimler* today require a much closer contact (Justice Ginsburg's "at home" language).

(e) ***True.***

(f) ***False.*** Transient service on individuals is valid *(Burnham);* application to corporations, through service on officer, is unclear (p. 64).

(g) ***Doubtful:*** see (b) above.

(h) ***False.*** The statement is overbroad. Fed. R. Civ. P. 4(k)(2) "permits the exercise of national-contacts jurisdiction" only "with respect to claims arising under federal law."

(i) ***True***. This the "theory." *Goodyear* did not apply it.

(j) ***False.*** The defendant's forum contact must relate to the cause of action. (See *Helicopteros.*)

(k) In general, it is irrelevant for a *forum non conveniens* decision whether a party would fare better or worse under whatever law that the foreign court would apply.

(a) The answer may depend on whether the injured party is a local party who would have a claim if the suit were kept, and the forum's conflicts rule referred to a law that would entertain such a claim. The forum court might think that dismissal under these circumstances would be a denial of access to justice. See *Lubbe.*

(b) The answer is clearer: what remedy is available under the foreign law, or in what amount, goes to the point in the first sentence above: this should not enter into the *forum non conveniens* decision.

(*l*) ***False.*** The statement in the question describes what happens in cases of federal **transfer**. When a case is dismissed for *forum non conveniens*, it starts all over again in the second court: it is an original case for that court, and it applies its own procedure (of course) and conflicts rules and the substantive law to which the latter directs it.

3. A court with *general jurisdiction* over the defendant may entertain all claims brought against the defendant. Absent general jurisdiction and absent the defendant's voluntary submission, a court may subject the defendant to its *specific jurisdiction* for claims ("specifically") arising from or substantially related to the defendant's forum contacts.

4. ***True.*** (*Shute*)

5. ***Probably not***. The plaintiff is asserting a personal right, but it arises from the offending domain name. By restricting the remedy to the elimination of the offending domain name or its transfer to the trademark owner, the ACPA essentially provides

for the vindication of a personal claim by means of an *in rem* action. Note that personal claims of the parties—e.g., for damages by either party—are not part of the ACPA's court jurisdiction and remain unaffected by its decision.

IV. RECOGNITION AND ENFORCEMENT OF FOREIGN JUDGMENTS AND DECREES

1. (a) ***True.***

   (b) ***True.***

   (c) ***True.***

   (d) ***True.***

   (e) ***False.*** Preclusion effect (here: collateral estoppel) can only arise when the court had jurisdiction, and the plaintiff could thus be expected to bring his or her claim. In the hypothetical, the court arguably had *specific* jurisdiction in tort (see Chapter III). *Tort* contacts do not make for jurisdictional contacts *for other matters,* such as *contract:* no contract jurisdiction, therefore no preclusion of the contract claim in the absence of waiver (e.g., voluntary submission).

   (f) ***True.*** The rule that a judgment merges the underlying claim, and therefore bars re-litigation, does not apply to foreign country judgments. For the rule in interstate practice, see 4(d), below.

2. (a) ***True.***

   (b) ***True.*** (Exception to *Shaffer).*

   (c) Past-due installments: ***True.*** Future installments: ***uncertain,*** older cases say "no" because a modifiable decree is not "final." Modern cases will recognize, subject to modification according to the law of the rendering state.

   (d) ***False.*** (The non-situs court is generally regarded as lacking subject matter jurisdiction).

   (e) ***Probably true:*** see *Durfee v. Duke,* but only as between the parties to the original litigation.

   (f) ***True.*** (*Durfee v. Duke*).

   (g) ***True.*** Subject matter jurisdiction: *Durfee v. Duke;* personal jurisdiction: *Treinies.*

   (h) ***True.*** Exception to *Shaffer,* same as (b).

   (i) ***False.*** Full Faith and Credit is due to sister state judgments only. Foreign country judgments are usually treated the same *as a matter of state law.*

   (j) ***Problematic: should be false.*** The implementing statute to the Full Faith and Credit Clause requires F-2 to accord the F-1 judgment the *same* effect as it has as where rendered (F-1). Decisions like *American Airlines* and *Hart* accord greater effect ("more" full faith and credit) in application of their own preclusion law. If F-1 law does not provide for such wider preclusion, does F-2's application of its standards violate the defendant's (now judgment debtor's) due process rights?

   (k) ***False.*** An antisuit injunction does not address the merits of the action in F-2 and therefore does not preclude it. It may bind the *parties* and subject the party violating it to sanctions. Any such sanctions would be imposed by F-1.

3. The general statute (28 U.S.C. § 1738) requires a state to give a sister state judgment the same effect as it has in the state "from which [it is] taken." Sections 1738A and B address specific situations—full faith and credit to child custody decrees (A) and to child support orders (B). § 1738C ("DOMA") authorized states to deny full faith and credit to same-sex marriages, was held to be unconstitutional in the *Obergefell* decision (Chapter V) and has been replaced by the 2022 Respect for Marriage Act.

4. (a) ***False.*** If F-1 had jurisdiction (see also (b)), errors of fact or substantive law must be raised by appeal, not collaterally.

   (b) ***False.*** Even the existence of jurisdiction becomes *res judicata* if it was or could have been litigated; the remedy is appeal, not collateral attack.

   (c) ***False.*** The parties are bound, and F-3 should recognize the judgment which is "last in time."

   (d) ***True.*** The (objectionable) claim has merged in the judgment. The present claim is for enforcement of a *judgment for money.*

   (e) ***True.*** Since F-1 would have applied the "substantive law of F-2," it thus viewed its Statute of Limitations as *procedural.* Its dismissal was therefore *not* "on the merits" and does not preclude litigation in F-2.

   (f) ***True.*** Under Full Faith and Credit, the F-1 judgment debtor has only the defenses available under F-1 law. Under the Uniform Act, the judgment debtor may also have *local* (F-2) defenses.

   (g) ***False.*** F-2 may provide an add-on, at least unless "unmistakable language" in the F-1 award seeks to preclude it (which, as a rule, will not be the case).

V. THE CREATION OF STATUS AND ITS CONSEQUENCES

1. ***True.***

2. The Respect for Marriage Act adopts the place-of-celebration rule to determine the validity of a marriage and prohibits denial of full faith and credit on the basis of race, ethnicity, or national origin. Consanguinity and religion are not mentioned. Presumably a marriage entered elsewhere that violates the forum's rules on consanguinity or is bigamous may be denied recognition, for instance because it violates the forum's public policy.

3. (a) ***True.***

   (b) ***True.***

   (c) ***False.*** Under the community property system, the surviving spouse might not inherit. There is no statutory share, as the surviving spouse already owns half of the community. The decedent may make other arrangements to dispose of his or her one-half interest in the community.

   (d) ***Technically true,*** but that law will generally apply the law of the marital domicile at the time of acquisition.

   (e) ***False***: domicile at the time of acquisition.

   (f) ***False***: the nature of property rights does not change. The new state's law applies to property acquired after the acquiring spouse became domiciled there.

   (g) ***True***: see (f), and example in the text.

(h) ***False***: under California's quasi-community property law, all property that would have been community property if acquired in California will be treated as such upon the owner's death, and the spouse will be entitled to retain his or her undivided one-half interest in the community.

4. ***True.***

5. (a) ***Yes.*** Local law establishes requirements for a license to marry, such as the parties being above a certain age, and usually, having been in-state residents for a certain time. European countries often refer to the parties' law of nationality; we do not. The applicants' nationality and the requirements under that law are irrelevant.

   (b) There is case law that says that we cannot recognize what we do not have. A better view would be to recognize such a relationship as equivalent to a local marriage, or analogous to a civil union or a common law marriage under the law of an American sister state.

VI. DISSOLUTION OF DOMESTIC RELATIONSHIPS AND ITS CONSEQUENCES (SUPPORT, CUSTODY)

1. ***True.***

2. (a) ***True.***

   (b) ***True.*** In the *Williams* cases, Nevada law required domicile, and the U.S. Supreme Court, in *Williams I,* only confirmed that this was a sufficient basis for divorce jurisdiction, not that it was *the only* one. The Restatement (Second) advocates the "close connection" basis.

3. ***True.*** The existence of jurisdiction could have been litigated. Any objections must be raised on appeal; they cannot be asserted in a collateral attack. See Chapter IV.

4. ***False.*** Full Faith and Credit does not apply to foreign-country judgments and decrees. Since the jurisdictional objection could not have been raised in a legal system with different jurisdictional requirements, it also cannot become res judicata.

5. ***True.***

6. ***False.*** In an *ex parte* divorce, the court's jurisdiction extends to the status determination only (the divorce). Since it lacks personal jurisdiction over the respondent (defendant), it has no power to determine personal rights and obligations.

7. ***True.*** It describes the problem discussed in the previous answer.

8. ***Probably True.*** If valid and effective where the divorce by *talaq* occurred, we would generally give it effect here. However, there have been recent denials of recognition on the ground that *talaq* divorces impermissibly disadvantage the woman.

9. ***False.*** The *get* is a requirement of Jewish religious law to effect a divorce and thereby to allow the parties to remarry. In New York (and all other states), parties must obtain a civil divorce to be free to remarry. An observant Jewish spouse may therefore need to satisfy both requirements.

10. ***True.***

11. ***Probably not.*** Despite jurisdictional rules, child snatching still occurs. Although bound by the decree, a disappointed parent might seek to get a different determination elsewhere and therefore, takes the child there. The federal act (No. 13 below) provides a *remedy* (return of the child), which might discourage child

snatching, but cannot prevent it. The Hague Convention on the Civil Aspects of International Child Abduction also provides for the return of the child in an international case. The Federal Parental Kidnapping Prevention Act provides for penalties.

12. ***True.***

13. The Uniform Act establishes jurisdictional standards that focus on the child (the child's "home state") and provide continuing jurisdiction for that state. Other courts (in the United States) must defer to the court with jurisdiction, so that taking a child to a different jurisdiction in the United States should not produce a different determination in the different jurisdiction's courts. Nonetheless, "child-snatching" occurs, and appeals and other procedural devices often delay resolution, which is counterproductive especially when the child is still very young. Internationally, the Hague Convention has been very successful, with some exceptions in cases in which the new state was the original home state of the abducting parent. See also above No. 11.

14. ***True.***

15. ***True.***

16. ***True.***

VII. PERVASIVE PROBLEMS

1. (a) ***False.*** As a matter of constitutional law (at least: theory), jurisdiction requires "*minimum* contacts," the choice of forum law "*significant* contacts." Forum choice-of-law rules or the forum's analysis of policy may also call for the application of a law other than the forum's.

   (b) ***True.*** Many of the facts connecting the parties and the cause of action to the forum will often be relevant for both inquiries.

   (c) ***True.*** There are only few federal statutory or treaty-based directives.

2. ***True.*** If, for instance, the right of a spouse to sue the other on a personal injury claim is considered part of the "tort" claim, the law of the place of injury may apply, while viewing the question as one of "family" law may result in the application of the law of the spouses' (common marital) domicile.

3. (a) ***True.***

   (b) (i) ***False.*** This approach may result in a "substantive" characterization at the forum and a "procedural" one in the other state. If the forum does not apply its own substantive law to out-of-state claims nor import foreign procedural law, neither state's rule would apply.

   (ii) ***True.*** To resolve the problem of the previous answer.

   (c) ***True.***

   (d) (i)–(iii) ***All True.*** Note that the question may have confused you because it put the proposition in the reverse from its usual formulation: a statute of limitations is "procedural" *unless* it is built-in the statutory cause of action or a borrowing statute calls for the application of another state's law. However, there is some important case law in a few states characterizing limitations as substantive, i.e., to follow the law applicable to the substantive claim. To the same effect: the Uniform Conflict of Laws Limitations Act and (e), immediately following).

(e) ***True.*** Note that they do *not* adopt a substantive characterization; rather, they loosen the procedural characterization to permit the application of another law.

4. ***True.*** Under the traditional, "jurisdiction-selective" approach to choice of law, the entire case would be decided under forum or another applicable law. Modern approaches advocate choices of law with respect to *issues* of the case, including for instance the "limitations" issue.

5. (a) ***True.***

(b) ***True.***

(c) ***True.*** See Chapter VII. When the foreign conflicts rule refers back to the forum *("remission")*, the forum—if it follows policy analysis—could conclude that the other state has "no interest" in the application of its law, leaving the forum as the only "interested" state and therefore fully justified in applying its own law.

6. ***True.*** Foreign law still is fact, but, under the Federal Rules and the Uniform Act, to be determined by the *court*. The resulting decision is appealable.

7. (a) ***False.*** See *Fauntleroy*, above Chapter IV.

(b) ***True.*** See the recent cases cited.

(c) ***True.***

(d) ***False.*** (Qualified). Public policy here is not a "defense," it does not undo a choice-of-law decision already made: it *shapes* it.

(e) Depends on the choice-of-law methodology used: same as (c) and (d). No difference.

VIII. APPROACHES TO CHOICE OF LAW: THEORY

1. ***False.*** The action will be governed by law of the place of the wrong, which is where the last element necessary to create a cause of action occurred. For the wrongful death action, that is P's death in state D. **Caveat:** The foregoing assumes that application of D law is constitutionally permissible. In fact, if the application of D law was not foreseeable for the defendant, constitutional limitations may require a different choice. See Chapter X.

2. ***True.*** The last act here is the destruction of the airplane, which took place in state C.

3. ***False.*** While the First Restatement does not distinguish between intentional and unintentional torts, at least some courts have held that as to intentional torts, the punitive element may dominate, and point to the place of wrongdoing, rather than of the injury, in cases where the former, but not the latter, allows recovery.

4. ***False.*** The action for breach of contract is governed by the law of the place where the breach occurred. The breach is the negligent performance in state A, not its effect in state B or C.

5. ***True.*** The rights and obligations of the parties "vested" at the place of wrong: see (a) above.

6. ***True.*** Under the Restatement (Second), A is the state of the most-significant-relationship to the issues of liability and amount of damages (§ 145: place of conduct, common domicile, place of the parties' relationship; see also the general principles of § 6). A's law would also apply under pure interest analysis (forum law, either because there is no interest in another state—false conflict—or because forum law prevails in

a true conflict) or under the "comparative impairment" approach. The law of A, as that of the parties' common domicile, would apply under New York's *Neumeier* rules, and A would probably consider its unlimited-damage approach (favoring compensation of injured persons) to represent the "better rule of law."

7. ***True.***

8. ***True.*** As to the individual defendant, there is a "false conflict" (A and C law are the same), and C law therefore applies. As to X, there is a true conflict (liability vs. limited liability); the courts of C may not weigh the competing interests but must apply forum law.

9. ***True.*** Unlimited liability provides compensation and deters negligent conduct.

10. Probably true under the third *Neumeier* rule, and under the decisions of the New York Court of Appeals in *Schultz v. Boy Scouts of America* and in *Cooney* (primary emphasis on domicile and place of injury). Query whether the law of C may apply to the individual defendant because of the existence of a false conflict (see No. 8).

11. Probably false, as to the individual defendant. The place of the most significant relationship to the *issue of liability* is his home state—where he acted and where application of local law would not unfairly surprise him. The policies underlying the laws of A and C are the same (compensation, perhaps deterrence). Whether approached from "false conflicts" analysis or the principles of §§ 6 and 145, the law of C applies. As to the other defendant X, policies differ, and contacts are more evenly balanced. A Restatement (Second) forum would probably tip the balance in favor of its own policy: apply the law of C, thereby displacing the law of the place of injury (§ 146).

12. ***True.*** False conflict as to the individual defendant; predominant forum interest in providing compensation as compared with furthering the policy of state B in shielding its manufacturers with respect to X.

13. A, as the forum, does not have the same plaintiff-favoring interest (as against X) as did C in No. 12. A might conclude that B's policy would be more impaired by non-application of its law than would C's. However, application of the compensation-favoring rule of C is more likely. Nos. 8–11 would be resolved the same way, and No. 7 also would not be affected by the change in forum.

14. ***False.*** When the fixed rules of the First Restatement refer to the law of another state without initial consideration of its content, rejection of that law on public policy grounds may be an important check (safety valve). In most modern approaches, policy considerations enter into the initial choice of law. A second policy review, after the choice has been made, is then unnecessary.

15. ***True.***

16. ***True.*** See the *American Motorist* decision, above at p. 211.

17. ***May be true.*** *But see* the discussion of *Schultz* and *P.V. v. Camp Jaycee* on the effect of the determination of a law's "scope."

18. ***True.***

19. **Suggested to be *true*,** although not expressly so provided in the new section itself.

20. ***True.*** See also No. 17 above.

21. ***Probably false.*** While facts and policies should be considered and evaluated (as in the Second Restatement, the Restatement (Third) appears to be more interest-analysis oriented.

22. ***More or less true.*** The first part of the question describes why "scope" is important. But the purpose is not to determine whether the other state's conflicts law refers back to the forum: the Restatement (Third) does not consider another state's conflicts law, except in rare circumstances. There will therefore to renvoi (remission).

IX. CHOICE OF LAW BY SUBJECT MATTER

1. (a) ***False.*** Some cases equate the place of conduct with the "place of injury" in selecting the law applicable to *intentional* torts.

   (b) ***True.***

2. *First Restatement:* The law of B (place of injury), including its grant of charitable immunity.

   Interest Analysis: C is a "disinterested" third state, and, as such *may* weigh interests. See next entry.

   Restatement (Second): In weighing interest and policies to determine the law of the most significant relationship (see also "Interest analysis" above), the court in C may be tempted *not* to grant charitable immunity (which is the modern trend). Under an approach like the second *Neumeier* rule, it may further be tempted to apply B's law, creating liability, since B is where the defendant acted. However, as between A and B there is really a kind of false conflict: had all facts and the suit occurred in A, the plaintiff could not have recovered. Similarly, there would not be a recovery if the case had arisen entirely within state B. State C should reach the same result and not use choice of law analysis to create an "interstate tort."

   Restatement (Third): The coming new Restatement states as the overriding principle that it is the law of the state with "the dominant interest" that should be applied to the particular issue in absence of a valid choice by the parties. § 6.01 (T.D.# 4, 2023). In its first topic of Chapter 6 it distinguishes between issues that relate to conduct and for which territorial connecting factors should be appropriate. In its second topic, the state with the dominant interest may be the one when personal issue of the parties are involved. § 6.03. See the discussion in the text at II(C). Here conduct is in one state, the loss allocation is a personal issue. Which state's law applies. § 6.08 (T.D.# 4) provides: if conduct and injury occur in the same state, then that state's law. Conduct regulation would overcome loss allocation— §§ 6.11 and 6.12, not relevant here, contain specific rules for strict liability and punitive damages.

3. (a) ***False.*** The last act necessary to form the contract was D's acceptance. Under the mailbox rule, it occurred when D mailed his letter in state B.

   (b) ***True.*** The law of the contemplated place of performance governs the remedies for breach of contract.

   (c) ***False.*** Some courts have held that the law of the place of performance also governs the validity of the contract as a result of implicit agreement of the parties.

4. (a) ***False.*** (Restatement (Second)): The law chosen by the parties must have a substantial relationship to the parties or the transaction. In addition, the Restatement (Second) would validate a choice for which there was a reasonable basis (e.g., a particularly well-developed legal system). The rule of the

Restatement (Third) is virtually the same. § 8.02(1) (T.D. # 6).Neither applies in a purely intrastate case. UCC § 1–301 (formerly 1–105) also requires a relationship to the chosen law. Otherwise, forum law applies. A proposed revision, later withdrawn, would have permitted parties to a "domestic" transaction to choose the law of any other U.S. state, even if unrelated to the transaction (but not the law of a foreign country).

(b) ***False.*** Courts departing from the First Restatement *will* use one of the modern approaches. But they will not necessarily do the same in tort and contract, i.e., a court may adhere to the First Restatement in contract but choose a new approach in tort, or it may be more interest-analysis oriented in tort while generally following the Restatement (Second) in contract. The same is of course with respect to the coming Restatement (Third).

(c) ***False.*** UCC § 1–105 provides for forum law, if there in an "appropriate relation" of the transaction to it.

(d) ***True.***

(e) ***False.*** They tend to decide these issues under the same law that applies to the contract.

(f) ***False.*** The non-situs court cannot directly affect title but can adjudicate the rights of the parties before it.

(g) ***True.*** UCC § 9–301(1).

5. (a) ***Probably false.*** Whether equitable conversion has occurred is up to the situs to decide, and a substantial number of (older) decisions reject it. Thus, land *and its proceeds* are treated as land. However, the situs, as a matter of its own choice of law, may apply domiciliary law for policy reasons. Note: The coming Restatement (Third) may seek to suggest adopting the civil-law type approach of treating an estate as a unit (combining real and personal property), to which only a single law would apply. Definite proposals are still coming and, if formulated in this way, would still need to be adopted by states (estate law being state law).

(b) ***Probably false.*** To effectuate (validate) the intent of the testator, most states utilize alternative references. Thus, the situs of land may uphold the will if it was validly executed under its law *or* under the law of the decedent's domicile (among others).

(c) ***Probably false.*** Situs law does not apply as an initial matter. However, as a matter of situs choice of law, domiciliary law is usually applicable to this issue.

(d) ***False.*** The personal representative is technically an officer of the appointing probate court and has no authority out of state. In the interest of unity of administration, most states give preference to the domiciliary representative to be appointed locally as ancillary representative and will also protect a local debtor who has made voluntary payment to a foreign domiciliary representative.

(e) ***Technically true.*** The situs may distribute local assets to creditors who filed locally. Its obligation is simply to let every creditor file, in-state or out-of-state. However, in some modern decisions, courts will often consider total assets (everywhere) and total liabilities, allow the appropriate percentage satisfaction, and remit the balance, if any, to the domicile.

6. (a) ***True.***

   (b) ***Two Views***: 1) A state may only regulate an out-of-state's company's doing of intrastate business by subjecting it to its "qualification statute." Complying with such a required filing requirement does not subject the corporation to general jurisdiction, i.e., for a claim that arose elsewhere. For the latter, the criteria for general jurisdiction must be met (*Goodyear* and *Daimler*). 2) If the qualification statute so provides, the company has "notice" and can be said to "consent" to jurisdiction by registering. So decided by the Supreme Court in *Malory v. Norfolk S. Ry. Co.,* discusses above in Chapter III (II(C)).

   (c) ***True.*** Note that these statutes only apply to corporations not listed on national stock exchanges.

   (d) ***False.*** *CTS* practically "constitutionalizes" the incorporation-law as the applicable law. The law of the state of effective operation/management is then left with a regulatory/supervisory function. See, e.g., *Haberman v. Washington Public Power Supply System*, 744 P.2d 1032 (Wash. 1987); *Hornbook* § 23.9. See also *Juul Labs. Inc. v. Grove*, 238 A.3d 904, 914 (Del. Ch. 2020).

X. CONSTITUTIONAL LIMITATIONS ON STATE CHOICE OF LAW

1. ***Basically true.*** However, you should note two points. First, a "limitation" may leave little room for choice. Thus, when, as in *Shutts and Wortman,* a court may not apply forum law, it will necessarily have to apply the law of the state that has the requisite connection with the case. Second, the U.S. Supreme Court's decision in *CTS Corp.* may have "constitutionalized" the reference to the law of incorporation as applicable to a corporation's "internal affairs." See No. 6(d) in Chapter IX above.

2. ***True.*** Qualification statutes may regulate a corporation's intrastate activities. With respect to a foreign corporation's "internal affairs," see No. 1 above.

3. ***Still uncertain.*** The Draft Restatement (Third) proposes to apply the issue-by-issue approach also to the determination of the principal place of business. If this became accepted (as distinguished from the principal place of business of the entire enterprise), then general jurisdiction would exist wherever the *particular* place of business is. This would expand today's definition of general jurisdiction or, put differently, blur the distinction between specific and general jurisdiction.

4. **(c)** *Bendix* rested in part on Commerce Clause grounds. But the absence of "general jurisdiction" contacts (see *Goodyear,* above p. 55) also makes assertion of general jurisdiction (along with the tolling of limitation periods applicable to general jurisdiction) a violation of the defendant's due process rights.

5. ***False.*** The question restates the due process requirement for the exercise of state court *jurisdiction (International Shoe, Shaffer, World-Wide Volkswagen, Asahi, J. McIntyre, Malory* in Chapter III above). *Hague* requires a "*significant* contact" or a "*significant* aggregation of contacts, creating state interest" (emphasis added) for the application of forum law to be permissible.

6. ***Usually false.*** The *claim* does not have the required connection to the forum; see the previous answer. In some circumstances, a state may and will regulate the extraterritorial conduct and activities of its citizens. An example is the taxation of income of U.S. citizens earned abroad. Special rules (and treaties) provide relief from the effects of double taxation. See also federal legislation providing for jurisdiction to pursue human rights violations committed abroad.

7. ***True.*** Remember that specific jurisdiction exists when *the claim arises from or is substantially related to the particular contact with the forum* (e.g., when a defective product, manufactured elsewhere, is marketed and causes harm in the forum state). See *Helicopteros, J. McIntyre* (if the defendant had introduced the machine into the forum state), Chapter III. See also *Ford*, same chapter, when the defendant did not introduce the product into the forum but maintained substantial contacts related to the product with the state.

XI. STATE LAW IN FEDERAL COURT

1. (a) ***False.*** The "outcome determinative" test is used to make the "substance/procedure" characterization when *Erie* applies. The constitutional aspect of *Erie* does *not* apply when there is federal lawmaking authority, for instance to promulgate Federal Rules of Civil Procedure. Thus, whenever a Federal Rule is meant to apply to the case, it governs, even if it affects the outcome of the case. Whether a Rule "is meant to apply" is a matter of interpretation in light of policy considerations *(Walker, Gasperini, Semtek).*

   (b) ***False.*** The federal court must make the same choice of law as the forum state. If the latter selects the law of a third state without regard to that state's interest (for instance, in application of the place-of-wrong rule), so must the federal court *(Challoner).* If the forum state uses interest analysis, then the federal court—using the forum state's standards and methodology—must do the same. The federal court should *not* make an *independent* determination of "interest."

   (c) ***True.*** There is no *general* federal power to create tort law (at least at the time of *Erie*; since the railroad tracks were used in interstate commerce, the answer perhaps is not so clear today). In contrast, the Rules Enabling Act—the source of the Federal Rules—is based on the Congressional power to establish federal courts combined with the Necessary and Proper Clause of the Constitution, which permits Congress to regulate how the courts that it has power to establish conduct their business.

   (d) ***False.*** The statement is overbroad. The Federal Rule displaces state law when it is *meant to apply* (not just "can be used") and clashes with state law. *Walker.* See also *Gasperini* and *Semtek.*

   (e) ***True.*** This is so despite the fact that a state court may have lacked jurisdiction in these circumstances. This result is therefore not required by the policy goal of achieving instate uniformity.

2. In state court. The federal court must follow the established decisions of the forum state. Only the state courts, ultimately the state supreme court, can adopt a new approach to choice of law.

3. The Federal Rule applies, since its purpose is to regulate the burden that frivolous appeals place upon the *federal* court system. *Burlington Northern R. Co. v. Woods,* 480 U.S. 1, 107 S. Ct. 967, 94 L. Ed. 2d 1 (1987).

XII. FEDERAL COMMON LAW AS THE RULE OF DECISION

1. ***False.*** In a way, decisional law interpreting and applying constitutional and statutory law is a form of common law. However, the term "federal common law" is used to describe decisional law *creating* rules of substantive or procedural law, when there is *no* applicable provision of written law. Case law interpreting and applying federal constitutional and statutory law is "federal courts law."

2. ***False.*** The "federal interest" test is used to determine whether the creation of federal common law is *appropriate.* The threshold question is whether it is constitutionally *permissible* to make federal common law. See No. 3.

3. ***True.***

4. ***True.***

5. ***False.*** It might be desirable, and there may even be federal lawmaking authority for the creation of federal common law for products liability (e.g., under the Commerce Clause), but the courts have consistently considered it inappropriate to do so.

Appendix B

Glossary

This Glossary, like a dictionary, addresses both terms and concepts used in statutes, decisions, and commentaries dealing with conflict-of-laws problems and issues. To make these terms and concepts more readily understandable and to tie them in to chapters and places where they are treated in detail, the entries here also contain brief explanations. As a result, this Glossary is like a small "Black Letter" of the Black Letter.

A

Act-of-State Doctrine Because the Constitution commits the conduct of foreign relations to the Executive, the United States Supreme Court established in the *Sabbatino* decision that the courts may not inquire into the legality of acts of foreign governments, done in their sovereign capacity within their own territory. This is known as the "act-of-state doctrine" and has subsequently been limited by legislation.

After-Acquired Domicile A person's domicile is an important connecting factor for both jurisdiction and choice of law. However, to be relevant for choice of law, the courts usually require that the domicile must have existed at the time that the relevant facts arose, i.e., that it not be "after-acquired."

Appearance By making a "general appearance" in a lawsuit (for instance, even when filing an answer that only contests the merits of the plaintiff's claim), the defendant waives any objection to the court's jurisdiction to hear the claim and to exercise its judicial power over the defendant. However, the defendant may choose to enter only a "special appearance" (not available in federal court). The sole purpose is to object to the court's jurisdiction. The defendant need address the merits of the plaintiff's claim only after the jurisdictional objection has been decided in the plaintiff's favor.

B

Bar (to claims) See also merger, res judicata. A valid and final judgment on the merits *against* a claimant bars the claimant and those in privity with him or her from suing on the same cause of action again, both in the state where the judgment was rendered and in all other states. A subsequent suit is barred even if new grounds are invoked, so long as the "new" grounds could have been raised in the original action.

Better Rule of Law One of the five choice-influencing considerations of Professor Leflar's approach to choice of law is that the court should select, as between two potentially applicable rules of law, the one which represents the "better rule of law."

Borrowing Statutes Borrowing statutes are a legislative exception to the traditional rule that statutes of limitation are procedural, i.e., that the forum state will apply its own statute of limitation. In circumstances specified in borrowing statutes, the forum state will "borrow" the (usually shorter) statute of limitations of another state.

C

Center-of-Gravity Approach This describes an early departure from the traditional approach of the First Restatement. The "center of gravity approach" was a precursor to today's "most-significant-relationship approach," but differed from it in that it often only counted contacts without considering the content of the foreign law or the policies underlying the laws of interested states.

Characterization Characterization is the process by which a court makes some basic decisions at the beginning of the choice-of-law process. There are three types of characterization: 1) a court will classify ("characterize") the case or an issue with respect to the legal subject matter it involves (e.g., tort, family law, contract, etc.). Especially when a court adheres to the traditional approach to choice of law, *subject matter characterization* has important consequences for the choice of the applicable law. 2) The *substance/procedure characterization* guides the court (especially when employing the traditional approach) in determining how much of the foreign law to apply; the court will apply foreign law only to substantive issues; it will apply its own law to procedural issues. 3) A federal court sitting in diversity will also make a substance/procedure characterization for *Erie purposes* to decide when it must apply the law of the state in which it sits. Note that the substance/procedure characterization for *Erie* purposes is different from the one under No. 2, above (see Chapter XI for details).

Civil Union A domestic relationship that may be contracted as provided by statute in some states. Civil union statutes (or their equivalents, such as registered domestic partnerships) originated when same-sex marriage was not yet possible. They were designed to provide the same rights and impose the same obligations on same-sex parties as does traditional marriage, except for the status of "marriage." Today, civil unions exist as an alternative to marriage in a few states and can be concluded regardless of the sex of the parties.

Class Action A lawsuit brought by or against a large number of individuals or organizations whose legal rights or obligations are closely enough related to make it more efficient to adjudicate them all in one proceeding. The class action often provides the only method of litigating numerous small claims or important social issues. The class sues or is sued through class representatives, and joinder of each class member is not required. A judgment in favor of or against a class binds all the class members. The prerequisites for the maintenance of a class action are set out in Federal Rule of Civil Procedure 23 and its state counterparts. They are: (1) an identifiable class; (2) representatives of the class must be class members; (3) the class must be so large that joinder is impracticable; (4) common questions of law or fact must exist; (5) the claims and defenses of the class representatives must be typical of those of the class members; (6) the representatives must be able to adequately represent the absent class members; and (7) the action must fall within one of the three types of class actions defined by the Rule. See *Philips Petroleum Co. v. Shutts* (U.S. 1985). Federal legislation in 2005 (the Class Action Fairness Act) significantly limited state court jurisdiction with respect to multistate, multiparty class actions.

***Clearfield Trust* Doctrine** The *Clearfield Trust* decision is an early example of the federal courts' power to make federal common law when there is federal lawmaking power to do so, combined with a strong federal interest in a nationally uniform rule. The decision itself involved the federal government's liability on commercial paper issued by it.

Cognovit Clause See also Consent. A clause by which a debtor or party to a contract agrees to submit to the jurisdiction of a particular court in the event of default or breach. Cognovit clauses often waive the right to receive notice of the proceedings, or authorize the entry of a judgment against the consenting party. See *D.H. Overmeyer Co. v. Frick Co.* (U.S. 1972).

Collateral Attack A challenge to the validity of a judgment in a proceeding other than one related to the entry or review of the judgment itself. A judgment, even if clearly erroneous or reversible on direct appeal, may not be attacked collaterally in the United States, except for the limited purpose of showing that the court that entered the judgment did not have proper personal or subject matter jurisdiction. Even an attack on the latter grounds is not permissible if both parties participated in the earlier proceeding. *Treinies.*

Collateral Estoppel See "Res Judicata (Issue Preclusion)."

Comity The comity doctrine, as a precursor to the vested-rights approach, explained why a state would recognize rights created under the law of a foreign country. Foreign-country judgments were also recognized on the basis of comity. Today, these judgments are ordinarily recognized much the same as sister-state judgments, and in choice of law in international cases the case law makes only occasional references to comity.

Comparative Impairment When, in interest analysis in choice of law (see that entry), a court weighs interests, it may be engaging in the "comparative impairment test." That approach asks which of two (or more) states' policies would be more impaired by *not* having its law applied. Its law should be applied.

Conduct-Regulating Rules (of a state's law) These help in selecting the applicable law for tort issues in the methodology for choice of law of the coming Restatement (Third). Distinguish from loss-allocating rules (see that entry for further discussion).

Confession-of-Judgment Clause See Cognovit Clause; see also Consent.

Consent to Jurisdiction A defendant can consent to jurisdiction by entering a (general) appearance or agreeing to jurisdiction in advance of litigation. The latter may take the form of a *cognovit* or *confession-of-judgment clause* or of a forum-selection clause in a contract. A plaintiff, by invoking the aid of the courts of the forum state, has thereby consented to jurisdiction over him or her with respect to counterclaims arising from the same transaction. A company's compliance with a state law that requires foreign corporations to register to do business and to appoint a local agent to receive service of process may amount to consent to be subject to general (i.e., even claim unrelated) jurisdiction in that state. If the registration statute provides that registration subjects the out-of-state company to the same jurisdiction as an in-state company, the Supreme Court has upheld the exercise of general jurisdiction (*Mallory*). It relied on a prior decision in which the state registration statute had not expressly so provided but had been so construed .

Constitutional Limitations The Due Process Clause of the Constitution sets limits to a state court's exercise of judicial jurisdiction over non-resident defendants as well as to its application of forum law. With respect to *jurisdiction,* the Due Process Clause requires that the forum state have "minimum contacts" with the defendant and the transaction (*International Shoe*). The *Mallory* decision of the Supreme Court (see previous paragraph) may have broadened the exercise of jurisdiction over an out-of-state defendant business. To permissibly apply *forum law,* the forum state must have a "significant contact" or an aggregation of contacts which are significant with the transaction. The Full Faith and Credit Clause has also been said to impose limitations on a court's freedom to choose its own law but, in practice, does not seem to impose limitations in addition to the Due Process Clause. Occasionally, the Equal Protection Clause, the Privileges and Immunities Clause, and the Commerce Clause will be important in choice of law.

Continuing Jurisdiction Once a court acquires jurisdiction over a particular dispute, its jurisdiction continues until the dispute is terminated, even if the defendant subsequently leaves the state. Continuing jurisdiction is most often invoked in matters of child custody, domestic relations, and probate, where litigation may go on over a long period of time and the court's orders are often amended or modified. The defendant must be given notice and an opportunity for a hearing if subsequent proceedings are held to modify the rights and duties of the parties under a prior order.

Covenant Marriage Three states (as of 2025) offer couples the option to contract a covenant marriage as an alternative to traditional marriage. Designed to curb the modern trend toward easy and quick dissolution, parties to a covenant marriage enter into a contract in which they choose forum law, undertake to undergo counseling in the advent of marital difficulties, and accept a waiting period before dissolution may be granted. Since American courts usually apply forum law to a petition of dissolution, it is doubtful that a subsequent state (in which one of the spouses has become domiciled subsequent to the marriage) will enforce the limitations of the covenant-marriage contract. Rather, it may be expected to proceed on the basis of forum law, leaving the respondent with a (speculative) claim for contract damages.

D

Defense of Marriage Act (DOMA) The trend to give a legal status to same-sex domestic relationships (that began in Hawaii and Alaska in the 1980s and 1990s) produced counter-movements (e.g., the "covenant marriage," see entry above) and strong opposition. The latter took the form of the Federal Defense of Marriage Act (DOMA). Enacted under the congressional power to define the "effects" of state law and judgments to be accorded by one state to another under the Constitution's Full Faith and Credit Clause, the statute defines marriage as being between a man and a woman. It also purports to authorize states to refuse other types of unions or rights or claims based on them. Forty states passed legislation or state constitutional amendments rejecting same-sex marriages. Nineteen of those states reject all same-sex domestic relations as conferring any legal status or rights and, accordingly, refuse to recognize those entered into in other states. The U.S. Supreme Court ultimately declared DOMA to be unconstitutional (*Obergefell*) so that same-sex marriage became legal throughout the United States. Such a marriage validly entered in one state became entitled to recognition in all other states of the Union. In late 2022, Congress passed the **Respect for Marriage Act** (described below) which repealed and replaced DOMA (thereby also guarding against a possible reversal of *Obergefell* (above)). Assuming final enactment of the law, marriage will now be valid and entitled to full faith and credit if valid under the law of the state of celebration.

Dépeçage Under modern approaches to choice of law, a court will not necessarily select *one* state whose law it will apply to the case before it (jurisdiction selection). Rather, it will examine the various issues presented by the case and make an individual choice of law for each one. This issue-by-issue approach splits the case up and is also called "dépeçage." Both the Restatement (Second) and the coming Restatement (Third) call for an issue-by-issue approach to choice of law.

Divisible Divorce In an *ex parte* divorce (see that entry), the court's jurisdiction extends only to granting the divorce itself. It lacks jurisdiction to affect the "incidents" (see that entry) of the divorce, such as support and property rights. To affect "incidents," the court needs personal jurisdiction over the defendant spouse. The divorce is "divisible" into the status aspect (dissolution of the marriage relationship) and the determination of "incidents."

Domicile The concept of domicile describes the closest connection that a natural person has to a state. While a person can have more than one residence, even more than one nationality, he or she has only a single domicile at any one time. "Domicile of origin" describes the domicile of a person at birth; it will be derivative of the custodial parent. "Domicile of choice" describes whatever domicile a person chooses subsequently (after reaching majority or being emancipated). The determination of a person's domicile of choice is a mixed question of fact and of the person's intent. The person must have left the previous domicile, have arrived at the new domicile, and have the intent to remain indefinitely (or must lack the intent to leave at a specified time). The coming Restatement (Third) will focus only on objective facts to determine a person's "center of life" and no longer seek to determine a person's "intent" (which, as in the case of a deceased person, would also need to be derived/assumed from objective facts). See also "Habitual Residence."—The domicile of a juridical person (e.g., a corporation) has been its state of incorporation or its principal place of business under traditional law and the Restatement (second). The coming Restatement (Third) equates a company's domicile with its principal place with respect to the *particular issue* involved. In other words, domicile is also subject to the issue by issue approach. See the entry for *dépeçage.*

Door Closing—Limiting Access to Court State statutes may close local courts to plaintiffs unless and until specified conditions have been met. "Qualification" statutes require foreign corporations to "qualify" before doing business in a state. Qualification usually includes registration with the Secretary of State, payment of a fee or tax, and the appointment of an agent to receive service of process. Application of qualifying statutes to corporations whose intrastate activities are merely incidental to interstate commerce is unconstitutional. However, registration, if required and performed. May subject the out-of-state company to general jurisdiction in the state. (See entry on *Consent to Jurisdiction.*)—In the area of medical malpractice, a number of states now require claimants to attempt to resolve their disputes by way of arbitration before being allowed to invoke the judicial process. Door Closing by contract (mandatory private arbitration in lieu of litigation) has been upheld by the U.S. Supreme Court.

Due Process of Law The Due Process Clause of the Federal Constitution is an important "Constitutional Limitation" (see that entry) on a state court's jurisdiction and on its choice of law.

E

***Erie*-Doctrine** The United States Supreme Court held in the *Erie* decision that the federal courts may not create rules of federal common law with respect to subject matter for which the federal government—in particular the Congress—lacks lawmaking authority under the Constitution. It also identified the important policy that there should be uniformity with respect to the law applied to a case as between state courts and federal courts sitting in the same state and hearing diversity cases. As a result of the *Erie* decision, and its progeny, federal courts must decide whether an issue is "outcome determinative." In the absence of federal lawmaking authority, the federal court must apply state law to an outcome-determinative issue. If there is federal lawmaking authority, the *Erie* policy may nevertheless speak in favor of the application of state law, unless there are "countervailing considerations." If there is federal lawmaking authority combined with a strong federal interest in a nationally uniform rule, federal common law may be created. See "*Clearfield Trust* Doctrine." The Federal Rules of Civil Procedure derive from federal lawmaking authority. If interpretation reveals that they were intended to apply to a particular issue, they then take precedence over inconsistent state law. When the purpose and scope of a federal and state rule on a like subject do not clash, the *Erie* policy favors application of the state rule. See *Walker*.

***Ex Parte* Divorce** A divorce granted in proceedings where only the petitioning spouse is before the court. The domicile of the petitioning spouse is a sufficient basis for divorce jurisdiction, and the divorce is entitled to full faith and credit. However, the divorce decree is subject to collateral attack on the grounds that the petitioner was not in fact domiciled in the state granting the divorce. However, a court must have personal jurisdiction over a respondent spouse to impose enforceable alimony or child support obligations, or to alter the respondent's rights to property not within the court's *in rem* jurisdiction.

F

False Conflict Modern approaches to choice of law inquire whether the case presents a conflict at all (see "True Conflict") or a "false conflict." The latter is the case when the potentially applicable laws do not differ, when their underlying policies have the same objectives, or when, by its own terms or underlying policy, the law of one of the states in question is not meant to apply to the case before the court. Whenever a court identifies a "false conflict," the choice-of-law problem disappears. The court will disregard the law of the state whose law is not meant to apply and apply the law of the interested state. See also "Interest Analysis." It is disputed whether the forum state also considers the other state's conflicts law, to see whether that law might refer back to the forum or to another state. In both cases, the other state is shown not have an interest, so that the case presents a false conflict. Maryland, for example, has proceeded that way. The coming Restatement (Third) rejects renvoi and therefore also its use for the determination of a possible false conflict. see also "Renvoi."

Federal Common Law The federal courts may create federal common law whenever there is federal lawmaking authority that the Congress has not yet exercised and when there is a federal interest in having a nationally uniform rule. See "*Clearfield Trust* Doctrine" and "*Erie* Doctrine," above.

Federal Interpleader Act The Federal Interpleader Act gives federal courts nationwide service of process for this purpose. The debtor functions as the stakeholder who admits liability but interpleads all interested parties for the purpose of determining to whom that liability exists. The federal court hearing the interpleader case applies the law of the state in which it sits. See also *Erie* and *Klaxon*.

Federal Question Jurisdiction Article III, Section 2 of the Constitution provides that the judicial power of the United States "shall extend to all cases, in Law and Equity, arising under this Constitution, the Laws of the United States, and Treaties made, or which shall be made, under their Authority." Accordingly, 28 U.S.C. § 1331 states that "The district courts shall have original jurisdiction of all civil actions arising under the Constitution, laws, or treaties of the United States," and various other statutes grant the federal courts subject matter jurisdiction over cases arising under them. Federal question jurisdiction may also be based on administrative regulations or executive orders made under authority from Congress, as well as federal common law.

Federal Tort Claims Act 28 U.S.C. § 1346(b) waives immunity and grants U.S. district courts jurisdiction against the United States "under circumstances where the United States, if a private person, would be liable to the claimant in accordance with the law of the place where the act or omission occurred."

Federal Transfer 28 U.S.C. § 1404(a) provides that a district court may transfer a civil action to any other district or division where it might have been brought. "Might have been brought" has been interpreted to require that the action be transferred only to a district where the plaintiff could have initiated the action originally. *Hoffman v. Blaski* (1960).

Foreign Sovereign Immunities Act (FSIA) This federal act confirms that foreign sovereigns (states) have immunity from suit in the United States unless the committed acts in violation of international law. Determining whether the exception applies may be precluded by the domestic taking/action rule: review of a country's public acts within its territory affecting its own nationals may not be undertaken. See *Sabbatino*.

Forum Non Conveniens Under the *forum non conveniens* doctrine, a court will decline to hear a case (even though it has jurisdiction to do so) when doing so would be seriously inconvenient for the defendant, witnesses, or the court. The *forum non conveniens* doctrine is part of both federal and state procedural law. In federal practice, it has been replaced by the federal *transfer statute* in interstate cases to which it applies. (See that entry and *Atlantic Marine*).

Forum Shopping Frequently, the plaintiff will be able to obtain personal jurisdiction over the defendant in more than one state. If, as a result of the several states' different approaches to choice of law, these states would each tend to apply their own forum law, the plaintiff will be able to influence the choice of law by his or her choice of the state in which to bring suit. The fixed choice-of-law rules of the First Restatement counteracted "forum shopping" attempts. Under the more flexible modern approaches to choice of law, forum shopping will often be a possibility. With few exceptions (such as the occasional selection of a plaintiff-favoring law in product liability), courts do not make choice-of-law decisions on the basis of the plaintiff's forum shopping, but rather on the basis of policy and interest-weighing considerations. The latter, however, may also favor certain parties or outcomes and therefore be the unspoken reason why suit is brought in that state.

Full Faith and Credit Clause Under the mandate of the Full Faith and Credit Clause of the Constitution, or in federal court, as a matter of constitutional tradition, all courts must give the same effect to the judgment of a court of a sister-state as that judgment has in the state where it was rendered, provided only that it was entered by a court with valid jurisdiction. In the area of choice of law, the Full Faith and Credit Clause today is co-extensive with the Due Process Clause for practical purposes, i.e., it does not place additional limitations on a state court's choice of law. The Full Faith and Credit Clause does not apply when the recognition of a foreign-country judgment is in issue nor with respect to the choice of law in international cases.

Full Faith and Credit for Child Support Orders Act See Uniform Interstate Family Support Act.

G

General Jurisdiction When a court has "general jurisdiction" over the defendant, it may hear all claims against the defendant, and there need not be a showing that a connection exists between the claim and the forum state. General jurisdiction exists at the individual defendant's domicile or, historically, when the defendant was served in the forum state. See also "Transient Jurisdiction." For business entities, the Supreme Court's decisions in *Goodyear* and *Daimler* have established qualitatively high requirements to be subject to general jurisdiction. The connection to the forum state must be so close that the business entity can be considered to be "at home" there. The Court mentioned that the states of incorporation and of the principal place of business satisfy that test. In addition, when an out-of-state corporation must register to do be able to do business in a state, registration may amount to consent to general jurisdiction in that state. See "Consent to Jurisdiction." See also "Jurisdiction," "Specific Jurisdiction."

H

Habitual Residence In international (especially European) practice, habitual residence connotes a person's close connection to a state for jurisdictional and choice-of-law purposes, just as "domicile" (see that entry) does in American law. Even when foreign law uses the term "domicile" (e.g., in European law on jurisdiction), the concept lacks the intent element of traditional American law.

Hague Conference on Private International Law An organization that drafts conflicts conventions and recommends them to the member states for adoption. The United States has ratified important Hague conventions and, as treaties, they are federal law. They include the Conventions on Service of Documents Abroad, on Taking Evidence Abroad, and on International Child Abduction (see immediately following).

Hague Convention on the Civil Aspects of International Child Abduction The United States is a party to this Convention, which seeks to counteract, on the international level, child-snatching by the non-custodial parent. Its goals are the same as those underlying the Uniform Child Custody Jurisdiction Act and its successor, the Uniform Child Custody Jurisdiction and Enforcement Act, but its provisions are not as far-reaching.

Hague Convention on the Recognition of Judgments After an earlier attempt to facilitate the international recognition of judgments through a treaty was abandoned, a new attempt succeeded in 2019, and the Hague Conference presented a new Convention for adoption. A number of countries signed, including the United States, but by 2025 only the European Union (on behalf of its member states), the United Kingdom, Ukraine, Uruguay, and three other states had ratified it. The Convention is limited in its scope: not included are judgments dealing with family law matters, maintenance obligations, intellectual property, defamation, and privacy, among others.

I

***In Rem* Jurisdiction** See also Personal Jurisdiction. When the subject matter of an action is property located within the state, a court may adjudicate *title* to interests in the property based on its power over the property itself. Since the court has control over the property, it need not have before it those whose interests may be affected. Its adjudication of the title to the property will be "good against the world." In the absence of personal jurisdiction, however, the court's *in rem* judgment affects only the property itself, not the underlying rights and claims of the parties.

"Incidents" The consequences of a status determination (validity of a marriage, decree of divorce, adoption, legitimation) are also called the "incidents" of the status. Examples: right to alimony and child support and to child custody upon divorce, right to inherit from the adoptive parent(s).

Interest Analysis "Pure" interest analysis, as advocated by Currie, resolves "true conflicts" in favor of the law of the forum because courts are not free to weigh interests, but must advance the legislative policies of the forum. (For "false conflicts" see the respective entry.) If the interests of the forum are not involved—if it is a "disinterested third state"—then it should apply the law of that interested state that most closely resembles its own. Modified approaches to interest analysis will permit the forum court to weigh interests. An example is the "comparative impairment" approach; see the respective entry.

Internal Affairs Rule The internal affairs of a corporation are governed by the law of the state of its incorporation. See also "Pseudo-Foreign Corporation."

International Sales The United States is a party to the United Nations Convention on Contracts for the International Sale of Goods ("Vienna Convention"). It applies to international sales contracts when the (business) parties have their places of business in different countries that have ratified the Convention or if the choice-of-law rules of the forum refer to the law of a contracting state. The United States has filed a reservation to the second of the foregoing: it applies the Convention only with respect to another contracting state.

Interpleader When more than one person lays claim to the same indebtedness in the hands of the debtor, the limits on state court jurisdiction may make it difficult or impossible for the debtor to get all the claimants into the same court. The *Federal Interpleader Act* now provides relief: see that entry.

J

Jurisdiction The term "jurisdiction" is used in a number of different senses in American law. A first, basic distinction is between "legislative" and "judicial" jurisdiction. *Legislative jurisdiction* describes the authority of a state to legislate, to make laws that apply to people, events, and transactions: it describes the reach of state law. *Judicial jurisdiction* (also: adjudicatory jurisdiction) describes the power of courts to adjudicate claims, rights between people, or to determine a person's status. To have that power, a court must have "subject matter jurisdiction." Thus, a small claims court cannot grant a divorce. *Judicial jurisdiction* also describes the court's power to determine the rights and obligations between the parties themselves or with respect to an interest they may have in property. For the former, the court needs "personal jurisdiction;" to affect an interest in property, the court needs "*in rem*" or "*quasi in rem*" jurisdiction. For the exercise of personal jurisdiction, the law distinguishes between "general" and "specific" jurisdiction. See the respective entries.

L

Last-Act Theory Under the traditional approach to choice of law in tort, the courts applies the law of the place of the wrong. This is the place where the last act occurred to give the plaintiff a claim, for instance, where the effects of food poisoning were felt by the plaintiff, not where the food was improperly prepared nor even where the plaintiff consumed it.

Last-in-Time Rule As between or among two or more inconsistent judgments in the same matter, the last judgment entered is entitled to recognition because it addressed and denied the valid effect of the previous judgment. *Treinies.* Many civil law countries have the opposite rule on the ground that after the first judgment there was nothing left to address.

Lex Fori Approach Under the approach to choice of law proposed by Ehrenzweig, the forum applies another state's law only when "formulated" or "unformulated" rules of forum law so direct. Otherwise, forum law applies in its own right or as the "subsidiary law." Since there are not many legislative choice-of-law rules (and few "unformulated" true rules), this approach favors the application of forum law.

Lex Loci (Delicti/Contractus) The traditional approach to choice of law identifies the place of the tort and then applies that state's law to the claim (lex loci delicti). Similarly, the place of the contract (lex loci contractus) governs questions of its validity under that approach.

Lex Mercatoria Also sometimes called "The New Law Merchant," the lex mercatoria encompasses international commercial custom and practice, whether in the form of new, and uniformly used, documents (for instance, form contracts) or legal arrangements (for instance, leases before their codification in many countries), or simply uniformly observed business practices. The lex mercatoria is too incomplete to be a source of legal solutions to an international problem, but can be useful in the interpretation of documents and transactions, i.e., by placing them into a commercial context. See also UNIDROIT Principles.

Lex Situs Traditionally, the law of the location (situs) of property applies to issues regarding that property. This is still true with respect to title to real property as well as to such questions as the validity of a transfer of movable property. However, a court with jurisdiction over the parties can adjudicate rights to property as between the parties themselves (and their privies) and may choose to apply a law other than that of the situs. Additionally, there exist legislative exceptions to the situs rule, for instance under the Uniform Commercial Code with respect to the perfection of security interests in accounts receivable. See further under "Situs Rule."

Long-Arm Statutes The Due Process Clause of the Constitution requires that, to exercise specific jurisdiction over a nonresident defendant, a state must show that there are minimum contacts between the defendant and the forum and that the claim arises out of or is related to these contacts. Long arm statutes are the legislative assertion of specific jurisdiction by specifying the types of contacts upon which jurisdiction will be asserted (for instance, doing business in the state, causing tortious injury in the state, and the like). A few states have adopted broad statutes in which they assert jurisdiction "to the limits of due process," leaving it to the courts to define these limits from case to case.

Loss-Allocating Rules The coming Restatement (Third) distinguishes between conduct-regulating rules (e.g., a rule establishing strict liability)—see that entry—and loss-allocating rules (e.g., guest statutes immunizing the driver or charitable immunity statutes) in its methodology for the determination of the applicable law to tort issues. It suggests some specific rules derived from this distinction and also suggests the latter to determine the applicable law when a rule is lacking. The goal is to find the "most appropriate law," as provide in the section dealing with contracts. A "manifestly more appropriate law" may also be applied to disregard an otherwise applicable specific rule.

M

Marriage The formal domestic relationship established between two persons according to formalities prescribed by the state, or in some states, an informal relationship accepted to be the equivalent ("common law marriage"). A marriage, valid where entered, traditionally is recognized everywhere as are its judicial dissolution and decrees regarding incidents, assuming proper jurisdiction. In the United States, same-sex marriage is legal, as it is in many foreign countries as well. See the "Respect for Marriage Act."

Merger See also Bar, Res Judicata. A valid and final judgment on the merits merges the original cause of action into the judgment. The original cause of action ceases to exist. The plaintiff is precluded from suing again on the original cause of action (for instance, in order to get a higher recovery), regardless of whether all matters were actually litigated. Any further suit must be brought on the judgment.

Minimum Contacts The defendant must have "minimum contacts" with the forum state and the cause of action must at least be "related" to these contacts before it may exercise specific jurisdiction over him or her. The claim for which the defendant may be subjected to personal jurisdiction must arise from, or closely relate to, the particular contact(s).

Most Significant Relationship For the problems and issues for which it departs from the fixed rules of the traditional approach, the Restatement (Second) provides for the application of the law of the place which has the "most significant relationship" to the parties and the particular issue. The Restatement Second provides general principles and enumerates specific contacts to aid in the determination of the place of the most significant relationship. The coming Restatement (Third) also provides rules in order to apply the "most appropriate law," with the latter also presenting its default rule.

Multiparty Multiforum Federal Jurisdiction Act To facilitate the exercise of federal jurisdiction in cases where many claims arise from the same accident, the Act (28 U.S.C. § 1369) provides for federal jurisdiction on the basis of "minimal diversity": when the accident resulted in the death of at least 75 persons, there need be diversity only with respect to one party on each side. The "minimal diversity" provision makes it more difficult to prevent removal to federal court by adding non-diverse parties.

N

Neoterritorialism This term is sometimes used to describe approaches and suggestions that seek a return to fixed, territorially-based rules of choice of law.

O

"On the Merits" In order to be entitled to preclusive effect in another state under the Full Faith and Credit Clause of the Constitution, a state's (otherwise valid) judgment must have been "on the merits." For instance, a dismissal on statute-of-limitations grounds is not "on the merits" and does not bar litigation in another state if the first state only closed the doors of its courts (procedural characterization) but did not intend to affect the claim (substantive characterization). See also the discussion of *Semtek.*

Outcome-Determinative Test An issue has to be "substantive" (rather than "procedural") for purposes of the "*Erie* Doctrine" (see that entry). To be substantive, it has to be "outcome determinative." If it is, the federal court sitting in diversity must apply the law of the forum state unless there is an applicable federal law, an applicable Federal Rule of Civil Procedure, or unless federal lawmaking authority combined with a federal interest permits the creation of federal common law. Note that the Federal Rules of Procedure must be valid under the Rules Enabling Act. That Act bars the making of rules that would impair substantive rights. For discussion of the distinction, see the different views of the majority and dissent in *Shady Grove.*

P

Parental Kidnapping Prevention Act The Federal Parental Kidnapping Prevention Act of 1980 requires courts to give full faith and credit to custody decisions entered by courts which exercised jurisdiction in accordance with the Uniform Child Custody Jurisdiction Act or Uniform Child Custody Jurisdiction and Enforcement Act (for which see the respective entries). See also Hague Convention on the Civil Aspects of International Child Abduction.

Penal Law Exception A state will not enforce the penal laws of another state. For conflicts purposes, a law is "penal" when a penalty is awarded to the state as distinguished from the individual victim. A statute providing for punitive damages thus is not a penal law. The penal law defense does not apply when a claim has been reduced to a money judgment, which is now sought to be recognized and enforced in the forum state.

Personal Jurisdiction The forum must have personal jurisdiction over the defendant in order to affect his or her personal rights and obligations. A judgment entered without valid personal jurisdiction is subject to collateral attack, on due process grounds, where rendered, and is not entitled to recognition under the Full Faith and Credit Clause in other states. A state may have "general" jurisdiction over the defendant (i.e., all issues), or the defendant may be subject to "specific" jurisdiction on a particular issue on the basis of "minimum contacts." A person's interest in property (title) can be affected without personal jurisdiction. However, the conclusive adjudication of underlying *claims* to title to the property does require personal jurisdiction. See also "Jurisdiction" and further references there.

Preclusion See "Res Judicata."

Privileges and Immunities The Privileges and Immunities Clause of the Constitution has rarely been invoked to limit a state's denial, under its law, of benefits to non-residents that are available to residents. The Supreme Court has held that the Privileges and Immunities Clause encompasses only "essential" activities and "basic" rights.

Pseudo-Foreign Corporation Statutes Some states (e.g., California and New York), by legislation, undertake to regulate foreign corporations which derive a specified high percentage of their income from the state or when a stated high percentage of the stock of such corporations is owned by residents of the forum but whose stock is not traded on national exchanges. Because of the close connection to the forum, the corporation is regarded to be a "pseudo-foreign corporation." The continued validity of some aspects of pseudo-foreign corporation legislation is in doubt. See the text.

Public Policy Exception The forum will not enforce a foreign law which violates its local public policy. This exception is extremely limited and does not encompass, for instance, mere differences between the law of the forum and that of the other state. The public policy exception does not apply (in interstate cases and litigation) when a claim has been reduced to a money judgment which is now sought to be recognized and enforced in the forum state. *Fauntleroy.*

R

Renvoi When the choice-of-law rules of the forum refer to the "whole" law of another state, and not only to its "internal" law, such a reference would then also include the choice-of-law rules of the other state. These could refer the forum court back to its own law (remission) or to the law of a third state (transmission). The forum court must decide whether to "accept" or to "reject" these references ("renvoi") contained in the other state's conflicts law. American courts ordinarily do not consider the conflicts law of another state. However, the Uniform Commercial Code contains several references to the "whole" law of the state to which reference is made, and the Restatement (Second) advocates a limited use of renvoi. If the conflicts law of another state should refer back to the forum state, this circumstance may aid the forum court in determining whether a "false conflict" exists (see that entry). The coming Restatement (Third)'s proposal is even more limited: another state's conflicts law should only be considered if both the forum and that state wish to have the same law applied to the issue. This really restricts *renvoi* to a few transmission situations. Excluding remission may prevent a determination that a "false conflict" is involved (see that entry).

Res Judicata (Claim Preclusion) See also Bar, Merger. Literally, "res judicata" means "a thing adjudicated," or settled by judgment. A final judgment on the merits by a court of competent jurisdiction precludes any subsequent action by the parties that involves the same cause of action or claim; the cause of action is "res judicata." Res judicata expresses the policy that for the sake of the parties, there be an end to litigation; that judicial time and resources should not be wasted by continuing litigation; and that the possibility of inconsistent judgments be minimized.

Res Judicata (Issue Preclusion) A party who participated in earlier litigation and had the opportunity to be heard on an issue will be precluded to litigate or relitigate the issue in a different subsequent case ("collateral estoppel").

Residence is different from domicile (see that entry), although statutory references to "residence" have sometimes been interpreted to mean "domicile." For purposes of divorce jurisdiction, state law may require in-state residence for a specified period in addition to the petitioner's domicile or may use a durational residence requirement for the purpose of proving the establishment of domicile.

Respect for Marriage Act In late 2022, Congress passed the Respect for Marriage Act which, as 28 U.S. Code § 1738C, repeals and replaces the previous § 1738C (DOMA)—for which see above, assuring full faith and credit to marriages that are valid under the law of the State of celebration and protecting them against discrimination on the basis of race, sex, ethnicity, and national origin. Thus, same-sex marriages will now be protected by federal statutory law if valid under the law where concluded. Bigamy and contiguity as grounds for denial of recognition are not mentioned: they would no doubt be against the public policy of the forum. However, an amendment to § 7 of U.S. Code title 1 provides that, "for purposes of Federal law," the validity of a marriage is determined by the law of the State of celebration, hence also the validity of a marriage that could not have been entered into in the recognizing State under its laws of consanguinity. As to foreign-country marriages, § 7(c) provides that "only the law of the jurisdiction applicable at the time the marriage was entered into may be considered," i.e. it is a choice-of-law provision.

Restatement (Second) of Conflict of Laws The First Restatement provided fixed, territorially-focused choice-of-law rules. The Restatement (Second) retains some of these rules, for instance with respect to immovable property, but for other areas of law, or for particular issues, provides for the application of law of the state of the "most significant relationship" (see that entry) with respect to the parties and the issue.

Restatement (Third) of Conflict of Laws Work is under way for the American Law Institute to promulgate a new Restatement. Like its predecessor, it will present a number of definite rules, provide a methodology (in some respects similar to its predecessor) for choice of law in tort and contract, redefine domicile in objective terms, abandon the distinction between real and personal property in succession, and maintain—indeed, reinforce—the issue-by-issue approach. Many provisions have already been approved by the ALI's Membership but it is still unclear when everything will be complete and the new Restatement will be promulgated. Consideration of it, adoption of it, or departure from it for other solutions by the appellate and highest courts of the states will of course become known only over a course of many years.

Revenue Rule See Tax-Law Exemption.

Revival of Judgments A judgment that is not properly executed within a period of time set out by statute becomes dormant. A dormant judgment must be revived before it can be enforced or executed. Revival is governed by statute in most jurisdictions and usually requires that the judgment be final, for a definite sum, and unsatisfied. A revival action must be brought before the expiration of the limitations period set out in the revival statute. According to the Restatement (Second), revival creates a new judgment which is entitled to full faith and credit.

Rules Enabling Act The Federal Rules of Civil Procedure and the Federal Rules of Evidence are promulgated pursuant to authority conferred by the Rules Enabling Act. It, in turn, is based on the congressional power to establish federal courts and, under the

Necessary and Proper Clause of the Constitution, to regulate the procedure to be followed in these courts.

Rules of Decision Act This federal statute provides that the federal courts, when sitting in diversity, shall apply the "law" of the state in which they sit. Following the *Erie* decision, the term "law" encompasses both state statutory and decisional law. Following *Klaxon*, state law also includes the state's conflicts law.

S

Same-Sex Marriage The *Obergefell* decision of the United States Supreme Court declared DOMA (see that entry) to be unconstitutional. Under that statute, states were free not to recognize same-sex marriage. Today, same-sex marriage is valid throughout the United States, and states must recognize such a marriage when validly entered in a sister state. See the entry, above, on **Respect for Marriage Act**.

Scope To determine whether another state's law is applicable (and perhaps inconsistent with forum law), the coming Restatement (Third) envisions a two-step approach. First, the "scope" of the other state's law must be determined. Second, if that law is found to be applicable, it must then be decided which law is to be given priority. The foregoing very much resembles current methodology, which asks whether there is a true or false conflict. The Restatement (Third) perhaps goes further, inasmuch as the forum is to determine the applicability of the other state's law not only by what that law provides, but also by what the other state's policies are that underlie its law. Of course, this can be guesswork, and might also be influenced by the result that one wants to achieve.

***Seider* Action** The New York decision in *Seider v. Roth* established a direct action procedure whereby an injured resident plaintiff could sue the non-resident tortfeasor's insurance carrier (subject to local jurisdiction on the basis of doing business in the forum state) for the value of the insured tortfeasor's insurance coverage. This procedure is an indirect attempt to gain personal jurisdiction over the non-resident defendant and, since the Supreme Court's decision in *Rush v. Savchuk,* is now unconstitutional.

Situs Rule Traditionally, only the situs of property, particularly immovable property, had jurisdiction to entertain claims relating to that property. Additionally, situs law applied to the adjudication of these claims. The situs continues to have exclusive jurisdiction to quiet title. However, states with personal jurisdiction over the parties may adjudicate their rights, as between them, with respect to property located elsewhere. When appropriate under the circumstances, for instance in the context of a divorce and support settlement, such a non-situs court might also apply a law other than that of the situs. See also "Lex Situs." The coming Restatement (Third) provides for a decedent's estate to be viewed as a single unit rather than to distinguish between personal property (law of decedent's domicile at death applies to the will or in case of intestacy) and real property (situs law). Abandoning the scission is to be welcomed; whether the courts will accept the new approach the future will show.

Sovereign Immunity The doctrine of sovereign immunity precludes any suit against the United States, an individual state, or their officers for claims arising from governmental activities. Governments can waive sovereign immunity by statute and consent to suit, as the federal government has done for tort cases through the Federal Tort Claims Act. The Federal Foreign Sovereign Immunities Act provides under what circumstances and for what claims United States courts may assert jurisdiction over foreign countries or entities owned or controlled by them (see that entry).

Specific Jurisdiction When a court lacks general jurisdiction over the defendant, it may exercise specific jurisdiction, for particular issues, on the basis of minimum contacts that the defendant has brought about between himself and the forum state. The claim that the court may hear on the basis of specific jurisdiction must arise out of, or be sufficiently related to, the defendant's particular contact(s) with the forum state (see *J. McIntyre*). For discussion of "relatedness," see *Ford v. Montana*.

Speech Act provides for the non-recognition of foreign country judgments in defamation cases when the law or procedures underlying such a judgment do not comport with American First Amendment standards, unless the claim would have resulted in the same outcome in this country. Note that the Uniform Foreign-Country Money Judgments Recognition Act of 2005, as well as its 1962 predecessor, is broader: they also envision non-recognition of a foreign country judgment if the foreign country's law or the procedure employed in the particular case are inconsistent with American public policy or constitutional guarantees.

Stream-of-Commerce Jurisdiction Courts held in earlier decisions that a defendant is subject to specific jurisdiction in the forum state when it placed a product into the stream of commerce, that product reached the forum state through ordinary commercial channels (which was foreseeable for the defendant), and the product then caused injury in the forum state. Exercise of this type of specific jurisdiction was drawn into question by the decision in *Asahi* and again rejected by the plurality in *J. McIntyre*. The most recent U.S. Supreme Court decision in *Ford v. Montana* permitted the exercise of jurisdiction on the basis of the relatedness of the claim to the defendant's activities in the forum, even though the particular product had not been introduced into the latter by the defendant. What constitutes required "relatedness" is an evaluation of facts and circumstances. To the extent that (forum) state interest is an important factor, the domicile of the plaintiff may also play an important role (see *Hague v. Allstate* and *Ford*).

Subject-Matter Jurisdiction The court's power to hear and decide particular categories of cases. Both constitutional provisions and statutes govern the types of cases a court can hear. For example, federal courts derive their authority to hear cases from Article III of the Constitution and Title 28 of the United States Code, as well as other statutory enactments.

Substance vs. Procedure When the forum's choice-of-law rule refers it to the law of another state, the forum will only apply foreign substantive law; it will use its own procedure. The forum court therefore "characterizes" an issue or a rule of law as being "substantive" or "procedural." Federal courts also undertake a substance/procedure characterization "for *Erie* purposes." See also "Characterization" and "Outcome Determinative Test." Note that "characterization" for *Erie* purposes is not the same as that for choice of law. See the discussion of *Shady Grove*.

T

Tax-Law Exception Traditionally, states did not enforce the revenue laws of another state. However, many states now do entertain tax claims brought by other states, and more than half of the states have reciprocal legislation. Moreover, the tax law exception does not apply when the foreign tax claim has been reduced to a money judgment whose recognition and enforcement is now sought in the forum state.

Territorialism The traditional approach to choice of law, as represented by the First Restatement, was territorially oriented. On the basis of a pre-determined connecting factor (such as the place of the injury in tort or the place where the contract was made), the case was localized in a state, and the forum court would then apply the law of that state. Modern approaches are less territorially focused and instead make the choice-of-law determination on the basis of other or additional considerations, such as underlying legal and social policies.

Tolling Statutes A tolling statute interrupts ("tolls") the running of a statute of limitations, for instance when the defendant cannot be served with process in the forum state.

Transfer See Federal Transfer.

Transient Jurisdiction As a matter of traditional jurisdiction theory, a court obtained personal jurisdiction over a nonresident defendant when the defendant was served with process while in the forum state, even if there only temporarily or in transit. Despite criticism of this rule (because it is inconsistent with the minimum contacts requirement for specific jurisdiction, let alone the "at home" standard for general jurisdiction (see entries), the U.S. Supreme court confirmed its continued validity in *Burnham*.

True Conflicts Under Currie's approach to interest analysis, the forum court must apply forum law to a case presenting a true conflict. Other approaches to interest analysis will weigh the interests of competing states. See also "Comparative Impairment," "False Conflicts," "Interest Analysis."

U

U.N. (Vienna) Convention on Contracts for the International Sale of Goods (CISG) See "International Sales."

UNIDROIT Principles The International Institute for the Unification of Private Law (UNIDROIT) in Rome, Italy, has established "Principles of International Contracts," drawn from national laws and designed to provide some uniform rules. When a legal system permits parties to stipulate the applicable law, the question may arise whether this freedom extends to the choice of non-state-based law, such as the Unidroit Principles or the lex mercatoria.

Uniform Certification of Questions of Law Act Under this Act, questions regarding a state's law on a particular issue may be certified to the Supreme Court of that state by a federal court or another state court.

Uniform Child Custody Jurisdiction Act (UCCJA) See also Parental Kidnapping Prevention Act (or its successor, Uniform Child Custody Jurisdiction and Enforcement Act (UCCJEA), see next entry). This act, now largely replaced by the UCCJEA, set out a standard by which a state court determines whether it has jurisdiction to decide a particular child custody matter. It also required the recognition of child custody decrees issued by other states' courts if jurisdiction was proper under the Act's standard. Its scope and effect were reinforced by the passage of the Parental Kidnapping Prevention Act by Congress in 1980. The PKPA sets forth standards for the recognition of decrees of other states and the exercise of jurisdiction to modify them.

Uniform Child Custody Jurisdiction and Enforcement Act (UCCJEA) Successor to the UCCJA (previous entry), in force in all states except Massachusetts (where it was introduced in 2025) and in Puerto Rico. An important difference to the UCCJA: the original home state retains exclusive jurisdiction for purposes of modification, i.e., it is not automatically replaced by a subsequent home state. It may lose its jurisdiction in very limited circumstances and may declare itself to be an inconvenient forum, e.g., when the child has moved away. See also the Federal Parental Kidnapping Act and the Hague Convention on the Civil Aspects of International Child Abduction.

Uniform Conflict of Laws-Limitations Act Traditionally, statutes of limitations have been considered to be "procedural," so that the forum's statute applied even if the claim itself was based on another state's law. This led to forum shopping and the enactment of borrowing statutes, which are confusing and difficult to apply. The Uniform Act provides that if a claim is substantively based on the law of another state or states, the limitations period of that state (or one of the states) applies. Note that the 1988 revision of § 142 of the Restatement (Second) also makes inroads on the traditional procedural characterization. So far the Act has been adopted only by Minnesota and Washington while some states have adopted their own rules.

Uniform Foreign-Country Money Judgments Recognition Act The Act closely resembles the interstate recognition act, except that public policy objections to the foreign country judgment (including due process concerns) may lead to a denial of recognition, when this would not be the case interstate (see *Fauntleroy*). See "Public Policy." The Act has been adopted by thirty states. Ten others and Puerto still follow the prior Act, while ren states have neither.

Uniform Interstate Family Support Act (UIFSA) Successor to Uniform Reciprocal Enforcement of Support Act (URESA) and now in force in all states. The Act provides a procedure by which alimony or child support decrees of one state can be enforced (or established in the first place) against a former spouse residing in another state. The claimant files a petition with the courts of his or her state of residence, which forward the petition for enforcement by the courts of the state where the former spouse resides. In child support the original court, with exceptions, retains continuing exclusive jurisdiction, also for modification. Awards benefit from the Federal Full Faith and Credit for Child Support Orders Act, further implementing the Full Faith and Credit Clause. In the case of spousal support, the enforcing state may undertake a review of the level of support on the basis of its standards.

Uniform Reciprocal Enforcement of Support Act (URESA) Predecessor to UIFSA (previous entry). On its basis, several states concluded reciprocal agreements with foreign countries.

Uniformity Uniformity of decision was long a principal policy goal in choice of law. The circumstance that the plaintiff brings suit in one state rather than in another should not affect the outcome of the case; the plaintiff should not be able to "forum shop." The First Restatement sought to advance this policy goal by providing fixed, pre-determined choice-of-law rules. Outside of international sales (see entry), modern approaches also favor uniformity but do not make it the dominant goal. Instead, courts may also take into account the policies of the forum and of other states, the needs of the interstate system, as well as other factors (e.g., consumer protection, unfairness).

V

Vienna Convention on Contracts for the International Sale of Goods See "International Sales."

W

Warsaw Convention The Convention on International Air Transport (Warsaw Convention) of 1933 (with subsequent modification) alleviates the complexity of potential litigation in multiple fora with differing choice-of-law rules and damage limitations. It thus limits the available places of suit and limits the maximum amount of damages recoverable for personal injury or death (the latter provisions have been subsequently amended). It does not cover all questions comprehensively. Examples of question not addressed include the definition of willful misconduct (which removes the damage limitation), the availability of contributory negligence as a defense, and the tolling of the statute of limitations. As a federal treaty, the Convention displaces state tort law in cases to which it applies.

Appendix C

Sample Examination Questions

Note: The sample exam questions are of various length. Three of them are too long and complex for in-class examinations; they are better suited for take-home examinations (perhaps with a page limitation). These questions are so identified below. The other questions have been used for in-class exams, with time limitations of up to 45 minutes.

I.

H and W, were married in a private ceremony in France some years ago, a ceremony conducted by themselves and attended by friends and family, including a law school friend of W's, who is now a French judge. All present signed the document W had prepared, declaring them to be married. H and W then returned to their home in New York and lived there for three years, after which happiness declined. In 2018, W had enough and, on short notice, flew to Haiti and there filed for divorce. A notice and date for an appearance was sent to H in New York by overnight FedEx: he signed a receipt and e-mailed W a message, saying "go ahead and bother me no more." W thereupon obtained a divorce and returned to New York.

H soon moved to California and there married Mary, also adopting Mary's two children from her prior marriage to X, now deceased. They lived in California and H, a physician, earned a considerable amount of money. In fact, he had already done quite well in New York. Part of his and W's money was used to purchase the couple's primary residence in California, some was placed in a certificate of deposit with a California bank, and some was used to purchase a second home in Scottsdale, Arizona. The rest was used as a 30% down payment on an apartment building in Pennsylvania, which appreciated in value and created additional income for the couple in the form of rent payments. Last year, the couple moved to Missouri, where the H died intestate a few months later. Both W and Mary claim to be H's surviving spouse. Who is it? Who gets what? What are the issues, and their probable resolutions?

II.

(Comprehensive Take-Home Exam Question)

Amy had lived in Florida for many years until she decided to move to Georgia in early 2023. she bought a house in Atlanta, registered to vote in DeKalb County and opened an office of her company Conflicts Solutions, Inc., incorporated in Delaware and operating since 2020 in Jacksonville, Florida. Amy maintains the Florida facility (as sole owner) as well as her house there, which is looked after periodically by a friend and which she occasionally rents out through Airbnb.

Earlier, in 2019, Jacques, a French citizen with homes in both Paris and Miami, had concluded a contract with Amy in Paris during one of her visits to France. The contract called for performance in France and required Jacques to give her an advance of 5,000 Euro, which he did. When she failed to perform, Jacques, currently living in his Miami place, decided to sue her for breach of contract in Florida. He sought return of the advance as well as damages for lost profits which he calculated at 65,000 Euro. In November 2021, Jacques filed suit in federal court in Miami, naming both Amy and Conflicts Solutions as defendants, serving Amy by registered mail sent to the Jacksonville address and there received by a 2-day Airbnb guest who told Amy about it. Amy did nothing. The secretary of Conflicts Solutions received the service on the company at its Florida office, but only a day before the hearing because of a delay in delivery by FedEx. Conflicts solution hurriedly filed a motion for an extension to file its objections to jurisdiction, but the motion was denied.

At the same time, Jacques also filed suit in Paris. Amy, who was in Paris at the time, received all necessary notices and papers. She appeared and, first of all, contested jurisdiction. The court rejected the defense, affirmed its jurisdiction on the basis of Jacques' citizenship and, after Amy had left in a huff, entered a default judgment against her, but only for the return of the EUR 5,000 advance.

Jacques now seeks to enforce the Paris judgment against her Georgian bank accounts (she has one in her name and another one jointly with Conflicts Solutions). In the meantime the Florida federal court had entered a default judgment against her and Conflicts Solutions last month which Jacques will now undoubtedly also seek to enforce, either in Florida or Georgia. A troubled Amy consults you and you are trying to sort things out: what are the issues? (please **outline** them). Their possible or probable solution?

III.

Federal Rule of Civil Procedure 6(a)(3), on computing time, provides to include the last day [of the filing period] in the computation unless that day is a legal holiday. "[W]hen [the] last day is excluded, the period runs until the next day . . ."

Rule 6(a)(4)(A): "Legal Holiday Defined," lists among other federal holidays, ". . . Columbus Day . . ." [Columbus Day is the second Monday in October.]

Assume that the last day of Hawaii's statute of limitation on plaintiff's contract claim fell on Columbus Day 2025. Hawaii does not observe Columbus Day as a legal holiday (i.e., its courts were open), but federal courts were closed: may plaintiff still bring his/her claim in federal court on Tuesday (assuming that there is proper diversity jurisdiction otherwise)?

Variation

The last day for filing a motion in federal court in Puerto Rico was January 11. That day was a legal holiday in Puerto Rico honoring Eugenio Maria de Hostos. The day is not a federal holiday and the federal district court's office was open. Would the motion be timely or late if filed in the federal court on January 12?

Another Variation

The suit is one in tort and is against the United States as the defendant. 28 U.S.C.A. § 1346(b) [Federal Tort Claims Act—FTCA] provides that federal district courts shall have exclusive jurisdiction over civil claims against the United States for money damages for injuries or losses caused by federal employees ". . . under circumstances where the

United States, if a private person, would be liable to the claimant in accordance with the law of the place where the act or omission occurred." The U.S. Supreme Court held in *Richards v. United States*, 369 U.S. 1 (1962), that the last phrase is to be taken as a reference the substantive and conflicts law of the state where the act or omission occurred.

28 USC § 2401(b) sets time limits on suits against the United States: a claim must have been submitted to the potentially responsible agency for review within two years from accrual (occurrence) and suit must be brought within 6 months from the mailing (by registered or certified mail) of the final denial of the claim.

Again, as above, suit is filed in federal court on the Tuesday after Columbus Day: Timely?

IV.

(Comprehensive Take-Home Type Exam Question)

Youth Campers, Inc., which is a charitable organization chartered in A, leases campgrounds in C, a beautiful state on the Northeastern seaboard. It sponsors a series of 2–3 week-long camp programs there. It advertises in and accepts applications from most Eastern and Midwestern states. Application forms are sent from, and are to be returned to A, and both the initial deposit and final payment are payable there. Campers from states other than A, however, need not travel there but are picked up in their home states.

On Camptrip #101-A, Youth Campers, Inc. gathered campers in A, and again in B, a state through which its buses pass to reach C. In B, Caterers, Inc., a local company, delivered spoiled food to Youth Campers. Through the negligence of Youth Camper's personnel, the food's condition went undetected, and it was served to all members of the group while they were in B. When reaching C, many had become very ill and had to be hospitalized. One A and one B resident died. Personnel resident in the community in C where the camp is located also experienced food poisoning after consuming some of the leftover food.

Under the law of C, a charitable organization has absolute immunity. Under the law of B, charitable immunity does not shield an organization which has been grossly negligent, while A law provides no immunity at all. A, B, and C law also differ with respect to the standard of care and to the issue whether punitive damages may be awarded.

Where and against whom should suit be filed on behalf of those who were injured or died, and what law should the court(s) apply?

V.

(Comprehensive Take-Home Type of Exam Question)

Willem is a member of the Netherlands national soccer team; he has been regarded as perhaps the most outstanding Dutch soccer player, and all-around athlete, in a decade or more. He suffered a severe knee injury while competing in a fierce match with a leading English club in Soccershire, England. The match was attended by Dr. Genoux, a French-Canadian permanent U.S. resident, whose principal medical practice is in Bloomington, Indiana, but who is also a member of orthopedic specialty clinics in New York City and Los Angeles. Dr. Genoux is a board-certified orthopedic surgeon, who specializes in sports medicine and widely disseminates information about his services, honors and recognition received, and his extensive surgical experience. He regularly lectures in England, advises the Soccershire club, and attends most of its games. He was in attendance when Willem was injured and gave first aid. He advised major knee surgery. Willem underwent such surgery in Indiana in late 2020 and returned to England for rehabilitation treatment. Six months later, it was clear that he was not improving. Dr. Genoux, on a visit to England, examined him and continued to express confidence; he advised adding Dr. Rodilla of New

York as a consultant. Willem saw Dr. Rodilla in New York and underwent some further treatment there. In late 2023, a desperate Willem sought yet another opinion and was told by a renowned New York specialist that the original operation was improperly done, that subsequent treatment had made his condition worse, and that, at this point, nothing further could be done to save Willem's knee. His career is over. Willem now wants to sue to recover his considerable expenses, damages for pain and suffering, and—especially—for the loss of his very substantial earning potential as an athlete. Soccershire Club, which advanced part of the expenses and also had continued to provide compensation to Willem, wants to be reimbursed for the moneys it has spent. Please advise both Willem and the Club where they should sue, obviously assessing—in so doing—their chances of recovery and collection.

Background information on points of law:

England: You may assume that English courts have jurisdiction over Dr. Genoux both under English law and for purposes of recognition of any judgment in the United States. Time limitations: three years from the injury or discovery. The time limitation of the applicable substantive law applies, but may be disregarded for reasons of public policy, including undue hardship.

California: There is no Medical Malpractice Compensation Fund in California (for which see "Indiana," below), but damages for non-economic injuries are capped at $500,000, but not otherwise. Attorneys' fees are capped, on a sliding scale (small to large recoveries) at 25–33%. Claims must be brought within one year from discovery of the injury or three years from the injury.

Indiana: The state has a Medical Malpractice Compensation Fund to which qualified medical providers contribute (Dr. Genoux does). The Fund will reimburse up to $1.3 million in damages for malpractice claims, the liability of the individual provider for compensatory damages beyond this is limited to another $500,000. Claims must first be submitted to a medical panel which issues non-binding opinions; they are admissible in evidence in any subsequent litigation (which, however, is subject to the cap for compensatory damages). Attorneys' fees are capped at 32%. Time limitation: two years from the alleged act or omission; some case law supports a "doctrine of continuing wrong" and would apply the limitation from the last act of wrongdoing, the same of course in the case of concealment.

New York: There is no Compensation Fund; recoveries are not capped, but attorneys' fees are limited to 30–10% on a sliding scale (small to large recovery). Time limits: 2½ years from the act or omission or from the end of continuous treatment.

VI.

Adam in State X owned and farmed land bordering on State Y. A little stream flowed from Y through Adam's property, helping with irrigation and sometimes providing some most welcome fish.

In Y, quite near to the state line, Bernardine family operated a small fertilizer factory. It emitted rather foul vapors, often carrying chemical particles. Because of the factory's location, most of the vapors and settling particles blew over and/or settled on Adam's land. He claims that both vapors and particles are toxic, requiring him to keep animals away from the area, preventing him from to use the land either for grazing or for planting, and that dead fish at times are floating in the little stream. The Bernardines live quite far away, are not bothered by any of the foregoing, and dispute all of Adam's complaints on the few occasions that they speak. In fact, last month when Bernardine visited Adam at the latter's request, their disagreement got so heated that Bernardine struck Adam and then stormed out of Adam's house.

Because of all this, Adam wants to sue the Bernardines. He wants damages for his injuries and lost work time, damages for the interference with and use of his land, and a permanent injunction against such future interference.

Under Y law, emissions of chemical vapors reaching another's land constitute only a tort of nuisance. A resulting "lack of enjoyment" may be compensated with damages for the emotional hurt, but not exceeding $ 2,000.—Under X law, such emissions can constitute trespass and damages may be awarded for all present and future losses of use and enjoyment, and injunctions may issue, with punitive damages for their violation.—Adam consults you: where can/should he sue?

VII.

The Adams Company is a Delaware Corporation, with principal place of business in New York.

It specializes in the manufacture of medical implant devices, all of which it sells through its wholly owned distributor, the Beta Company of New Jersey, incorporated in that state. The implant devices are widely known, in part as a result of vigorous advertising by both Adams and Beta in all national media, in part also because of very favorable published medical evaluations. The implants are widely used and both companies maintain offices or contact persons in most states.

One of the implant devices that Adams Co. makes and sells includes a mesh, cut to a specific shape. The mesh is woven from filaments of polypropylene and other non-biological substances. The mesh, as part of the device, will be permanently implanted in the human body through surgery. This mesh is made by Cee, LLC, in Georgia, from materials supplied to it by Adams.

An Adams thigh and pelvic implant caused severe injury to an Indiana resident patient when it failed within days after the surgery was performed in Atlanta. After further surgery and months of (mainly ineffective) rehabilitation, the patient is now moving to Georgia. She now wishes to sue Adams, Beta, and Cee for damages and wishes to do so in Georgia.

Litigation in the courts below has been contradictory on jurisdictional issues. The Chief Justice of the United States Supreme Court has now assigned you the task to draft a comprehensive majority opinion for the Court.

SUGGESTED ANSWERS TO SAMPLE EXAMINATION QUESTIONS

I.

To whom was H married when he died? First, what about his marriage to W in France? If valid there, it would be recognized in the United States (and probably elsewhere). But most countries require observance of a formal (civil) procedure. (In the United States, a member of the clergy can perform a civil and a religious ceremony in one.) Very few jurisdictions allow a private ceremony, i.e., without an officiant who is appointed or licensed for this purpose. France does not allow a private marriage (also known as self-solemnization or self-uniting). That a judge was present is irrelevant; nothing "official" took place. H and W's subsequent life in New York, holding themselves out as married, also has no legal effect because New York is one of the many states that do not provide for "common law marriage." Haiti, in granting W a divorce, seems to have recognized the attempted French marriage. H, however, is not bound by that. He did not appear/

participate in the Haitian proceeding (his message was directed to W, not the court), and, in light of *Williams II*, Haiti may not have had *ex parte* divorce jurisdiction since W was not domiciled there. Without a valid French marriage, there was nothing to dissolve in Haiti. Even if the Haitian court seemingly accepted the French "marriage," it did divorce W, and she is now estopped from challenging that. W is not the surviving wife of H; Mary is.

New York, where H and W lived (and can be presumed to have been domiciled since no moving plans are indicated), is a common law property state. The assets of each of the parties acquired there were their own separate property. It remained as such when H moved to California, a community property state. Assets acquired in California by H, now his domicile, after he married W, are community property and remain as such (see below). Assets acquired with a mixture of separate and community property—commingled funds—are presumed to be community property. Evidence of the separate nature of an identifiable portion of a commingled asset can rebut this presumption (tracing).

In cases of intestacy, succession to personal property is governed by the law of the decedent's domicile at death, real property by the law of its situs. When H died intestate in Missouri, he was presumably domiciled there (the "couple [had] moved [there]"). H's intestate estate will consist of whatever separate property he owned at the time of his death, as well as his one-half interest in the community property.

In purchasing various assets during his lifetime, H used commingled funds. Tracing is not addressed in the facts, so community property is presumed. California and Arizona situs law applies to the real property in those states. Both are community property states: Mary obtained a one-half interest in the real property at the time it was acquired. [Since not addressed in the facts, it is assumed that the California residence had not yet been sold when the couple moved to Missouri.] Whatever part/percentage of these properties the evidence can establish he acquired with separate funds (brought with him from New York) does not go to Mary as part of her share of the community but becomes part of his intestate estate and will be distributed by California and Arizona succession law (as the situs of that property).

The certificate of deposit account is a contract, which might name a beneficiary to whom the account is payable upon the death of the account holder(s). If H and Mary were joint account holders, then the account would become Mary's at the time of H's death.

The facts are silent about any beneficiary designation or joint account holder. Presuming community property, one-half of the account belongs to Mary and H's half becomes part of the intestate estate, as part of H's share of the community. The move to Missouri (a common law property state) did not change the character of the certificate of deposit.

Mary's interest in the apartment house in Pennsylvania is less clear. The facts are silent as to how title to the house was held. The situs is a common law property state: if titled in H's name alone, separate property might be presumed. However, this is not the end of the inquiry. Again, it is important to determine whether H used separate or community assets to acquire the apartment house, since the nature of assets does not change (see *Rozan v. Rozan,* 317 P.2d 11 (Cal. 1957), and 25 Ariz. Rev. Stat. § 211). To the extent that community funds were used, Mary has a one-half interest. Any part of the interest acquired with separate funds becomes part of the intestate estate, and would pass according to the succession law at the situs of the real property.

To determine the separate or community character of appreciation in value, California (where H and Mary were domiciled at the time acquisition of the apartment house) looks to whether the appreciation was "active" (one or both of the spouses did something to cause the asset to appreciate) or "passive." Active appreciation is community property, without regard to the nature of the underlying asset. Passive appreciation retains the character of the underlying property. Here, the facts are silent as to participation in the apartment building undertaking, so passive appreciation is presumed. Appreciation on each interest described in the preceding paragraph would retain the separate or community character of the underlying interest.

The characterization of rents earned by the real property as separate or community property also follows from the character of the underlying interest. However, the same presumption about commingling applies: it must be possible to identify the underlying interest that gives rise to the income, or the presumption of community property will apply. And even if this is possible, the rents themselves must not be commingled once characterized, or the presumption of community property might again apply.

The intestate estate, with whatever it contains from the Pennsylvania apartment house interest and the halves of the California and Arizona real properties, will be distributed according to Pennsylvania, California, and Arizona (situs states) succession laws; any personal property, wherever located, will go by Missouri (domicile at death) succession law. Under both Pennsylvania and Arizona law, Mary will inherit one-half of H's intestate estate. 20 Pa. Stats. § 2102); 14 Ariz. Rev. Stats. § 2102(1). Under Missouri succession law, she will get the first $20,000 plus one half of the rest of the estate. Missouri Rev. Stats. § 474.010(1)(a). Under Pennsylvania law, she will get the first 30K, then one half of the rest. In all states, the children split the rest: adopted children inherit the same as biological children (see, for instance, Missouri Rev. Stats. § 453.090; § 453.190 also requires recognition of out-of-state adoptions).

Note that if part of H's estate in Arizona and Pennsylvania was acquired with community property funds, Mary's percentage of what she gets from all local assets may be higher in those states than in Missouri. This is so because Mary is entitled to her share of the community property in addition to her share of the intestate estate, which includes H's one-half interest in the community property. None of the states involved here has adopted the Uniform Disposition of Community Property at Death Act (see p. 130). What remains unclear is whether the couple had acquired a house in Missouri and, if so, with what funds. If a house had been acquired, succession would be the same as, or similar to, the Pennsylvania analysis.

II.

Personal jurisdiction

Over Amy

The parties dealt with each other in Paris. Their contract was made there and called for performance there. Amy's alleged breach therefore also occurred there. Jacques' claim thus did not arise from anything that Amy did or was to do in Florida, which might have supported *specific jurisdiction*. The question thus becomes: was she subject to *general jurisdiction* in Florida? This raises the question where she was domiciled at the time of suit.

She had lived in Florida for many years (without known intent to leave) and thus was domiciled there at least until "early 2020." Did she then change her domicile to Georgia? To change one's domicile, traditional law requires abandoning the previous domicile, arriving at the new, and intending to stay there, i.e., not having plans to leave. The first and third elements involve a person's intent, but how does one know that? Courts have usually deduced it from objective facts (see, e.g., *Estate of Dorrance*, 163 A. 303 (Pa. 1932)).

The Draft Restatement (Third) of Conflict of Laws will drop the intent element and focus on a person's "center of life," i.e., again evaluating objective facts.

In this case, Amy did retain her Florida house, and her company (Conflicts Solutions) may be said to have its principal place of business in Jacksonville. On the other hand, she has now acquired a house in Atlanta, in which she lives (while renting out the Florida one), has registered to vote in Georgia (thereby giving up her right to vote in Florida when exercising her Georgia registration), and has opened an office of her company in Georgia (thereby moving part of her involvement with it there). In objective terms, she now lives—has the center of her life—in Georgia. If this is so, Florida would no longer have general jurisdiction over here.

Assuming, for a moment, that there was jurisdiction in Florida, there is also the further question whether service was correct. Fed. R. Civ. P. 4(2)(B) permits handing service to someone residing at the defendant's "dwelling or usual place of abode." Rule 5(b)(2)(ii) provides more or less the same, and Rule 5(b)(2)(C) permits mailing "to the person's last known address." The Airbnb renter who received the certified letter perhaps satisfies Rule 4(e)(2)(B) as someone who "resided" there, albeit for only a brief period. Additionally, Rule 5 permits mailing and provides that it is effective upon dispatch. The latter is questionable when the document is the initial service. Furthermore, Rule 4 (e)(1) also permits service in accordance with state law. Florida state law is stricter than the provisions just discussed. However, if applicable, the Federal Rules would prevail (see *Hanna v. Plumer*).

Proposed Solution. It is indeed questionable whether there was general jurisdiction over Amy. Indeed, one should conclude that there was not. In addition, the way process was (attempted to be) served raises questions. The latter is irrelevant when there was no jurisdiction in the first place. And lack of jurisdiction of the rendering court is a defense when enforcement of a default judgment is sought. See below.

Over the company "Conflicts Solutions"

If the principal place of business was (and probably continues to be) in Florida, as suggested above, then Florida and Delaware, its place of incorporation, may exercise general jurisdiction over the company: Delaware because it created and maintains its corporate existence, Florida because the company is "at home" there, in the language of *Goodyear* and *Daimler*. Service may be effected by delivering it to an "officer" or other authorized agent of the company. Fed. R. Civ. P. 4(h)(1)(B). A question might be whether "the secretary of the company" was an office worker or a company official. However, this may not make a difference: whatever the person's capacity was, he or she was probably authorized to receive documents for the company.

Service initiates the exercise of jurisdiction and fulfills the important due process requirement of giving notice to the defendant in sufficient time for preparation. Due process does not require actual notice, but only that the party giving notice do so in a way that will "reasonably . . . accomplish" this goal. See *Mullane v. Central Hanover Bank & Trust Co.* The delay in Conflicts Solutions receiving notice was not occasioned by plaintiff but by a third party, who acted for the plaintiff, in a way as its agent. The provision in Fed. R. Civ. P. 5, that mailing is effective upon dispatch, was discounted earlier and should be here as well. The facts remain that plaintiff did what he could do, thereby perhaps satisfying *Mullane*, but that defendant received notice in insufficient time. For the latter reason, the court might (perhaps should) have granted the request for an extension. It declined to exercise its discretion. The defendant company sought no further relief, either by formulating its objections to jurisdiction, or by appealing the denial of its motion (perhaps on grounds of abuse of discretion). It apparently did nothing: having been in court, *Treinies* now prevents raising the issue collaterally. The default judgment should stand.

Jacques' Suit in Paris

Jurisdiction of French court over Amy

Jacques sued Amy on the basis of Code Civil art. 14 which gives a court jurisdiction on the basis of the plaintiff's French citizenship. Amy appeared and contested jurisdiction, but of course lost on this issue since the court's exercise of jurisdiction complied with French law. Appealing the denial (on what grounds?) would not have changed the result. However, a judgment based on *plaintiff's* relationship to the forum (here Jacques' citizenship) will not be recognized in the United States. See *Schibsby v. Westenholz* (for England). However, Amy had been physically present in Paris, had received notice and had appeared . . . and then walked away when her objections to jurisdictions failed. Had this happened in the United States, a court would have had jurisdiction—not on the ground of the plaintiff's citizenship, but on the ground of service on the defendant while present in the jurisdiction (see *Burnham v. Superior Court*) and her appearance. Hence, if the recognizing American court reviews a foreign court's jurisdiction by American due process standards, the result in this case should be recognition of proper exercise of jurisdiction by the French court on the basis of *Burnham* and her appearance, even though the French court invoked a different ground.

Substance of French Judgment

The French court rendered a default judgment when Amy left. As discussed, it had jurisdiction, the judgment therefore stands and cannot be challenged collaterally. See *Treinies* (by analogy). The French court, however, only entered a judgment for the advance Amy had failed to return, i.e., € 5,000. There is no information on whether the court rejected Jacques' claim for damages or did not consider it. If it did not consider it, then the judgment is res judicata only with respect to the € 5,000 because civil law countries do not regard issues that *could* have been litigated as res judicata but allow these to be litigated in further proceedings. More below.

Florida and French Judgments before the Georgia Court for Recognition

French Judgment and Uncompensated Claims

Georgia has adopted the Uniform Foreign-Country Money Judgments Recognition Act and will enforce a foreign money judgment that is valid in the country where rendered and does not offend the forum's public policy. See Georgia Code §§ 9–12–112 and 9–12–113. These conditions are fulfilled in this case—the French judgment is enforceable against Amy's own Georgia bank account. Amy's Georgia joint account with Conflicts Solutions may also be reached for her personal obligations. [It might also be considered—although a bit far-fetched—whether the company and Amy should be considered as one, given Amy's sole ownership and control of the company, i.e., disregarding Conflicts Solutions' corporate veil. In such a case, the joint account should be reachable in full. See further below.]

If Jacques should also sue in Georgia for the € 65,000 not mentioned in the French judgment (for instance, in case the Florida default judgment might/would not be recognized in Georgia for lack of jurisdiction), the first question is whether the issue is res judicata and relitigation therefore precluded. It would be res judicata, if the French court had rejected the claim and the rejection was not appealed. If, on the other hand, the issue was not addressed by the French court, it would not be res judicata under French law. Does the French or the Georgia definition of res judicata apply? On this question, the authorities are split. It is suggested here that a judgment, if recognized, should have the same effect as it has where rendered—that would mean here that the limited French res judicata effect leaves the other claim untouched. Jacques could bring it again. If he may and does, what law applies to the claim?

Under the traditional—Restatement (First)—view, it would be French law (place of making and intended performance of the contract). The law of the state of the "most significant relationship" under Restatement (Second) § 188 is probably also French law since all contacts are with France and no contract-law principles or policies speak in favor of a different law. The coming Restatement (Third), seeking the "most appropriate" law, would probably come to the same result. The only exception might be a state following Currie or the "more impairment" test, if Georgia law where to provide for damages for lost profits and French law did not (which we do not know). In such a "true conflict," forum law might apply. However, why should Georgia law apply (or be considered impaired if not applied) when the person who would go uncompensated is not a Georgia resident?

Florida Default Judgment

As mentioned earlier, the Florida default judgment against Amy should not be recognized (is not entitled to Full Faith and Credit) because the Florida court lacked jurisdiction. Since Amy, though notified, did not appear, *Treinies* does not apply.

It is different in the case of Conflicts Solutions. The Florida federal court did have diversity jurisdiction. In November 2021, the average exchange rate of Euro to Dollar was 1:1329. Jacques' claim (total of Euro 70,000) thus came to US $ 79,303 satisfying the jurisdictional amount criterion. However, a problem was that, while properly served and given some notice, circumstances beyond the control of the parties gave the defendant very little notice which might have supported its motion for an extension. By not following up on this issue, it is now precluded. The judgment should be recognized in Georgia.

Enforcement can be satisfied from Conflict Solutions' Georgia bank account (held jointly with Amy). If Conflicts Solutions' interest in the account is insufficient the question mentioned earlier arises again, viz. whether the company and Amy can be considered as one so that Conflicts Solutions' debts can be satisfied from assets shown or registered in either of their names.

<u>Florida Assets</u>

If the Georgia assets are insufficient to satisfy Jacques' enforcement of his French or Florida judgment for possibly obtaining an additional Georgia judgment, he can seek further relief from the parties' Florida assets. Property owned by Conflicts Solutions can be used to satisfy the Florida default judgment or the Georgia recognition of it (judgments do not merge). Amy's Florida house cannot be affected directly by the Georgia decree (i.e., Georgia cannot give Jacques title to it), but her personal obligation would have to be recognized and result in a Florida *in rem* decree against the house. See *Fall v. Eastin.*

III.

Basic Question

The question involves a problem addressed in *Hanna v. Plumer*, 380 U.S. 460, 85 S. Ct. 1136, 14 L. Ed.2d 8 (1965), p. 249, *supra*, and *Walker v. Armco Steel Corp.*, 446 U.S. 740, 100 S. Ct. 1978 (1980), p. 250, *supra*: the relationship between the Federal Rules and state law in a case in which the federal court sits in diversity. There does seems to be a "direct collision" between the Federal Rule and state law and practice (as the U.S. Supreme Court later explained in *Hanna*): if the Federal Rule applies, plaintiff can file; if state law applies, plaintiff can no longer file <u>and</u>, if state law is also applicable to the merits, *may* be precluded from suing elsewhere. [The last conclusion very much depends on a subsequent court's view of a statute of limitations as "substantive" or "procedural"—see, e.g., *Keeton v. Hustler Magazine, Inc.*, 465 U.S. 770, 104 S. Ct. 1473, 79 L. Ed.2d 790 (1984).]

Walker counsels that a "direct collision" should not be assumed just because the texts of federal and state law differ: for a Federal Rule to have the preemptive effect (as federal law under the Supremacy Clause), it must be applicable to (in the sense of: intended to cover) a case like the one at bar: this is essentially a "false conflict"-inquiry (for which see p. 204 *supra*): in *Walker*, the Federal Rule did not apply (probably *could not* apply because of *Guaranty Trust*, p. 215, *supra*), its intended scope of application was different from (therefore did not collide with, therefore represented a false conflict with respect to) state law.

The *Walker* Court, in fine-tuning *Hanna*, sought an accommodation between state and federal law (when in doubt, tilting to the former).

Applied to our hypothetical case this should mean that, true to *Walker* and that opinion's regard for a state's interest in its statutes of limitations and repose (and people's—albeit hypothetical—reliance on them):

The state limitation should apply and the federal action, filed on Tuesday, should be dismissed as time-barred.

Note: Whether plaintiff can bring another action elsewhere depends on the effect of the dismissal under *state* preclusion law as incorporated into federal law: *Semtek International Inc. v. Lockheed Martin Corp.,* 531 U.S. 497, 121 S. Ct. 1021, 149 L. Ed.2d 32 (2001).

Variation

Under *Erie*, a federal court generally must apply the substantive law of the state in which it sits, but it follows its own procedural rules, established under the Rules Enabling Act and a legitimate exercise of federal power so long as they do not abridge constitutionally protected rights. Whenever there is a "clash" between a state and a federal rule, the latter prevails. *Hanna*, above. In order to determine whether there is a clash, one looks at the underlying purpose of the particular rule. *Walker*, above.

Here, the purpose of the federal rule is to provide a schedule for the litigation of cases. It has nothing with establishing limitations on claims. Puerto Rican state holidays close public state offices, including courts. The holiday closing of a court may have an effect on the limitations of claims but holidays are not established for such purposes. Both—the federal rule and the closing of state courts on state holidays—have no substantive purpose. They have a procedural purpose (the federal rule) and a procedural effect (the state court closing). So, one should conclude that the federal rule, and with it, the federal deadline apply.

Another Variation

This case is much more difficult because the cause of action is a claim based on federal law (the Federal Tort Claims Act, FTCA), its adjudication moreover committed to the exclusive jurisdiction of the federal courts. Federal law, on the one hand, permits tort actions against the government (thus "creates them," in contrast to the common law's absolute immunity of the sovereign), also establishes time limits for the bringing of actions (28 U.S.C.A. § 2401(b), see facts), but—on the other hand—also specifically refers to state law, viz. the law of the place of occurrence, for the law applicable to liability. A first reaction that this is all federal law and therefore necessarily preempts state law thus must be double-checked against the FTCA's own reference to liability "in accordance with the law of the place where the act or omission occurred," the "law of that place" also to include that state's conflicts law (*Richards*, see facts).

Walker arose in and applied to litigation in diversity. Its resolution (bringing about an accommodation of the federal and state rules by focusing on their—different—purposes) advanced the "twin aims of *Erie*," viz. the avoidance of forum shopping and the equal administration of justice. Technically, *Walker* does not apply in federal question cases, but that does not mean that the policy goals of *Erie* (as distinguished from its "constitutional leg") are also not relevant.

In this case, the FTCA's reference to state law standards of liability is in fact a legislative decision in favor of an *Erie*-type (parallel) disposition of tort claims against the federal government even though it is federal law that makes the claim actionable. This would then mean, in *Walker*-like fashion, that a defendant should have the same freedom from liability ("repose") in federal court as s/he has in state court.

So far so good. Only: (a) federal law permits ("gives") the cause of action and also provides a limitation (here: an extra day): is the limitation "built-in"? If so, the federal limitation (and its extension) should apply, even though the content of the liability, if any, has been referred—by the same federal law—to state law, i.e. incorporates/adopts state-law standards for the case at bar.—(b) This case could not have been brought in state court in the first place (see the FTCA), so that state court (state law) limitations should be irrelevant. This case is not analogous to *Marrese v. American Academy of Ortho*. Surgeons, 470 U.S. 373, 105 S. Ct. 1327, 84 L. Ed.2d 274 (1985). In that case, the issue concerned the res judicata effect of a judgment on a later case, and the U.S. Supreme Court required the federal court to inquire into the res judicata effect under state law (although entirely hypothetical for lack of jurisdiction of state courts in the first place). However, difficult (or strange) *Marrese* may be, it arose in the full-faith-and-credit-to-judgments context. The present case involves choice of the applicable procedural law to an original action. While *Guaranty Trust* characterized limitations to be "substantive for *Erie* purposes," it did so for diversity cases to which both the constitutional and the policy concerns of *Erie* apply. The former do not apply in the present case, the latter do not favor state standards in the absence of state jurisdiction: there was nothing for plaintiff to rely on. In fact, if—as it might seem—the resolution turns on the assessment of policy concerns, "countervailing considerations" (to those in favor of the application of state law) here argue in favor of the application of the federal standard to insure uniform exposure to (and limitation of) liability of the federal government throughout the United States. For "countervailing considerations," see *Byrd v. Blue Ridge Rural Electric Cooperative, Inc.*, 356 U.S. 525, 78 S. Ct. 893, 2 L. Ed.2d 953 (1958). Cf. also *Clearfield Trust Co. v. United States*, 318 U.S. 363, 63 S. Ct. 573 (1943) (federal common law to assure uniform standards for federal government liability—not quite apposite here, because the FTCA expressly adopts state law standards for *substantive* liability). Result: the federal time limitation should prevail, i.e., filing on Tuesday was still timely.

IV.

Youth Campers is subject to jurisdiction in A, its home state. Under long arm statutes, asserting jurisdiction on the basis of the "commission of a tort" within the forum state, Youth Campers probably is also subject to jurisdiction in B and C since, for jurisdictional purposes, the "commission of a tort" may be defined alternatively to include the place where the negligent conduct took place and the place where its effects were felt (when the latter place was foreseeable, as it was here; in C jurisdiction can be based on the "relatedness" factor established by *Ford*). A has the most favorable law for a plaintiff with respect to the immunity issue. The plaintiffs will therefore attempt to get the benefit of that law by suing in A (whether A will in fact apply its own law, is another question which is addressed below). Youth Campers might suggest to the A court that it is an inconvenient forum to hear the claims of B and C residents who were injured in their respective states. See *Gulf Oil Corp. v. Gilbert*, 330 U.S. 501 (1947). To anticipate a *forum non conveniens* motion, B and C plaintiffs might invoke the diversity jurisdiction of the A federal court (assuming that the jurisdictional amount is met) since a § 1404 transfer from A to either B or C would require the transferee court to apply the same law that the transferor (A) would apply. *Van Dusen v. Barrack*, 376 U.S. 612 (1964).

Suit against Caterers can be brought in B where it does business (is "at home"). Assuming that C law is more favorable than B law with respect to the issue of punitive damages, plaintiffs suing Caterers might wish to do so in C. However, it is unclear whether C will have jurisdiction since Caterers its described as a "local" B company. Was it foreseeable for Caterers that its negligence in B might cause injury in C? And how does "foreseeability of injury" in C translate into "foreseeability of being haled into court in C," as required by *World-Wide Volkswagen* (U.S. 1980)? For "stream-of-commerce" jurisdiction, see *Asahi*. And there is hardly the substantial "relatedness" to C which supported specific jurisdiction in *Ford*.

The foreseeability and relatedness elements for specific jurisdiction are even much more difficult with respect to A, should jurisdiction over Caterers be sought to be exercised there. Youth Campers' buses were destined to C, not to A. Arguably, the "stream of commerce" does not flow "backwards."

Yet Youth Campers, should it be sued in A—as seems likely—, will have an interest in bringing Caterers in as a third party defendant in order to seek indemnification from Caterers for any liability it may be held to have incurred. If Caterers is not subject to jurisdiction in A (see *Asahi*, 480 U.S. 102 (1987) and above), this may strengthen Youth Campers' motion for transfer (if B and C plaintiffs sue in A federal court, as mentioned above) of some cases to a jurisdiction where Caterers is subject to jurisdiction. Note, however, that, as a prerequisite for transfer, the transferee court must have been able to entertain the case in the first place. As a result, Youth Campers will be able to bring in Caterers in B only with respect to C plaintiffs (A plaintiffs were not in federal court in A for lack of diversity, and Caterers cannot be brought in with respect to B plaintiffs, also for lack of diversity). Thus, for Youth Campers to bring in Caterers in B or C with respect to all plaintiffs presupposes that the original action was brought in A *state* court and there dismissed or stayed in favor of states B or C on *forum non conveniens* grounds. However, B and C plaintiffs of course control whether to sue Youth Campers initially in A state or federal court.

Even assuming that jurisdiction could be invoked in C or A, it would be a further question whether Caterers' connection with those states is sufficient to allow the application of forum law (discussed below).

A. Suit Against Youth Campers

1. In State A

If A continues to adhere to the First Restatement, it will apply the law of the place of the tort. In the case of negligent torts, this will ordinarily be the place where the injury was suffered (State C). *Alabama Great Southern Railroad Company* (Ala. 1892). Under the law of C, Youth Campers has immunity, and the A court should therefore dismiss the tort actions. The A court will perhaps avoid this result by characterizing immunity either as an issue separate from tort or as relating to procedure rather than substantive liability.

In the first case, the court might treat "immunity" as part of the law applicable to Youth Campers as an organization (regardless of whether the question arises in a tort, contract, or other context). Since Youth Campers is chartered in A, it is the law of that state which governs it as an organization (in application of, or in analogy to the "internal affairs" rule). Similarly, immunity may also be regarded as presenting a procedural issue (who may sue whom in the A forum?), to which A, and not C, law applies. In either case, A law applies: it does not provide immunity, the suit proceeds, and C substantive law will now apply with respect to liability (standard of care, etc.). Punitive damages may be considered as bound up with liability itself (so that C law would apply) or as going only to the remedy, as do damages generally, so that A law—procedural *characterization*—would apply: *Kilberg* (N.Y. 1961). Assuming that punitive damages are regarded as substantive (= C law), and in the absence of a statutory prohibition against the application of another law (see *Kilberg*), the provision for punitive damages by the law of C will not be regarded as violative of A's public policy (*Loucks*, N.Y. 1918).

If A follows interest analysis, A law will apply to the immunity issue. First, the case may present a "false conflict." The purpose of C's immunity rule is not to deny compensation to tort victims (its own or those from other states). Instead, it seeks to protect its charities; Youth Campers, however, is not a C but an A charity. Even assuming that C also seeks to shield foreign charities from liability (in order to encourage their charitable work in C)—so that the issue now presents a "true conflict"—, A will resolve the immunity question under A law. Pure interest analysis (Currie) dictates this resolution of a true conflict.

The "comparative impairment" approach will also apply A law, certainly with respect to plaintiffs from A, but possibly also as to B and C plaintiffs because A's liability rule (lack of immunity) is both conduct-regulating and, as a result, compensation-favoring. A's policy of regulating its own charities would be more impaired by the non-application of its rule then would be C's policy of shielding charities (since C presumably also does not condone negligent conduct). Interest-analysis states would also apply forum (A) law to the issues of liability and damages. The comparative impairment approach, however, might distinguish between A plaintiffs, on the one hand, and B and C plaintiffs, on the other, in circumstances where the laws of B and C should show significant differences with respect to the liability and damages issues.

Application of the *Neumeier-Rules* (N.Y. 1972) would lead to the selection of the law of A with respect to A plaintiffs (*Neumeier* # 1: common domicile of the parties; if this result would not be changed by *Schultz, infra,* because the court there held that charitable immunity is a loss-allocating rule). The law of B will apply to B plaintiffs under the second part of *Neumeier* #2 if "acting at the plaintiffs domicile" means *conduct* rather than injury, as in the traditional approach (the N.Y. Court of Appeals) continues to speak of the "locus of the tort" (*Schultz*, 1985). If *Neumeier* #2 does not focus on conduct, *Neumeier* #3 becomes applicable to *both* B and C plaintiffs (parties from different states): law of the place of the tort applies *unless* there are important reasons for displacing that law and doing so would not disturb the smooth working of the interstate system or produce uncertainty for litigants. The considerations reviewed above in connection with interest analysis could constitute the important reasons for displacing the law of the place of the tort (= C). However, the New York Court of Appeals emphasized in *Schultz, supra,* that "the significant contacts are, almost exclusively, the parties' domiciles and the locus of the tort." See also *Cooney* (N.Y. 1993). The Neumeier-Rules will select the applicable law for the issues of immunity and liability. It is unclear whether they extend also to the issue of damages or whether, in circumstances akin to *Kilberg, supra,* forum (A) law will apply to B and C plaintiffs as well.

The "Better Law" approach would select A law: limitations on liability (complete immunity, as in C, or limited immunity, as in B) are "anachronistic;" the law of A, providing avenues for redress and compensation, is to be preferred. Assuming that C provides for greater (or punitive) damages than A, the question may arise whether C law is "better" as to that issue. However, A may continue to regard its law as "better" because it strikes a *balance* between liability and the extent of liability (i.e., regarding the higher C limit as irrelevant because plaintiffs could not sue there in view of Youth Campers' immunity).

Selection of the applicable law in accordance with the Second Restatement also requires an initial characterization: Section 145 refers to the "rights and liabilities . . . with respect to an issue in tort." Is charitable immunity "an issue in tort" or an issue of organizational capacity (the "internal affairs" rule mentioned above)? The characterization issue is discussed in connection with the First Restatement, *supra*. Assuming that all issues in this case relate to "tort," § 146 calls for the application of the law of the place of the tort (State C), *unless* another state has a more significant relationship to the occurrence and to the parties. Section 146 thus is only the starting point: its reference to the place of the tort is weaker than *Neumeier*-Rule #3 since there is no suggestion that place-of-tort law applies as a matter of course unless "displaced," and that limits must be observed before such displacement may occur.

Section 145, in conjunction with the general principles established by § 6, aids in the determination of the law of the place of the most significant relationship in tort. That determination is to be made for *each issue* and, in the instant case, for each set of plaintiffs. The contacts listed in § 145 (place of conduct—State B—, place of injury State C—, domicile of the parties—all three states, except for identity in the case of A plaintiffs—, place where relationship was centered—everywhere campers were picked up, where the camp was located?) are divided and hence inconclusive by themselves. The principles of § 6 provide additional help. [Note that the Draft Restatement (Third) places greater emphasis on the place of conduct for personal injury torts.]

A plaintiffs: The forum's policy in favor of compensation and of holding local organizations liable for their negligence, the general tort-law policy in favor of compensation, the expectation of the parties (if there was any) to have home state law apply, the ease of application of forum law, and the absence of another state's interest in denying compensation—all point to the law of A for the issues of immunity, liability, *and* damages. In addition, a fact that all plaintiffs on behalf of campers have in common—, prospective campers dealt with Youth Campers in A, through the application and payment process. While these may be thought of as mainly jurisdictional contacts, they do relate the parties to A, in the context of this occurrence, within the meaning of § 145. C was the state of injury. For A plaintiffs, who consumed the food in B, this is a fortuitous contact. A's contacts are more significant.

B plaintiffs: In the main, the same considerations apply. However, the expectation to have home state law apply seemingly is a variant. At closer look, a false conflict may be present. B law does not immunize charities, it protects them only against ordinary negligence claims. There is no reason why B law would seek to immunize a foreign charity as against its own claimants. Similarly, B's law would not be frustrated; indeed, its basic compensation-favoring policy would be furthered if A would also apply any higher (or punitive) damage principles its law might contain. Once again, C's contact is not significant. A law applies (probably to all issues).

C plaintiffs: Quite possibly, the contacts of C are not insignificant as to these plaintiffs, and their contact to A, in turn, is also not enough to warrant a departure from the starting point provided by § 146 (place of tort). For C plaintiffs, the *place of injury* was not fortuitous. They consumed the food in C and fell ill there. They were employed (and suffered the injury) at their *domicile* and would *expect* local law to apply (if they had any expectation at all). C does not have a compensation-favoring policy in the case of charities (a policy which, with differences, B has in common with A), but perhaps seeks to encourage charitable organizations to be active in its state as a trade-off. Nonapplication of its immunity rule might therefore frustrate this policy. A's compensation-favoring policy (which is shared by B, hence the false conflict noted in that context above) does not necessarily extend to foreign plaintiffs, and its sole concern to regulate the conduct of organizations chartered by it (conduct which, moreover, occurred in B) seems insufficient to make it a state more significantly related to the occurrence and the parties than C. Therefore C law should apply to the immunity issue. The liability and damages issues therefore need not be reached.

2. In State B

The initial assumption was that suit would be brought in A. For reasons of their own (e.g., convenience), the parties may choose to sue in B, especially if they believe that they can show gross negligence. What law will B apply?

In states adhering to the First Restatement, the answer will be the same as under No. 1, above: A law (by way of characterization) to the immunity issue, C law to liability, A or C law to the damage issue.

(Pure) interest-analysis states will apply B law either because the case presents a "false conflict" or because pure interest analysis mandates the application of forum law in cases of true conflicts which cannot be resolved through a restrained view of forum law, when the forum is an interested state and application of its law is constitutionally permissible (see Section B below). For the foregoing, see also No. 1 above. "Comparative impairment" states may reach the same result (= B law) for essentially similar reasons as outlined in No. 1 above: B's interest is that of a conduct-regulating state.

Neumeier-Rules: See No. 1 above.

"Better Law" states: B law, for reasons outlined in No. 1 above.

Restatement Second: See general discussion under No. 1 above. A *plaintiffs:* A law (for reasons given under No. 1 above) or B law because (1) some A policy concerns have been replaced by B concerns or (2) there is a false conflict as between A and B which suggests an application of forum law (= ease of application of the law, § 6, Restatement Second). *B plaintiffs:* A or B law, see No. 1 above. C *plaintiffs: C* law, see No. 1 above.

3. In State C

It is most unlikely that suit would be brought in C. Assuming this were the case, what law should the C court apply?

First Restatement and (pure) interest-analysis states: C law (place of tort or mandated application of forum law). Comparative impairment: see No. 1 above—the question is whether *this* forum will agree that it is "less" impaired by the application of B or C law than by the nonapplication of its own. *Neumeier-Rules*: same as under No. 1, above. "Better Law:" compensation-limiting rules *should* be anachronistic, so that A or B law *should* appear to be the "better law." The case law of "better law" states overwhelmingly finds the "better law" at home. Hence: C law?

Restatement Second: In a state following this approach, the result could be dramatically different from those summarized in the preceding paragraph. Thus, a Restatement

Second state might conclude that charitable immunity is a liability-limiting or corporate-affairs rule (not related to—local—procedure nor governed by local liability or capacity rules, absent additional contacts), with the result that the *foreign* (State A), and *not* the forum (State C), rule should apply. In that event, C would come out like A (No. 1, above), perhaps with different emphases on the weight and significance of the various contacts.

B. Suit Against Caterers, Inc.

Introductory Note

The order of states is changed in this analysis to reflect (a) the likely place of suit for reasons of jurisdiction and (b) the emergence of constitutional problems concerning the application of forum law. For Restatement (Third) see the discussion at the end of this subsection.

1. In State B

Application of the First Restatement will again lead to the law of C, as the state of injury. Decisions focusing on the place of conduct as the place of the tort ordinarily do so only with respect to intentional torts and are therefore inapposite here. Whether B will also apply C's measure of damages (including punitive damages, as would Restatement (Third), see above) is a matter of characterization (discussed above at A(1)). For the constitutionality of applying the law of C, see No. 3 below.

Interest analysis would point to forum (B) law for reasons analogous to those discussed in Section A. Application of the Restatement Second would also lead to B law for A and B plaintiffs: State B is more significantly related to the parties and the occurrence than the (fortuitous) state of the injury. For the interplay of §§ 145 and 146, see the discussion in A(1) above. As also discussed earlier, C law may apply to C plaintiffs.

The "Better Law" approach will once again ordinarily lead to B law. Exceptionally however, a "better law" state will apply a foreign rule favoring the local plaintiff (see *Lichter v. Fritsch*, 77 Wis.2d 178, 252 N.W.2d 360 (1977)). In the instant case, B might select a higher (or punitive) measure of damage which A or C might provide (assuming the constitutionality of applying either of these to determine the extent of Caterers' liability, see below at No. 3).

2. In State C

C will be inclined to apply its law to all plaintiffs if it is a First Restatement (= place of injury), an interest analysis, or a "better law" state (in the last case subject to the qualification in the preceding paragraph). The constitutionality of doing so will be discussed in No. 3 below.

Application of the Restatement Second will lead to C law for C plaintiffs (§ 146 will not be displaced in view of the congruence of place of injury, plaintiff expectation, ease of application of forum law and concomitant lack of a more significant relationship to another state). B law will apply to B plaintiffs (the law of the more significantly related state B—§ 145—displaces the law of the place of injury—§ 146). As to A plaintiffs: The occurrence is not related to A, nor is the defendant; A law is therefore not more significantly related to the case than the law of the place of injury. The A plaintiffs do have contacts with B (consumption of the spoiled food) but probably not enough to displace the law of the place of injury C. For the Restatement (Third) see below.

3. In State A

For reasons of their own (more favorable measure of damages, longer statute of limitations, or what not), some or all plaintiffs may wish to sue Caterers in State A. It was noted initially that A probably lacks jurisdiction over Caterers: the action does not arise out of any contact which Caterers has with A (including causing injury there, as required by the *stream-of-commerce* jurisprudence), and general jurisdiction is of course also lacking. However, assuming that A did have jurisdiction (for instance, because Caterers appeared and thereby consented to the exercise of jurisdiction), what law would A apply?

As a Restatement (First) state, A would be inclined to look to C, as the state of injury. Pure interest analysis would require the application of A law, as would (probably) the "Better Law" approach. Comparative impairment analysis would differentiate among the plaintiffs, perhaps applying A law for the benefit of A plaintiffs but yielding to B or C law in cases brought by residents of those states. The Restatement Second would similarly differentiate among the plaintiffs: A law would not apply for reasons given in No. 2 above.

As a result, C law would probably apply to A and C plaintiffs under § 146, and B law to B plaintiffs.

C. Restatement (Third)

Both Youth Campers and Caterers (the producers of the food) were negligent and the specific rule of § 6.11(a)(1) calls for the application of the law of the defendant manufacturer's (Caterers') domicile (state B) when sued by state D domiciliaries as well when sued by state A domiciliaries if the product was also available in state A (same section), as well as if sued by other plaintiff's if state B was also the state of injury (§ 6.11(a)(3)), although the facts are not entirely clear where the illness of the campers began. In all probability, the Restatement (Third) would all for the application of B law when suits are brought by B and C domiciliaries. State B law would shield Youth Campers, unless its personnel had been grossly negligent (see facts) but no charitable immunity law would excuse Caterers.

D. Constitutional Limitations on Choice of Law

As demonstrated in Section A, Youth Campers has sufficient contact with all three states so that the application of any one of their laws presents only choice-of-law, but not constitutional problems. Caterers, in contrast, is a "local" company of State B and has acted only in that state. This raises the questions (1) whether A (this section) or C (section #2, above) may apply C law (state of injury) and (2) whether A or C (where suit is most unlikely) may apply A law, for instance as a result of an interest-analysis approach to choice of law, as suggested in the preceding paragraph.

The constitutional limits to choice of law are defined by *Home Ins. v. Dick* (U.S. 1930), *Allstate Ins. Co. v. Hague* (U.S. 1981), and *Phillips Petroleum Co. v. Shutts* (U.S. 1985). They teach that a state may *not* apply its law when it has *no* contact with the transaction or occurrence (*Home Ins., Shutts*). Rather, forum law may be applied only when the forum has "a significant contact or significant aggregation of contacts, creating state interests, such that choice of its law is neither arbitrary nor fundamentally unfair" (*Allstate Ins. v. Hague,* reaffirmed in *Shutts*).

A,—in the second question posed above—, has no contact with the transaction: the negligent conduct occurred in B, the conduct was directed (in stream-of-commerce terms) toward C, and caused injury there. The fact that A may have jurisdiction (= the assumption in the introductory paragraph) is not enough for the application of its unrelated law: *Shutts.* State A is therefore restricted to the application of B and possibly (see below) C law.

B law may of course be applied by A, B, and C. Caterers' conduct occurred in B, that state has an interest in regulating local conduct, and the application of home-state law to home-state conduct therefore cannot be "arbitrary [or] fundamentally unfair."

The permissibility of the application of C law by either A or C,—the first question posed above—, falls within the gray area left by *Hague*. C does have a state interest (the injuries were suffered there). But where or what is the "significant contact or aggregation of contacts creating [that] state interest?" It would have to be the causing of injury in C, even though Caterers had no control over when the plaintiffs would be stricken or, for that matter, where Youth Campers' buses would be at the time plaintiffs would be stricken (possibly even while being taken on a detour through state D). Choice of law thus would track the jurisdictional inquiry along stream-of-commerce lines.

Caterers acted in its home state, just as the accident in *Hague* took place in the common home state of victim and tortfeasor. Tenuous contacts with the forum, including the defendant's amenability to jurisdiction there (and the consequent lack of unfair surprise with respect to the application of forum law), sanctioned the forum's application of its own law in *Hague* (despite the court's formulation that there must be a *"significant"* contact or aggregation of contacts). Both the running together of the jurisdictional and choice-of-law inquiries as well as the application of the *Hague* test to the facts of the case have been criticized. Nevertheless, if Caterers is—or could be—subject to jurisdiction in C, it is probable that the application of C law would pass constitutional scrutiny. This is especially so because C law is the law of the place of injury, and the choice of that law (First Restatement) has never been questioned on constitutional grounds when there was jurisdiction over the defendant. "Tradition" is not a particularly good argument, at least standing alone, but it was an element in the Supreme Court's decision in *Sun Oil Co. v. Wortman* (U.S. 1988) which permitted the forum to apply its own unrelated longer statute of limitations as a matter of procedural characterization.

As a result, only the application of A law to Caterers may be constitutionally impermissible. The use of B or C law is a matter of each forum's approach to choice of law.

V.

This question raises issues from all three major areas of the course (as did Question II)—jurisdiction, choice of law, and judgment recognition, including how these interrelate and affect answers to each other. An analysis could proceed by topic or by possible forum. This discussion chooses the latter.

Indiana. As Dr. Genoux's principal place of practice and the place where the operation was performed, Indiana obviously has jurisdiction (general jurisdiction if it is Dr. Genoux's domicile or he was served there or because of his principal business activity there, specific jurisdiction because the claim arises from his acts (or omissions) in the state). In the absence of any facts, it is assumed that there is no jurisdiction over Dr. Rodilla in Indiana. The following therefore deals only with Dr. Genoux.

Indiana, following a significant-contacts approach, would apply its own law—as the place of the alleged tort, the contacts of Dr. Genoux with the state, the fact that Willem sought out Dr. Genoux in the state, and that it has an interest in the application of its liability-limiting law (see further below). The time limit for bringing actions (applicable regardless of whether these are characterized as substantive or procedural) are also governed by Indiana law and are 2 years from the act or omission. On the facts, it is difficult to say exactly from when that time runs. Indians courts have held that the statute applies from the "occurrence," not from "discovery." *Havens v. Ritchey*, 582 N.E.2d 792 (Ind. 1991); *Brinkman v. Bueter et al.*, 879 N.E.2d 549 (Ind. 2008). However, the period does not start running in cases of concealment or, as some cases have suggested, when the "doctrine of continuing wrong" applies (with the limitation then applicable from the last wrong). Cf. *Boggs v. Tri-State Radiology*, 730 N.E.2d 692, 699 (Ind. 2000). Assuming that malpractice is proved, Indiana limits the recovery of compensatory damages to a total of $1.25 million. IC 34–18–14–3(a)(3) and (b); attorneys' fees are limited to 15%. IC 34–18–18–1. The purpose of the statutory limitation to assure that everyone has access to medical services by preventing the reduction of services as a result of burdensome damage awards or high costs of insurance. *Johnson v. St. Vincent Hosp.*, 273 Ind. 374, 404 N.E.2d 585, 590, 597 (1980). At the same time, Indiana law is not intended to shield egregious conduct: the jury is therefore not precluded from awarding punitive damages in addition to the (limited) compensatory damages. See *Cacdac v. West*, 705 N.E.2d 506 (Ind. App. 1999).

If the malpractice claim is reduced to judgment elsewhere, recognition of that judgment might be sought in Indiana (if assets are insufficient to satisfy it in the state or country of rendition). Indiana has the Uniform Enforcement of Foreign Judgments Act for *sister-state judgments*. Such a judgment (e.g., a California or New York judgment in this case), when properly filed, has the same effect as an Indiana judgment. IC 34–54–11–1 (but see further below). Alternatively, the judgment creditor could of course seek recognition by suit on the judgment under the Constitution's Full Faith and Credit Clause and the Implementing Statute. The Indiana Act does not address recognition of foreign-country judgments (2003 Ind. P.L. 40 § 1); Indiana does not have the Uniform Foreign Money-Judgments Recognition Act or its successor, the Uniform Foreign Country Judgments Recognition Act. Recognition of such judgments therefore follows the common-law approach: suit on the foreign judgment (as a claim), recognition on the basis of res judicata and comity, no objectionable foreign procedures (such as lack of adequate notice), and no violation of local public policy. There are relatively few modern Indiana decision on foreign-country judgment recognition. In *Glaverbel S.A. v. Northlake Marketing & Supply, Inc.*, 1998 48 U.S.P.Q.2d 1344 (N.D. Ind. 1998), the court recognized the res judicata effect of the Belgian judgment as a matter of comity and found that the fact that Belgian procedure did not provide American-style discovery did not violate the Indiana forum's public policy. Indiana does not seem to have a reciprocity requirement; even if it did, reciprocity with respect to England would be assured. We will need to return to judgment recognition in Indiana again below.

England. Whether English courts have jurisdiction over Dr. Genoux is first of all a question of English law. England asserts jurisdiction on the basis of transient service as well as by "service out of the jurisdiction" when the tort occurred in England or has a direct effect in England (see Cheshire, North, Fawcett, Private International Law 386 (14th ed. 2008)). Assertion of jurisdiction in England seems possible, especially if the doctor can ever be served there. Second, transient service or the doctor's activities in England and initial treatment of Willem there would both satisfy American due process standards for the purpose of recognizing assertion of jurisdiction of an English court as proper if a judgment were sought to be in Indiana (or elsewhere in the United States).

As in the case of Indiana, it is assumed—for lack of facts—that there is no jurisdiction over Dr. Rodilla in England. The following is therefore limited to Dr. Genoux.

In England, choice of law in tort is governed by European Union's Rome II Regulation (which the United Kingdom continued in force as national law after leaving the EU—"Brexit"). That law looks to the place of the tort (presumably Indiana, where *both* the alleged negligent conduct *and* the injury occurred). It also permits a departure from the otherwise applicable law if the case is "manifestly" more closely connected to another state. It is questionable whether, in the absence of American-type interest analysis, an

English court would depart from the place-of-tort rule under the circumstances of the case. If not, the applicable substantive law is that of Indiana.

Is the Indiana limitation on damages a matter of substance or procedure? At common law, the quantification of damages was generally considered to be procedural (calling for the application of forum law). A statutory limitation—specific to a particular type of claim—might be considered to be so closely related to the question of liability that it should be considered to be "substantive" (in analogy to "built in" time limitations). Limitations of time or otherwise, however, have been considered substantive when the cause of action itself was created by statute ("unknown to the common law"), which is not true in the case of medical malpractice. In similar circumstance, the House of Lords, in construing sec. 14(3)(b) of Part III of the United Kingdom Private International Law Act of 1995, disregarded statutory damage limitations of New South Wales (Australia), considered the quantification of damages to be procedural and applied (the 30% more favorable) English law. *Harding v. Wealands*, [2007] 2 A.C. 1 (H.L.). The English court would disregard the Indiana limitation.—Similarly, the time limitation for the bringing of an action might be considered to be procedural; even if, as under new EC law, it were to be considered as substantive (= Indiana law applies), the flexible standard of Indiana case law suggests that an action would still be timely.

New York. The facts are too scant to allow a conclusion concerning jurisdiction over Dr. Genoux on the basis of his activities there. Surely, however, he can be served at some time while in New York. There is no question regarding jurisdiction over Dr. Rodilla.

Choice of law in tort by New York courts calls for the application of the *Neumeier Rules*, as refined in *Schultz*. Following an issue-by-issue approach (see Restatement (Second) of Conflict of Laws § 145(2))—*dépeçage*—, New York would inquire whether a damage limitation (like Indiana's) is loss-allocating or conduct-regulating. From Indiana's perspective, it is quite clearly the former—a smaller recovery for some injured parties to provide more extensive medical service to others (see above). For New York, the absence of limits—resulting in potential unlimited liability—may be conduct-regulating (see the dissent in *Schultz*), but there was no conduct by Dr. Genoux in New York. If damage limits are loss-allocating in the absence of a New York regulatory interest, the *Neumeiner Rules*, apply—specifically the first part of Rule #2. It leads to Indiana law. The second part of Rule #2 contains a proviso that the first part does not. Even if one were to read it into the first part, it seems inapplicable here: There are no special reasons for the application of New York law (such an interest in providing compensation for a local plaintiff who might otherwise become a public ward). As a result the Indiana limitation applies.

The matter is different in the case of Dr. Rodilla. She treated Willem in New York and the worsening of Willem's condition was its result. A claim against her has no connection to Indiana and only through Willem to England. However, contacts need to be the defendant's own, not established through the plaintiff. In *Schultz*, the New York court chose not to apply the third *Neumeier Rule* as to the second defendant and ended up applying the same law to both defendants. This exception does not apply here. As to Dr. Rodilla, the liability limitation issue is conduct-regulating (see above) and New York law applies as such. Even if this were not so, *Neumeier Rule* #3 (also calling for New York) would not call for an exception here since Dr. Rodilla had no connection to the liability-limiting law. New York law applies.

The applicable time limitations are those of New York law (as the result of a procedural characterization). Both actions are still timely.

California. Jurisdiction over Dr. Genoux: same comment as under "New York," above. The facts present no grounds on which jurisdiction could be asserted over Dr. Rodilla.

An action against Dr. Genoux will still be timely under California's 3-year rule. It applies either as a result of a traditional procedural characterization or even as a result of false-conflict analysis: one function of limitations is to protect courts against entertaining state claims. This case is in a California court, not Indiana. Indiana's protective policy (even if it statute should have run) applies to its courts and is inapplicable here. Another function of limitations is to free defendants, to bring about closure. Indiana law (if applicable—on which see the following) already provides the defendant with peace of mind by (a) requiring insurance in the amount of $250,000 as a condition of participation in the Compensation Fund and then (b) limiting his liability to the amount of that coverage.

With respect to the applicable law, a first question should what choice(s) is/are involved. California has contact(s) with the defendant, but not with Willem (other than in his capacity as potential plaintiff). As the U.S. Supreme Court concluded in application of *Home Ins. Co. v. Dick*, p. 231 *supra*, in *John Hancock Mut. Life Ins. Co. v. Yates,* 299 U.S. 178, 182 (1936): "there was no occurrence, nothing done, to which the law of Georgia could apply." See also *Allstate Ins. Co. v. Hague*, p. 234 *supra*. Arguably, therefore, the California court may only apply either Indiana or New York (possibly English) law, but not its own.

California follows the "comparative impairment"-approach to choice of law. In considering the interests of Indiana and New York in the application of their laws, respectively, California should conclude that Indiana's interests would be more impaired than New York's, hence its law should be applied: for Indiana's interests, see above under "Indiana." New York, in contrast, has an interest in compensating local injured parties and to counteract negligent conduct in New York. Neither interest is implicated here: New York's interests would not be impaired, let alone more than Indiana's by non-application of its law.

[The same result should follow if, for some reason (e.g., on the basis of additional facts), one should reach the conclusion that it would be constitutional to apply California law. In view of such a change of facts, the quote from *John Hancock v. Yates, supra* would not be a bar, but California's lack of an impaired interest would still require the application of Indiana law.]

<u>Public policy</u>. California itself places some restrictions on recoveries in malpractice actions, e.g. on the amount of attorneys' fees recoverable by contract or contingent fee and especially on recoveries for no-economic losses—principally, pain and suffering, thus does not object to the *principle* of a limitation. The absence of a limitation on recoveries may serve to regulate physicians' conduct in California and to benefit local claimants (see above). Neither reason for the application of California forum law applies here: Indiana interests predominate and its law applies.

Lawsuits and judgment recognition and enforcement. As the state-by-state discussion shows, Willem faces problems in each of the three American states. While all might have jurisdiction of Dr. Genoux, only New York has jurisdiction over Dr. Rodilla. As to Dr. Genoux, all three states would probably apply Indiana law, including its damage cap. California and New York would not have a reason to award punitive damages against Dr. Genoux, since no conduct occurred or was suffered in those states. Indiana, as the state of conduct, might award punitive damages: but it is a close call whether Willem's action might be time-barred there. The result: only New York presents the possibility of suing both defendants, with an unlimited recovery and punitive damages possible as against Dr. Rodilla, but Indiana limits apply and no punitive damages as to Dr. Genoux may be awarded. California promises the least recovery (none against Dr. Rodilla for lack of jurisdiction, Indiana limits without punitive damages as to Dr. Genoux). For Indiana, see the previous comment.

England also lacks jurisdiction over Dr. Rodilla. But as to Dr. Genoux, an English court might apply English law to the quantification of damages and, because part of Dr. Genoux's conduct occurred in England, might award exemplary damages under English law. Cf. Cheshire, North, Fawcett, *supra,* at 851–52. Willem's best chance may therefore be to sue Dr. Genoux in England and Dr. Rodilla in New York. Assuming that his English action succeeds, the question then becomes whether the ensuing judgment will be recognized and enforced in the United States (if Dr. Genoux's English assets should prove insufficient).

Recognition of an English judgment. California and New York have the Uniform Foreign-Money Judgment Recognition Act (California has its 2005 successor), Indiana does not (foreign country judgment recognition follows the common-law approach, enunciated by the U.S. Supreme Court in *Hilton*, but made substantially "recognition friendlier" in U.S. state case law since). By and large, the English judgment will not face greater hurdles under the common-law approach than under the Uniform Act (assuming, as posited, no objections to jurisdiction of the English court or to the opportunity to be heard there).

New York or California therefore should have no objection to the recognition of an English judgments if it were sought there (e.g., to reach local assets there). All recognition prerequisites are satisfied and there is no public policy objection.

What about recognition in Indiana? Indiana public policy might well be invoked to limit enforcement of *compensatory* damages to the maximum allowed by Indiana law. Since Indiana itself does not include punitive damages within its statutory cap, a foreign award of exemplary damages should not offend its public policy.

Interstate recognition. If, because of Indiana's possible limitation on recognition, the English judgment creditor first seeks recognition in New York and, if New York assets should prove insufficient to satisfy the (now recognized) English judgment, subsequently seeks to enforce the deficiency in Indiana, what result? The New York recognition of the English judgment reduces "the claim on the foreign judgment" to a domestic (here: New York) judgment which is now entitled to recognition (as an interstate judgment) under the Constitution's Full Faith and Credit command—without reexamination as to the underlying merits. *Treinies v. Sunshine Mining Co.* (1939); *Fauntleroy v. Lum* (1908). The contrary decision in *Reading and Bates Const. Co. v. Baker Energy Resources Corp.*, 976 S.W.2d 702 (Tex. App.-Hous. (1 Dist.) 1998) (refusing recognition of a previously recognized judgment because this would amount to recognition through the "back door"), appears to be wrongly decided.

A New York judgment against Dr. Rodilla can be enforced against her property anywhere in the United States. Personal jurisdiction over her in the state of recognition and enforcement is not required for that purpose. *Shaffer v. Heitner* (1977).

Other issues. The above does not explore the issue of joint and several liability of the physicians for the entire damage nor the issue of contribution claims between them (and the law applicable to such claims).

VI.

Obviously, A could sue B in Y, where B lives, and which has general jurisdiction. He could sue in Y state or federal court (diversity of citizenship is met but A must claim more than $75,000, the jurisdictional amount). Both the Y state and federal courts would apply Y conflicts law (*Klaxon*) unless the federal court applies federal common law interstitially (under the Clean Air Act, which the Question did not mention, and which may not be likely after the recent Supreme Court decision in *West Virginia v. EPA*, 597 U.S. 697, 142 S.Ct. 2587 (2022)), explained further in *Biden v. Nebraska*, 600 U.S. 477, 501–506 (2023).Under Y conflicts law, the question is which law applies: the state of injury (presumably state X under traditional law), or the state with the most significant relationship to the issue (Restatement (Second) §§ 145, 146, depending on the issue)? Or do we use the distinction between loss allocation and conduct regulation in the coming Restatement (Third)? The last of these seems easy: Y's limitation allocates losses (see *Schultz*) and therefore applies to its resident. X's rule of course regulates conduct, and X would apply it if suit were brought there (as New York should probably have done in *Schultz*, see *P.V. ex rel. T.V. v. Camp Jaycee*, 962 A.2d 453 (N.J. 2008)). See more below on Restatement (Third),

If Y follows the Restatement (Second), which is the state of the most significant relationship? The contacts (§ 145) are pretty evenly divided; both states have policies in favor of their own laws (see § 6). Their policies agree that there should be compensation, but Y severely limits the amount, and might reject higher amounts as violative of its public policy (see *Kilberg*). The rejection of X law on public policy grounds might also occur if Y followed the traditional approach and first looked to X as the state of injury. (The Reporters of Restatement (Third) discuss the (European) notion of "the polluter pays." Nonetheless, the *Kilberg* public policy consideration might overcome an application of X law by Y.) However, Section 6.09 of the coming Restatement (Third) (T.D. #4) deals with Cross-Border Torts and provides in subsection (a) that the law of the state of conduct applies when conduct causes injury in another state. However, and relevant here, subsection (b) provides for the application of the law of the state of injury (here state X) if the injured party shows that "the location of the injury was reasonably foreseeable." Here, injury was foreseeable since Adams had complained about it on some occasions. If Y courts turn to (adopt) Restatement (Third), they should then also apply X law.

To be on the safe side, A should seek to sue in X, if possible. Does X have jurisdiction over B? It of course has specific jurisdiction over B for A's battery claim: B entered A's house in X and hit and injured him there. This is the classic situation addressed by the old (non-resident motorist) long-arm statutes and the broader modern statutes. X would also apply its law under any of the choice-of-law approaches (place of injury, Restatement (Second) § 146, conduct-regulating forum tort liability law).

What about the more important (because vastly bigger) pollution claim? Would X have specific jurisdiction over B? (Specific jurisdiction over one claim does not provide jurisdiction over a different claim.) B's conduct (permitting and controlling polluting emissions) occurred in Y. It caused injury to A in X, but B did not introduce the emissions into X, the wind and the little stream did.

Suppose B discharged a firearm across the state line. Conduct and injury would happen in different states, but B would have directly caused the injury; X could exercise jurisdiction over him. In the instant case, B's activities in Y produced polluting emissions, and he knew of their effect on A's property (at the latest through A's complaints). In the previous hypothetical, had B tolerated his employee shooting across the state line in the course of the latter's employment, vicarious liability might have subjected him to specific jurisdiction in X. The same should be the answer in the instant case: knowingly permitting one's emissions to injure the neighbor's property permits the exercise of jurisdiction in the latter state "within the limits of due process." (The question might be closer if B's fertilizer factory were located at considerable distance from A's land, but this was not the case here.)

In entertaining the case, X would apply its own law under all the above approaches. Recommended solution: suit in X, application of X law.

VII.

This question raises complex questions of jurisdiction. To sue Cee in Georgia is easy, although perhaps not the most promising for the plaintiff. Cee is a Georgia company and is therefore subject to general jurisdiction there. However, it is not the deep pocket, nor did it manufacture the implant. If the mesh was in fact faulty, Cee might face liability but surely would wish to implead Adams Company, which manufactured the implant, and Beta Company, which sold it. And the (now Georgia) plaintiff would prefer to sue these companies in Georgia rather than in their respective states of incorporation.

The Adams Company manufactured the implant that failed but it did not sell it to the plaintiff (who was injured in Georgia) and did not even sell it into Georgia (presumably Beta did). That both companies may have maintained offices in Georgia does not subject them to general jurisdiction there unless, as out-of-state companies, they had to register in Georgia and that registration constitutes consent to jurisdiction (see *Mallory* and the older Georgia case to which the Supreme Court referred). Specific jurisdiction over Beta may exist if it introduced the specific implant into Georgia itself, rather than having sold it to a wholesaler outside of the state. If the latter had been the case, it had put the implant into the stream of commerce, as did Adams, the manufacturer, which used Beta as its sole distributor. In fact, Beta was wholly owned by Adams—the two were one—and piercing the corporate veil might be appropriate (as the U.S. Supreme Court permitted Illinois to do in *Schlunk*).

In *Ford v. Montana* and in the companion case, the defective cars had not been brought into the states where they caused injuries by the defendant manufacturer. But Ford did sell the same models in those states, and its products were well-known and sold nationally. Given its nationwide business, subjecting it to jurisdiction in Montana (and Minnesota) was not unfair. The injuries suffered in each state were not caused by Ford there, but were sufficiently related to its in-state activities. The same can be said for Beta in this case.

Adams' connection to Georgia is not what Ford's was in Montana nor Beta's in this case. However, it directly provided the materials to Cee, which the latter used in manufacturing the mesh used in this (as in all) implants. The material did not cause the injury, but it became part of the faulty implant; it surely was related to the injury. Furthermore, as discussed, Adams and Beta can be considered as one, so that which applies to one can be applied to the other.

Finally, in both *Hague* (with respect to choice of law) and *Ford* (with respect to jurisdiction), the Court gave some weight to the forum state's interest. It is obvious that Georgia has an interest in ensuring that safe and successful surgeries are performed in its state. It also has an interest in providing a legal remedy to its resident, but this last point might be disregarded because the plaintiff changed her residence after the injury. However, so had Mrs. Hague, and the Court found that she had done so in good faith, meaning that there was no evidence of forum shopping.

Table of Cases

1st Summit Bank v. Samuelson, 61
A v. M, 134
Abbott v. Abbott, 153
Abernathy v. Carlyle Group, Inc., 58
Adam v. Saenger, 59
Addison v. Addison, 129
Adjei v. Mayorkas, 150
ADT Security Services, Inc. v. Apex Alarm, LLC, 252
Advance Products & Systems, Inc. v. CCI Piping Systems, L.L.C., 107
AdvanFort Co. v. Zamil Offshore Services Co., 80
Aerospatiale see Areelik A.S. v. E.I. DuPont der Nemours and Co., 252
Agent Orange Product Liability Litigation, In re, 268
Air Crash Disaster Near Chicago, Illinois on May 25, In re, 250
Air Crash Near Clarence Center, In re, 186
Alabama Great Southern R.R. Co. v. Carroll, 175
Al-Ajmi v. Turki, 152
Alaska Packers Association v. Industrial Accident Commission, 233
Alberta Securities Commission v. Ryckman, 115
Albright v. Vining Sparks Securities, Inc, 239
Aldrich v. Aldrich, 102
Aleem v. Aleem, 151
Allergy Research Group LLC v. Rez Candles, Inc., 75
Alliance for Fair Board Recruitment v. Securities and Exchange Commission, 268
Allstate Insurance Co. v. Hague, 189, 230, 234, 235, 318, 322
American Dredging Co. v. Miller, 82
American Insurance Association v. Garamendi, 264
American Motorists Ins. Co. v. ARTRA Group, Inc., 166, 179, 211
American Surety Co. v. Baldwin, 101
Angel v. Bullington, 104, 247
Animal Science Products v. Hebei Welcome Pharmaceutical Co., 167
Ansello v. Wisconsin Central, Ltd., 106
Anwar v. Fairfield Greenwich Ltd., 77
Applebaum v. Lyft, Inc., 78
Aranda v. Philip Morris, 81
Armstrong v. Atrium Med. Corp. et al., 63
Armstrong v. Manzo, 134
Artis v. District of Columbia, 162
Asahi Metal Industry Co. v. Superior Court, 67, 70
Ashfaq v. Ashfaq, 151
Atlantic Marine Const. Co. v. U.S. District Court, 78, 79
Attorney General of Canada v. R.J. Reynolds Tobacco Holdings, Inc., 109
Austria GmbH v. Hectronic International, Inc., 58
Avena and Other Mexican Nationals (Mexico v. United States), 265
Aybar v. Aybar, 60
Babcock v. Jackson, 183, 192
Badilla v. Midwest Air Traffic Control Serv., Inc., 262
Baker v. General Motors Corp., 97, 112
Baldwin v. Iowa Traveling Men's Association, 99, 101
Banco Nacional de Cuba v. Sabbatino, 265
Bank of Am. Nat'l Trust & Savings Ass'n v. Parnell, 261, 263
Bano v. Union of India, 151
Barber v. Barber, 97
Barefield, People v., 124
Bassi, In re Estate of, 133
Bates Construction Co. v. Baker Energy Resources Corp., 323
Begay v. Miller, 152
Belfast, United States v., 53
Beller ex rel. Beller v. U.S., 152
Bendix Autolite Corp. v. Midwesco Enter., Inc., 162, 240
Benes v. Luis de la Aguilera et al., 234
Berk v. Choy, 76
Berkson v. Gogo LLC, 78
Bernhard v. Harrah's Club, 180
Bernkrant v. Fowler, 211
Biden v. Nebraska, 324
Binning v. State, 108
Birchfield v. Armstrong, 132
Black Canyon Irrigation District, United States v., 105
Blackburn v. Blackburn, 125
Blackmer v. United States, 53
Blake v. McClung, 225
Bledsoe v. Crowley, 239
Boettger ex rel. Boettger v. Roberts, 133
Boggs v. Tri-State Radiology, 320
Boghosian v. Boghosian, 98
Boing Co. v. KB Yuzhnoye, 267
Bonebrake v. Cox, 207
Bonsu v. Holder, 168
Bordes v. Deveaux, 186
Boyle v. United Tech. Corp., 262
Boyles, Ex parte, 63
Bradford Electric Light Co. v. Clapper, 232
Breard v. Greene, 264

Bridgestone/Firestone Inc., In re, 80
Brinkman v. Bueter, et al., 319
Brown v. Kansas City Live, LLC, 93
Bryant v. Finnish National Airline, 55
Burger King v. Rudzewicz, 60, 62, 67, 73
Burlington Northern R. Co. v. Woods, 281
Burnham v. Superior Court, 54
BY Equities, LLC v. Carver Theater Productions, 261
Byrd v. Blue Ridge Rural Electric, Cooperative, 248, 312
C&C Inv. Props., L.L.C. v. Trustmark Nat'l Bank, 261
Cacdac v. West, 320
Cadence Design Sys., Inc. v. Pounce Consulting, Inc., 53
Calder v. Jones, 72
California v. Texas, 38
Campion v. State, Dep't of Community & Regional Affairs, Hous. Assistance Div., 145
Cardenas v. Stephens, 265
Cargill Financial Services International, Inc. v. Barshchovkij, 115
Cargill, Inc. v. Sabine Trading & Shipping Co., 58
Carnival Cruise Lines, Inc. v. Shute, 78
Carnival Cruise Lines, Inc. v. Superior Court, 78
Carpenter, In re, 113
Carroll v. Lanza, 233
Casavant v. Norwegian Cruise Line, Ltd., 78
Castano v. American Tobacco Co., 255
CBF Industria de Gusa S/A v. AMCI Holdings, Inc., 117
CC/Devas (Mauritius) Ltd. v. Antrix Corp. Ltd., 65
Chappell, In re, 222
China Agritech, Inc. v. Resh, 250
Chirag v. MT Marida Marguerite Schiffahrts, 80
Ciampa v. Nichols, 148
Claimsolution, Inc. v. Claim Solutions, LLC, 75
Clark v. Podesta, 73
Clark, Estate of, 131, 222
Clarke v. Clarke, 218, 219
Clay v. Sun Insurance Office, Ltd., 232
Clearfield Trust Co. v. United States, 261, 312
Cohen v. Key Safety Systems, Inc., 80
Colby v. Colby, 144
Coleman v. California Bd. of Prison Terms, 94
Colvin v. Hutchison, 222
CompuServe Inc. v. Patterson, 75
Cook v. Cook, 144
Cooney v. Osgood Machinery, Inc., 185
Cooper Tire & Rubber Co. v. McCall, 60
Corporacion Venezolana de Fomento v. Vintero Sales Corp., 256
Crane v. Merriman, 148
Crescent Int'l, Inc. v. Avatar Cmty., Inc., 266
Crichton v. Succession of Crichton, 128
Crichton, Estate of, 128
Crider v. Zurich Insurance Co., 239
Csepel v. Republic of Hungary, 267
CTS Corp. v. Dynamics Corp. of America, 225, 226, 233
Custody of a Minor (No. 3), 152
D.H. Overmyer Co. v. Frick Co., 60, 285
D'Oench, Duhme & Co. v. FDIC, 261
Daimler AG v. Bauman, 52, 55
Dalip Singh Bir's Estate, In re, 126
Dawson v. Sonju, 113
Day & Zimmermann, Inc. v. Challoner, 253
Day v. Henry, 239
Dedie & Springston, In re Marriage of, 147
Del Prado v. B.N. Development Co., 102
Delaware v. New York, 225
Demaree v. Fulton Cnty. School Dist., 94
Dorrance, Estate of, 38, 307
Douglas v. New York, New Haven & Hartford Railroad Co., 240
Draper v. Gardner Defined Plan Trust, 226
Drip Capital Inc. v. JY Imports of NY, Inc., 115
Dubin v. City of Philadelphia, 63
Duckwall v. Lease, 221
Durfee v. Duke, 98, 102, 218, 220
Dyke v. Dyke, 263
Dynamic Software Services v. Cyberbest Technology, Inc., 60
EBF Partners, LLC v. Novabella, Inc., 108
Edelson v. Soricelli, 239
Edgar v. MITE Corp., 226
Edwards v. Erie Coach Lines Co., 186
El Al Israel Airlines Ltd. v. Tseng, 267
Elali v. Marchoud, In re Marriage of, 126
Eldon Industries v. Paradies & Co., 217
Electronic Frontier Found. v. Global Equity Mgmt. (SA) Pty Ltd., 116
Elkaiat v. Mawashi, 148
Ellerton v. Ellerton, 206
EMA Financial, LLC v. NFusz, Inc., 166
Emery v. Burbank, 208
Enis v. State, 124
Erickson v. Pharmacia LLC, 184, 194
Erie R.R. Co. v. Tompkins, 246, 260
Esfeld v. Costa Crociere, Sp.A., 79, 81
Estin v. Estin, 74, 143, 149
European Community v. RJR Nabisco, Inc., 109
Exercise Tax Litigation, In re, 94
F. Hoffmann-La Roche Ltd. v. Empagran S.A., 58
F.D.I.C. v. Deglau, 261
F.D.I.C. v. Estrada-Rivera, 261
Fall v. Eastin, 97, 98, 218
Fauntleroy v. Lum, 107, 276
Federal Republic of Germany v. Philipp, 266
Federative Republic of Brazil, United States v., 110
Feeney v. Dunham, 251
Ferens v. John Deere Co., 255
Ferreira v. Ferreira, 146
Fitch v. Huntington, 84
Florida Dep't of Children & Families v. Adoption of X.X.G., 134

Ford Motor Co. v. Montana, 71
Ford v. Ford, 221
Franchise Tax Bd. of California v. Hyatt, 109
Franchise Tax Board of California v. Hyatt, 233
Fresh Results, LLC v. ASF Holland, B.V., 80
Frummer v. Hilton Hotels Int'l, Inc., 63
Fuld v. Palestine Liberation Organization, 69
Galeotti v. Cianbro Corp., 166
Galvan v. NCO Financial Systems, Inc., 256
Garcia v. Chiquita Brands International, Inc., 253
Gasperini v. Center for Humanities, Inc., 248
George v. George, 124
Giancaspro v. Congleton, 135
Girsberger v. Kresz, 115
GITA Sports Ltd. v. SG Sensortechnik GmbH & Co. KG, 79
Gitter v. Gitter, 40, 53
Glasford v. Schreier, 36
Glaverbel S.A. v. Northlake Marketing & Supply, Inc., 320
Golan v. Saada, 153
Golden v. Quality Life Services, LLC, 255
Goldsmith v. Sotheby's, Inc., 63
Goodyear Dunlop Tire Operations, S.A. v. Brown, 52, 55, 56
Gordon v. Parker, 202
Gourdine v. Karl Storz Endoscopy-America, Inc., 179
Grace v. MacArthur, 54
Grant v. McAuliffe, 160
Graves, State v., 125
Gray v. American Radiator & Standard Sanitary Corp., 62
Griffin v. McCoach, 254
Griswold, Matter of Estate of, 135
Guaranty Trust Co. v. York, 247
Guidi v. Inter-Continental Hotels Corp., 80
Gulf Oil Corp. v. Gilbert, 80, 313
Gustavia Home, LLC v. Rutty, 226
Guzzo v. Cristofano, 40
Haberman v. Washington Public Power Supply System, 280
Halvey, People ex rel. v. Halvey, 146
Hanna v. Plumer, 249, 310
Hanson v. Denckla, 67
Harding v. Wealands, 321
Harnischfeger Sales Corp. v. Sternberg Dredging Co., 94, 104
Harpur v. Bich, 116
Harpur v. Rich, 116
Harris v. Balk, 63, 85
Harris v. Polskie Linie Lotnicze, 267
Harrison's Estate, In re, 36
Hart v. American Airlines, 94
Hartford Fire Ins. Co. v. California, 58
Haumschild v. Continental Casualty Co., 160, 203
Havens v. Ritchey, 319
Headen v. Pope & Talbot, Inc., 126
Heart of Adoptions, Inc. v. J.A., 134
Hearts with Haiti, Inc. v. Kendrick, 38
Heavner v. Uniroyal, Inc., 162
Helbrans, United States v., 148
Helicopteros Nacionales de Colombia, S.A. v. Hall, 50, 51, 55
Hellenic Lines Ltd. v. Rhoditis, 206
Hennefeld v. Township of Montclair, 133
Hernandez v. Grisham, 255
Hess v. Pawloski, 59
Hicklin v. Orbeck, 239
Hieston v. National City Bank of Chicago, 108
Hilton v. Guyot, 95, 113
Hinderlider v. La Plata River & Cherry Creek Ditch Co., 253, 260
Hirsch's Estate, In re, 225
Hoffman v. Blaski, 289
Holmes v. Syntex Laboratories, Inc., 81
Home Ins. v. Dick, 231, 318
Hondros v. Hewlett Packard Enterprises, 262
Hornblower v. Hornblower, 145
Hughes v. Fetter, 80, 109, 238
Hughes v. Hughes, 128
Huntington v. Attrill, 109, 167
Hutchison v. Ross, 223
Illinois v. City of Milwaukee, 261
Incubadora Mexicana, SA de CV v. Zoetis, Inc., 80
Industrial Commission of Wisconsin v. McCartin, 105
Insurance Corp. of Ireland, Ltd. v. Compagnie des Bauxites de Guinee, 57, 58
Interamerican Trade Corp. v. Companhia Fabricadora de Pecas, 79
International Paper Co. v. Ouellette, 268
International Shoe Co. v. Washington, 64, 85
Iragorri v. United Technologies Corp., 80
ISI Int'l, Inc. v. Borden Ladner Gervais LLP, 69
J. McIntyre Machinery, Ltd. v. Nicastro, 70
Jackson v. Johns-Manville Sales Corp., 268
Jacob, In re, 134
Jacobs Private Equity, LLC v. <JPE.com>, 75
Jaeglin v. Moakley, 223
James v. Grand Trunk Western R. Co., 108
Jang v. Trustees of St. Johnsbury Academy, 116
Jarvison, United States v., 152
Jepson v. General Casualty Co. of Wisconsin, 189
Jiminez v. De La Cruz, 150
John Hancock Mutual Life Ins. Co. v. Yates, 231, 237, 322
Johnson v. Chrysler Canada, Inc., 70
Johnson v. Muelberger, 144
Johnson v. St. Vincent Hosp., 320
Jones v. Cannizzaro, 94
Juul Labs. Inc. v. Grove, 226, 280
Kansas v. Kennedy, 268
Kantor v. Wellesley Galleries, Ltd., 38
Kaplinsky v. Kaplinsky, 151

Karim v. Finch Shipping Co., 160
Kee v. Hines, 147
Keeton v. Hustler Magazine, Inc., 72, 237, 311
Kilberg v. Northeast Airlines, Inc., 160, 203
Kimbell Foods, Inc., United States v., 262
Kiobel v. Royal Dutch Petroleum Co., 58
KL Group v. Case, Kay & Lynch, 213, 217
Klaxon Co. v. Stentor Electric Mfg. Co., 114, 253
Kohler v. Bank of Bermuda, Ltd., 58
Kowalewski, In re Marriage of, 84, 98
Kraus v. Mummau, 110
Kremer v. Chemical Construction Corp., 102
Kulko v. Superior Court, 66, 145, 150
Kushnick v. Kushnick, 150
Kwiecinski v. Medi-Tech International Corp., 106
L.S., In re, 147
LaFleur v. Pyfer, 124
LaGrand Case (Germany v. United States), 265
Lakeside Surfaces, Inc. v. Cambria Co., LLC, 79
Lambert v. Kysar, 78
Lams v. F.H. Smith Co., 208
Landry v. Carlson Mooring Service, 106
Lauritzen v. Larsen, 206
Lauterbach v. Lauterbach, 142
Lawrence, United States v., 53
Leary v. Gledhill, 168
Lee Memorial Healoth System v. Martinez, 252
Legum v. Brown, 102
Lehr v. Robertson, 134
Leonard v. Lentz, 153
Levin v. Gladstein, 110
Lewis v. Vail Results, 64
Liberty Synergistics, Inc. v. Microflo Ltd., 214
Lichter v. Fritsch, 317
Lilienthal v. Kaufman, 177, 193, 212
Lofton v. Secretary of Florida Dept. of Children & Family Services, 134
Loucks v. Standard Oil Co. of New York, 166
Lowe v. Richards, 102
Lozano v. Montoya Alvarez, 153
Lubbe v. Cape plc, 81
Lutheran Social Services of New Jersey v. Doe, 134
M/S Bremen v. Zapata Off-Shore Co., 77
Mack, Matter of Estate of, 98
Macsherry v. Sparrows Point, LLC, 179
Magnolia Petroleum Co. v. Hunt, 105
Mahindra, USA Inc., In re, 81
Makaeff v. Trump University, LLC, 251
Mallory v. Norfolk So. Ry. Co., 56, 60
Malpeso v. Malpeso, 145
Manetti-Farrow, Inc. v. Gucci Am., Inc., 266
Marie v. Garrison, 161
Marina de Ponce, Inc. v. Federal deposit Insurance Corporation, 261
Marks ex rel. SM v. Hochhauser, 53
Marra v. Bushee, 202
Marrese v. American Academy of Orthopaedic Surgeons, 107, 312
Martinez v. N. Ariz. Univ., 73
Massie v. Watts, 97
Masterpiece Cakeshop v. Colorado Civil Rights Commission, 132
Mattel, Inc. v. Barbie-Club.com, 75
Matusevitch v. Telnikoff, 116
May v. Anderson, 74, 146
May's Estate, In re, 124, 126
Mayer-Kolker v. Kolker, 152
McCarrell v. Hoffman-La Roche, Inc., 162
McCormack v. Medcor, Inc., 180
McGee v. International Life Insurance Co., 62
McGinnes Indus. Maint. Corp. v. Phoenix Ins. Co., 261
McKay v. Novartis Pharmaceutical Corp., 256
McKinley v. United States, 164
McManaway v. KRB, Inc., 262
Medellin v. Texas, 265
Medical Marijuana, Inc. v. Horn, 58
Mehdi Ahmad, In re Estate of, 151
Meier's Estate, In re, 225
Melki v. Melki, 125
Mendoza, United States v., 94
Michigan Trust Co. v. Ferry, 83
Milliken v. Meyer, 52, 64
Milliken v. Pratt, 207
Milwaukee County v. M.E. White Co., 109
Milwaukee, City of v. Illinois, 267
Ministri Family, LLC v. Bell, 254
Miree v. DeKalb Cnty., 263
Mitchell v. Lumpkin, 265
Mitchell v. Mackey, 36
Mitsubishi Motors Corp. v. Soler Chrysler-Plymouth, Inc., 78
MKM Healthcare Solutions, LLC v. Biotronic Inc., 79
Mohamad v. Rajoub, 95
Moki Mac River Expeditions v. Drugg, 66
Monasky v. Taglieri, 40
Monegasque de Reassurances S.A.M. v. NAK Naftogaz of Ukraine, 117
Monroe Staffing Services, LLC v. Whitaker, 166
Monsanto Co. v. McFarling, 78
Moore v. Livingston, 221
Moore, Estate of v. Carroll, 71
Mullane v. Central Hannover Bank & Trust Co., 49, 57
Murphy v. Beck, 261
Murphy v. F.D.I.C., 261
Murphy, United States v., 152
Mutual Life Insurance Co. v. Liebing, 231
Mwani v. Osama Bin Laden, 69
National Equipment Rental, Ltd. v. Szukhent, 60
National Security Counselors v. C.I.A., 262
Navani v. Shahani, 148
Neely v. Club Med Management Services, Inc., 206
Nelson v. Hix, 203

Netherlands Shipmortgage Corp. v. Madias, 226
Neumeier v. Kuehner, 184, 192
New York Life Insurance Co. v. Dodge, 231
New York Life Insurance Co. v. Dunlevy, 75
New York, City of v. BP P.L.C., 267
New York, City of v. Chevron Corp., 263
Nodak Mutual Ins. Co. v. American Family Mutual Ins. Co., 190
O'Reilly v. Curtis Pub. Co., 204
Obergefell v. Hodges, 131
Ofer v. Sirota, 143, 152
Offshore Rental Co. v. Continental Oil Co., 180
Olberding v. Illinois Central R. Co., 59
Olga Sugey Centano Aguirre v. Hernandez, 148
OneWest Bank, FSB v. Erickson, 84
Order of United Commercial Travelers of America v. Wolfe, 233
Oswalt v. Scripto, Inc., 70
Ou Kullasadu Invest v. Kark, 130
Oulette v. Int'l Paper Co., 268
P.V. ex rel. T.V. v. Camp Jaycee, 186, 324
Pacific Employers Insurance Co. v. Industrial Accident Commission, 233
Pacific States Cut Stone Co. v. Goble, 130
Palmer v. Hoffman, 247
Parke-Bernet Galleries, Inc. v. Franklyn, 62
Parker v. Perdue Foods, LLC, 236
Parrott v. Abraham, 142
Parsons v. Chesapeake & Ohio Ry. Co., 82
Pasquantino v. United States, 110
Patel, United States v., 148
Paulo v. Bepex Corp., 180
Paulowina Plantations v. Rajamannan, 81
Penn Fire Ins. Co, v. Gold Mining & Milling Co., 56
Penn Mutual Life Insurance Co. v. Fields, 37, 38
Pennoyer v. Neff, 54, 57
Perito v. Perito, 142
Perkins v. Benguet Consolidated Mining Co., 52, 55
Philipp v. Fed. Republic of Germany, 266
Philipp v. Stiftung Preussischer Kulturbesitz, 266
Phillips Petroleum Co. v. Shutts, 76, 98, 236, 284, 318
Phillips v. Metropolitan Transportation Authority, 104
Pink, United States v., 265
Piper Aircraft Co. v. Reyno, 80
Pittman v. Rutherford, 109
Plazza, In re Estate of, 223
Pritchard v. Norton, 208
Promenade D'Iberville, LLC v. Jacksonville Electric Authority, 233
Ragan v. Merchants Transfer & Warehouse Co., 250
Ranolls v. Dewling, 124
Reading & Bates Construction Co. v. Baker Energy Resources Corp., 115
Reed v. General Motors Corp., 250
Reeder v. Williams, 94
Reeves v. Schulmeier, 159, 174
Rein v. ESS Group, Inc., 227
Renard, Estate of, 222
Republic of Colombia v. Diageo North America, Inc., 109
Republic of Hungary v. Simon, 266
Republic Technologies (NA), LLC v. BBK Tobacco & Foods, LLP, 236
Rhoades, In re Estate of, 222
Richards v. United States, 27, 164, 256, 303
Risdal & Anderson, Inc., In re, 263
RJR Nabisco, Inc. v. European Community, 58
Robinson v. Robinson, 128
Roche v. McDonald, 102
Rodriguez-Diaz v. Sierra-Martinez, 38
Rosenstiel v. Rosenstiel, 74, 149
Rozan v. Rozan, 306
Rush v. Savchuk, 51, 76, 86
S.K.G., In re Adoption of, 134
S.L.S., People In Interest of, 147
Sabal Trail Transmission, LLC v. Real Estate, 262
Sabal Trail Transmissions, LLC v. 3.921 Acres of Land in Lake County Florida, 263
Safra v. Palestinian Authority, 69
Salesky v. CRMNEXT, Inc., 168
Salini Construttori S.p.A. v. Kingdom of Morocco, 109
Sampsell v. Superior Court, 146
Sanchez v. State Farm Fire & Cas. Co., 73
Sarasota Wine Market, LLC v. Schmitt, 239
Satz v. Satz, 152
Schalliol v. Fare, 27
Scherk v. Alberto-Culver Co., 78
Schettler v. RalRon Capital Corp., 261
Schmierer v. The Tribal Trust, 113
Schultz v. Boy Scouts of America, Inc., 185
Schwartz v. Schwartz, 151
Scianella v. AstraZeneca UK Ltd., 226
Scola v. Publix Supermarkets, Inc., 77
Scotts Co. v. Hacienda Loma Linda, 81
SEC v. Sabhlok, 53
Secretary of U.S. Dep't of Labor v. American Made Bags, LLC, 77
Seguros Universales, S.A. v. Microsoft Corp., 79
Seider v. Roth, 86
Semtek International Inc. v. Lockheed Martin Corp., 251, 311
Senior Health Ins. Company of Pennsylvania, In re, 233
Shady Grove in Berk v. Choy, 250
Shady Grove Orthopedic Associates, P.A. v. Allstate Ins. Co., 76, 250

Shaffer v. Heitner, 51, 63, 83, 84, 85, 87, 141, 145
Shanghai Yongrun Inv. Mgmt. Co., Ltd. v. Kashi Galazy Venture Capital, Ltd., 116
Shanghai Yongrun Inv. Mgt. Co., Ltd. v. Xu, 116
Shanks, In re Marriage of, 110
Shannon v. Irving Trust Co., 223
Shen v. Garland, 168
Sherrer v. Sherrer, 74, 144
Shrader v. Biddinger, 75
Sibaja v. Dow Chemical Co., 252
Sierra Estate of Romagosa v. Trafigura Trading LLC, 266
Simler v. Conner, 248
Simons v. Miami Beach First National Bank, 143
Sims v. BMW of North America, LLC, 71
Sky Cable, LLC v. Coley, 256
Slater v. Mexican National Railroad Co., 173, 239
Slaughter-House Cases, In re, 54
Societe Nationale Industrielle Aerospatiale v. U.S. District Court, 252
Society of Lloyd's v. Ashenden, 117
Society of Lloyd's v. Siemon-Netto, 116
Soria v. Chrysler Canada, Inc., 70
Sosna v. Iowa, 142
St. Stephen's School v. PriceWaterhouse Coopers Accountants N.V., 77
Standard Oil Co., United States v., 262
Stangvik v. Shiley Inc., 81
Stearns v. Stearns, 110
Stencel Aero Eng'g Corp. v. United States, 262
Stephens v. Stephens, 128
Sterba, In re, 267
Stewart Organization, Inc. v. Ricoh Corp., 78, 266
Storey v. Cello Holdings, L.L.C., 95
Stovall v. Preston, 125
Sudholt v. County Mutual Ins. Co., 234
SUEZ Water N.Y. Inc. v. E.I. du Pont de Nemours & Co., 60
Sun Oil Co. v. Wortman, 162, 236, 319
Supreme Court of New Hampshire v. Piper, 239
Sutton v. Leib, 145
Swarb v. Lennox, 61
Swift v. Tyson, 246
Taca Int'l Airlines v. Rolls-Royce of England, Ltd., 63
Taracorp, Ltd. v. Dailey, 113
Tarikonda v. Pinjari, 151
Tazziz v. Tazziz, 152
Tennessee ex rel. Sizemore v. Surety Bank, 85
Tennessee Gas Pipeline Co., LLC v. Permanent Easement for 7.053 Acres, 262
Terrorist Attacks on September 11, 2001, In re, 186
Texas v. Florida, 38
Texas v. New Jersey, 85
Texas v. Pankey, 261, 263
The Pep Boys Manny Moe & Jack of California v. Old Republic Ins. Co., 211
Thomas v. Washington Gas Light Co., 106
Thompson v. Thompson, 147
Thornton's Estate, In re, 129
TMI, In re, 255
Toledo Society for Crippled Children v. Hickok, 221
TopstepTrader, LLC v. OneUp Trader, LLC, 78
Townley and Carraz, In re Marraiage of, 142
Traversi's Estate, In re, 220
Treinies v. Sunshine Mining Co., 93, 101
Triple Up Ltd. v. Youku Tudou Inc., 69
Trout Point Lodge, Ltd. v. Handshoe, 116
Trower v. Blinken, 168
Trueblood v. MMIC Ins. Co., Inc., 106
Udny v. Udny, 35
Underwriters National Assurance Co. v. North Carolina Life & Accident, 107
Union Carbide Corp. Gas Plant Disaster, In re, 80
United Air Lines, Inc. v. Wiener, 94
United Air Lines, Inc., United States v., 94
V.L. v. E.L., 134, 135
Van Averment, United States v., 252
Van Dusen v. Barrack, 255, 313
VantagePoint Venture Partners 1996 v. Examen, Inc., 226
Vimar Seguros y Reaseguros, S.A. v. M/V Sky Reefer, 78
Vivendi Universal S.A. Securities Litigation, In re, 77
Volkswagenwerk Aktiengesellschaft v. Schlunk, 64
Volkswagenwerk Aktiengesellschaft, Ex parte, 63
Walker v. Armco Steel Corp., 250, 310
Wallace v. Louisiana Citizens Property Ins. Corp., 77
Wallis v. Pan Am. Petroleum Corp., 262
Walton v. Arabian American Oil Co., 168
Waranka v. Wadena Ins. Co., 109
Watkins v. Conway, 113
Watson v. Employers Liability Assurance Corp., 232
Wave Studio, LLC v. General Hotel Management Ltd., 80
Weaver v. Weaver, 142
Weber v. Jolly Hotels, 74
Weesner v. Weesner, 97
Wells v. Simonds Abrasive Co., 237, 238
West Virginia v. E.P.A., 267, 324
Western Union Tel. Co. v. Pennsylvania, 220
Whealton v. Whealton, 74, 148
Wheat v. Wheat, 142
White Lumber Sales, Inc., State ex rel. v. Sulmonetti, 62
Wilkins v. Ellett, 224
Wilkins v. Zelichowski, 125
Williams v. North Carolina (Williams I), 140
Williams v. North Carolina (Williams II), 73, 140
Williams v. Tech Mahindra (Americas) Inc., 250

Wimbledon Financing Master Fund, Ltd. v. Molner, 81
Winans v. Winans, 36
Windsor, United States v., 131
Windt v. Qwest Communications Int'l, Inc., 80
Winkler v. Stowe, 145
Woll v. Dugas, 208
World-Wide Volkswagen Corp. v. Woodson, 57, 65, 69
Wyatt v. Fulrath, 131
Young v. F.D.I.C., 261
Yousef v. James River Ins. Co., 39
Yuriiovych v. Hryhorivna, 148
Zanghi v. Ritella, 80
Zippo Mfg. Co. v. Zippo Dot Com, Inc., 75
Z-Modular, LLC v. MCN Build, Inc., 207
Zschernig v. Miller, 117, 264
Zuniga v. Bernalillo County, 255